CW01645258

The 1560

GENEVA BIBLE

ILLUSTRATED **APOCRYPHA**

By Dr Lewis Spencer

ISBN: 979-8-89587-193-5

This edition of The Geneva Bible Apocrypha in traditional orthography was meticulously edited to the highest precision, drawing upon historical texts and extensive scholarly research. Special acknowledgment is due to the Oxford Theology Society for their invaluable support and contributions, ensuring the utmost accuracy and integrity of this work

Dear Reader,

This book is a labour of love and dedication by many devoted individuals. If this work has enriched your understanding and faith, your thoughts would mean the world to me.

Please consider leaving a review via the QR code to support this publication and future endeavours.

Thank you!

Dr Lewis Spencer

FREE AUDIOBOOK

The Oxford Theology Society is pleased to present a complimentary two-audiobook collection, yours to download and enjoy, the professionally narrated:

"Allegories of Enoch" *and* ***"The Book of Watchers"***

To download the audio file, please go to the ***<u>last page</u>*** ***of the book***

May these sacred materials prove invaluable in your studies!

TABLE OF CONTENT

I ESDRAS

CHAPTER 1

[1]And Josias held the feast of the
passover in Jerusalem unto his Lord,
and offered the passover the fourteenth
day of the first month; [2]Having set the
priests according to their daily courses,
being arrayed in long garments, in the
temple of the Lord. [3]And he spake unto
the Levites, the holy ministers of Israel,
that they should hallow themselves
unto the Lord, to set the holy ark of the
Lord in the house that king Solomon
the son of David had built: [4]And said,
Ye shall no more bear the ark upon
your shoulders: now therefore serve the
Lord your God, and minister unto his
people Israel, and prepare you after
your families and kindreds, [5]According
as David the king of Israel prescribed,
and according to the magnificence of
Solomon his son: and standing in the
temple according to the several dignity
of the families of you the Levites, who
minister in the presence of your
brethren the children of Israel,
[6]Offer the passover in order, and make
ready the sacrifices for your brethren,
and keep the passover according to
the commandment of the Lord, which
was given unto Moses. [7]And unto the
people that was found there Josias gave
thirty thousand lambs and kids, and
three thousand calves: these things
were given of the king's allowance,
according as he promised, to the
people, to the priests, and to the
Levites. [8]And Helkias, Jeconias, and
Samaias, and Nathanael his brother,
and Assabias, and Ochiel, and Joram,
captains over thousands, gave to the
Levites for the passover five thousand
sheep, and seven hundred calves. [9]And
Zacharias, and Syelus, the governors of
the temple, gave to the priests for the
passover two thousand and six hundred
sheep, and three hundred calves.
[10]And when these things were done, the
priests and Levites, having the
unleavened bread, stood in very comely
order according to the kindreds, [11]And
according to the several dignities of the
fathers, before the people, to offer to
the Lord, as it is written in the book of
Moses: and thus did they in the
morning. [12]And they roasted the
passover with fire, as appertaineth: as
for the sacrifices, they sod them in
brass pots and pans with a good savour,
[13]And set them before all the people:
and afterward they prepared for
themselves, and for the priests their
brethren, the sons of Aaron. [14]For the
priests offered the fat until night: and
the Levits prepared for themselves, and
the priests their brethren, the sons of
Aaron.
[15]The holy singers also, the sons of
Asaph, were in their order, according to
the appointment of David, to wit,
Asaph, Zacharias, and Jeduthun, who
was of the king's retinue. [16]Moreover
the porters were at every gate; it was
not lawful for any to go from his
ordinary service: for their brethren the
Levites prepared for them. [17]Thus were
the things that belonged to the
sacrifices of the Lord accomplished in
that day, that they might hold the
passover, [18]And offer sacrifices upon
the altar of the Lord, according to the
commandment of king Josias. [19]So the
children of Israel which were present
held the passover at that time, and the
feast of sweet bread seven days. [20]And
such a passover was not kept in Israel
since the time of the prophet Samuel.

21Yea, all the kings of Israel held not
such a passover as Josias, and the
priests, and the Levites, and the Jews,
held with all Israel that were found
dwelling at Jerusalem. 22In the
eighteenth year of the reign of Josias
was this passover kept. 23And the
works or Josias were upright before his
Lord with an heart full of godliness.
24As for the things that came to pass in
his time, they were written in former
times, concerning those that sinned, and
did wickedly against the Lord above all
people and kingdoms, and how they
grieved him exceedingly, so that the
words of the Lord rose up against Israel.
25Now after all these acts of Josias it
came to pass, that Pharaoh the king of
Egypt came to raise war at Carchamis
upon Euphrates: and Josias went out
against him. 26But the king of Egypt
sent to him, saying, What have I to do
with thee, O king of Judea? 27I am not
sent out from the Lord God against
thee; for my war is upon Euphrates: and
now the Lord is with me, yea, the Lord
is with me hasting me forward: depart
from me, and be not against the Lord.
28Howbeit Josias did not turn back his
chariot from him, but undertook to
fight with him, not regarding the words
of the prophet Jeremy spoken by the
mouth of the Lord: 29But joined battle
with him in the plain of Magiddo, and
the princes came against king Josias.
30Then said the king unto his servants,
Carry me away out of the battle; for I am
very weak. And immediately his
servants took him away out of the
battle. 31Then gat he up upon his
second chariot; and being brought back
to Jerusalem died, and was buried in his
father's sepulchre.
32And in all Jewry they mourned for
Josias, yea, Jeremy the prophet
lamented for Josias, and the chief men
with the women made lamentation for
him unto this day: and this was given
out for an ordinance to be done
continually in all the nation of Israel.
33These things are written in the book
of the stories of the kings of Judah, and
every one of the acts that Josias did, and
his glory, and his understanding in the
law of the Lord, and the things that he
had done before, and the things now
recited, are reported in the book of the
kings of Israel and Judea. 34And the
people took Joachaz the son of Josias,
and made him king instead of Josias his
father, when he was twenty and three
years old. 35And he reigned in Judea
and in Jerusalem three months: and
then the king of Egypt deposed him
from reigning in Jerusalem.
36And he set a tax upon the land of an
hundred talents of silver and one talent
of gold. 37The king of Egypt also made
king Joacim his brother king of Judea
and Jerusalem. 38And he bound Joacim
and the nobles: but Zaraces his brother
he apprehended, and brought him
out of Egypt. 39Five and twenty years
old was Joacim when he was made king
in the land of Judea and Jerusalem; and
he did evil before the Lord.
40Wherefore against him
Nabuchodonosor the king of Babylon
came up, and bound him with a chain
of brass, and carried him into Babylon.
41Nabuchodonosor also took of the
holy vessels of the Lord, and carried
them away, and set them in his own
temple at Babylon. 42But those things
that are recorded of him, and of his
uncleanness and impiety, are written in
the chronicles of the kings. 43And
Joacim his son reigned in his stead: he
was made king being eighteen years
old; 44And reigned but three months

and ten days in Jerusalem; and did evil
before the Lord. 45So after a year
Nabuchodonosor sent and caused him
to be brought into Babylon with the
holy vessels of the Lord; 46And made
Zedechias king of Judea and Jerusalem,
when he was one and twenty years old;
and he reigned eleven years: 47And he
did evil also in the sight of the Lord,
and cared not for the words that were
spoken unto him by the prophet Jeremy
from the mouth of the Lord. 48And
after that king Nabuchodonosor had
made him to swear by the name of the
Lord, he forswore himself, and
rebelled; and hardening his neck, his
heart, he transgressed the laws of the
Lord God of Israel. 49The governors
also of the people and of the priests did
many things against the laws, and
passed all the pollutions of all nations,
and defiled the temple of the Lord,
which was sanctified in Jerusalem.
50Nevertheless the God of their fathers
sent by his messenger to call them back,
because he spared them and his
tabernacle also.
51But they had his messengers in
derision; and, look, when the Lord
spake unto them, they made a sport of
his prophets:
52So far forth, that he, being wroth with
his people for their great ungodliness,
commanded the kings of the Chaldees
to come up against them; 53Who slew
their young men with the sword, yea,
even within the compass of their holy
temple, and spared neither young man
nor maid, old man nor child, among
them; for he delivered all into their
hands. 54And they took all the holy
vessels of the Lord, both great and
small, with the vessels of the ark of
God, and the king's treasures, and
carried them away into Babylon. 55As
for the house of the Lord, they burnt it,
and brake down the walls of Jerusalem,
and set fire upon her towers: 56And as
for her glorious things, they never
ceased till they had consumed and
brought them all to nought: and the
people that were not slain with the
sword he carried unto Babylon: 57Who
became servants to him and his
children, till the Persians reigned, to
fulfil the word of the Lord spoken by
the mouth of Jeremy: 58Until the land
had enjoyed her sabbaths, the whole
time of her desolation shall she rest,
until the full term of seventy years.

CHAPTER 2

1In the first year of Cyrus king of the
Persians, that the word of the Lord
might be accomplished, that he had
promised by the mouth of Jeremy; 2The
Lord raised up the spirit of Cyrus the king
of the Persians, and he made
proclamation through all his kingdom,
and also by writing, 3Saying, Thus saith
Cyrus king of the Persians; The Lord of
Israel, the most high Lord, hath made
me king of the whole world, 4And
commanded me to build him an house
at Jerusalem in Jewry. 5If therefore
there be any of you that are of his
people, let the Lord, even his Lord, be
with him, and let him go up to
Jerusalem that is in Judea, and build the
house of the Lord of Israel: for he is the
Lord that dwelleth in Jerusalem.
6Whosoever then dwell in the places
about, let them help him, those, I say,
that are his neighbours, with gold, and
with silver, 7With gifts, with horses,
and with cattle, and other things, which
have been set forth by vow, for the
temple of the Lord at Jerusalem. 8Then
the chief of the families of Judea and of

the tribe of Benjamin stood up; the
priests also, and the Levites, and all
they whose mind the Lord had moved
to go up, and to build an house for the
Lord at Jerusalem, 9 And they that dwelt
round about them, and helped them in
all things with silver and gold, with
horses and cattle, and with very many
free gifts of a great number whose
minds were stirred up thereto.
10 King Cyrus also brought forth the
holy vessels, which Nabuchodonosor
had carried away from Jerusalem, and
had set up in his temple of idols.
11 Now when Cyrus king of the Persians
had brought them forth, he delivered
them to Mithridates his treasurer:
12 And by him they were delivered to
Sanabassar the governor of Judea.
13 And this was the number of them; A
thousand golden cups, and a thousand of
silver, censers of silver twenty nine,
vials of gold thirty, and of silver two
thousand four hundred and ten, and a
thousand other vessels.
14 So all the vessels of gold and of silver,
which were carried away, were five
thousand four hundred threescore and
nine. 15 These were brought back by
Sanabassar, together with them of the
captivity, from Babylon to Jerusalem.
16 But in the time of Artexerxes king of
the Persians Belemus, and Mithridates,
and Tabellius, and Rathumus, and
Beeltethmus, and Semellius the
secretary, with others that were in
commission with them, dwelling in
Samaria and other places, wrote unto
him against them that dwelt in Judea
and Jerusalem these letters following;
17 To king Artexerxes our lord, Thy
servants, Rathumus the storywriter, and
Semellius the scribe, and the rest of
their council, and the judges that are in
Celosyria and Phenice. 18 Be it now
known to the lord king, that the Jews
that are up from you to us, being come
into Jerusalem, that rebellious and
wicked city, do build the marketplaces,
and repair the walls of it and do lay the
foundation of the temple. 19 Now if this
city and the walls thereof be made up
again, they will not only refuse to give
tribute, but also rebel against kings.
20 And forasmuch as the things
pertaining to the temple are now in
hand, we think it meet not to neglect
such a matter,
21 But to speak unto our lord the king,
to the intent that, if it be thy pleasure it
may be sought out in the books of thy
fathers: 22 And thou shalt find in the
chronicles what is written concerning
these things, and shalt understand that
that city was rebellious, troubling both
kings and cities: 23 And that the Jews
were rebellious, and raised always wars
therein; for the which cause even this
city was made desolate. 24 Wherefore
now we do declare unto thee, O lord
the king, that if this city be built again,
and the walls thereof set up anew, thou
shalt from henceforth have no passage
into Celosyria and Phenice. 25 Then the
king wrote back again to Rathumus the
storywriter, to Beeltethmus, to
Semellius the scribe, and to the rest that
were in commission, and dwellers in
Samaria and Syria and Phenice, after
this manner; 26 I have read the epistle
which ye have sent unto me: therefore I
commanded to make diligent search,
and it hath been found that that city was
from the beginning practising against
kings; 27 And the men therein were
given to rebellion and war: and that
mighty kings and fierce were in
Jerusalem, who reigned and exacted
tributes in Celosyria and Phenice.
28 Now therefore I have commanded

to hinder those men from building the
city, and heed to be taken that there be
no more done in it; 29 And that those
wicked workers proceed no further
to the annoyance of kings, 30 Then
king Artexerxes his letters being
read, Rathumus, and Semellius the
scribe, and the rest that were in
commission with them, removing in
haste toward Jerusalem with a troop of
horsemen and a multitude of people in
battle array, began to hinder the
builders; and the building of the temple
in Jerusalem ceased until the second
year of the reign of Darius king of the
Persians.

CHAPTER 3

1 Now when Darius reigned, he made a
great feast unto all his subjects, and
unto all his household, and unto all the
princes of Media and Persia,
2 And to all the governors and captains
and lieutenants that were under him,
from India unto Ethiopia, of an hundred
twenty and seven provinces.
3 And when they had eaten and drunken,
and being satisfied were gone home,
then Darius the king went into his
bedchamber, and slept, and soon after
awaked.
4 Then three young men, that were of
the guard that kept the king's body,
spake one to another;
5 Let every one of us speak a sentence:
he that shall overcome, and whose
sentence shall seem wiser than the
others, unto him shall the king Darius
give great gifts, and great things in
token of victory:
6 As, to be clothed in purple, to drink in
gold, and to sleep upon gold, and a
chariot with bridles of gold, and an
headtire of fine linen, and a chain about
his neck:
7 And he shall sit next to Darius because
of his wisdom, and shall be called
Darius his cousin. 8 And then every one
wrote his sentence, sealed it, and laid
it under king Darius his pillow; 9 And
said that, when the king is risen, some
will give him the writings; and of
whose side the king and the three
princes of Persia shall judge that his
sentence is the wisest, to him shall the
victory be given, as was appointed.
10 The first wrote, Wine is the strongest.
11 The second wrote, The king is
strongest.
12 The third wrote, Women are
strongest: but above all things Truth
beareth away the victory. 13 Now when
the king was risen up, they took their
writings, and delivered them unto him,
and so he read them: 14 And sending
forth he called all the princes of Persia
and Media, and the governors, and the
captains, and the lieutenants, and the
chief officers;
15 And sat him down in the royal seat of
judgment; and the writings were read
before them. 16 And he said, Call the
young men, and they shall declare their
own sentences. So they were called,
and came in. 17 And he said unto them,
Declare unto us your mind concerning
the writings. Then began the first, who
had spoken of the strength of wine;
18 And he said thus, O ye men, how
exceeding strong is wine! it causeth all
men to err that drink it: 19 It maketh the
mind of the king and of the fatherless
child to be all one; of the bondman and
of the freeman, of the poor man and of
the rich: 20 It turneth also every thought
into jollity and mirth, so that a man
remembereth neither sorrow nor debt:
21 And it maketh every heart rich, so that
a man remembereth neither king nor

governor; and it maketh to speak all
things by talents: 22And when they are
in their cups, they forget their love both
to friends and brethren, and a little after
draw out swords: 23But when they are
from the wine, they remember not what
they have done. 24O ye men, is not
wine the strongest, that enforceth to do
thus? And when he had so spoken, he
held his peace.

CHAPTER 4

1Then the second, that had spoken of
the strength of the king, began to say,
2O ye men, do not men excel in strength
that bear rule over sea and land and
allthings in them? 3But yet the king is
more mighty: for he is lord of all these
things, and hath dominion over them;
and whatsoever he commandeth them
they do. 4If he bid them make war the
one against the other, they do it: if he
send them out against the enemies, they
go, and break down mountains walls
and towers. 5They slay and are slain,
and transgress not the king's
commandment: if they get the victory,
they bring all to the king, as well the
spoil, as all things else.
6Likewise for those that are no soldiers,
and have not to do with wars, but use
husbandry, when they have reaped
again that which they had sown, they
bring it to the king, and compel one
another to pay tribute unto the king.
7And yet he is but one man: if he
command to kill, they kill; if he
command to spare, they spare; 8If he
command to smite, they smite; if he
command to make desolate, they make
desolate; if he command to build, they
build; 9If he command to cut down,
they cut down; if he command to plant,
they plant. 10So all his people and his
armies obey him: furthermore he lieth
down, he eateth and drinketh, and
taketh his rest: 11And these keep watch
round about him, neither may any one
depart, and do his own business, neither
disobey they him in any thing. 12O ye
men, how should not the king be
mightiest, when in such sort he is
obeyed? And he held his tongue.
13Then the third, who had spoken of
women, and of the truth, (this was
Zorobabel) began to speak.
14O ye men, it is not the great king, nor
the multitude of men, neither is it wine,
that excelleth; who is it then that ruleth
them, or hath the lordship over them?
are they not women? 15Women have
borne the king and all the people that
bear rule by sea and land. 16Even of
them came they: and they nourished
them up that planted the vineyards,
from whence the wine cometh. 17These
also make garments for men; these
bring glory unto men; and without
women cannot men be. 18Yea, and if
men have gathered together gold and
silver, or any other goodly thing, do
they not love a woman which is comely
in favour and beauty? 19And letting all
those things go, do they not gape, and
even with open mouth fix their eyes fast
on her; and have not all men more desire
unto her than unto silver or gold, or any
goodly thing whatsoever? 20A man
leaveth his own father that brought him
up, and his own country, and cleaveth
unto his wife. 21He sticketh not to
spend his life with his wife. and
remembereth neither father, nor mother,
nor country. 22By this also ye must
know that women have dominion over
you: do ye not labour and toil, and give
and bring all to the woman? 23Yea, a
man taketh his sword, and goeth his
way to rob and to steal, to sail upon the

sea and upon rivers; 24And looketh
upon a lion, and goeth in the darkness;
and when he hath stolen, spoiled, and
robbed, he bringeth it to his love.
25Wherefore a man loveth his wife
better than father or mother. 26Yea,
many there be that have run out of their
wits for women, and become servants
for their sakes.
27Many also have perished, have erred,
and sinned, for women. 28And now do
ye not believe me? is not the king great
in his power? do not all regions fear to
touch him? 29Yet did I see him and
Apame the king's concubine, the
daughter of the admirable Bartacus,
sitting at the right hand of the king,
30And taking the crown from the king's
head, and setting it upon her own head;
she also struck the king with her left
hand.
31And yet for all this the king gaped and
gazed upon her with open mouth: if she
laughed upon him, he laughed also: but
if she took any displeasure at him, the
king was fain to flatter, that she might
be reconciled to him again.
32O ye men, how can it be but women
should be strong, seeing they do
thus?
33Then the king and the princes looked
one upon another: so he began to speak
of the truth. 34O ye men, are not
women strong? great is the earth, high
is the heaven, swift is the sun in his
course, for he compasseth the heavens
round about, and fetcheth his course
again to his own place in one day. 35Is
he not great that maketh these things?
therefore great is the truth, and stronger
than all things. 36All the earth crieth
upon the truth, and the heaven blesseth
it: all works shake and tremble at it, and
with it is no unrighteous thing. 37Wine
is wicked, the king is wicked, women
are wicked, all the children of men are
wicked, and such are all their wicked
works; and there is no truth in them; in
their unrighteousness also they shall
perish. 38As for the truth, it endureth,
and is alwaYs strong; it liveth and
conquereth for evermore. 39With her
there is no accepting of persons or
rewards; but she doeth the things that
are just, and refraineth from all unjust
and wicked things; and all men do well
like of her works. 40Neither in her
judgment is any unrighteousness; and
she is the strength, kingdom, power,
and majesty, of all ages. Blessed be the
God of truth. 41And with that he held
his peace. And all the people then
shouted, and said, Great is Truth, and
mighty above all things. 42Then said
the king unto him, Ask what thou wilt
more than is appointed in the writing,
and we will give it thee, because thou
art found wisest; and thou shalt sit next
me, and shalt be called my cousin.
43Then said he unto the king,
Remember thy vow, which thou hast
vowed to build Jerusalem, in the day
when thou camest to thy kingdom,
44And to send away all the vessels that
were taken away out of Jerusalem,
which Cyrus set apart, when he vowed
to destroy Babylon, and to send them
again thither. 45Thou also hast vowed
to build up the temple, which the
Edomites burned when Judea was
made desolate by the Chaldees. 46And
now, O lord the king, this is that which
I require, and which I desire of thee,
and this is the princely liberality
proceeding from thyself: I desire
therefore that thou make good the vow,
the performance whereof with thine
own mouth thou hast vowed to the
King of heaven.
47Then Darius the king stood up, and

kissed him, and wrote letters for him
unto all the treasurers and lieutenants
and captains and governors, that they
should safely convey on their way both
him, and all those that go up with him to
build Jerusalem. 48 He wrote letters also
unto the lieutenants that were in
Celosyria and Phenice, and unto them
in Libanus, that they should bring cedar
wood from Libanus unto Jerusalem,
and that they should build the city with
him. 49 Moreover he wrote for all the
Jews that went out of his realm up into
Jewry, concerning their freedom, that
no officer, no ruler, no lieutenant, nor
treasurer, should forcibly enter into
their doors; 50 And that all the country
which they hold should be free without
tribute; and that the Edomites should
give over the villages of the Jews which
then they held: 51 Yea, that there should
be yearly given twenty talents to the
building of the temple, until the time
that it were built; 52 And other ten
talents yearly, to maintain the burnt
offerings upon the altar every day, as
they had a commandment to offer
seventeen: 53 And that all they that went
from Babylon to build the city should
have free liberty, as well they as their
posterity, and all the priests that went
away. 54 He wrote also concerning. the
charges, and the priests' vestments
wherein they minister; 55 And likewise
for the charges of the Levites, to be
given them until the day that the house
were finished, and Jerusalem builded
up. 56 And he commanded to give to all
that kept the city pensions and wages.
57 He sent away also all the vessels from
Babylon, that Cyrus had set apart; and
all that Cyrus had given in
commandment, the same charged he
also to be done, and sent unto
Jerusalem. 58 Now when this young
man was gone forth, he lifted up his
face to heaven toward Jerusalem, and
praised the King of heaven, 59 And said,
From thee cometh victory, from thee
cometh wisdom, and thine is the glory,
and I am thy servant. 60 Blessed art
thou, who hast given me wisdom: for
to thee I give thanks, O Lord of our
fathers. 61 And so he took the letters,
and went out, and came unto Babylon,
and told it all his brethren. 62 And they
praised the God of their fathers,
because he had given them freedom
and liberty 63 To go up, and to build
Jerusalem, and the temple which is
called by his name: and they feasted
with instruments of musick and
gladness seven days.

CHAPTER 5

1 After this were the principal men of
the families chosen according to their
tribes, to go up with their wives and
sons and daughters, with their
menservants and maidservants, and
their cattle.
2 And Darius sent with them a thousand
horsemen, till they had brought them
back to Jerusalem safely, and with
musical [instruments] tabrets and flutes.
3 And all their brethren played, and he
made them go up together with them.
4 And these are the names of the men
which went up, according to their
families among their tribes, after their
several heads.
5 The priests, the sons of Phinees the
son of Aaron: Jesus the son of Josedec,
the son of Saraias, and Joacim the son
of Zorobabel, the son of Salathiel, of
the house of David, out of the kindred
of Phares, of the tribe of Judah; 6 Who
spake wise sentences before Darius the
king of Persia in the second year of his

reign, in the month Nisan, which is the
first month. [7]And these are they of
Jewry that came up from the captivity,
where they dwelt as strangers, whom
Nabuchodonosor the king of Babylon
had carried away unto Babylon. [8]And
they returned unto Jerusalem, and to
the other parts of Jewry, every man to
his own city, who came with
Zorobabel, with Jesus, Nehemias, and
Zacharias, and Reesaias, Enenius,
Mardocheus. Beelsarus, Aspharasus,
Reelius, Roimus, and Baana, their
guides. [9]The number of them of the
nation, and their governors, sons of
Phoros, two thousand an hundred
seventy and two; the sons of Saphat,
four hundred seventy and two: [10]The
sons of Ares, seven hundred fifty and
six: [11]The sons of Phaath Moab, two
thousand eight hundred and twelve:
[12]The sons of Elam, a thousand two
hundred fifty and four: the sons of
Zathul, nine hundred forty and five: the
sons of Corbe, seven hundred and five:
the sons of Bani, six hundred forty and
eight: [13]The sons of Bebai, six hundred
twenty and three: the sons of Sadas,
three thousand two hundred twenty and
two: [14]The sons of Adonikam, six
hundred sixty and seven: the sons of
Bagoi, two thousand sixty and six: the
sons of Adin, four hundred fifty and
four: [15]The sons of Aterezias, ninety
and two: the sons of Ceilan and Azetas
threescore and seven: the sons of
Azuran, four hundred thirty and two:
[16]The sons of Ananias, an hundred
and one: the sons of Arom, thirty two:
and the sons of Bassa, three hundred
twenty and three: the sons of
Azephurith, an hundred and two: [17]The
sons of Meterus, three thousand and
five: the sons of Bethlomon, an hundred
twenty and three: [18]They of
Netophah, fifty and five: they of
Anathoth, an hundred fifty and eight:
they of Bethsamos, forty and two:
[19]They of Kiriathiarius, twenty and
five: they of Caphira and Beroth, seven
hundred forty and three: they of Pira,
seven hundred: [20]They of Chadias and
Ammidoi, four hundred twenty and
two: they of Cirama and Gabdes, six
hundred twenty and one:
[21]They of Macalon, an hundred twenty
and two: they of Betolius, fifty and two:
the sons of Nephis, an hundred fifty and
six: [22]The sons of Calamolalus and
Onus, seven hundred twenty and five:
the sons of Jerechus, two hundred
forty and five: [23]The sons of Annas,
three thousand three hundred and thirty.
[24]The priests: the sons of Jeddu, the son
of Jesus among the sons of Sanasib,
nine hundred seventy and two: the sons
of Meruth, a thousand fifty and two:
[25]The sons of Phassaron, a thousand
forty and seven: the sons of Carme, a
thousand and seventeen.
[26]The Levites: the sons of Jessue, and
Cadmiel, and Banuas, and Sudias,
seventy and four. [27]The holy singers:
the sons of Asaph, an hundred twenty
and eight.
[28]The porters: the sons of Salum, the
sons of Jatal, the sons of Talmon, the
sons of Dacobi, the sons of Teta, the sons
of Sami, in all an hundred thirty and
nine. [29]The servants of the temple: the
sons of Esau, the sons of Asipha, the
sons of Tabaoth, the sons of Ceras, the
sons of Sud, the sons of Phaleas, the
sons of Labana, the sons of Graba,
[30]The sons of Acua, the sons of Uta, the
sons of Cetab, the sons of Agaba, the sons
of Subai, the sons of Anan, the sons of
Cathua, the sons of Geddur, [31]The sons
of Airus, the sons of Daisan, the sons of
Noeba, the sons of Chaseba, the sons of

Gazera, the sons of Azia, the sons of
Phinees, the sons of Azare, the sons of
Bastai, the sons of Asana, the sons of
Meani, the sons of Naphisi, the sons of
Acub, the sons of Acipha, the sons of
Assur, the sons of Pharacim, the sons of
Basaloth, 32The sons of Meeda, the
sons of Coutha, the sons of Charea, the
sons of Charcus, the sons of Aserer, the
sons of Thomoi, the sons of Nasith, the
sons of Atipha. 33The sons of the
servants of Solomon: the sons of
Azaphion, the sons of Pharira, the sons
of Jeeli, the sons of Lozon, the sons of
Israel, the sons of Sapheth, 34The sons
of Hagia, the sons of Pharacareth, the
sons of Sabi, the sons of Sarothie, the
sons of Masias, the sons of Gar, the
sons of Addus, the sons of Suba, the
sons of Apherra, the sons of Barodis,
the sons of Sabat, the sons of Allom.
35All the ministers of the temple, and
the sons of the servants of Solomon,
were three hundred seventy and two.
36These came up from Thermeleth and
Thelersas, Charaathalar leading them,
and Aalar; 37Neither could they shew
their families, nor their stock, how they
were of Israel: the sons of Ladan, the
son of Ban, the sons of Necodan, six
hundred fifty and two. 38And of the
priests that usurped the office of the
priesthood, and were not found: the
sons of Obdia, the sons of Accoz, the
sons of Addus, who married Augia one
of the daughters of Barzelus, and was
named after his name. 39And when the
description of the kindred of these
men was sought in the register, and
was not found, they were removed
from executing the office of the
priesthood: 40For unto them said
Nehemias and Atharias, that they
should not be partakers of the holy
things, till there arose up an high priest
clothed with doctrine and truth. 41So of
Israel, from them of twelve years old and
upward, they were all in number forty
thousand, beside menservants and
womenservants two thousand three
hundred and sixty. 42Their menservants
and handmaids were seven thousand
three hundred forty and seven: the
singing men and singing women, two
hundred forty and five: 43Four
hundred thirty and five camels, seven
thousand thirty and six horses, two
hundred forty and five mules, five
thousand five hundred twenty and five
beasts used to the yoke. 44And certain of
the chief of their families, when they
came to the temple of God that is in
Jerusalem, vowed to set up the
house again in his own place according
to their ability, 45And to give into the
holy treasury of the works a
thousand pounds of gold, five
thousand of silver, and an hundred
priestly vestments.
46And so dwelt the priests and the
Levites and the people in Jerusalem,
and in the country, the singers also and
the porters; and all Israel in their
villages. 47But when the seventh month
was at hand, and when the children of
Israel were every man in his own place,
they came all together with one consent
into the open place of the first gate
which is toward the east.
48Then stood up Jesus the son of
Josedec, and his brethren the priests and
Zorobabel the son of Salathiel, and his
brethren, and made ready the altar of
the God of Israel, 49To offer burnt
sacrifices upon it, according as it is
expressly commanded in the book of
Moses the man of God.
50And there were gathered unto them
out of the other nations of the land, and
they erected the altar upon his own

place, because all the nations of the land
were at enmity with them, and
oppressed them; and they offered
sacrifices according to the time, and
burnt offerings to the Lord both
morning and evening. 51 Also they held
the feast of tabernacles, as it is
commanded in the law, and offered
sacrifices daily, as was meet: 52 And
after that, the continual oblations, and
the sacrifice of the sabbaths, and of the
new moons, and of all holy feasts.
53 And all they that had made any vow
to God began to offer sacrifices to God
from the first day of the seventh month,
although the temple of the Lord was
not yet built. 54 And they gave unto the
masons and carpenters money, meat,
and drink, with cheerfulness.
55 Unto them of Zidon also and Tyre
they gave carrs, that they should bring
cedar trees from Libanus, which should
be brought by floats to the haven of
Joppa, according as it was commanded
them by Cyrus king of the Persians.
56 And in the second year and second
month after his coming to the temple of
God at Jerusalem began Zorobabel the
son of Salathiel, and Jesus the son of
Josedec, and their brethren, and the
priests, and the Levites, and all they
that were come unto Jerusalem out of
the captivity:
57 And they laid the foundation of the
house of God in the first day of the
second month, in the second year after
they were come to Jewry and
Jerusalem.
58 And they appointed the Levites from
twenty years old over the works of the
Lord. Then stood up Jesus, and his sons
and brethren, and Cadmiel his brother,
and the sons of Madiabun, with the
sons of Joda the son of Eliadun, with
their sons and brethren, all Levites, with
one accord setters forward of the
business, labouring to advance the
works in the house of God. So the
workmen built the temple of the Lord.
59 And the priests stood arrayed in their
vestments with musical instruments
and trumpets; and the Levites the sons
of Asaph had cymbals, 60 Singing songs
of thanksgiving, and praising the Lord,
according as David the king of Israel
had ordained. 61 And they sung with
loud voices songs to the praise of the
Lord, because his mercy and glory is
for ever in all Israel. 62 And all the
people sounded trumpets, and shouted
with a loud voice, singing songs of
thanksgiving unto the Lord for the
rearing up of the house of the Lord.
63 Also of the priests and Levites, and of
the chief of their families, the ancients
who had seen the former house came to
the building of this with weeping and
great crying. 64 But many with trumpets
and joy shouted with loud voice,
65 Insomuch that the trumpets might not
be heard for the weeping of the people:
yet the multitude sounded
marvellously, so that it was heard afar
off. 66 Wherefore when the enemies of
the tribe of Judah and Benjamin heard
it, they came to know what that noise of
trumpets should mean. 67 And they
perceived that they that were of the
captivity did build the temple unto the
Lord God of Israel. 68 So they went to
Zorobabel and Jesus, and to the chief of
the families, and said unto them, We
will build together with you. 69 For we
likewise, as ye, do obey your Lord,
and do sacrifice unto him from the days
of Azbazareth the king of the
Assyrians, who brought us hither.
70 Then Zorobabel and Jesus and the
chief of the families of Israel said unto
them, It is not for us and you to build

together an house unto the Lord our
God. 71 We ourselves alone will build
unto the Lord of Israel, according as
Cyrus the king of the Persians hath
commanded us. 72 But the heathen of
the land lying heavy upon the
inhabitants of Judea, and holding them
strait, hindered their building; 73 And
by their secret plots, and popular
persuasions and commotions, they
hindered the finishing of the building
all the time that king Cyrus lived: so
they were hindered from building for
the space of two years, until the reign
of Darius.

CHAPTER 6

1 Now in the second year of the reign of
Darius Aggeus and Zacharias the son of
Addo, the prophets, prophesied unto
the Jews in Jewry and Jerusalem in the
name of the Lord God of Israel, which
was upon them. 2 Then stood up
Zorobabel the son of Salatiel, and Jesus
the son of Josedec, and began to build
the house of the Lord at Jerusalem, the
prophets of the Lord being with them,
and helping them. 3 At the same time
came unto them Sisinnes the governor
of Syria and Phenice, with
Sathrabuzanes and his companions,
and said unto them, 4 By whose
appointment do ye build this house and
this roof, and perform all the other
things? and who are the workmen that
perform these things? 5 Nevertheless
the elders of the Jews obtained favour,
because the Lord had visited the
captivity; 6 And they were not hindered
from building, until such time as
signification was given unto Darius
concerning them, and an answer
received. 7 The copy of the letters
which Sisinnes, governor of Syria and
Phenice, and Sathrabuzanes, with their
companions, rulers in Syria and
Phenice, wrote and sent unto Darius;
To king Darius, greeting: 8 Let all
things be known unto our lord the king,
that being come into the country of
Judea, and entered into the city of
Jerusalem we found in the city of
Jerusalem the ancients of the Jews that
were of the captivity 9 Building an
house unto the Lord, great and new, of
hewn and costly stones, and the timber
already laid upon the walls. 10 And
those works are done with great speed,
and the work goeth on prosperously in
their hands, and with all glory and
diligence is it made. 11 Then asked we
these elders, saying, By whose
commandment build ye this house, and
lay the foundations of these works?
12 Therefore to the intent that we might
give knowledge unto thee by writing,
we demanded of them who were the
chief doers, and we required of them
the names in writing of their principal
men. 13 So they gave us this answer, We
are the servants of the Lord which made
heaven and earth. 14 And as for this
house, it was builded many years ago
by a king of Israel great and strong, and
was finished. 15 But when our fathers
provoked God unto wrath, and sinned
against the Lord of Israel which is
in heaven, he gave them over into the
power of Nabuchodonosor king of
Babylon, of the Chaldees; 16 Who
pulled down the house, and burned it,
and carried away the people captives
unto Babylon. 17 But in the first year
that king Cyrus reigned over the
country of Babylon Cyrus the king
wrote to build up this house. 18 And the
holy vessels of gold and of silver, that
Nabuchodonosor had carried away out
of the house at Jerusalem, and had set

them in his own temple those Cyrus the
king brought forth again out of the
temple at Babylon, and they were
delivered to Zorobabel and to
Sanabassarus the ruler, [19]With
commandment that he should carry
away the same vessels, and put them in
the temple at Jerusalem; and that the
temple of the Lord should be built in
his place. [20]Then the same
Sanabassarus, being come hither, laid
the foundations of the house of the
Lord at Jerusalem; and from that time
to this being still a building, it is not yet
fully ended. [21]Now therefore, if it seem
good unto the king, let search be made
among the records of king Cyrus:
[22]And if it be found that the building of
the house of the Lord at Jerusalem hath
been done with the consent of king
Cyrus, and if our lord the king be so
minded, let him signify unto us thereof.
[23]Then commanded king Darius to seek
among the records at Babylon: and so at
Ecbatane the palace, which is in the
country of Media, there was found a
roll wherein these things were
recorded. [24]In the first year of the reign
of Cyrus king Cyrus commanded that
the house of the Lord at Jerusalem
should be built again, where they do
sacrifice with continual fire: [25]Whose
height shall be sixty cubits and the
breadth sixty cubits, with three rows of
hewn stones, and one row of new wood
of that country; and the expences
thereof to be given out of the house of
king Cyrus: [26]And that the holy vessels
of the house of the Lord, both of gold
and silver, that Nabuchodonosor took
out of the house at Jerusalem, and
brought to Babylon, should be restored
to the house at Jerusalem, and be set in
the place where they were before.
[27]And also he commanded that Sisinnes
the governor of Syria and Phenice, and
Sathrabuzanes, and their companions,
and those which were appointed rulers
in Syria and Phenice, should be careful
not to meddle with the place, but suffer
Zorobabel, the servant of the Lord, and
governor of Judea, and the elders of the
Jews, to build the house of the Lord in
that place. [28]I have commanded also
to have it built up whole again; and that
they look diligently to help those that
be of the captivity of the Jews, till the
house of the Lord be finished: [29]And
out of the tribute of Celosyria and
Phenice a portion carefully to be given
these men for the sacrifices of the Lord,
that is, to Zorobabel the governor, for
bullocks, and rams, and lambs; [30]And
also corn, salt, wine, and oil, and that
continually every year without further
question, according as the priests that be
in Jerusalem shall signify to be daily
spent: [31]That offerings may be made to
the most high God for the king and for
his children, and that they may pray for
their lives. [32]And he commanded that
whosoever should transgress, yea, or
make light of any thing afore spoken or
written, out of his own house should a
tree be taken, and he thereon be
hanged, and all his goods seized for the
king. [33]The Lord therefore, whose
name is there called upon, utterly
destroy every king and nation, that
stretcheth out his hand to hinder or
endamage that house of the Lord in
Jerusalem.
[34]I Darius the king have ordained that
according unto these things it be done
with diligence.

CHAPTER 7

[1]Then Sisinnes the governor of
Celosyria and Phenice, and

Sathrabuzanes, with their companions
following the commandments of king
Darius, 2 Did very carefully oversee the
holy works, assisting the ancients of the
Jews and governors of the temple.
3 And so the holy works prospered,
when Aggeus and Zacharias the
prophets prophesied. 4 And they
finished these things by the
commandment of the Lord God of
Israel, and with the consent of Cyrus,
Darius, and Artexerxes, kings of Persia.
5 And thus was the holy house finished
in the three and twentieth day of the
month Adar, in the sixth year of Darius
king of the Persians 6 And the children
of Israel, the priests, and the Levites,
and others that were of the captivity, that
were added unto them, did according to
the things written in the book of Moses.
7 And to the dedication of the temple of
the Lord they offered an hundred
bullocks two hundred rams, four
hundred lambs;
8 And twelve goats for the sin of all
Israel, according to the number of the
chief of the tribes of Israel. 9 The priests
also and the Levites stood arrayed in
their vestments, according to their
kindreds, in the service of the Lord
God of Israel, according to the book of
Moses: and the porters at every gate.
10 And the children of Israel that were of
the captivity held the passover the
fourteenth day of the first month, after
that the priests and the Levites were
sanctified. 11 They that were of the
captivity were not all sanctified
together: but the Levites were all
sanctified together. 12 And so they
offered the passover for all them of the
captivity, and for their brethren the
priests, and for themselves. 13 And the
children of Israel that came out of the
captivity did eat, even all they that had
separated themselves from the
abominations of the people of the land,
and sought the Lord. 14 And they kept
the feast of unleavened bread seven
days, making merry before the Lord,
15 For that he had turned the counsel of
the king of Assyria toward them, to
strengthen their hands in the works of
the Lord God of Israel.

CHAPTER 8

1 And after these things, when
Artexerxes the king of the Persians
reigned came Esdras the son of Saraias,
the son of Ezerias, the son of Helchiah,
the son of Salum, 2 The son of Sadduc,
the son of Achitob, the son of Amarias,
the son of Ezias, the son of Meremoth,
the son of Zaraias, the son of Savias,
the son of Boccas, the son of Abisum,
the son of Phinees, the son of Eleazar,
the son of Aaron the chief priest.
3 This Esdras went up from Babylon, as
a scribe, being very ready in the law of
Moses, that was given by the God of
Israel.
4 And the king did him honour: for he
found grace in his sight in all his
requests.
5 There went up with him also certain of
the children of Israel, of the priest of the
Levites, of the holy singers, porters,
and ministers of the temple, unto
Jerusalem, 6 In the seventh year of the
reign of Artexerxes, in the fifth month,
this was the king's seventh year; for
they went from Babylon in the first day
of the first month, and came to
Jerusalem, according to the prosperous
journey which the Lord gave them.
7 For Esdras had very great skill, so
that he omitted nothing of the law and
commandments of the Lord, but taught
all Israel the ordinances and judgments.

8Now the copy of the commission,
which was written from Artexerxes the
king, and came to Esdras the priest and
reader of the law of the Lord, is this that
followeth; 9King Artexerxes unto
Esdras the priest and reader of the law
of the Lord sendeth greeting: 10Having
determined to deal graciously, I have
given order, that such of the nation of
the Jews, and of the priests and Levites
being within our realm, as are willing
and desirous should go with thee unto
Jerusalem. 11As many therefore as
have a mind thereunto, let them
depart with thee, as it hath seemed
good both to me and my seven friends
the counsellors; 12That they may look
unto the affairs of Judea and Jerusalem,
agreeably to that which is in the law of
the Lord; 13And carry the gifts unto the
Lord of Israel to Jerusalem, which I and
my friends have vowed, and all the gold
and silver that in the country of
Babylon can be found, to the Lord in
Jerusalem, 14With that also which is
given of the people for the temple of the
Lord their God at Jerusalem: and that
silver and gold may be collected for
bullocks, rams, and lambs, and things
thereunto appertaining; 15To the end
that they may offer sacrifices unto the
Lord upon the altar of the Lord their
God, which is in Jerusalem. 16And
whatsoever thou and thy brethren will
do with the silver and gold, that do,
according to the will of thy God. 17And
the holy vessels of the Lord, which are
given thee for the use of the temple of
thy God, which is in Jerusalem, thou
shalt set before thy God in Jerusalem.
18And whatsoever thing else thou shalt
remember for the use of the temple of
thy God, thou shalt give it out of the
king's treasury. 19And I king
Artexerxes have also commanded the
keepers of the treasures in Syria and
Phenice, that whatsoever Esdras the
priest and the reader of the law of the
most high God shall send for, they
should give it him with speed, 20To
the sum of an hundred talents of silver,
likewise also of wheat even to an
hundred cors, and an hundred pieces of
wine, and other things in abundance.
21Let all things be performed after the
law of God diligently unto the most
high God, that wrath come not upon the
kingdom of the king and his sons. 22I
command you also, that ye require no
tax, nor any other imposition, of any of
the priests, or Levites, or holy singers,
or porters, or ministers of the temple, or
of any that have doings in this temple,
and that no man have authority to
impose any thing upon them. 23And
thou, Esdras, according to the wisdom
of God ordain judges and justices, that
they may judge in all Syria and Phenice
all those that know the law of thy God;
and those that know it not thou shalt
teach.

24And whosoever shall transgress the
law of thy God, and of the king, shall
be punished diligently, whether it be by
death, or other punishment, by penalty
of money, or by imprisonment. 25Then
said Esdras the scribe, Blessed be the
only Lord God of my fathers, who hath
put these things into the heart of the
king, to glorify his house that is in
Jerusalem: 26And hath honoured me in
the sight of the king, and his
counsellors, and all his friends and
nobles. 27Therefore was I encouraged
by the help of the Lord my God, and
gathered together men of Israel to go
up with me. 28And these are the chief
according to their families and several
dignities, that went up with me from
Babylon in the reign of king

Artexerxes: 29 Of the sons of Phinees,
Gerson: of the sons of Ithamar,
Gamael: of the sons of David, Lettus
the son of Sechenias: 30 Of the sons of
Pharez, Zacharias; and with him were
counted an hundred and fifty men: 31 Of
the sons of Pahath Moab, Eliaonias, the
son of Zaraias, and with him two
hundred men: 32 Of the sons of Zathoe,
Sechenias the son of Jezelus, and with
him three hundred men: of the sons of
Adin, Obeth the son of Jonathan, and
with him two hundred and fifty men:
33 Of the sons of Elam, Josias son of
Gotholias, and with him seventy men:
34 Of the sons of Saphatias, Zaraias son
of Michael, and with him threescore
and ten men: 35 Of the sons of Joab,
Abadias son of Jezelus, and with him
two hundred and twelve men: 36 Of the
sons of Banid, Assalimoth son of
Josaphias, and with him an hundred
and threescore men: 37 Of the sons of
Babi, Zacharias son of Bebai, and with
him twenty and eight men: 38 Of the
sons of Astath, Johannes son of Acatan,
and with him an hundred and ten men:
39 Of the sons of Adonikam the last, and
these are the names of them, Eliphalet,
Jewel, and Samaias, and with them
seventy men: 40 Of the sons of Bago,
Uthi the son of Istalcurus, and with him
seventy men. 41 And these I gathered
together to the river called Theras,
where we pitched our tents three days:
and then I surveyed them. 42 But
when I had found there none of the
priests and Levites, 43 Then sent I unto
Eleazar, and Iduel, and Masman, 44 And
Alnathan, and Mamaias, and Joribas,
and Nathan, Eunatan, Zacharias, and
Mosollamon, principal men and
learned. 45 And I bade them that they
should go unto Saddeus the captain,
who was in the place of the treasury:
46 And commanded them that they
should speak unto Daddeus, and to
his brethren, and to the treasurers in
that place, to send us such men as might
execute the priests' office in the house
of the Lord. 47 And by the mighty hand
of our Lord they brought unto us skilful
men of the sons of Moli the son of Levi,
the son of Israel, Asebebia, and his
sons, and his brethren, who were
eighteen. 48 And Asebia, and Annus,
and Osaias his brother, of the sons of
Channuneus, and their sons, were
twenty men. 49 And of the servants of
the temple whom David had ordained,
and the principal men for the service
of the Levites to wit, the servants of the
temple two hundred and twenty, the
catalogue of whose names were
shewed. 50 And there I vowed a fast
unto the young men before our Lord, to
desire of him a prosperous journey both
for us and them that were with us, for
our children, and for the cattle: 51 For
I was ashamed to ask the king footmen,
and horsemen, and conduct for
safeguard against our adversaries. 52 For
we had said unto the king, that the
power of the Lord our God should be
with them that seek him, to support
them in all ways. 53 And again we
besought our Lord as touching these
things, and found him favourable unto
us. 54 Then I separated twelve of the
chief of the priests, Esebrias, and
Assanias, and ten men of their brethren
with them: 55 And I weighed them the
gold, and the silver, and the holy vessels
of the house of our Lord, which the king,
and his council, and the princes, and all
Israel, had given. 56 And when I had
weighed it, I delivered unto them six
hundred and fifty talents of silver, and
silver vessels of an hundred talents, and
an hundred talents of gold, 57 And

twenty golden vessels, and twelve
vessels of brass, even of fine brass,
glittering like gold. 58 And I said unto
them, Both ye are holy unto the Lord,
and the vessels are holy, and the gold
and the silver is a vow unto the Lord,
the Lord of our fathers. 59 Watch ye,
and keep them till ye deliver them to
the chief of the priests and Levites, and
to the principal men of the families of
Israel, in Jerusalem, into the chambers
of the house of our God. 60 So the
priests and the Levites, who had
received the silver and the gold and the
vessels, brought them unto Jerusalem,
into the temple of the Lord. 61 And
from the river Theras we departed the
twelfth day of the first month, and came
to Jerusalem by the mighty hand of our
Lord, which was with us: and from the
beginning of our journey the Lord
delivered us from every enemy, and so
we came to Jerusalem.

62 And when we had been there three
days, the gold and silver that was
weighed was delivered in the house of
our Lord on the fourth day unto
Marmoth the priest the son of Iri.
63 And with him was Eleazar the son of
Phinees, and with them were Josabad
the son of Jesu and Moeth the son of
Sabban, Levites: all was delivered them
by number and weight. 64 And all the
weight of them was written up the same
hour.

65 Moreover they that were come out of
the captivity offered sacrifice unto
the Lord God of Israel, even twelve
bullocks for all Israel, fourscore and
sixteen rams, 66 Threescore and twelve
lambs, goats for a peace offering,
twelve; all of them a sacrifice to the
Lord. 67 And they delivered the king's
commandments unto the king's
stewards' and to the governors of
Celosyria and Phenice; and they
honoured the people and the temple of
God. 68 Now when these things were
done, the rulers came unto me, and
said, 69 The nation of Israel, the princes,
the priests and Levites, have not put
away from them the strange people of
the land, nor the pollutions of the
Gentiles to wit, of the Canaanites,
Hittites, Pheresites, Jebusites, and the
Moabites, Egyptians, and Edomites.

70 For both they and their sons have
married with their daughters, and the
holy seed is mixed with the strange
people of the land; and from the
beginning of this matter the rulers and
the great men have been partakers of
this iniquity. 71 And as soon as I had
heard these things, I rent my clothes, and
the holy garment, and pulled off the hair
from off my head and beard, and sat me
down sad and very heavy. 72 So all they
that were then moved at the word of the
Lord God of Israel assembled unto me,
whilst I mourned for the iniquity: but I sat
still full of heaviness until the evening
sacrifice. 73 Then rising up from the fast
with my clothes and the holy garment
rent, and bowing my knees, and
stretching forth my hands unto the
Lord, 74 I said, O Lord, I am
confounded and ashamed before thy
face; 75 For our sins are multiplied
above our heads, and our ignorances
have reached up unto heaven. 76 For
ever since the time of our fathers we
have been and are in great sin, even unto
this day. 77 And for our sins and our
fathers' we with our brethren and our
kings and our priests were given up
unto the kings of the earth, to the
sword, and to captivity, and for a prey
with shame, unto this day. 78 And now
in some measure hath mercy been
shewed unto us from thee, O Lord, that

there should be left us a root and a name
in the place of thy sanctuary; 79 And to
discover unto us a light in the house of
the Lord our God, and to give us food
in the time of our servitude. 80 Yea,
when we were in bondage, we were not
forsaken of our Lord; but he made us
gracious before the kings of Persia, so
that they gave us food;
81 Yea, and honoured the temple of our
Lord, and raised up the desolate Sion,
that they have given us a sure abiding in
Jewry and Jerusalem. 82 And now, O
Lord, what shall we say, having these
things? for we have transgressed thy
commandments, which thou gavest by
the hand of thy servants the prophets,
saying, 83 That the land, which ye enter
into to possess as an heritage, is a land
polluted with the pollutions of the
strangers of the land, and they have
filled it with their uncleanness.
84 Therefore now shall ye not join your
daughters unto their sons, neither shall
ye take their daughters unto your sons.
85 Moreover ye shall never seek to have
peace with them, that ye may be
strong, and eat the good things of the
land, and that ye may leave the
inheritance of the land unto your
children for evermore. 86 And all that is
befallen is done unto us for our wicked
works and great sins; for thou, O Lord,
didst make our sins light, 87 And didst
give unto us such a root: but we have
turned back again to transgress thy law,
and to mingle ourselves with the
uncleanness of the nations of the land.
88 Mightest not thou be angry with us to
destroy us, till thou hadst left us neither
root, seed, nor name? 89 O Lord of
Israel, thou art true: for we are left a
root this day. 90 Behold, now are we
before thee in our iniquities, for we
cannot stand any longer by reason of
these things before thee. 91 And as
Esdras in his prayer made his
confession, weeping, and lying flat
upon the ground before the temple,
there gathered unto him from
Jerusalem a very great multitude of
men and women and children: for there
was great weeping among the
multitude. 92 Then Jechonias the son of
Jeelus, one of the sons of Israel, called
out, and said, O Esdras, we have sinned
against the Lord God, we have married
strange women of the nations of the
land, and now is all Israel aloft. 93 Let
us make an oath to the Lord, that we will
put away all our wives, which we have
taken of the heathen, with their
children, 94 Like as thou hast decreed,
and as many as do obey the law of the
Lord. 95 Arise and put in execution: for
to thee doth this matter appertain, and
we will be with thee: do valiantly. 96 So
Esdras arose, and took an oath of the
chief of the priests and Levites of all
Israel to do after these things; and so
they sware.

CHAPTER 9

1 Then Esdras rising from the court of
the temple went to the chamber of
Joanan the son of Eliasib, 2 And
remained there, and did eat no meat nor
drink water, mourning for the great
iniquities of the multitude. 3 And there
was a proclamation in all Jewry and
Jerusalem to all them that were of the
captivity, that they should be gathered
together at Jerusalem: 4 And that
whosoever met not there within two or
three days according as the elders that
bare rule appointed, their cattle should
be seized to the use of the temple, and
himself cast out from them that were of
the captivity. 5 And in three days were

all they of the tribe of Judah and
Benjamin gathered together at
Jerusalem the twentieth day of the ninth
month. 6And all the multitude sat
trembling in the broad court of the
temple because of the present foul
weather. 7So Esdras arose up, and said
unto them, Ye have transgressed the
law in marrying strange wives, thereby
to increase the sins of Israel. 8And now
by confessing give glory unto the Lord
God of our fathers, 9And do his will,
and separate yourselves from the
heathen of the land, and from the
strange women.
10Then cried the whole multitude, and
said with a loud voice, Like as thou hast
spoken, so will we do. 11But
forasmuch as the people are many, and
it is foul weather, so that we cannot
stand without, and this is not a work of
a day or two, seeing our sin in these
things is spread far:
12Therefore let the rulers of the
multitude stay, and let all them of our
habitations that have strange wives
come at the time appointed, 13And with
them the rulers and judges of every
place, till we turn away the wrath of the
Lord from us for this matter. 14Then
Jonathan the son of Azael and Ezechias
the son of Theocanus accordingly took
this matter upon them: and Mosollam
and Levis and Sabbatheus helped them.
15And they that were of the captivity
did according to all these things. 16And
Esdras the priest chose unto him the
principal men of their families, all by
name: and in the first day of the tenth
month they sat together to examine the
matter. 17So their cause that held
strange wives was brought to an end in
the first day of the first month. 18And
of the priests that were come together,
and had strange wives, there were
found:
19Of the sons of Jesus the son of
Josedec, and his brethren; Matthelas
and Eleazar, and Joribus and Joadanus.
20And they gave their hands to put
away their wives and to offer rams to
make reconcilement for their errors.
21And of the sons of Emmer; Ananias,
and Zabdeus, and Eanes, and Sameius,
and Hiereel, and Azarias. 22And of the
sons of Phaisur; Elionas, Massias
Israel, and Nathanael, and Ocidelus and
Talsas. 23And of the Levites; Jozabad,
and Semis, and Colius, who was called
Calitas, and Patheus, and Judas, and
Jonas. 24Of the holy singers; Eleazurus,
Bacchurus. 25Of the porters; Sallumus,
and Tolbanes.
26Of them of Israel, of the sons of
Phoros; Hiermas, and Eddias, and
Melchias, and Maelus, and Eleazar, and
Asibias, and Baanias. 27Of the sons of
Ela; Matthanias, Zacharias, and
Hierielus, and Hieremoth, and Aedias.
28And of the sons of Zamoth; Eliadas,
Elisimus, Othonias, Jarimoth, and
Sabatus, and Sardeus. 29Of the sons of
Babai; Johannes, and Ananias and
Josabad, and Amatheis. 30Of the sons
of Mani; Olamus, Mamuchus, Jedeus,
Jasubus, Jasael, and Hieremoth. 31And
of the sons of Addi; Naathus, and
Moosias, Lacunus, and Naidus, and
Mathanias, and Sesthel, Balnuus, and
Manasseas.
32And of the sons of Annas; Elionas and
Aseas, and Melchias, and Sabbeus, and
Simon Chosameus.
33And of the sons of Asom; Altaneus,
and Matthias, and Baanaia, Eliphalet,
and Manasses, and Semei. 34And of
the sons of Maani; Jeremias, Momdis,
Omaerus, Juel, Mabdai, and Pelias,
and Anos, Carabasion, and Enasibus,
and Mamnitanaimus, Eliasis, Bannus,

Eliali, Samis, Selemias, Nathanias: and
of the sons of Ozora; Sesis, Esril,
Azaelus, Samatus, Zambis, Josephus.
35 And of the sons of Ethma; Mazitias,
Zabadaias, Edes, Juel, Banaias. 36 All
these had taken strange wives, and they
put them away with their children.
37 And the priests and Levites, and they
that were of Israel, dwelt in Jerusalem,
and in the country, in the first day of the
seventh month: so the children of Israel
were in their habitations. 38 And the
whole multitude came together with
one accord into the broad place of the
holy porch toward the east: 39 And they
spake unto Esdras the priest and reader,
that he would bring the law of Moses,
that was given of the Lord God of
Israel. 40 So Esdras the chief priest
brought the law unto the whole
multitude from man to woman, and to all
the priests, to hear law in the first day of
the seventh month. 41 And he read in the
broad court before the holy porch from
morning unto midday, before both men
and women; and the multitude gave
heed unto the law. 42 And Esdras the
priest and reader of the law stood up
upon a pulpit of wood, which was made
for that purpose. 43 And there stood up
by him Mattathias, Sammus, Ananias,
Azarias, Urias, Ezecias, Balasamus,
upon the right hand: 44 And upon his left
hand stood Phaldaius, Misael, Melchias,
Lothasubus, and Nabarias. 45 Then took
Esdras the book of the law before the
multitude: for he sat honourably in the
first place in the sight of them all. 46 And
when he opened the law, they stood all
straight up. So Esdras blessed the Lord
God most High, the God of hosts,
Almighty. 47 And all the people
answered, Amen; and lifting up their
hands they fell to the ground, and
worshipped the Lord.
48 Also Jesus, Anus, Sarabias, Adinus,
Jacubus, Sabateas, Auteas, Maianeas,
and Calitas, Asrias, and Joazabdus, and
Ananias, Biatas, the Levites, taught the
law of the Lord, making them withal to
understand it.
49 Then spake Attharates unto Esdras
the chief priest. and reader, and to the
Levites that taught the multitude, even
to all, saying, 50 This day is holy unto
the Lord; (for they all wept when they
heard the law:) 51 Go then, and eat the
fat, and drink the sweet, and send part to
them that have nothing; 52 For this day
is holy unto the Lord: and be not
sorrowful; for the Lord will bring you
to honour. 53 So the Levites published
all things to the people, saying, This day
is holy to the Lord; be not sorrowful.
54 Then went they their way, every one
to eat and drink, and make merry, and
to give part to them that had nothing,
and to make great cheer; 55 Because
they understood the words wherein
they were instructed, and for the which
they had been assembled

II ESDRAS

CHAPTER 1

1 The second book of the prophet
Esdras, the son of Saraias, the son of
Azarias, the son of Helchias, the son of
Sadamias, the sou of Sadoc, the son of
Achitob, 2 The son of Achias, the son of
Phinees, the son of Heli, the son of
Amarias, the son of Aziei, the son of
Marimoth, the son of And he spake
unto the of Borith, the son of Abisei,
the son of Phinees, the son of Eleazar,
3 The son of Aaron, of the tribe of Levi;
which was captive in the land of the
Medes, in the reign of Artexerxes king
of the Persians.
4 And the word of the Lord came unto
me, saying, 5 Go thy way, and shew
my people their sinful deeds, and their
children their wickedness which they
have done against me; that they may
tell their children's children: 6 Because
the sins of their fathers are increased in
them: for they have forgotten me, and
have offered unto strange gods. 7 Am
not I even he that brought them out of
the land of Egypt, from the house of
bondage? but they have provoked me
unto wrath, and despised my counsels.
8 Pull thou off then the hair of thy head,
and cast all evil upon them, for they
have not been obedient unto my law, but
it is a rebellious people. 9 How long shall
I forbear them, into whom I have done
so much good? 10 Many kings have I
destroyed for their sakes; Pharaoh with
his servants and all his power have I
smitten down. 11 All the nations have I
destroyed before them, and in the east I
have scattered the people of two
provinces, even of Tyrus and Sidon,
and have slain all their enemies.
12 Speak thou therefore unto them,
saying, Thus saith the Lord, 13 I led you
through the sea and in the beginning
gave you a large and safe passage; I
gave you Moses for a leader, and
Aaron for a priest. 14 I gave you light in
a pillar of fire, and great wonders have
I done among you; yet have ye forgotten
me, saith the Lord.
15 Thus saith the Almighty Lord, The
quails were as a token to you; I gave
you tents for your safeguard:
nevertheless ye murmured there,
16 And triumphed not in my name for
the destruction of your enemies, but
ever to this day do ye yet murmur.
17 Where are the benefits that I have
done for you? when ye were hungry and
thirsty in the wilderness, did ye not cry
unto me, 18 Saying, Why hast thou
brought us into this wilderness to kill
us? it had been better for us to have
served the Egyptians, than to die in this
wilderness. 19 Then had I pity upon
your mournings, and gave you manna
to eat; so ye did eat angels' bread.
20 When ye were thirsty, did I not cleave
the rock, and waters flowed out to your
fill? for the heat I covered you with the
leaves of the trees. 21 I divided among
you a fruitful land, I cast out the
Canaanites, the Pherezites, and the
Philistines, before you: what shall I yet
do more for you? saith the Lord. 22 Thus
saith the Almighty Lord, When ye were
in the wilderness, in the river of the
Amorites, being athirst, and
blaspheming my name, 23 I gave you
not fire for your blasphemies, but cast
a tree in the water, and made the river
sweet. 24 What shall I do unto thee, O
Jacob? thou, Juda, wouldest not obey
me: I will turn me to other nations, and
unto those will I give my name, that

they may keep my statutes. 25 Seeing ye
have forsaken me, I will forsake you
also; when ye desire me to be gracious
unto you, I shall have no mercy upon
you. 26 Whensoever ye shall call upon
me, I will not hear you: for ye have
defiled your hands with blood, and your
feet are swift to commit manslaughter.
27 Ye have not as it were forsaken me, but
your own selves, saith the Lord.
28 Thus saith the Almighty Lord, Have I
not prayed you as a father his sons,
as a mother her daughters, and a nurse
her young babes, 29 That ye would be
my people, and I should be your God;
that ye would be my children, and I
should be your father? 30 I gathered you
together, as a hen gathereth her
chickens under her wings: but now,
what shall I do unto you? I will cast you
out from my face. 31 When ye offer unto
me, I will turn my face from you: for
your solemn feastdays, your new
moons, and your circumcisions, have I
forsaken. 32 I sent unto you my servants
the prophets, whom ye have taken and
slain, and torn their bodies in pieces,
whose blood I will require of your
hands, saith the Lord. 33 Thus saith the
Almighty Lord, Your house is desolate,
I will cast you out as the wind doth
stubble. 34 And your children shall not be
fruitful; for they have despised my
commandment, and done the thing that
is an evil before me. 35 Your houses will
I give to a people that shall come;
which not having heard of me yet shall
believe me; to whom I have shewed no
signs, yet they shall do that I have
commanded them. 36 They have seen no
prophets, yet they shall call their sins to
remembrance, and acknowledge them.
37 I take to witness the grace of the
people to come, whose little ones
rejoice in gladness: and though they
have not seen me with bodily eyes, yet
in spirit they believe the thing that I say.
38 And now, brother, behold what glory;
and see the people that come from the
east: 39 Unto whom I will give for
leaders, Abraham, Isaac, and Jacob,
Oseas, Amos, and Micheas, Joel,
Abdias, and Jonas, 40 Nahum, and
Abacuc, Sophonias, Aggeus, Zachary,
and Malachy, which is called also an
angel of the Lord.

CHAPTER 2

1 Thus saith the Lord, I brought this
people out of bondage, and I gave them
my commandments by menservants the
prophets; whom they would not hear,
but despised my counsels. 2 The mother
that bare them saith unto them, Go your
way, ye children; for I am a widow
and forsaken. 3 I brought you up with
gladness; but with sorrow and
heaviness have I lost you: for ye have
sinned before the Lord your God, and
done that thing that is evil before him.
4 But what shall I now do unto you? I
am a widow and forsaken: go your way,
O my children, and ask mercy of the
Lord. 5 As for me, O father, I call upon
thee for a witness over the mother of
these children, which would not keep
my covenant, 6 That thou bring them to
confusion, and their mother to a spoil,
that there may be no offspring of them.
7 Let them be scattered abroad among
the heathen, let their names be put out
of the earth: for they have despised my
covenant. 8 Woe be unto thee, Assur,
thou that hidest the unrighteous in thee!
O thou wicked people, remember what
I did unto Sodom and Gomorrha;
9 Whose land lieth in clods of pitch and
heaps of ashes: even so also will I do unto
them that hear me not, saith the

Almighty Lord. [10]Thus saith the Lord
unto Esdras, Tell my people that I will
give them the kingdom of Jerusalem,
which I would have given unto Israel.
[11]Their glory also will I take unto me,
and give these the everlasting
tabernacles, which I had prepared
for them. [12]They shall have the tree of
life for an ointment of sweet savour;
they shall neither labour, nor be weary.
[13]Go, and ye shall receive: pray for few
days unto you, that they may be
shortened: the kingdom is already
prepared for you: watch. [14]Take heaven
and earth to witness; for I have broken
the evil in pieces, and created the good:
for I live, saith the Lord. [15]Mother,
embrace thy children, and bring them
up with gladness, make their feet as fast
as a pillar: for I have chosen thee, saith
the Lord. [16]And those that be dead will
I raise up again from their places, and
bring them out of the graves: for I have
known my name in Israel. [17]Fear not,
thou mother of the children: for I have
chosen thee, saith the Lord. [18]For thy
help will I send my servants Esau and
Jeremy, after whose counsel I have
sanctified and prepared for thee twelve
trees laden with divers fruits, [19]And as
many fountains flowing with milk and
honey, and seven mighty mountains,
whereupon there grow roses and lilies,
whereby I will fill thy children with joy.
[20]Do right to the widow, judge for the
fatherless, give to the poor, defend the
orphan, clothe the naked, [21]Heal the
broken and the weak, laugh not a lame
man to scorn, defend the maimed, and
let the blind man come into the sight of
my clearness. [22]Keep the old and
young within thy walls. [23]Wheresoever
thou findest the dead, take them and bury
them, and I will give thee the first place
in my resurrection. [24]Abide still, O my
people, and take thy rest, for thy
quietness still come. [25]Nourish thy
children, O thou good nurse; stablish
their feet. [26]As for the servants whom I
have given thee, there shall not one of
them perish; for I will require them
from among thy number.

[27]Be not weary: for when the day of
trouble and heaviness cometh, others
shall weep and be sorrowful, but thou
shalt be merry and have abundance.
[28]The heathen shall envy thee, but they
shall be able to do nothing against thee,
saith the Lord.

[29]My hands shall cover thee, so that thy
children shall not see hell. [30]Be joyful,
O thou mother, with thy children; for I
will deliver thee, saith the Lord.

[31]Remember thy children that sleep, for
I shall bring them out of the sides of the
earth, and shew mercy unto them: for I
am merciful, saith the Lord Almighty.

[32]Embrace thy children until I come
and shew mercy unto them: for my
wells run over, and my grace shall not
fail.

[33]I Esdras received a charge of the Lord
upon the mount Oreb, that I should go
unto Israel; but when I came unto them,
they set me at nought, and despised
the commandment of the Lord. [34]And
therefore I say unto you, O ye heathen,
that hear and understand, look for your
Shepherd, he shall give you everlasting
rest; for he is nigh at hand, that shall
come in the end of the world. [35]Be
ready to the reward of the kingdom, for
the everlasting light shall shine upon
you for evermore. [36]Flee the shadow of
this world, receive the joyfulness of
your glory: I testify my Saviour openly.
[37]O receive the gift that is given you,
and be glad, giving thanks unto him that
hath led you to the heavenly kingdom.
[38]Arise up and stand, behold the

number of those that be sealed in the
feast of the Lord; 39Which are departed
from the shadow of the world, and have
received glorious garments of the Lord.
40Take thy number, O Sion, and shut up
those of thine that are clothed in white,
which have fulfilled the law of the Lord.
41The number of thy children, whom
thou longedst for, is fulfilled: beseech
the power of the Lord, that thy people,
which have been called from the
beginning, may be hallowed. 42I Esdras
saw upon the mount Sion a great people,
whom I could not number, and they all
praised the Lord with songs. 43And in
the midst of them there was a young man
of a high stature, taller than all the rest,
and upon every one of their heads he set
crowns, and was more exalted; which I
marvelled at greatly. 44So I asked the
angel, and said, Sir, what are these?
45He answered and said unto me, These
be they that have put off the mortal
clothing, and put on the immortal, and
have confessed the name of God: now
are they crowned, and receive palms.
46Then said I unto the angel, What
young person is it that crowneth them,
and giveth them palms in their hands?
47So he answered and said unto me, It
is the Son of God, whom they have
confessed in the world. Then began I
greatly to commend them that stood so
stiffly for the name of the Lord. 48Then
the angel said unto me, Go thy way, and
tell my people what manner of things,
and how great wonders of the Lord thy
God, thou hast seen.

CHAPTER 3

1In the thirtieth year after the ruin of the
city I was in Babylon, and lay troubled
upon my bed, and my thoughts came up
over my heart: 2For I saw the
desolation of Sion, and the wealth of
them that dwelt at Babylon. 3And my
spirit was sore moved, so that I began
to speak words full of fear to the most
High, and said,

4O Lord, who bearest rule, thou spakest
at the beginning, when thou didst plant
the earth, and that thyself alone, and
commandedst the people, 5And gavest
a body unto Adam without soul, which
was the workmanship of thine hands,
and didst breathe into him the breath of
life, and he was made living before thee.
6And thou leadest him into paradise,
which thy right hand had planted,
before ever the earth came forward.
7And unto him thou gavest
commandment to love thy way: which
he transgressed, and immediately thou
appointedst death in him and in his
generations, of whom came nations,
tribes, people, and kindreds, out of
number. 8And every people walked
after their own will, and did wonderful
things before thee, and despised thy
commandments. 9And again in process
of time thou broughtest the flood upon
those that dwelt in the world, and
destroyedst them. 10And it came to pass
in every of them, that as death was to
Adam, so was the flood to these.
11Nevertheless one of them thou leftest,
namely, Noah with his household, of
whom came all righteous men. 12And
it happened, that when they that
dwelt upon the earth began to multiply,
and had gotten them many children,
and were a great people, they began
again to be more ungodly than the first.
13Now when they lived so wickedly
before thee, thou didst choose thee a
man from among them, whose name
was Abraham. 14Him thou lovedst, and
unto him only thou shewedst thy will:
15And madest an everlasting covenant

with him, promising him that thou
wouldest never forsake his seed.
[16]And unto him thou gavest Isaac, and
unto Isaac also thou gavest Jacob and
Esau. As for Jacob, thou didst choose
him to thee, and put by Esau: and so
Jacob became a great multitude. [17]And
it came to pass, that when thou leadest
his seed out of Egypt, thou broughtest
them up to the mount Sinai. [18]And
bowing the heavens, thou didst set fast
the earth, movedst the whole world, and
madest the depths to tremble, and
troubledst the men of that age. [19]And
thy glory went through four gates, of
fire, and of earthquake, and of wind,
and of cold; that thou mightest give the
law unto the seed of Jacob, and
diligence unto the generation of Israel.
[20]And yet tookest thou not away from
them a wicked heart, that thy law might
bring forth fruit in them. [21]For the first
Adam bearing a wicked heart
transgressed, and was overcome; and so
be all they that are born of him. [22]Thus
infirmity was made permanent; and the
law (also) in the heart of the people with
the malignity of the root; so that the
good departed away, and the evil
abode still. [23]So the times passed
away, and the years were brought to an
end: then didst thou raise thee up a
servant, called David: [24]Whom thou
commandedst to build a city unto thy
name, and to offer incense and
oblations unto thee therein. [25]When
this was done many years, then they
that inhabited the city forsook thee,
[26]And in all things did even as Adam
and all his generations had done: for
they also had a wicked heart: [27]And
so thou gavest thy city over into the
hands of thine enemies. [28]Are their
deeds then any better that inhabit
Babylon, that they should therefore
have the dominion over Sion? [29]For
when I came thither, and had seen
impieties without number, then my soul
saw many evildoers in this thirtieth
year, so that my heart failed me. [30]For
I have seen how thou sufferest them
sinning, and hast spared wicked doers:
and hast destroyed thy people, and hast
preserved thine enemies, and hast not
signified it. [31]I do not remember how
this way may be left: Are they then of
Babylon better than they of Sion? [32]Or
is there any other people that knoweth
thee beside Israel? or what generation
hath so believed thy covenants as
Jacob? [33]And yet their reward
appeareth not, and their labour hath no
fruit: for I have gone here and there
through the heathen, and I see that they
flow in wealth, and think not upon thy
commandments. [34]Weigh thou
therefore our wickedness now in the
balance, and their's also that dwell the
world; and so shall thy name no where
be found but in Israel. [35]Or when was it
that they which dwell upon the earth
have not sinned in thy sight? or what
people have so kept thy
commandments? [36]Thou shalt find that
Israel by name hath kept thy precepts;
but not the heathen.

CHAPTER 4

[1]And the angel that was sent unto me,
whose name was Uriel, gave me an
answer, [2]And said, Thy heart hath gone
to far in this world, and thinkest thou
to comprehend the way of the most
High? [3]Then said I, Yea, my lord. And
he answered me, and said, I am sent to
shew thee three ways, and to set forth
three similitudes before thee: [4]Whereof
if thou canst declare me one, I will
shew thee also the way that thou desirest

to see, and I shall shew thee from
whence the wicked heart cometh. 5And
I said, Tell on, my lord. Then said he
unto me, Go thy way, weigh me the
weight of the fire, or measure me the
blast of the wind, or call me again the
day that is past. 6Then answered I and
said, What man is able to do that, that
thou shouldest ask such things of me?
7And he said unto me, If I should ask
thee how great dwellings are in the
midst of the sea, or how many springs
are in the beginning of the deep, or how
many springs are above the firmament,
or which are the outgoings of paradise:
8Peradventure thou wouldest say unto
me, I never went down into the deep,
nor as yet into hell, neither did I ever
climb up into heaven. 9Nevertheless
now have I asked thee but only of the
fire and wind, and of the day
wherethrough thou hast passed, and of
things from which thou canst not be
separated, and yet canst thou give me no
answer of them. 10He said moreover
unto me, Thine own things, and such as
are grown up with thee, canst thou not
know; 11How should thy vessel then be
able to comprehend the way of the
Highest, and, the world being now
outwardly corrupted to understand the
corruption that is evident in my sight?
12Then said I unto him, It were better
that we were not at all, than that we
should live still in wickedness, and to
suffer, and not to know wherefore.
13He answered me, and said, I went into
a forest into a plain, and the trees took
counsel, 14And said, Come, let us go
and make war against the sea that it may
depart away before us, and that we may
make us more woods. 15The floods of
the sea also in like manner took
counsel, and said, Come, let us go up
and subdue the woods of the plain, that
there also we may make us another
country. 16The thought of the wood
was in vain, for the fire came and
consumed it. 17The thought of the
floods of the sea came likewise to
nought, for the sand stood up and
stopped them. 18If thou wert judge now
betwixt these two, whom wouldest thou
begin to justify? or whom wouldest
thou condemn? 19I answered and said,
Verily it is a foolish thought that they
both have devised, for the ground is
given unto the wood, and the sea also
hath his place to bear his floods. 20Then
answered he me, and said, Thou hast
given a right judgment, but why judgest
thou not thyself also? 21For like as the
ground is given unto the wood, and the
sea to his floods: even so they that
dwell upon the earth may understand
nothing but that which is upon the
earth: and he that dwelleth above the
heavens may only understand the
things that are above the height of the
heavens. 22Then answered I and said, I
beseech thee, O Lord, let me have
understanding: 23For it was not my
mind to be curious of the high things,
but of such as pass by us daily, namely,
wherefore Israel is given up as a
reproach to the heathen, and for what
cause the people whom thou hast loved
is given over unto ungodly nations, and
why the law of our forefathers is
brought to nought, and the written
covenants come to none effect, 24And
we pass away out of the world as
grasshoppers, and our life is
astonishment and fear, and we are not
worthy to obtain mercy. 25What will he
then do unto his name whereby we are
called? of these things have I asked.
26Then answered he me, and said, The
more thou searchest, the more thou
shalt marvel; for the world hasteth fast

to pass away, 27And cannot
comprehend the things that are
promised to the righteous in time to
come: for this world is full of
unrighteousness and infirmities. 28But
as concerning the things whereof thou
askest me, I will tell thee; for the evil is
sown, but the destruction thereof is not
yet come. 29If therefore that which is
sown be not turned upside down, and if
the place where the evil is sown pass not
away, then cannot it come that is sown
with good. 30For the grain of evil seed
hath been sown in the heart of Adam
from the beginning, and how much
ungodliness hath it brought up unto this
time? and how much shall it yet bring
forth until the time of threshing come?
31Ponder now by thyself, how great
fruit of wickedness the grain of evil
seed hath brought forth. 32And when
the ears shall be cut down, which are
without number, how great a floor shall
they fill? 33Then I answered and said,
How, and when shall these things come
to pass? wherefore are our years few
and evil? 34And he answered me,
saying, Do not thou hasten above the
most Highest: for thy haste is in vain to
be above him, for thou hast much
exceeded. 35Did not the souls also of
the righteous ask question of these
things in their chambers, saying, How
long shall I hope on this fashion? when
cometh the fruit of the floor of our
reward? 36And unto these things Uriel
the archangel gave them answer, and
said, Even when the number of seeds
is filled in you: for he hath weighed the
world in the balance. 37By measure
hath he measured the times; and by
number hath he numbered the times;
and he doth not move nor stir them,
until the said measure be fulfilled.
38Then answered I and said, O Lord that
bearest rule, even we all are full of
impiety. 39And for our sakes
peradventure it is that the floors of the
righteous are not filled, because of the
sins of them that dwell upon the earth.
40So he answered me, and said, Go thy
way to a woman with child, and ask of
her when she hath fulfilled her nine
months, if her womb may keep the birth
any longer within her. 41Then said I,
No, Lord, that can she not. And he said
unto me, In the grave the chambers of
souls are like the womb of a woman:
42For like as a woman that travaileth
maketh haste to escape the necessity of
the travail: even so do these places
haste to deliver those things that are
committed unto them. 43From the
beginning, look, what thou desirest to
see, it shall be shewed thee. 44Then
answered I and said, If I have found
favour in thy sight, and if it be possible,
and if I be meet therefore, 45Shew me
then whether there be more to come
than is past, or more past than is to
come. 46What is past I know, but
what is for to come I know not. 47And
he said unto me, Stand up upon the
right side, and I shall expound the
similitude unto thee. 48So I stood, and
saw, and, behold, an hot burning oven
passed by before me: and it happened
that when the flame was gone by I
looked, and, behold, the smoke
remained still. 49After this there passed
by before me a watery cloud, and sent
down much rain with a storm; and
when the stormy rain was past, the
drops remained still. 50Then said he
unto me, Consider with thyself; as the
rain is more than the drops, and as the
fire is greater than the smoke; but the
drops and the smoke remain behind: so
the quantity which is past did more
exceed. 51Then I prayed, and said, May

I live, thinkest thou, until that time? or
what shall happen in those days? 52 He
answered me, and said, As for the
tokens whereof thou askest me, I may
tell thee of them in part: but as touching
thy life, I am not sent to shew thee; for
I do not know it.

CHAPTER 5

1 Nevertheless as coming the tokens,
behold, the days shall come, that they
which dwell upon earth shall be taken
in a great number, and the way of truth
shall be hidden, and the land shall be
barren of faith. 2 But iniquity shall be
increased above that which now thou
seest, or that thou hast heard long ago.
3 And the land, that thou seest now to
have root, shalt thou see wasted
suddenly.
4 But if the most High grant thee to live,
thou shalt see after the third trumpet
that the sun shall suddenly shine again
in the night, and the moon thrice in the
day:
5 And blood shall drop out of wood, and
the stone shall give his voice, and the
people shall be troubled: 6 And even he
shall rule, whom they look not for that
dwell upon the earth, and the fowls
shall take their flight away together:
7 And the Sodomitish sea shall cast out
fish, and make a noise in the night,
which many have not known: but they
shall all hear the voice thereof. 8 There
shall be a confusion also in many
places, and the fire shall be oft sent out
again, and the wild beasts shall change
their places, and menstruous women
shall bring forth monsters: 9 And salt
waters shall be found in the sweet, and all
friends shall destroy one another; then
shall wit hide itself, and understanding
withdraw itself into his secret chamber,
10 And shall be sought of many, and yet
not be found: then shall
unrighteousness and incontinency be
multiplied upon earth. 11 One land also
shall ask another, and say, Is
righteousness that maketh a man
righteous gone through thee? And it
shall say, No. 12 At the same time shall
men hope, but nothing obtain: they
shall labour, but their ways shall not
prosper. 13 To shew thee such tokens I
have leave; and if thou wilt pray again,
and weep as now, and fast even days,
thou shalt hear yet greater things.
14 Then I awaked, and an extreme
fearfulness went through all my body,
and my mind was troubled, so that it
fainted. 15 So the angel that was come to
talk with me held me, comforted me,
and set me up upon my feet. 16 And in
the second night it came to pass, that
Salathiel the captain of the people came
unto me, saying, Where hast thou been?
and why is thy countenance so heavy?
17 Knowest thou not that Israel is
committed unto thee in the land of their
captivity?
18 Up then, and eat bread, and forsake us
not, as the shepherd that leaveth his
flock in the hands of cruel wolves.
19 Then said I unto him, Go thy ways
from me, and come not nigh me. And
he heard what I said, and went from me.
20 And so I fasted seven days, mourning
and weeping, like as Uriel the angel
commanded me.
21 And after seven days so it was, that
the thoughts of my heart were very
grievous unto me again, 22 And my soul
recovered the spirit of understanding,
and I began to talk with the most High
again, 23 And said, O Lord that bearest
rule, of every wood of the earth, and of
all the trees thereof, thou hast chosen
thee one only vine: 24 And of all lands of

the whole world thou hast chosen thee
one pit: and of all the flowers thereof
one lily: 25 And of all the depths of the
sea thou hast filled thee one river: and
of all builded cities thou hast hallowed
Sion unto thyself: 26 And of all the
fowls that are created thou hast named
thee one dove: and of all the cattle that
are made thou hast provided thee one
sheep: 27 And among all the multitudes
of people thou hast gotten thee one
people: and unto this people, whom
thou lovedst, thou gavest a law that is
approved of all. 28 And now, O Lord,
why hast thou given this one people
over unto many? and upon the one root
hast thou prepared others, and why hast
thou scattered thy only one people
among many? 29 And they which did
gainsay thy promises, and believed not
thy covenants, have trodden them
down. 30 If thou didst so much hate thy
people, yet shouldest thou punish them
with thine own hands. 31 Now when I
had spoken these words, the angel that
came to me the night afore was sent
unto me, 32 And said unto me, Hear
me, and I will instruct thee; hearken to
the thing that I say, and I shall tell thee
more. 33 And I said, Speak on, my Lord.
Then said he unto me, Thou art sore
troubled in mind for Israel's sake:
lovest thou that people better than he
that made them? 34 And I said, No,
Lord: but of very grief have I spoken:
for my reins pain me every hour, while
I labour to comprehend the way of the
most High, and to seek out part of his
judgment. 35 And he said unto me, Thou
canst not. And I said, Wherefore, Lord?
whereunto was I born then? or why was
not my mother's womb then my grave,
that I might not have seen the
travail of Jacob, and the wearisome toil
of the stock of Israel? 36 And he said
unto me, Number me the things that are
not yet come, gather me together the
dross that are scattered abroad, make me
the flowers green again that are
withered, 37 Open me the places that are
closed, and bring me forth the winds
that in them are shut up, shew me the
image of a voice: and then I will
declare to thee the thing that thou
labourest to know. 38 And I said, O Lord
that bearest rule, who may know these
things, but he that hath not his dwelling
with men? 39 As for me, I am unwise:
how may I then speak of these things
whereof thou askest me? 40 Then said
he unto me, Like as thou canst do none
of these things that I have spoken of,
even so canst thou not find out my
judgment, or in the end the love that I
have promised unto my people. 41 And
I said, Behold, O Lord, yet art thou nigh
unto them that be reserved till the end:
and what shall they do that have been
before me, or we that be now, or they
that shall come after us? 42 And he said
unto me, I will liken my judgment unto
a ring: like as there is no slackness of
the last, even so there is no swiftness of
the first. 43 So I answered and said,
Couldest thou not make those that have
been made, and be now, and that are
for to come, at once; that thou mightest
shew thy judgment the sooner? 44 Then
answered he me, and said, The creature
may not haste above the maker; neither
may the world hold them at once that
shall be created therein. 45 And I said,
As thou hast said unto thy servant, that
thou, which givest life to all, hast given
life at once to the creature that thou hast
created, and the creature bare it: even so
it might now also bear them that now
be present at once. 46 And he said unto
me, Ask the womb of a woman, and say
unto her, If thou bringest forth children,

why dost thou it not together, but one
after another? pray her therefore to bring
forth ten children at once. [47]And I said,
She cannot: but must do it by distance
of time. [48]Then said he unto me, Even
so have I given the womb of the earth
to those that be sown in it in their times.
[49]For like as a young child may not
bring forth the things that belong to the
aged, even so have I disposed the world
which I created. [50]And I asked, and
said, Seeing thou hast now given me the
way, I will proceed to speak before
thee: for our mother, of whom thou hast
told me that she is young, draweth now
nigh unto age. [51]He answered me, and
said, Ask a woman that beareth
children, and she shall tell thee. [52]Say
unto her, Wherefore are unto they
whom thou hast now brought forth like
those that were before, but less of
stature? [53]And she shall answer thee,
They that be born in the the strength of
youth are of one fashion, and they that
are born in the time of age, when the
womb faileth, are otherwise.
[54]Consider thou therefore also, how
that ye are less of stature than those that
were before you. [55]And so are they that
come after you less than ye, as the
creatures which now begin to be old,
and have passed over the strength of
youth. [56]Then said I, Lord, I beseech
thee, if I have found favour in thy sight,
shew thy servant by whom thou visitest
thy creature.

CHAPTER 6

[1]And he said unto me, In the beginning,
when the earth was made, before the
borders of the world stood, or ever the
winds blew, [2]Before it thundered and
lightened, or ever the foundations of
paradise were laid, [3]Before the fair
flowers were seen, or ever the
moveable powers were established,
before the innumerable multitude of
angels were gathered together, [4]Or ever
the heights of the air were lifted up,
before the measures of the firmament
were named, or ever the chimneys in
Sion were hot, [5]And ere the present
years were sought out, and or ever the
inventions of them that now sin were
turned, before they were sealed that
have gathered faith for a treasure:
[6]Then did I consider these things, and
they all were made through me alone,
and through none other: by me also they
shall be ended, and by none other.
[7]Then answered I and said, What shall
be the parting asunder of the times? or
when shall be the end of the first, and
the beginning of it that followeth?
[8]And he said unto me, From Abraham
unto Isaac, when Jacob and Esau were
born of him, Jacob's hand held first the
heel of Esau. [9]For Esau is the end of
the world, and Jacob is the beginning of
it that followeth. [10]The hand of man is
betwixt the heel and the hand: other
question, Esdras, ask thou not. [11]I
answered then and said, O Lord that
bearest rule, if I have found favour in
thy sight, [12]I beseech thee, shew thy
servant the end of thy tokens, whereof
thou shewedst me part the last night.
[13]So he answered and said unto me,
Stand up upon thy feet, and hear a
mighty sounding voice. [14]And it shall
be as it were a great motion; but the
place where thou standest shall not be
moved. [15]And therefore when it
speaketh be not afraid: for the word
is of the end, and the foundation of the
earth is understood. [16]And why?
because the speech of these things
trembleth and is moved: for it knoweth
that the end of these things must be

changed. 17 And it happened, that when
I had heard it I stood up upon my feet,
and hearkened, and, behold, there was
a voice that spake, and the sound of it
was like the sound of many waters.
18 And it said, Behold, the days come,
that I will begin to draw nigh, and to
visit them that dwell upon the earth,
19 And will begin to make inquisition of
them, whatthey be that have hurt
unjustly with their unrighteousness,
and when the affliction of Sion shall
be fulfilled; 20 And when the world, that
shall begin to vanish away, shall be
finished, then will I shew these tokens:
the books shall be opened before the
firmament, and they shall see all
together: 21 And the children of a year
old shall speak with their voices, the
women with child shall bring forth
untimely children of three or four
months old, and they shall live, and be
raised up. 22 And suddenly shall the
sown places appear unsown, the full
storehouses shall suddenly be found
empty: 23 And tha trumpet shall give a
sound, which when every man heareth,
they shall be suddenly afraid. 24 At that
time shall friends fight one against
another like enemies, and the earth shall
stand in fear with those that dwell
therein, the springs of the fountains
shall stand still, and in three hours they
shall not run. 25 Whosoever remaineth
from all these that I have told thee shall
escape, and see my salvation, and the
end of your world. 26 And the men that
are received shall see it, who have not
tasted death from their birth: and the
heart of the inhabitants shall be
changed, and turned into another
meaning. 27 For evil shall be put out,
and deceit shall be quenched.

28 As for faith, it shall flourish,
corruption shall be overcome, and the
truth, which hath been so long without
fruit, shall be declared. 29 And when he
talked with me, behold, I looked by
little and little upon him before whom I
stood. 30 And these words said he unto
me; I am come to shew thee the time of
the night to come. 31 If thou wilt pray yet
more, and fast seven days again, I shall
tell thee greater things by day than I
have heard. 32 For thy voice is heard
before the most High: for the Mighty
hath seen thy righteous dealing, he hath
seen also thy chastity, which thou hast
had ever since thy youth. 33 And
therefore hath he sent me to shew thee
all these things, and to say unto thee, Be
of good comfort and fear not 34 And
hasten not with the times that are past,
to think vain things, that thou mayest
not hasten from the latter times. 35 And
it came to pass after this, that I wept
again, and fasted seven days in like
manner, that I might fulfil the three
weeks which he told me. 36 And in the
eighth night was my heart vexed within
me again, and I began to speak before
the most High. 37 For my spirit was
greatly set on fire, and my soul was in
distress.

38 And I said, O Lord, thou spakest from
the beginning of the creation, even the
first day, and saidst thus; Let heaven
and earth be made; and thy word was a
perfect work. 39 And then was the spirit,
and darkness and silence were on every
side; the sound of man's voice was not
yet formed. 40 Then commandedst thou
a fair light to come forth of thy
treasures, that thy work might appear.
41 Upon the second day thou madest the
spirit of the firmament, and
commandedst it to part asunder, and to
make a division betwixt the waters, that
the one part might go up, and the other
remain beneath. 42 Upon the third day

thou didst command that the waters
should be gathered in the seventh part
of the earth: six pats hast thou dried up,
and kept them, to the intent that of these
some being planted of God and tilled
might serve thee. 43 For as soon as thy
word went forth the work was made.
44 For immediately there was great and
innumerable fruit, and many and divers
pleasures for the taste, and flowers of
unchangeable colour, and odours of
wonderful smell: and this was done the
third day. 45 Upon the fourth day thou
commandedst that the sun should shine,
and the moon give her light, and the
stars should be in order: 46 And gavest
them a charge to do service unto man,
that was to be made. 47 Upon the fifth
day thou sadist unto the seventh part,
where the waters were gathered that it
should bring forth living creatures,
fowls and fishes: and so it came to pass.
48 For the dumb water and without life
brought forth living things at the
commandment of God, that all people
might praise thy wondrous works.
49 Then didst thou ordain two living
creatures, the one thou calledst Enoch,
and the other Leviathan; 50 And didst
separate the one from the other: for the
seventh part, namely, where the water
was gathered together, might not hold
them both. 51 Unto Enoch thou gavest
one part, which was dried up the third
day, that he should dwell in the same
part, wherein are a thousand hills: 52 But
unto Leviathan thou gavest the seventh
part, namely, the moist; and hast kept
him to be devoured of whom thou wilt,
and when. 53 Upon the sixth day thou
gavest commandment unto the earth,
that before thee it should bring forth
beasts, cattle, and creeping things:
54 And after these, Adam also, whom
thou madest lord of all thy creatures: of
him come we all, and the people also
whom thou hast chosen. 55 All this have
I spoken before thee, O Lord, because
thou madest the world for our sakes
56 As for the other people, which also
come of Adam, thou hast said that they
are nothing, but be like unto spittle: and
hast likened the abundance of them unto
a drop that falleth from a vessel.
57 And now, O Lord, behold, these
heathen, which have ever been reputed
as nothing, have begun to be lords over
us, and to devour us. 58 But we thy
people, whom thou hast called thy
firstborn, thy only begotten, and thy
fervent lover, are given into their
hands. 59 If the world now be made
for our sakes, why do we not possess an
inheritance with the world? how long
shall this endure?

CHAPTER 7

1 And when I had made an end of
speaking these words, there was sent
unto me the angel which had been sent
unto me the nights afore: 2 And he said
unto me, Up, Esdras, and hear the words
that I am come to tell thee. 3 And I said,
Speak on, my God. Then said he unto
me, The sea is set in a wide place, that it
might be deep and great. 4 But put the
case the entrance were narrow, and like
a river; 5 Who then could go into the sea
to look upon it, and to rule it? if he went
not through the narrow, how could he
come into the broad? 6 There is also
another thing; A city is builded, and set
upon a broad field, and is full of all
good things: 7 The entrance thereof is
narrow, and is set in a dangerous place
to fall, like as if there were a fire on the
right hand, and on the left a deep water:
8 And one only path between them both,
even between the fire and the water, so

small that there could but one man go
there at once. 9 If this city now were
given unto a man for an inheritance, if
he never shall pass the danger set before
it, how shall he receive this inheritance?
10 And I said, It is so, Lord. Then said he
unto me, Even so also is Israel's
portion. 11 Because for their sakes I
made the world: and when Adam
transgressed my statutes, then was
decreed that now is done. 12 Then
were the entrances of this world made
narrow, full of sorrow and travail: they
are but few and evil, full of perils,: and
very painful. 13 For the entrances of the
elder world were wide and sure, and
brought immortal fruit. 14 If then they
that live labour not to enter these strait
and vain things, they can never receive
those that are laid up for them. 15 Now
therefore why disquietest thou thyself,
seeing thou art but a corruptible man?
and why art thou moved, whereas thou
art but mortal? 16 Why hast thou not
considered in thy mind this thing that is
to come, rather than that which is
present? 17 Then answered I and said, O
Lord that bearest rule, thou hast
ordained in thy law, that the righteous
should inherit these things, but that the
ungodly should perish. 18 Nevertheless
the righteous shall suffer strait things,
and hope for wide: for they that have
done wickedly have suffered the strait
things, and yet shall not see the wide.
19 And he said unto me. There is no
judge above God, and none that hath
understanding above the Highest. 20 For
there be many that perish in this life,
because they despise the law of God
that is set before them. 21 For God hath
given strait commandment to such as
came, what they should do to live, even
as they came, and what they should
observe to avoid punishment.
22 Nevertheless they were not obedient
unto him; but spake against him, and
imagined vain things;
23 And deceived themselves by their
wicked deeds; and said of the most
High, that he is not; and knew not his
ways: 24 But his law have they
despised, and denied his covenants; in
his statutes have they not been faithful,
and have not performed his works.
25 And therefore, Esdras, for the empty
are empty things, and for the full are the
full things.

26 Behold, the time shall come, that
these tokens which I have told thee
shall come to pass, and the bride shall
appear, and she coming forth shall be
seen, that now is withdrawn from the
earth. 27 And whosoever is delivered
from the foresaid evils shall see my
wonders. 28 For my son Jesus shall be
revealed with those that be with him,
and they that remain shall rejoice
within four hundred years. 29 After these
years shall my son Christ die, and all
men that have life. 30 And the world
shall be turned into the old silence
seven days, like as in the former
judgments: so that no man shall
remain. 31 And after seven days the
world, that yet awaketh not, shall be
raised up, and that shall die that is
corrupt 32 And the earth shall restore
those that are asleep in her, and so shall
the dust those that dwell in silence, and
the secret places shall deliver those
souls that were committed unto
them.
33 And the most High shall appear upon
the seat of judgment, and misery shall
pass away, and the long suffering shall
have an end: 34 But judgment only shall
remain, truth shall stand, and faith shall
wax strong: 35 And the work shall
follow, and the reward shall be shewed,

and the good deeds shall be of force,
and wicked deeds shall bear no rule.
36 Then said I, Abraham prayed first for
the Sodomites, and Moses for the
fathers that sinned in the wilderness:
37 And Jesus after him for Israel in the
time of Achan: 38 And Samuel and
David for the destruction: and Solomon
for them that should come to the
sanctuary: 39 And Helias for those that
received rain; and for the dead, that he
might live: 40 And Ezechias for the
people in the time of Sennacherib: and
many for many. 41 Even so now, seeing
corruption is grown up, and wickedness
increased, and the righteous have
prayed for the ungodly: wherefore shall
it not be so now also? 42 He answered
me, and said, This present life is not the
end where much glory doth abide;
therefore have they prayed for the
weak. 43 But the day of doom shall be
the end of this time, and the beginning
of the immortality for to come, wherein
corruption is past, 44 Intemperance is at
an end, infidelity is cut off,
righteousness is grown, and truth is
sprung up. 45 Then shall no man be able
to save him that is destroyed, nor to
oppress him that hath gotten the
victory. 46 I answered then and said,
This is my first and last saying, that it
had been better not to have given the
earth unto Adam: or else, when it was
given him, to have restrained him from
sinning. 47 For what profit is it for men
now in this present time to live in
heaviness, and after death to look for
punishment? 48 O thou Adam, what hast
thou done? for though it was thou that
sinned, thou art not fallen alone, but we
all that come of thee. 49 For what profit
is it unto us, if there be promised us an
immortal time, whereas we have done
the works that bring death? 50 And that
there is promised us an everlasting
hope, whereas ourselves being most
wicked are made vain? 51 And that there
are laid up for us dwellings of health
and safety, whereas we have lived
wickedly? 52 And that the glory of the
most High is kept to defend them
which have led a wary life, whereas we
have walked in the most wicked ways
of all? 53 And that there should be
shewed a paradise, whose fruit
endureth for ever, wherein is security
and medicine, since we shall not enter
into it? 54 (For we have walked in
unpleasant places.) 55 And that the faces
of them which have used abstinence shall
shine above the stars, whereas our faces
shall be blacker than darkness? 56 For
while we lived and committed iniquity,
we considered not that we should begin
to suffer for it after death. 57 Then
answered he me, and said, This is the
condition of the battle, which man that
is born upon the earth shall fight;
58 That, if he be overcome, he shall
suffer as thou hast said: but if he get the
victory, he shall receive the thing that I
say. 59 For this is the life whereof Moses
spake unto the people while he lived,
saying, Choose thee life, that thou
mayest live. 60 Nevertheless they
believed not him, nor yet the prophets
after him, no nor me which have
spoken unto them, 61 That there should
not be such heaviness in their
destruction, as shall be joy over them
that are persuaded to salvation. 62 I
answered then, and said, I know, Lord,
that the most High is called merciful, in
that he hath mercy upon them which
are not yet come into the world, 63 And
upon those also that turn to his law;
64 And that he is patient, and long
suffereth those that have sinned, as his
creatures; 65 And that he is bountiful,

for he is ready to give where it needeth;
66 And that he is of great mercy, for he
multiplieth more and more mercies to
them that are present, and that are past,
and also to them which are to come.
67 For if he shall not multiply his
mercies, the world would not continue
with them that inherit therein. 68 And he
pardoneth; for if he did not so of his
goodness, that they which have
committed iniquities might be eased of
them, the ten thousandth part of men
should not remain living. 69 And being
judge, if he should not forgive them that
are cured with his word, and put out the
multitude of contentions, 70 There
should be very few left peradventure in
an innumerable multitude.

CHAPTER 8

1 And he answered me, saying, The
most High hath made this world for
many, but the world to come for few. 2 I
will tell thee a similitude, Esdras; As
when thou askest the earth, it shall say
unto thee, that it giveth much mould
whereof earthen vessels are made, but
little dust that gold cometh of: even so
is the course of this present world.
3 There be many created, but few shall
be saved. 4 So answered I and said,
Swallow then down, O my soul,
understanding, and devour wisdom.
5 For thou hast agreed to give ear, and art
willing to prophesy: for thou hast no
longer space than only to live. 6 O Lord,
if thou suffer not thy servant, that we
may pray before thee, and thou give us
seed unto our heart, and culture to our
understanding, that there may come
fruit of it; how shall each man live that
is corrupt, who beareth the place of a
man? 7 For thou art alone, and we all
one workmanship of thine hands, like
as thou hast said. 8 For when the body is
fashioned now in the mother's womb,
and thou givest it members, thy
creature is preserved in fire and water,
and nine months doth thy workmanship
endure thy creature which is created in
her. 9 But that which keepeth and is kept
shall both be preserved: and when the
time cometh, the womb preserved
delivereth up the things that grew in it.
10 For thou hast commanded out of the
parts of the body, that is to say, out of
the breasts, milk to be given, which is
the fruit of the breasts,
11 That the thing which is fashioned may
be nourished for a time, till thou
disposest it to thy mercy. 12 Thou
broughtest it up with thy
righteousness, and nurturedst it in thy
law, and reformedst it with thy
judgment. 13 And thou shalt mortify it
as thy creature, and quicken it as thy
work. 14 If therefore thou shalt destroy
him which with so great labour was
fashioned, it is an easy thing to be
ordained by thy commandment, that the
thing which was made might be
preserved. 15 Now therefore, Lord, I will
speak; touching man in general, thou
knowest best; but touching thy people,
for whose sake I am sorry; 16 And for
thine inheritance, for whose cause I
mourn; and for Israel, for whom I am
heavy; and for Jacob, for whose sake I
am troubled; 17 Therefore will I begin
to pray before thee for myself and for
them: for I see the falls of us that dwell
in the land. 18 But I have heard the
swiftness of the judge which is to come.
19 Therefore hear my voice, and
understand my words, and I shall speak
before thee. This is the beginning of the
words of Esdras, before he was taken
up: and I said, 20 O Lord, thou that
dwellest in everlastingness which

beholdest from above things in the
heaven and in the air; 21 Whose throne
is inestimable; whose glory may not be
comprehended; before whom the hosts
of angels stand with trembling,
22 Whose service is conversant in wind
and fire; whose word is true, and
sayings constant; whose
commandment is strong, and ordinance
fearful; 23 Whose look drieth up the
depths, and indignation maketh the
mountains to melt away; which the
truth witnesseth: 24 O hear the prayer of
thy servant, and give ear to the petition
of thy creature. 25 For while I live I will
speak, and so long as I have
understanding I will answer. 26 O look
not upon the sins of thy people; but on
them which serve thee in truth. 27 Regard
not the wicked inventions of the
heathen, but the desire of those that
keep thy testimonies in afflictions.
28 Think not upon those that have
walked feignedly before thee: but
remember them, which according to
thy will have known thy fear. 29 Let it
not be thy will to destroy them which
have lived like beasts; but to look upon
them that have clearly taught thy law.
30 Take thou no indignation at them
which are deemed worse than beasts;
but love them that always put their trust
in thy righteousness and glory. 31 For
we and our fathers do languish of such
diseases: but because of us sinners thou
shalt be called merciful. 32 For if thou
hast a desire to have mercy upon us,
thou shalt be called merciful, to us
namely, that have no works of
righteousness. 33 For the just, which
have many good works laid up with
thee, shall out of their own deeds
receive reward. 34 For what is man, that
thou shouldest take displeasure at him?
or what is a corruptible generation, that
thou shouldest be so bitter toward it?
35 For in truth them is no man among
them that be born, but he hath dealt
wickedly; and among the faithful there is
none which hath not done amiss. 36 For in
this, O Lord, thy righteousness and thy
goodness shall be declared, if thou be
merciful unto them which have not the
confidence of good works. 37 Then
answered he me, and said, Some things
hast thou spoken aright, and according
unto thy words it shall be. 38 For indeed I
will not think on the disposition of
them which have sinned before death,
before judgment, before destruction:
39 But I will rejoice over the disposition
of the righteous, and I will remember
also their pilgrimage, and the salvation,
and the reward, that they shall have.
40 Like as I have spoken now, so shall it
come to pass. 41 For as the husbandman
soweth much seed upon the ground, and
planteth many trees, and yet the thing
that is sown good in his season cometh
not up, neither doth all that is planted
take root: even so is it of them that are
sown in the world; they shall not all be
saved. 42 I answered then and said, If I
have found grace, let me speak. 43 Like
as the husbandman's seed perisheth, if
it come not up, and receive not thy rain
in due season; or if there come too
much rain, and corrupt it: 44 Even so
perisheth man also, which is formed
with thy hands, and is called thine own
image, because thou art like unto him,
for whose sake thou hast made all
things, and likened him unto the
husbandman's seed. 45 Be not wroth
with us but spare thy people, and have
mercy upon thine own inheritance: for
thou art merciful unto thy creature.
46 Then answered he me, and said,
Things present are for the present, and
things to cometh for such as be to come.

47For thou comest far short that thou
shouldest be able to love my creature
more than I: but I have ofttimes drawn
nigh unto thee, and unto it, but never to
the unrighteous. 48In this also thou art
marvellous before the most High: 49In
that thou hast humbled thyself, as it
becometh thee, and hast not judged
thyself worthy to be much glorified
among the righteous. 50For many great
miseries shall be done to them that in
the latter time shall dwell in the world,
because they have walked in great
pride. 51But understand thou for
thyself, and seek out the glory for such
as be like thee. 52For unto you is paradise
opened, the tree of life is planted, the
time to come is prepared, plenteousness
is made ready, a city is builded, and rest
is allowed, yea, perfect goodness and
wisdom. 53The root of evil is sealed up
from you, weakness and the moth is hid
from you, and corruption is fled into
hell to be forgotten: 54Sorrows are
passed, and in the end is shewed the
treasure of immortality. 55And
therefore ask thou no more questions
concerning the multitude of them that
perish. 56For when they had taken
liberty, they despised the most High,
thought scorn of his law, and forsook
his ways. 57Moreover they have
trodden down his righteous, 58And said
in their heart, that there is no God; yea,
and that knowing they must die. 59For
as the things aforesaid shalt receive
you, so thirst and pain are prepared for
them: for it was not his will that men
should come to nought: 60But they
which be created have defiled the name
of him that made them, and were
unthankful unto him which prepared
life for them. 61And therefore is my
judgment now at hand. 62These things
have I not shewed unto all men, but
unto thee, and a few like thee. Then
answered I and said, 63Behold, O Lord,
now hast thou shewed me the multitude
of the wonders, which thou wilt begin
to do in the last times: but at what time,
thou hast not shewed me.

CHAPTER 9

1He answered me then, and said,
Measure thou the time diligently in itself:
and when thou seest part of the signs
past, which I have told thee before,
2Then shalt thou understand, that it is
the very same time, wherein the
Highest will begin to visit the world
which he made. 3Therefore when there
shall be seen earthquakes and uproars
of the people in the world: 4Then shalt
thou well understand, that the most
High spake of those things from the
days that were before thee, even from
the beginning. 5For like as all that is
made in the world hath a beginning and
an end, and the end is manifest: 6Even
so the times also of the Highest have
plain beginnings in wonder and
powerful works, and endings in effects
and signs. 7And every one that shall be
saved, and shall be able to escape by his
works, and by faith, whereby ye have
believed, 8Shall be preserved from the
said perils, and shall see my salvation in
my land, and within my borders: for I
have sanctified them for me from the
beginning. 9Then shall they be in pitiful
case, which now have abused my ways:
and they that have cast them away
despitefully shall dwell in torments.
10For such as in their life have received
benefits, and have not known me;
11And they that have loathed my law,
while they had yet liberty, and, when as
yet place of repentance was open unto
them, understood not, but despised it;

[12]The same must know it after death by
pain. [13]And therefore be thou not
curious how the ungodly shall be
punished, and when: but enquire how
the righteous shall be saved, whose the
world is, and for whom the world is
created. [14]Then answered I and said, [15]I
have said before, and now do speak,
and will speak it also hereafter, that there
be many more of them which perish, than
of them which shall be saved: [16]Like as
a wave is greater than a drop. [17]And
he answered me, saying, Like as the
field is, so is also the seed; as the
flowers be, such are the colours also;
such as the workman is, such also is the
work; and as the husbandman ls
himself, so is his husbandry also: for it
was the time of the world. [18]And now
when I prepared the world, which was
not yet made, even for them to dwell in
that now live, no man spake against me.
[19]For then every one obeyed: but now
the manners of them which are created
in this world that is made are corrupted
by a perpetual seed, and by a law which
is unsearchable rid themselves. [20]So I
considered the world, and, behold,
there was peril because of the devices
that were come into it. [21]And I saw, and
spared it greatly, and have kept me a
grape of the cluster, and a plant of a
great people. [22]Let the multitude perish
then, which was born in vain; and let
my grape be kept, and my plant; for
with great labour have I made it perfect.
[23]Nevertheless, if thou wilt cease yet
seven days more, (but thou shalt not fast
in them, [24]But go into a field of
flowers, where no house is builded, and
eat only the flowers of the field; taste
no flesh, drink no wine, but eat flowers
only;)
[25]And pray unto the Highest
continually, then will I come and talk
with thee.
[26]So I went my way into the field which
is called Ardath, like as he commanded
me; and there I sat among the flowers,
and did eat of the herbs of the field, and
the meat of the same satisfied me.
[27]After seven days I sat upon the grass,
and my heart was vexed within me, like
as before: [28]And I opened my mouth,
and began to talk before the most High,
and said, [29]O Lord, thou that
shewest thyself unto us, thou wast
shewed unto our fathers in the
wilderness, in a place where no man
treadeth, in a barren place, when they
came out of Egypt.
[30]And thou spakest saying, Hear me, O
Israel; and mark my words, thou seed
of Jacob. [31]For, behold, I sow my law
in you, and it shall bring fruit in you, and
ye shall be honoured in it for ever. [32]But
our fathers, which received the law,
kept it not, and observed not thy
ordinances: and though the fruit of thy
law did not perish, neither could it, for
it was thine; [33]Yet they that received it
perished, because they kept not the
thing that was sown in them. [34]And, lo,
it ls a custom, when the ground hath
received seed, or the sea a ship, or any
vessel meat or drink, that, that being
perished wherein it was sown or cast
into, [35]That thing also which was sown,
or cast therein, or received, doth perish,
and remaineth not with us: but with us
it hath not happened so. [36]For we that
have received the law perish by sin, and
our heart also which received it
[37]Notwithstanding the law perisheth
not, but remaineth in his force. [38]And
when I spake these things in my heart,
I looked back with mine eyes, and upon
the right side I saw a woman, and,
behold, she mourned and wept with a
loud voice, and was much grieved in

heart, and her clothes were rent, and she had ashes upon her head. 39 Then let I my thoughts go that I was in, and turned me unto her, 40 And said unto her, Wherefore weepest thou? why art thou so grieved in thy mind?

41 And she said unto me, Sir, let me alone, that I may bewail myself, and add unto my sorrow, for I am sore vexed in my mind, and brought very low. 42 And I said unto her, What aileth thee? tell me. 43 She said unto me, I thy servant have been barren, and had no child, though I had an husband thirty years, 44 And those thirty years I did nothing else day and night, and every hour, but make my, prayer to the Highest. 45 After thirty years God heard me thine handmaid, looked upon my misery, considered my trouble, and gave me a son: and I was very glad of him, so was my husband also, and all my neighbours: and we gave great honour unto the Almighty. 46 And I nourished him with great travail. 47 So when he grew up, and came to the time that he should have a wife, I made a feast.

CHAPTER 10

1 And it so came to pass, that when my son was entered into his wedding chamber, he fell down, and died. 2 Then we all overthrew the lights, and all my neighbours rose up to comfort me: so I took my rest unto the second day at night. 3 And it came to pass, when they had all left off to comfort me, to the end I might be quiet; then rose I up by night and fled, and came hither into this field, as thou seest. 4 And I do now purpose not to return into the city, but here to stay, and neither to eat nor drink, but continually to mourn and to fast until I die. 5 Then left I the meditations wherein I was, and spake to her in anger, saying, 6 Thou foolish woman above all other, seest thou not our mourning, and what happeneth unto us? 7 How that Sion our mother is full of all heaviness, and much humbled, mourning very sore? 8 And now, seeing we all mourn and are sad, for we are all in heaviness, art thou grieved for one son? 9 For ask the earth, and she shall tell thee, that it is she which ought to mourn for the fall of so many that grow upon her. 10 For out of her came all at the first, and out of her shall all others come, and, behold, they walk almost all into destruction, and a multitude of them is utterly rooted out. 11 Who then should make more mourning than she, that hath lost so great a multitude; and not thou, which art sorry but for one? 12 But if thou sayest unto me, My lamentation is not like the earth's, because I have lost the fruit of my womb, which I brought forth with pains, and bare with sorrows;

13 But the earth not so: for the multitude present in it according to the course of the earth is gone, as it came: 14 Then say I unto thee, Like as thou hast brought forth with labour; even so the earth also hath given her fruit, namely, man, ever since the beginning unto him that made her. 15 Now therefore keep thy sorrow to thyself, and bear with a good courage that which hath befallen thee. 16 For if thou shalt acknowledge the determination of God to be just, thou shalt both receive thy son in time, and shalt be commended among women. 17 Go thy way then into the city to thine husband. 18 And she said unto me, That will I not do: I will not go into the city, but here will I die. 19 So I proceeded to speak further unto her, and said, 20 Do not so, but be counselled. by me: for

how many are the adversities of Sion?
be comforted in regard of the sorrow of
Jerusalem. 21 For thou seest that our
sanctuary is laid waste, our altar broken
down, our temple destroyed; 22 Our
psaltery is laid on the ground, our song
is put to silence, our rejoicing is at an
end, the light of our candlestick is put
out, the ark of our covenant is spoiled,
our holy things are defiled, and the
name that is called upon us is almost
profaned: our children are put to shame,
our priests are burnt, our Levites are
gone into captivity, our virgins are
defiled, and our wives ravished; our
righteous men carried away, our little
ones destroyed, our young men are
brought in bondage, and our strong
men are become weak; 23 And, which is
the greatest of all, the seal of Sion hath
now lost her honour; for she is
delivered into the hands of them that
hate us. 24 And therefore shake off thy
great heaviness, and put away the
multitude of sorrows, that the Mighty
may be merciful unto thee again, and the
Highest shall give thee rest and ease
from thy labour.

25 And it came to pass while I was
talking with her, behold, her face upon
a sudden shined exceedingly, and her
countenance glistered, so that I was
afraid of her, and mused what it might
be. 26 And, behold, suddenly she made a
great cry very fearful: so that the earth
shook at the noise of the woman. 27 And
I looked, and, behold, the woman
appeared unto me no more, but there
was a city builded, and a large place
shewed itself from the foundations:
then was I afraid, and cried with a loud
voice, and said, 28 Where is Uriel the
angel, who came unto me at the first?
for he hath caused me to fall into many
trances, and mine end is turned into
corruption, and my prayer to rebuke.
29 And as I was speaking these words
behold, he came unto me, and looked
upon me. 30 And, lo, I lay as one that
had been dead, and mine understanding
was taken from me: and he took me by
the right hand, and comforted me, and
set me upon my feet, and said unto me,
31 What aileth thee? and why art thou so
disquieted? and why is thine
understanding troubled, and the
thoughts of thine heart? 32 And I said,
Because thou hast forsaken me, and yet
I did according to thy words, and I went
into the field, and, lo, I have seen, and
yet see, that I am not able to express.
33 And he said unto me, Stand up
manfully, and I will advise thee. 34 Then
said I, Speak on, my lord, in me; only
forsake me not, lest I die frustrate of my
hope. 35 For I have seen that I knew not,
and hear that I do not know. 36 Or is my
sense deceived, or my soul in a dream?
37 Now therefore I beseech thee that
thou wilt shew thy servant of this
vision. 38 He answered me then, and
said, Hear me, and I shall inform thee,
and tell thee wherefore thou art afraid:
for the Highest will reveal many secret
things unto thee. 39 He hath seen that thy
way is right: for that thou sorrowest
continually for thy people, and makest
great lamentation for Sion. 40 This
therefore is the meaning of the vision
which thou lately sawest: 41 Thou
sawest a woman mourning, and thou
begannest to comfort her: 42 But now
seest thou the likeness of the woman no
more, but there appeared unto thee a
city builded. 43 And whereas she told
thee of the death of her son, this is the
solution: 44 This woman, whom thou
sawest is Sion: and whereas she said
unto thee, even she whom thou seest as
a city builded, 45 Whereas, I say, she

said unto thee, that she hath been thirty
years barren: those are the thirty years
wherein there was no offering made in
her. [46]But after thirty years Solomon
builded the city and offered offerings:
and then bare the barren a son. [47]And
whereas she told thee that she
nourished him with labour: that was the
dwelling in Jerusalem. [48]But whereas
she said unto thee, That my son coming
into his marriage chamber happened to
have a fail, and died: this was the
destruction that came to Jerusalem.
[49]And, behold, thou sawest her likeness,
and because she mourned for her son,
thou begannest to comfort her: and of
these things which have chanced, these
are to be opened unto thee. [50]For now
the most High seeth that thou art
grieved unfeignedly, and sufferest from
thy whole heart for her, so hath he
shewed thee the brightness of her glory,
and the comeliness of her beauty:
[51]And therefore I bade thee remain in
the field where no house was builded:
[52]For I knew that the Highest would
shew this unto thee. [53]Therefore I
commanded thee to go into the field,
where no foundation of any building
was. [54]For in the place wherein the
Highest beginneth to shew his city,
there can no man's building be able to
stand. [55]And therefore fear not, let not
thine heart be affrighted, but go thy
way in, and see the beauty and
greatness of the building, as much as
thine eyes be able to see: [56]And then
shalt thou hear as much as thine ears
may comprehend. [57]For thou art
blessed above many other, and art
called with the Highest; and so are but
few. [58]But to morrow at night thou shalt
remain here; [59]And so shall the Highest
shew thee visions of the high things,
which the most High will do unto them
that dwell upon the earth in the last
days. So I slept that night and another,
like as he commanded me.

CHAPTER 11

[1]Then saw I a dream, and, behold, there
came up from the sea an eagle, which
had twelve feathered wings, and three
heads. [2]And I saw, and, behold, she
spread her wings over all the earth, and
all the winds of the air blew on her, and
were gathered together. [3]And I beheld,
and out of her feathers there grew other
contrary feathers; and they became
little feathers and small. [4]But her heads
were at rest: the head in the midst was
greater than the other, yet rested it with
the residue. [5]Moreover I beheld, and,
lo, the eagle flew with her feathers, and
reigned upon earth, and over them that
dwelt therein. [6]And I saw that all things
under heaven were subject unto her,
and no man spake against her, no, not
one creature upon earth. [7]And I beheld,
and, lo, the eagle rose upon her talons,
and spake to her feathers, saying,
[8]Watch not all at once: sleep every one
in his own place, and watch by course:
[9]But let the heads be preserved for the
last. [10]And I beheld, and, lo, the voice
went not out of her heads, but from the
midst of her body.
[11]And I numbered her contrary
feathers, and, behold, there were eight
of them. [12]And I looked, and, behold,
on the right side there arose one feather,
and reigned over all the earth; [13]And so
it was, that when it reigned, the end of
it came, and the place thereof appeared
no more: so the next following stood
up. and reigned, and had a great time;
[14]And it happened, that when it reigned,
the end of it came also, like as the first,
so that it appeared no more. [15]Then

came there a voice unto it, and said,
16 Hear thou that hast borne rule over the
earth so long: this I say unto thee,
before thou beginnest to appear no
more, 17 There shall none after thee
attain unto thy time, neither unto the
half thereof. 18 Then arose the third, and
reigned as the other before, and
appeared no more also. 19 So went it
with all the residue one after another, as
that every one reigned, and then
appeared no more.
20 Then I beheld, and, lo, in process of
time the feathers that followed stood up
upon the right side, that they might rule
also; and some of them ruled, but
within a while they appeared no more:
21 For some of them were set up, but
ruled not. 22 After this I looked, and,
behold, the twelve feathers appeared no
more, nor the two little feathers: 23 And
there was no more upon the eagle's
body, but three heads that rested,
and six little wings. 24 Then saw I also
that two little feathers divided
themselves from the six, and remained
under the head that was upon the right
side: for the four continued in their
place. 25 And I beheld, and, lo, the
feathers that were under the wing
thought to set up themselves and to
have the rule. 26 And I beheld, and, lo,
there was one set up, but shortly it
appeared no more. 27 And the second
was sooner away than the first. 28 And I
beheld, and, lo, the two that remained
thought also in themselves to reign:
29 And when they so thought, behold,
there awaked one of the heads that were
at rest, namely, it that was in the midst;
for that was greater than the two other
heads. 30 And then I saw that the two
other heads were joined with it. 31 And,
behold, the head was turned with them
that were with it, and did eat up the two
feathers under the wing that would
have reigned. 32 But this head put the
whole earth in fear, and bare rule in it
over all those that dwelt upon the earth
with much oppression; and it had the
governance of the world more than all
the wings that had been. 33 And after
this I beheld, and, lo, the head that was
in the midst suddenly appeared no
more, like as the wings. 34 But there
remained the two heads, which also in
like sort ruled upon the earth, and over
those that dwelt therein. 35 And I
beheld, and, lo, the head upon the right
side devoured it that was upon the left
side. 36 Then I head a voice, which said
unto me, Look before thee, and
consider the thing that thou seest.
37 And I beheld, and lo, as it were a
roaring lion chased out of the wood:
and I saw that he sent out a man's voice
unto the eagle, and said, 38 Hear thou, I
will talk with thee, and the Highest
shall say unto thee, 39 Art not thou it that
remainest of the four beasts, whom I
made to reign in my world, that the
end of their times might come through
them? 40 And the fourth came, and
overcame all the beasts that were past,
and had power over the world with
great fearfulness, and over the whole
compass of the earth with much wicked
oppression; and so long time dwelt he
upon the earth with deceit. 41 For the
earth hast thou not judged with truth.
42 For thou hast afflicted the meek, thou
hast hurt the peaceable, thou hast loved
liars, and destroyed the dwellings of
them that brought forth fruit, and hast
cast down the walls of such as did thee
no harm. 43 Therefore is thy wrongful
dealing come up unto the Highest, and
thy pride unto the Mighty.
44 The Highest also hath looked upon
the proud times, and, behold, they are

ended, and his abominations are
fulfilled. 45 And therefore appear no
more, thou eagle, nor thy horrible
wings, nor thy wicked feathers nor thy
malicious heads, nor thy hurtful claws,
nor all thy vain body: 46 That all the
earth may be refreshed, and may return,
being delivered from thy violence, and
that she may hope for the judgment and
mercy of him that made her.

CHAPTER 12

1 And it came to pass, whiles the lion
spake these words unto the eagle, I saw,
2 And, behold, the head that remained
and the four wings appeared no more,
and the two went unto it and set
themselves up to reign, and their
kingdom was small, and fill of uproar.
3 And I saw, and, behold, they appeared
no more, and the whole body of the
eagle was burnt so that the earth was in
great fear: then awaked I out of the
trouble and trance of my mind, and
from great fear, and said unto my spirit,
4 Lo, this hast thou done unto me, in that
thou searchest out the ways of the
Highest. 5 Lo, yet am I weary in my
mind, and very weak in my spirit; and
little strength is there in me, for the
great fear wherewith I was afflicted this
night. 6 Therefore will I now beseech
the Highest, that he will comfort me
unto the end. 7 And I said, Lord that
bearest rule, if I have found grace before
thy sight, and if I am justified with thee
before many others, and if my prayer
indeed be come up before thy face;
8 Comfort me then, and shew me thy
servant the interpretation and plain
difference of this fearful vision, that
thou mayest perfectly comfort my soul.
9 For thou hast judged me worthy to
shew me the last times. 10 And he said
unto me, This is the interpretation of
the vision: 11 The eagle, whom thou
sawest come up from the sea, is the
kingdom which was seen in the vision
of thy brother Daniel. 12 But it was not
expounded unto him, therefore now I
declare it unto thee. 13 Behold, the days
will come, that there shall rise up a
kingdom upon earth, and it shall be
feared above all the kingdoms that
were before it. 14 In the same shall
twelve kings reign, one after another:
15 Whereof the second shall begin to
reign, and shall have more time than
any of the twelve. 16 And this do the
twelve wings signify, which thou
sawest. 17 As for the voice which thou
heardest speak, and that thou sawest
not to go out from the heads but from
the midst of the body thereof, this is the
interpretation: 18 That after the time of
that kingdom there shall arise great
strivings, and it shall stand in peril of
failing: nevertheless it shall not then
fall, but shall be restored again to his
beginning. 19 And whereas thou sawest
the eight small under feathers sticking
to her wings, this is the interpretation:
20 That in him there shall arise eight
kings, whose times shall be but small,
and their years swift. 21 And two of
them shall perish, the middle time
approaching: four shall be kept until
their end begin to approach: but two
shall be kept unto the end. 22 And
whereas thou sawest three heads
resting, this is the interpretation: 23 In
his last days shall the most High raise
up three kingdoms, and renew many
things therein, and they shall have the
dominion of the earth, 24 And of those
that dwell therein, with much
oppression, above all those that were
before them: therefore are they called
the heads of the eagle. 25 For these are

they that shall accomplish his
wickedness, and that shall finish his last
end. 26And whereas thou sawest that
the great head appeared no more, it
signifieth that one of them shall die
upon his bed, and yet with pain. 27For
the two that remain shall be slain with
the sword. 28For the sword of the one
shall devour the other: but at the last
shall he fall through the sword himself.
29And whereas thou sawest two
feathers under the wings passing over
the head that is on the right side; 30It
signifieth that these are they, whom the
Highest hath kept unto their end: this is
the small kingdom and full of trouble,
as thou sawest. 31And the lion, whom
thou sawest rising up out of the wood,
and roaring, and speaking to the eagle,
and rebuking her for her
unrighteousness with all the words
which thou hast heard; 32This is the
anointed, which the Highest hath kept
for them and for their wickedness unto
the end: he shall reprove them, and
shall upbraid them with their cruelty.
33For he shall set them before him alive
in judgment, and shall rebuke them,
and correct them. 34For the rest of my
people shall he deliver with mercy,
those that have been pressed upon my
borders, and he shall make them joyful
until the coming of the day of
judgment, whereof I have spoken unto
thee from the the beginning. 35This is
the dream that thou sawest, and these
are the interpretations. 36Thou only hast
been meet to know this secret of the
Highest. 37Therefore write all these
things that thou hast seen in a book, and
hide them: 38And teach them to the wise
of the people, whose hearts thou knowest
may comprehend and keep these
secrets. 39But wait thou here thyself yet
seven days more, that it may be
shewed thee, whatsoever it pleaseth the
Highest to declare unto thee. And with
that he went his way. 40And it came to
pass, when all the people saw that the
seven days were past, and I not come
again into the city, they gathered them
all together, from the least unto the
greatest, and came unto me, and said,
41What have we offended thee? and
what evil have we done against thee,
that thou forsakest us, and sittest here
in this place? 42For of all the prophets
thou only art left us, as a cluster of the
vintage, and as a candle in a dark place,
and as a haven or ship preserved from
the tempest. 43Are not the evils which
are come to us sufficient? 44If thou
shalt forsake us, how much better had it
been for us, if we also had been burned
in the midst of Sion? 45For we are not
better than they that died there. And
they wept with a loud voice. Then
answered I them, and said, 46Be of
good comfort, O Israel; and be not
heavy, thou house of Jacob: 47For the
Highest hath you in remembrance, and
the Mighty hath not forgotten you in
temptation. 48As for me, I have not
forsaken you, neither am I departed
from you: but am come into this place,
to pray for the desolation of Sion, and
that I might seek mercy for the low
estate of your sanctuary. 49And now go
your way home every man, and after
these days will I come unto you. 50So
the people went their way into the city,
like as I commanded them: 51But I
remained still in the field seven days, as
the angel commanded me; and did eat
only in those days of the flowers of the
field, and had my meat of the herbs

CHAPTER 13

1And it came to pass after seven days,

I dreamed a dream by night: 2And, lo,
there arose a wind from the sea, that it
moved all the waves thereof. 3And I
beheld, and, lo, that man waxed strong
with the thousands of heaven: and when
he turned his countenance to look, all
the things trembled that were seen
under him. 4And whensoever the voice
went out of his mouth, all they burned
that heard his voice, like as the earth
faileth when it feeleth the fire. 5And
after this I beheld, and, lo, there was
gathered together a multitude of men,
out of number, from the four winds of
the heaven, to subdue the man that
came out of the sea 6But I beheld,
and, lo, he had graved himself a great
mountain, and flew up upon it. 7But I
would have seen the region or place
whereout the hill was graven, and I
could not. 8And after this I beheld,
and, lo, all they which were gathered
together to subdue him were sore
afraid, and yet durst fight. 9And, lo, as
he saw the violence of the multitude
that came, he neither lifted up his hand,
nor held sword, nor any instrument of
war: 10But only I saw that he sent out of
his mouth as it had been a blast of fire,
and out of his lips a flaming breath, and
out of his tongue he cast out sparks and
tempests. 11And they were all mixed
together; the blast of fire, the flaming
breath, and the great tempest; and fell
with violence upon the multitude which
was prepared to fight, and burned them
up every one, so that upon a sudden of
an innumerable multitude nothing was
to be perceived, but only dust and smell
of smoke: when I saw this I was
afraid. 12Afterward saw I the same man
come down from the mountain, and call
unto him another peaceable Multitude.
13And there came much people unto
him, whereof some were glad, some were
sorry, and some of them were bound,
and other some brought of them that
were offered: then was I sick through
great fear, and I awaked, and said,
14Thou hast shewed thy servant these
wonders from the beginning, and hast
counted me worthy that thou shouldest
receive my prayer: 15Shew me now yet
the interpretation of this dream. 16For
as I conceive in mine understanding,
woe unto them that shall be left in those
days and much more woe unto them
that are not left behind! 17For they that
were not left were in heaviness. 18Now
understand I the things that are laid up
in the latter days, which shall happen
unto them, and to those that are left
behind. 19Therefore are they come into
great perils and many necessities, like
as these dreams declare. 20Yet is it
easier for him that is in danger to come
into these things, than to pass away as
a cloud out of the world, and not to see
the things that happen in the last days.
And he answered unto me, and said,
21The interpretation of the vision shall
I shew thee, and I will open unto thee
the thing that thou hast required.
22Whereas thou hast spoken of them
that are left behind, this is the
interpretation: 23He that shall endure
the peril in that time hath kept himself:
they that be fallen into danger are such
as have works, and faith toward the
Almighty. 24Know this therefore, that
they which be left behind are more
blessed than they that be dead. 25This
is the meaning of the vision: Whereas
thou sawest a man coming up from the
midst of the sea: 26The same is he
whom God the Highest hath kept a
great season, which by his own self
shall deliver his creature: and he shall
order them that are left behind. 27And
whereas thou sawest, that out of his
mouth there came as a blast of wind,
and fire, and storm; 28And that he held

neither sword, nor any instrument of
war, but that the rushing in of him
destroyed the whole multitude that
came to subdue him; this is the
interpretation: [29]Behold, the days
come, when the most High will begin
to deliver them that are upon the earth.
[30]And he shall come to the astonishment
of them that dwell on the earth. [31]And
one shall undertake to fight against
another, one city against another, one
place against another, one people
against another, and one realm against
another. [32]And the time shall be when
these things shall come to pass, and the
signs shall happen which I shewed thee
before, and then shall my Son be
declared, whom thou sawest as a man
ascending. [33]And when all the people
hear his voice, every man shall in their
own land leave the battle they have one
against another. [34]And an innumerable
multitude shall be gathered together, as
thou sawest them, willing to come, and
to overcome him by fighting. [35]But he
shall stand upon the top of the mount
Sion. [36]And Sion shall come, and shall
be shewed to all men, being prepared
and builded, like as thou sawest the
hill graven without hands. [37]And this
my Son shall rebuke the wicked
inventions of those nations, which for
their wicked life are fallen into the
tempest; [38]And shall lay before them
their evil thoughts, and the torments
wherewith they shall begin to be
tormented, which are like unto a flame:
and he shall destroy them without
labour by the law which is like unto
me. [39]And whereas thou sawest that he
gathered another peaceable multitude
unto him; [40]Those are the ten tribes,
which were carried away prisoners out
of their own land in the time of Osea
the king, whom Salmanasar the king of
Assyria led away captive, and he
carried them over the waters, and so
came they into another land. [41]But they
took this counsel among themselves,
that they would leave the multitude of
the heathen, and go forth into a further
country, where never mankind dwelt,
[42]That they might there keep their
statutes, which they never kept in their
own land. [43]And they entered into
Euphrates by the narrow places of the
river. [44]For the most High then shewed
signs for them, and held still the flood,
till they were passed over. [45]For
through that country there was a great
way to go, namely, of a year and a
half: and the same region is called
Arsareth. [46]Then dwelt they there until
the latter time; and now when they shall
begin to come, [47]The Highest shall stay
the springs of the stream again, that
they may go through: therefore sawest
thou the multitude with peace. [48]But
those that be left behind of thy people
are they that are found within my
borders. [49]Now when he destroyeth the
multitude of the nations that are
gathered together, he shall defend his
people that remain. [50]And then shall he
shew them great wonders. [51]Then said
I, O Lord that bearest rule, shew me
this: Wherefore have I seen the man
coming up from the midst of the sea?
[52]And he said unto me, Like as thou
canst neither seek out nor know the
things that are in the deep of the sea:
even so can no man upon earth see my
Son, or those that be with him, but in
the day time. [53]This is the interpretation
of the dream which thou sawest, and
whereby thou only art here lightened.
[54]For thou hast forsaken thine own way,
and applied thy diligence unto my law,
and sought it. [55]Thy life hast thou
ordered in wisdom, and hast called
understanding thy mother.

[56]And therefore have I shewed thee the

treasures of the Highest: after other
three days I will speak other things unto
thee, and declare unto thee mighty and
wondrous things.
57 Then went I forth into the field,
giving praise and thanks greatly unto
the most High because of his wonders
which he did in time; 58 And because he
governeth the same, and such things as
fall in their seasons: and there I sat
three days.

CHAPTER 14

1 And it came to pass upon the third day,
I sat under an oak, and, behold, there
came a voice out of a bush over against
me, and said, Esdras, Esdras. 2 And I
said, Here am I, Lord And I stood up
upon my feet. 3 Then said he unto me,
In the bush I did manifestly reveal
myself unto Moses, and talked with
him, when my people served in Egypt:
4 And I sent him and led my people out
of Egypt, and brought him up to the
mount of where I held him by me a long
season, 5 And told him many wondrous
things, and shewed him the secrets of
the times, and the end; and commanded
him, saying, 6 These words shalt thou
declare, and these shalt thou hide. 7 And
now I say unto thee, 8 That thou lay up
in thy heart the signs that I have
shewed, and the dreams that thou hast
seen, and the interpretations which thou
hast heard: 9 For thou shalt be taken
away from all, and from henceforth
thou shalt remain with my Son, and
with such as be like thee, until the times
be ended. 10 For the world hath lost his
youth, and the times begin to wax old.
11 For the world is divided into twelve
parts, and the ten parts of it are gone
already, and half of a tenth part: 12 And
there remaineth that which is after the
half of the tenth part. 13 Now therefore
set thine house in order, and reprove
thy people, comfort such of them as be
in trouble, and now renounce
corruption, 14 Let go from thee mortal
thoughts, cast away the burdens of
man, put off now the weak nature,
15 And set aside the thoughts that are
most heavy unto thee, and haste thee to
flee from these times. 16 For yet greater
evils than those which thou hast seen
happen shall be done hereafter. 17 For
look how much the world shall be
weaker through age, so much the more
shall evils increase upon them that
dwell therein. 18 For the time is fled far
away, and leasing is hard at hand: for
now hasteth the vision to come, which
thou hast seen. 19 Then answered I
before thee, and said, 20 Behold, Lord, I
will go, as thou hast commanded me,
and reprove the people which are
present: but they that shall be born
afterward, who shall admonish them?
thus the world is set in darkness, and
they that dwell therein are without
light. 21 For thy law is burnt, therefore
no man knoweth the things that are
done of thee, or the work that shall
begin. 22 But if I have found grace
before thee, send the Holy Ghost into
me, and I shall write all that hath been
done in the world since the beginning,
which were written in thy law, that men
may find thy path, and that they which
will live in the latter days may live.
23 And he answered me, saying, Go thy
way, gather the people together, and say
unto them, that they seek thee not for
forty days. 24 But look thou prepare thee
many box trees, and take with thee
Sarea, Dabria, Selemia, Ecanus, and
Asiel, these five which are ready to
write swiftly; 25 And come hither, and I
shall light a candle of understanding in

thine heart, which shall not be put out, till the things be performed which thou shalt begin to write. 26 And when thou hast done, some things shalt thou publish, and some things shalt thou shew secretly to the wise: to morrow this hour shalt thou begin to write. 27 Then went I forth, as he commanded, and gathered all the people together, and said, 28 Hear these words, O Israel. 29 Our fathers at the beginning were strangers in Egypt, from whence they were delivered: 30 And received the law of life, which they kept not, which ye also have transgressed after them. 31 Then was the land, even the land of Sion, parted among you by lot: but your fathers, and ye yourselves, have done unrighteousness, and have not kept the ways which the Highest commanded you. 32 And forasmuch as he is a righteous judge, he took from you in time the thing that he had given you. 33 And now are ye here, and your brethren among you. 34 Therefore if so be that ye will subdue your own understanding, and reform your hearts, ye shall be kept alive and after death ye shall obtain mercy. 35 For after death shall the judgment come, when we shall live again: and then shall the names of the righteous be manifest, and the works of the ungodly shall be declared. 36 Let no man therefore come unto me now, nor seek after me these forty days. 37 So I took the five men, as he commanded me, and we went into the field, and remained there. 38 And the next day, behold, a voice called me, saying, Esdras, open thy mouth, and drink that I give thee to drink. 39 Then opened I my mouth, and, behold, he reached me a full cup, which was full as it were with water, but the colour of it was like fire. 40 And I took it, and drank: and when I had drunk of it, my heart uttered understanding, and wisdom grew in my breast, for my spirit strengthened my memory: 41 And my mouth was opened, and shut no more. 42 The Highest gave understanding unto the five men, and they wrote the wonderful visions of the night that were told, which they knew not: and they sat forty days, and they wrote in the day, and at night they ate bread. 43 As for me. I spake in the day, and I held not my tongue by night. 44 In forty days they wrote two hundred and four books. 45 And it came to pass, when the forty days were filled, that the Highest spake, saying, The first that thou hast written publish openly, that the worthy and unworthy may read it: 46 But keep the seventy last, that thou mayest deliver them only to such as be wise among the people: 47 For in them is the spring of understanding, the fountain of wisdom, and the stream of knowledge. 48 And I did so.

CHAPTER 15

1 Behold, speak thou in the ears of my people the words of prophecy, which I will put in thy mouth, saith the Lord: 2 And cause them to be written in paper: for they are faithful and true. 3 Fear not the imaginations against thee, let not the incredulity of them trouble thee, that speak against thee. 4 For all the unfaithful shall die in their unfaithfulness. 5 Behold, saith the Lord, I will bring plagues upon the world; the sword, famine, death, and destruction. 6 For wickedness hath exceedingly polluted the whole earth, and their hurtful works are fulfilled. 7 Therefore saith the Lord, 8 I will hold my tongue no more as touching their wickedness,

which they profanely commit, neither
will I suffer them in those things, in
which they wickedly exercise
themselves: behold, the innocent and
righteous blood crieth unto me, and the
souls of the just complain continually.
9 And therefore, saith the Lord, I will
surely avenge them, and receive unto
me all the innocent blood from among
them. 10 Behold, my people is led as a
flock to the slaughter: I will not suffer
them now to dwell in the land of Egypt:
11 But I will bring them with a mighty
hand and a stretched out arm, and smite
Egypt with plagues, as before, and will
destroy all the land thereof. 12 Egypt
shall mourn, and the foundation of it
shall be smitten with the plague and
punishment that God shall bring upon
it. 13 They that till the ground shall
mourn: for their seeds shall fail through
the blasting and hail, and with a fearful
constellation. 14 Woe to the world and
them that dwell therein! 15 For the
sword and their destruction draweth
nigh, and one people shall stand up and
fight against another, and swords in
their hands. 16 For there shall be sedition
among men, and invading one another;
they shall not regard their kings nor
princes, and the course of their actions
shall stand in their power. 17 A man
shall desire to go into a city, and shall
not be able. 18 For because of their pride
the cities shall be troubled, the houses
shall be destroyed, and men shall be
afraid. 19 A man shall have no pity upon
his neighbour, but shall destroy their
houses with the sword, and spoil their
goods, because of the lack of bread, and
for great tribulation. 20 Behold, saith
God, I will call together all the kings of
the earth to reverence me, which are
from the rising of the sun, from the
south, from the east, and Libanus; to
turn themselves one against another,
and repay the things that they have done
to them. 21 Like as they do yet this day
unto my chosen, so will I do also, and
recompense in their bosom. Thus saith
the Lord God; 22 My right hand shall not
spare the sinners, and my sword shall
not cease over them that shed innocent
blood upon the earth. 23 The fire is gone
forth from his wrath, and hath
consumed the foundations of the earth,
and the sinners, like the straw that is
kindled. 24 Woe to them that sin, and
keep not my commandments! saith the
Lord. 25 I will not spare them: go your
way, ye children, from the power,
defile not my sanctuary. 26 For the Lord
knoweth all them that sin against him,
and therefore delivereth he them unto
death and destruction. 27 For now are
the plagues come upon the whole earth
and ye shall remain in them: for God
shall not deliver you, because ye have
sinned against him. 28 Behold an
horrible vision, and the appearance
thereof from the east: 29 Where the
nations of the dragons of Arabia shall
come out with many chariots, and the
multitude of them shall be carried as the
wind upon earth, that all they which hear
them may fear and tremble. 30 Also the
Carmanians raging in wrath shall go
forth as the wild boars of the wood, and
with great power shall they come, and
join battle with them, and shall waste
a portion of the land of the Assyrians.
31 And then shall the dragons have the
upper hand, remembering their
nature; and if they shall turn
themselves, conspiring together in
great power to persecute them, 32 Then
these shall be troubled bled, and keep
silence through their power, and shall
flee. 33 And from the land of the
Assyrians shall the enemy besiege

them, and consume some of them, and
in their host shall be fear and dread, and
strife among their kings. 34 Behold
clouds from the east and from the north
unto the south, and they are very
horrible to look upon, full of wrath and
storm. 35 They shall smite one upon
another, and they shall smite down a
great multitude of stars upon the earth,
even their own star; and blood shall be
from the sword unto the belly, 36 And
dung of men unto the camel's hough.
37 And there shall be great fearfulness
and trembling upon earth: and they that
see the wrath shall be afraid, and
trembling shall come upon them. 38 And
then shall there come great storms from
the south, and from the north, and
another part from the west. 39 And
strong winds shall arise from the east,
and shall open it; and the cloud which
he raised up in wrath, and the star stirred
to cause fear toward the east and west
wind, shall be destroyed. 40 The great
and mighty clouds shall be puffed up
full of wrath, and the star, that they may
make all the earth afraid, and them that
dwell therein; and they shall pour out
over every high and eminent place an
horrible star, 41 Fire, and hail, and flying
swords, and many waters, that all fields
may be full, and all rivers, with the
abundance of great waters. 42 And they
shall break down the cities and walls,
mountains and hills, trees of the wood,
and grass of the meadows, and their
corn. 43 And they shall go stedfastly
unto Babylon, and make her afraid.
44 They shall come to her, and besiege
her, the star and all wrath shall they
pour out upon her: then shall the dust
and smoke go up unto the heaven, and
all they that be about her shall bewail
her. 45 And they that remain under her
shall do service unto them that have put
her in fear. 46 And thou, Asia, that art
partaker of the hope of Babylon, and art
the glory of her person: 47 Woe be unto
thee, thou wretch, because thou hast
made thyself like unto her; and hast
decked thy daughters in whoredom,
that they might please and glory in thy
lovers, which have always desired to
commit whoredom with thee. 48 Thou
hast followed her that is hated in all her
works and inventions: therefore saith
God, 49 I will send plagues upon thee;
widowhood, poverty, famine, sword,
and pestilence, to waste thy houses
with destruction and death. 50 And the
glory of thy Power shall be dried up as
a flower, the heat shall arise that is sent
over thee. 51 Thou shalt be weakened as
a poor woman with stripes, and as one
chastised with wounds, so that the
mighty and lovers shall not be able to
receive thee. 52 Would I with jealousy
have so proceeded against thee, saith
the Lord, 53 If thou hadst not always
slain my chosen, exalting the stroke of
thine hands, and saying over their dead,
when thou wast drunken, 54 Set forth the
beauty of thy countenance? 55 The
reward of thy whoredom shall be in thy
bosom, therefore shalt thou receive
recompence. 56 Like as thou hast done
unto my chosen, saith the Lord, even so
shall God do unto thee, and shall
deliver thee into mischief 57 Thy
children shall die of hunger, and thou
shalt fall through the sword: thy cities
shall be broken down, and all thine
shall perish with the sword in the field.
58 They that be in the mountains shall
die of hunger, and eat their own flesh,
and drink their own blood, for very
hunger of bread, and thirst of water.
59 Thou as unhappy shalt come through
the sea, and receive plagues again.
60 And in the passage they shall rush on

the idle city, and shall destroy some
portion of thy land, and consume part
of thy glory, and shall return to
Babylon that was destroyed. 61 And
thou shalt be cast down by them as
stubble, and they shall be unto thee as
fire; 62 And shall consume thee, and thy
cities, thy land, and thy mountains; all
thy woods and thy fruitful trees shall
they burn up with fire. 63 Thy children
shall they carry away captive, and,
look, what thou hast, they shall spoil it,
and mar the beauty of thy face.

CHAPTER 16

1 Woe be unto thee, Babylon, and Asia!
woe be unto thee, Egypt and Syria!
2 Gird up yourselves with cloths of sack
and hair, bewail your children, and be
sorry; for your destruction is at hand.
3 A sword is sent upon you, and who
may turn it back? 4 A fire is sent among
you, and who may quench it? 5 Plagues
are sent unto you, and what is he that
may drive them away? 6 May any man
drive away an hungry lion in the wood?
or may any one quench the fire in
stubble, when it hath begun to burn?
7 May one turn again the arrow that is
shot of a strong archer? 8 The mighty
Lord sendeth the plagues and who is he
that can drive them away? 9 A fire shall
go forth from his wrath, and who is he
that may quench it? 10 He shall cast
lightnings, and who shall not fear? he
shall thunder, and who shall not be
afraid? 11 The Lord shall threaten, and
who shall not be utterly beaten to
powder at his presence? 12 The earth
quaketh, and the foundations thereof;
the sea ariseth up with waves from the
deep, and the waves of it are troubled,
and the fishes thereof also, before the
Lord, and before the glory of his power:
13 For strong is his right hand that
bendeth the bow, his arrows that he
shooteth are sharp, and shall not miss,
when they begin to be shot into the ends
of the world. 14 Behold, the plagues are
sent, and shall not return again, until
they come upon the earth. 15 The fire is
kindled, and shall not be put out, till it
consume the foundation of the earth.
16 Like as an arrow which is shot of a
mighty archer returneth not backward:
even so the plagues that shall be sent
upon earth shall not return again.
17 Woe is me! woe is me! who will
deliver me in those days? 18 The
beginning of sorrows and great
mournings; the beginning of famine and
great death; the beginning of wars, and
the powers shall stand in fear; the
beginning of evils! what shall I do
when these evils shall come? 19 Behold,
famine and plague, tribulation and
anguish, are sent as scourges for
amendment. 20 But for all these things
they shall not turn from their
wickedness, nor be always mindful of
the scourges. 21 Behold, victuals shall
be so good cheap upon earth, that they
shall think themselves to be in good
case, and even then shall evils grow
upon earth, sword, famine, and great
confusion. 22 For many of them that
dwell upon earth shall perish of famine;
and the other, that escape the hunger,
shall the sword destroy. 23 And the dead
shall be cast out as dung, and there shall
be no man to comfort them: for the
earth shall be wasted, and the cities
shall be cast down. 24 There shall be no
man left to till the earth, and to sow it
25 The trees shall give fruit, and who
shall gather them? 26 The grapes shall
ripen, and who shall tread them? for all
places shall be desolate of men: 27 So
that one man shall desire to see another,

and to hear his voice. 28For of a city
there shall be ten left, and two of the
field, which shall hide themselves in the
thick groves, and in the clefts of the
rocks. 29As in an orchard of Olives
upon every tree there are left three or
four olives; 30Or as when a vineyard is
gathered, there are left some clusters of
them that diligently seek through the
vineyard: 31Even so in those days there
shall be three or four left by them that
search their houses with the sword.
32And the earth shall be laid waste, and
the fields thereof shall wax old, and her
ways and all her paths shall grow full of
thorns, a 33The virgins shall mourn,
having no bridegrooms; the women
shall mourn, having no husbands; their
daughters shall mourn, having no
helpers. 34In the wars shall their
bridegrooms be destroyed, and their
husbands shall perish of famine. 35Hear
now these things and understand them,
ye servants of the Lord. 36Behold, the
word of the Lord, receive it: believe not
the gods of whom the Lord spake.
37Behold, the plagues draw nigh, and
are not slack. 38As when a woman with
child in the ninth month bringeth forth
her son, with two or three hours of her
birth great pains compass her womb,
which pains, when the child cometh
forth, they slack not a moment: 39Even
so shall not the plagues be slack to
come upon the earth, and the world
shall mourn, and sorrows shall come
upon it on every side. 40O my people,
hear my word: make you ready to thy
battle, and in those evils be even as
pilgrims upon the earth. 41He that
selleth, let him be as he that fleeth
away: and he that buyeth, as one that
will lose: 42He that occupieth
merchandise, as he that hath no profit
by it: and he that buildeth, as he that
shall not dwell therein: 43He that
soweth, as if he should not reap: so also
he that planteth the vineyard, as he that
shall not gather the grapes: 44They that
marry, as they that shall get no
children; and they that marry not, as the
widowers. 45And therefore they that
labour labour in vain: 46For strangers
shall reap their fruits, and spoil their
goods, overthrow their houses, and take
their children captives, for in
captivity and famine shall they get
children. 47And they that occupy their
merchandise with robbery, the more
they deck their cities, their houses, their
possessions, and their own persons:
48The more will I be angry with them
for their sin, saith the Lord. 49Like as a
whore envieth a right honest and
virtuous woman: 50So shall
righteousness hate iniquity, when she
decketh herself, and shall accuse her to
her face, when he cometh that shall
defend him that diligently searcheth
out every sin upon earth. 51And
therefore be ye not like thereunto, nor
to the works thereof. 52For yet a little,
and iniquity shall be taken away out of
the earth, and righteousness shall reign
among you. 53Let not the sinner say that
he hath not sinned: for God shall burn
coals of fire upon his head, which saith
before the Lord God and his glory, I
have not sinned. 54Behold, the Lord
knoweth all the works of men, their
imaginations, their thoughts, and their
hearts: 55Which spake but the word, Let
the earth be made; and it was made: Let
the heaven be made; and it was created.
56In his word were the stars made, and
he knoweth the number of them. 57He
searcheth the deep, and the treasures
thereof; he hath measured the sea, and
what it containeth. 58He hath shut the
sea in the midst of the waters, and with

his word hath he hanged the earth upon
the waters. [59]He spreadeth out the
heavens like a vault; upon the waters
hath he founded it. [60]In the desert hath
he made springs of water, and pools
upon the tops of the mountains, that the
floods might pour down from the high
rocks to water the earth. [61]He made
man, and put his heart in the midst of
the body, and gave him breath, life, and
understanding. [62]Yea and the Spirit of
Almighty God, which made all things,
and searcheth out all hidden things in
the secrets of the earth, [63]Surely he
knoweth your inventions, and what ye
think in your hearts, even them that sin,
and would hide their sin. [64]Therefore
hath the Lord exactly searched out all
your works, and he will put you all to
shame. [65]And when your sins are
brought forth, ye shall be ashamed
before men, and your own sins shall be
your accusers in that day. [66]What will
ye do? or how will ye hide your sins
before God and his angels? [67]Behold,
God himself is the judge, fear him:
leave off from your sins, and forget
your iniquities, to meddle no more with
them for ever: so shall God lead you
forth, and deliver you from all trouble.
[68]For, behold, the burning wrath of a
great multitude is kindled over you, and
they shall take away certain of you, and
feed you, being idle, with things
offered unto idols. [69]And they that
consent unto them shall be had in
derision and in reproach, and trodden
under foot. [70]For there shall be in every
place, and in the next cities, a great
insurrection upon those that fear the
Lord. [71]They shall be like mad men,
sparing none, but still spoiling and
destroying those that fear the Lord.
[72]For they shall waste and take away
their goods, and cast them out of their
houses. [73]Then shall they be known,
who are my chosen; and they shall be
tried as the gold in the fire. [74]Hear, O ye
my beloved, saith the Lord: behold, the
days of trouble are at hand, but I will
deliver you from the same. [75]Be ye not
afraid neither doubt; for God is your
guide, [76]And the guide of them who
keep my commandments and precepts,
saith the Lord God: let not your sins
weigh you down, and let not your
iniquities lift up themselves. [77]Woe be
unto them that are bound with their
sins, and covered with their iniquities
like as a field is covered over with
bushes, and the path thereof covered
with thorns, that no man may travel
through! [78]It is left undressed, and is
cast into the fire to be consumed
therewith.

TOBIT

CHAPTER 1

[1]The book of the words of Tobit, son of
Tobiel, the son of Ananiel, the son of
Aduel, the son of Gab´ael, of the seed
of Asael, of the tribe of Naph´tali; [2]who
in the time of Shalmane´ser king of the
Assyrians was led captive out of
Thisbe, which is at the right hand of
that city, which is called properly
Naph´tali in Galilee above Asher.
[3]I Tobit have walked all the days of my
life in the ways of truth and justice, and
I did many almsdeeds to my brethren,
and my nation, who came with me to
Nin´eveh, into the land of the Assyrians.
[4]And when I was in mine own country,
in the land of Israel, being but young,
all the tribe of Naph´tali my father fell
from the house of Jerusalem, which
was chosen out of all the tribes of
Israel, that all the tribes should sacrifice
there, where the temple of the
habitation of the most High was
consecrated and built for all ages.
[5]Now all the tribes which together
revolted, and the house of my father
Naph´tali, sacrificed unto the heifer
Ba´al. [6]But I alone went often to
Jerusalem at the feasts, as it was
ordained unto all the people of Israel by
an everlasting decree, having the
firstfruits and tenths of increase, with
that which was first shorn; and them
gave I at the altar to the priests the
children of Aaron. [7]The first tenth part
of all increase I gave to the sons of
Aaron, who ministered at Jerusalem:
another tenth part I sold away, and
went, and spent it every year at
Jerusalem: [8]and the third I gave unto
them to whom it was meet, as Deborah
my father's mother had commanded
me, because I was left an orphan by my
father. [9]Furthermore, when I was come
to the age of a man, I married Anna of
mine own kindred, and of her I begot
Tobias.
[10]And when we were carried away
captives to Nin´eveh, all my brethren and
those that were of my kindred did eat of
the bread of the Gentiles. [11]But I kept
myself from eating; [12]because I
remembered God with all my heart.
[13]And the most High gave me grace and
favor before Shalmane´ser, so that I
was his purveyor. [14]And I went into
Me´di-a, and left in trust with Gab´ael,
the brother of Gabrias, at Rages a city
of Me´di-a ten talents of silver. [15]Now
when Shalmane´ser was dead,
Sennach´erib his son reigned in his
stead; whose estate was troubled, that I
could not go into Me´di-a. [16]And in the
time of Shalmane´ser I gave many alms
to my brethren, and gave my bread to
the hungry, [17]and my clothes to the
naked: and if I saw any of my nation
dead, or cast about the walls of Nin´eveh,
I buried him. [18]And if the king
Sennach´erib had slain any, when he
was come, and fled from Judea, I buried
them privily; for in his wrath he killed
many; but the bodies were not found,
when they were sought for of the king.
[19]And when one of the Nin´evites went
and complained of me to the king, that
I buried them, and hid myself;
understanding that I was sought for to
be put to death, I withdrew myself for
fear. [20]Then all my goods were forcibly
taken away, neither was there any thing
left me, beside my wife Anna and my
son Tobias. [21]And there passed not five
and fifty days, before two of his sons
killed him, and they fled into the

mountains of Ar′arat; and Esar–
had′don his son reigned in his stead;
who appointed over his father's
accounts, and over all his affairs,
Ach′ia-cha′rus my brother Anael's
son.
22 And Ach′ia-cha′rus intreating for
me, I returned to Nin′eveh. Now
Ach′ia- cha′rus was cupbearer, and
keeper of the signet, and steward, and
overseer of the accounts: and
Sarchedonus appointed him next unto
him: and he was my brother's son.

CHAPTER 2

1 Now when I was come home again, and
my wife Anna was restored unto me,
with my son Tobias, in the feast of
Pentecost, which is the holy feast of the
seven weeks, there was a good dinner
prepared me, in the which I sat down
to eat. 2 And when I saw abundance of
meat, I said to my son, Go and bring
what poor man soever thou shalt find
out of our brethren, who is mindful of
the Lord; and, lo, I tarry for thee. 3 But
he came again, and said, Father, one of
our nation is strangled, and is cast out
in the market place. 4 Then before I had
tasted of any meat, I started up, and
took him up into a room until the going
down of the sun. 5 Then I returned, and
washed myself, and ate my meat in
heaviness, 6 remembering that prophecy
of Amos, as he said, Your feasts shall
be turned into mourning, and all your
mirth into lamentation.
7 Therefore I wept: and after the going
down of the sun I went and made a
grave, and buried him. 8 But my
neighbors mocked me, and said, This
man is not yet afraid to be put to death
for this matter: who fled away; and yet,
lo, he burieth the dead again. 9 The same
night also I returned from the burial,
and slept by the wall of my courtyard,
being polluted, and my face was
uncovered: 10 and I knew not that there
were sparrows in the wall, and mine
eyes being open, the sparrows muted
warm dung into mine eyes, and a
whiteness came in mine eyes; and I
went to the physicians, but they helped
me not: moreover Ahikar did nourish
me, until I went into Elyma′is.
11 And my wife Anna did take women's
works to do. 12 And when she had
sent them home to the owners, they
paid her wages, and gave her also
besides a kid. 13 And when it was in my
house, and began to cry, I said unto her,
From whence is this kid? is it not stolen?
render it to the owners; for it is not
lawful to eat any thing that is stolen.
14 But she replied upon me, It was given
for a gift more than the wages. Howbeit
I did not believe her, but bade her render
it to the owners: and I was abashed at
her. But she replied upon me, Where
are thine alms and thy righteous deeds?
behold, thou and all thy works are
known.

CHAPTER 3

1 Then I being grieved did weep, and in
my sorrow prayed, saying, 2 O Lord,
thou art just, and all thy works and all thy
ways are mercy and truth, and thou
judgest truly and justly for ever.
3 Remember me, and look on me,
punish me not for my sins and
ignorances, and the sins of my fathers,
who have sinned before thee: 4 for they
obeyed not thy commandments:
wherefore thou hast delivered us for
a spoil, and unto captivity, and unto
death, and for a proverb of reproach to
all the nations among whom we are

dispersed. 5 And now thy judgments are many and true: deal with me according to my sins and my fathers': because we have not kept thy commandments, neither have walked in truth before thee. 6 Now therefore deal with me as seemeth best unto thee, and command my spirit to be taken from me, that I may be dissolved, and become earth: for it is profitable for me to die rather than to live, because I have heard false reproaches, and have much sorrow: command therefore that I may now be delivered out of this distress, and go into the everlasting place: turn not thy face away from me.

7 It came to pass the same day, that in Ecbatana a city of Me′di-a Sara the daughter of Ragu′el was also reproached by her father's maids; 8 because that she had been married to seven husbands, whom Asmode′us the evil spirit had killed, before they had lain with her. Dost thou not know, said they, that thou hast strangled thine husbands? thou hast had already seven husbands, neither wast thou named after any of them. 9 Wherefore dost thou beat us for them? if they be dead, go thy ways after them, let us never see of thee either son or daughter. 10 When she heard these things, she was very sorrowful, so that she thought to have strangled herself; and she said, I am the only daughter of my father, and if I do this, it shall be a reproach unto him, and I shall bring his old age with sorrow unto the grave.

11 Then she prayed toward the window, and said, Blessed art thou, O Lord my God, and thine holy and glorious name is blessed and honorable for ever: let all thy works praise thee for ever. 12 And now, O Lord, I set mine eyes and my face toward thee, 13 and say, Take me out of the earth, that I may hear no more the reproach. 14 Thou knowest, Lord, that I am pure from all sin with man, 15 and that I never polluted my name, nor the name of my father, in the land of my captivity: I am the only daughter of my father, neither hath he any child to be his heir, neither any near kinsman, nor any son of his alive, to whom I may keep myself for a wife: my seven husbands are already dead; and why should I live? but if it please not thee that I should die, command some regard to be had of me, and pity taken of me, that I hear no more reproach.

16 So the prayers of them both were heard before the majesty of the great God. 17 And Raphael was sent to heal them both, that is, to scale away the whiteness of Tobit's eyes, and to give Sara the daughter of Ragu′el for a wife to Tobias the son of Tobit; and to bind Asmode′us the evil spirit; because she belonged to Tobias by right of inheritance. The selfsame time came Tobit home, and entered into his house, and Sara the daughter of Ragu′el came down from her upper chamber.

CHAPTER 4

1 In that day Tobit remembered the money which he had committed to Gab′ael in Rages of Me′di-a, 2 and said with himself, I have wished for death; wherefore do I not call for my son Tobias, that I may signify to him of the money before I die? 3 And when he had called him, he said, My son, when I am dead, bury me; and despise not thy mother, but honor her all the days of thy life, and do that which shall please her, and grieve her not. 4 Remember, my son, that she saw many dangers for thee, when thou wast in her womb; and

when she is dead, bury her by me in one
grave.
5 My son, be mindful of the Lord our God
all thy days, and let not thy will be set to
sin, or to transgress his
commandments: do uprightly all thy
life long, and follow not the ways of
unrighteousness. 6 For if thou deal truly,
thy doings shall prosperously succeed
to thee, and to all them that live justly.
7 Give alms of thy substance; and when
thou givest alms, let not thine eye be
envious, neither turn thy face from any
poor, and the face of God shall not be
turned away from thee. 8 If thou hast
abundance, give alms accordingly: if
thou have but a little, be not afraid to
give according to that little: 9 for thou
layest up a good treasure for thyself
against the day of necessity. 10 Because
that alms do deliver from death, and
suffereth not to come into darkness.
11 For alms is a good gift unto all that
give it in the sight of the most High.
12 Beware of all whoredom, my son, and
chiefly take a wife of the seed of thy
fathers, and take not a strange woman
to wife, which is not of thy father's
tribe: for we are the children of the
prophets, Noah, Abraham, Isaac, and
Jacob: remember, my son, that our
fathers from the beginning, even that
they all married wives of their own
kindred, and were blessed in their
children, and their seed shall inherit the
land. 13 Now therefore, my son, love thy
brethren, and despise not in thy heart
thy brethren, the sons and daughters of
thy people, in not taking a wife of them:
for in pride is destruction and much
trouble, and in lewdness is decay and
great want: for lewdness is the mother
of famine. 14 Let not the wages of any
man, which hath wrought for thee, tarry
with thee, but give him it out of hand:
for if thou serve God, he will also repay
thee: be circumspect, my son, in all
things thou doest, and be wise in all thy
conversation. 15 Do that to no man
which thou hatest: drink not wine to
make thee drunken: neither let
drunkenness go with thee in thy
journey. 16 Give of thy bread to the
hungry, and of thy garments to them
that are naked; and according to thine
abundance give alms; and let not thine
eye be envious, when thou givest alms.
17 Pour out thy bread on the burial of the
just, but give nothing to the wicked.
18 Ask counsel of all that are wise, and
despise not any counsel that is
profitable. 19 Bless the Lord thy God
alway, and desire of him that thy ways
may be directed, and that all thy paths
and counsels may prosper: for every
nation hath not counsel; but the Lord
himself giveth all good things, and he
humbleth whom he will, as he will;
now therefore, my son, remember my
commandments, neither let them be put
out of thy mind.
20 And now I signify this to thee, that I
committed ten talents to Gab´ael the son of
Gabrias at Rages in Me´di-a. 21 And fear
not, my son, that we are made poor: for
thou hast much wealth, if thou fear
God, and depart from all sin, and do that
which is pleasing in his sight.

CHAPTER 5

1 Tobias then answered and said, Father,
I will do all things which thou hast
commanded me: 2 but how can I receive
the money, seeing I know him not?
3 Then he gave him the handwriting, and
said unto him, Seek thee a man which
may go with thee, while I yet live, and
I will give him wages: and go and
receive the money.

[4]Therefore when he went to seek a man,
he found Raphael that was an angel.
[5]But he knew not; and he said unto him,
Canst thou go with me to Rages? and
knowest thou those places well? [6]To
whom the angel said, I will go with
thee, and I know the way well: for I
have lodged with our brother Gab'ael.
[7]Then Tobias said unto him, Tarry for
me, till I tell my father. [8]Then he said
unto him, Go, and tarry not. So he went
in and said to his father, Behold, I have
found one which will go with me. Then
he said, Call him unto me, that I may
know of what tribe he is, and whether he
be a trusty man to go with thee.
[9]So he called him, and he came in, and
they saluted one another. [10]Then Tobit
said unto him, Brother, show me of
what tribe and family thou art. [11]To
whom he said, Dost thou seek for a tribe
or family, or an hired man to go with thy
son? Then Tobit said unto him, I would
know, brother, thy kindred and name.
[12]Then he said, I am Azari'as, the son
of Anani'as the great, and of thy
brethren. [13]Then Tobit said, Thou art
welcome, brother; be not now angry
with me, because I have inquired to
know thy tribe and thy family; for thou
art my brother, of an honest and good
stock: for I know Anani'as and
Jonathas, sons of that great Shemai'ah,
as we went together to Jerusalem to
worship, and offered the firstborn, and
the tenths of the fruits; and they were
not seduced with the error of our
brethren: my brother, thou art of a
good stock. [14]But tell me, what wages
shall I give thee? wilt thou a drachm a
day, and things necessary, as to mine
own son? [15]Yea, moreover, if ye return
safe, I will add something to thy wages.
[16]So they were well pleased. Then said
he to Tobias, Prepare thyself for the
journey, and God send you a good
journey. And when his son had
prepared all things for the journey, his
father said, Go thou with this man, and
God, which dwelleth in heaven,
prosper your journey, and the angel of
God keep you company. So they went
forth both, and the young man's dog
with them.
[17]But Anna his mother wept, and said
to Tobit, Why hast thou sent away our
son? is he not the staff of our hand, in
going in and out before us? [18]Be not
greedy to add money to money: but let
it be as refuse in respect of our child.
[19]For that which the Lord hath given us
to live with doth suffice us. [20]Then said
Tobit to her, Take no care, my sister; he
shall return in safety, and thine eyes
shall see him. [21]For the good angel will
keep him company, and his journey
shall be prosperous, and he shall return
safe. [22]Then she made an end of
weeping.

CHAPTER 6

[1]And as they went on their journey,
they came in the evening to the river
Tigris, and they lodged there. [2]And
when the young man went down to
wash himself, a fish leaped out of the
river, and would have devoured him.
[3]Then the angel said unto him, Take the
fish. And the young man laid hold of
the fish, and drew it to land. [4]To whom
the angel said, Open the fish, and take
the heart and the liver and the gall, and
put them up safely. [5]So the young man
did as the angel commanded him; and
when they had roasted the fish, they did
eat it: then they both went on their way,
till they drew near to Ecbatana. [6]Then
the young man said to the angel,
Brother Azari'as, to what use is the

heart and the liver and the gall of the
fish? 7And he said unto him, Touching
the heart and the liver, if a devil or an
evil spirit trouble any, we must make a
smoke thereof before the man or the
woman, and the party shall be no more
vexed. 8As for the gall, it is good to
anoint a man that hath whiteness in his
eyes, and he shall be healed.
9And when they were come near to
Rages, 10the angel said to the young
man, Brother, today we shall lodge
with Ragu´el, who is thy cousin; he also
hath one only daughter, named Sara; I
will speak for her, that she may be
given thee for a wife. 11For to thee doth
the right of her appertain, seeing thou
only art of her kindred. 12And the maid
is fair and wise: now therefore hear me,
and I will speak to her father; and when
we return from Rages we will celebrate
the marriage: for I know that Ragu´el
cannot marry her to another according
to the law of Moses, but he shall be
guilty of death, because the right of
inheritance doth rather appertain to
thee than to any other.
13Then the young man answered the
angel, I have heard, brother Azari´as,
that this maid hath been given to seven
men, who all died in the marriage
chamber. 14And now I am the only son
of my father, and I am afraid, lest if I
go in unto her, I die, as the other before:
for a wicked spirit loveth her, which
hurteth nobody, but those which come
unto her: wherefore I also fear lest I die,
and bring my father's and my mother's
life because of me to the grave with
sorrow: for they have no other son to
bury them.
15Then the angel said unto him, Dost
thou not remember the precepts which
thy father gave thee, that thou shouldest
marry a wife of thine own kindred?
wherefore hear me, O my brother; for
she shall be given thee to wife; and
make thou no reckoning of the evil
spirit; for this same night shall she be
given thee in marriage. 16And when
thou shalt come into the marriage
chamber, thou shalt take the ashes of
perfume, and shalt lay upon them some
of the heart and liver of the fish, and
shalt make a smoke with it: 17and the
devil shall smell it, and flee away, and
never come again any more: but when
thou shalt come to her, rise p both of
you, and pray to God which is merciful,
who will have pity on you, and save
you: fear not, for she is appointed unto
thee from the beginning; and thou shalt
preserve her, and she shall go with thee.
Moreover I suppose that she shall bear
thee children. Now when Tobias had
heard these things, he loved her, and his
heart was effectually joined to her.

CHAPTER 7

1And when they were come to
Ecbatana, they came to the house of
Ragu´el, and Sara met them: and after
they had saluted one another, she
brought them into the house. 2Then said
Ragu´el to Edna his wife, How like is
this young man to Tobit my cousin!
3And Ragu´el asked them, From
whence are ye, brethren? To whom
they said, We are of the sons of
Naph´tali, which are captives in
Nin´eveh. 4Then he said to them, Do ye
know Tobit our kinsman? And they
said, We know him. Then said he, Is he
in good health? 5And they said, He is
both alive, and in good health: and
Tobias said, He is my father. 6Then
Ragu´el leaped up, and kissed him, and
wept, 7and blessed him, and said unto
him, Thou art the son of an honest and

good man. But when he had heard that
Tobit was blind, he was sorrowful, and
wept. 8And likewise Edna his wife and
Sara his daughter wept. Moreover they
entertained them cheerfully; and after
that they had killed a ram of the flock,
they set store of meat on the table.
Then said Tobias to Raphael, Brother
Azari´as, speak of those things of
which thou didst talk in the way, and
let this business be dispatched. 9So he
communicated the matter with Ragu´el:
and Ragu´el said to Tobias, Eat and
drink, and make merry: 10for it is meet
that thou shouldest marry my daughter:
nevertheless I will declare unto thee
the truth. 11I have given my daughter in
marriage to seven men, who died
that night they came in unto her:
nevertheless for the present be merry.
But Tobias said, I will eat nothing here,
till we agree and swear one to another.
12Ragu´el said, Then take her from
henceforth according to the manner, for
thou art her cousin, and she is thine, and
the merciful God give you good
success in all things. 13Then he called
his daughter Sara, and she came to her
father, and he took her by the hand, and
gave her to be wife to Tobias, saying,
Behold, take her after the law of Moses,
and lead her away to thy father. And he
blessed them; 14and called Edna his
wife, and took paper, and did write an
instrument of covenants, and sealed it.
15Then they began to eat.
16After Ragu´el called his wife Edna,
and said unto her, Sister, prepare
another chamber, and bring her in
thither. 17Which when she had done as
he had bidden her, she brought her
thither: and she wept, and she received
the tears of her daughter, and said unto
her, 18Be of good comfort, my
daughter; the Lord of heaven and earth
give thee joy for this thy sorrow: be of
good comfort, my daughter.

CHAPTER 8

1And when they had supped, they
brought Tobias in unto her. 2And as he
went, he remembered the words of
Raphael, and took the ashes of the
perfumes, and put the heart and the liver
of the fish thereupon, and made a
smoke therewith. 3The which smell
when the evil spirit had smelled, he fled
into the utmost parts of Egypt, and the
angel bound him.
4And after that they were both shut
in together, Tobias rose out of the bed,
and said, Sister, arise, and let us pray
that God would have pity on us. 5Then
began Tobias to say, Blessed art thou, O
God of our fathers, and blessed is thy
holy and glorious name for ever; let the
heavens bless thee, and all thy
creatures. 6Thou madest Adam, and
gavest him Eve his wife for an helper
and stay: of them came mankind: thou
hast said, It is not good that man should
be alone; let us make unto him an aid
like unto himself. 7And now, O Lord, I
take not this my sister for lust, but
uprightly: therefore mercifully ordain
that we may become aged together.
8And she said with him, Amen. 9So
they slept both that night.
And Ragu´el arose, and went and made
a grave, 10saying, I fear lest he also be
dead. 11But when Ragu´el was come
into his house, 12he said unto his wife
Edna, Send one of the maids, and let
her see whether he be alive: if he be not,
that we may bury him, and no man
know it. 13So the maid opened the door,
and went in, and found them both asleep,
14and came forth, and told them that he
was alive. 15Then Ragu´el praised God,
and said, O God, thou art worthy to be

praised with all pure and holy praise;
therefore let thy saints praise thee with
all thy creatures; and let all thine
angels and thine elect praise thee for
ever. [16]Thou art to be praised, for thou
hast made me joyful; and that is not
come to me which I suspected; but thou
hast dealt with us according to thy great
mercy. [17]Thou art to be praised,
because thou hast had mercy of two
that were the only begotten children of
their fathers: grant them mercy, O Lord,
and finish their life in health with joy
and mercy. [18]Then Ragu´el bade his
servants to fill the grave. [19]And he kept
the wedding feast fourteen days. [20]For
before the days of the marriage were
finished, Ragu´el had said unto him by
an oath, that he should not depart till the
fourteen days of the marriage were
expired; [21]and then he should take the
half of his goods, and go in safety to his
father; and should have the rest when I
and my wife be dead.

CHAPTER 9

[1]Then Tobias called Raphael, and said
unto him, [2]Brother Azari´as, take with
thee a servant, and two camels, and go
to Rages of Me´di-a to Gab´ael, and
bring me the money, and bring him to
the wedding. [3]For Ragu´el hath sworn
that I shall not depart. [4]But my father
counteth the days; and if I tarry long, he
will be very sorry. [5]So Raphael went
out, and lodged with Gab´ael, and gave
him the handwriting: who brought forth
bags which were sealed up, and gave
them to him. [6]And early in the morning
they went forth both together, and came
to the wedding: and Tobias blessed his
wife.

CHAPTER 10

[1]Now Tobit his father counted every
day: and when the days of the journey
were expired, and they came not, [2]then
Tobit said, Are they detained? or is
Gab´ael dead, and there is no man to
give him the money? [3]Therefore he
was very sorry. [4]Then his wife said
unto him, My son is dead, seeing he
stayeth long; and she began to bewail
him, and said, [5]Now I care for nothing,
my son, since I have let thee go, the
light of mine eyes. [6]To whom Tobit
said, Hold thy peace, take no care, for he
is safe. [7]But she said, Hold thy peace,
and deceive me not; my son is dead.
And she went out every day into the
way which they went, and did eat no
meat on the daytime, and ceased not
whole nights to bewail her son Tobias,
until the fourteen days of the wedding
were expired, which Ragu´el had sworn
that he should spend there.
Then Tobias said to Ragu´el, Let me
go, for my father and my mother look no
more to see me. [8]But his father-in-law
said unto him, Tarry with me, and I will
send to thy father, and they shall declare
unto him how things go with thee. [9]But
Tobias said, No; but let me go to my
father. [10]Then Ragu´el arose, and gave
him Sara his wife, and half his goods,
servants, and cattle, and money: [11]and
he blessed them, and sent them away,
saying, The God of heaven give you a
prosperous journey, my children. [12]And
he said to his daughter, Honor thy father
and thy mother-in-law, which are now
thy parents, that I may hear good report
of thee. And he kissed her. Edna also
said to Tobias, The Lord of heaven
restore thee, my dear brother, and grant
that I may see thy children of my
daughter Sara before I die, that I may

rejoice before the Lord: behold, I commit my daughter unto thee of special trust; wherefore do not treat her evil.

CHAPTER 11

1 After these things Tobias went his way, praising God that he had given him a prosperous journey, and blessed Ragu´el and Edna his wife, and went on his way till they drew near unto Nin´eveh. 2 Then Raphael said to Tobias, Thou knowest, brother, how thou didst leave thy father: 3 let us haste before thy wife, and prepare the house. 4 And take in thine hand the gall of the fish. So they went their way, and the dog went after them.

5 Now Anna sat looking about toward the way for her son. 6 And when she espied him coming, she said to his father, Behold, thy son cometh, and the man that went with him.

7 Then said Raphael, I know, Tobias, that thy father will open his eyes.

8 Therefore anoint thou his eyes with the gall, and being pricked therewith, he shall rub, and the whiteness shall fall away, and he shall see thee.

9 Then Anna ran forth, and fell upon the neck of her son, and said unto him, Seeing I have seen thee, my son, from henceforth I am content to die. And they wept both. 10 Tobit also went forth toward the door, and stumbled: but his son ran unto him, 11 and took hold of his father: and he strake of the gall on his father's eyes, saying, Be of good hope, my father. 12 And when his eyes began to smart, he rubbed them; 13 and the whiteness pilled away from the corners of his eyes: and when he saw his son, he fell upon his neck. 14 And he wept, and said, Blessed art thou, O God, and blessed is thy name for ever; and blessed are all thine holy angels: 15 for thou hast scourged, and hast taken pity on me: for, behold, I see my son Tobias. And his son went in rejoicing, and told his father the great things that had happened to him in Me´di-a.

16 Then Tobit went out to meet his daughter-in-law at the gate of Nin´eveh, rejoicing, and praising God: and they which saw him go marveled, because he had received his sight. 17 But Tobit gave thanks before them, because God had mercy on him. And when he came near to Sara his daughter-in-law, he blessed her, saying, Thou art welcome, daughter: God be blessed, which hath brought thee unto us, and blessed be thy father and thy mother. And there was joy among all his brethren which were at Nin´eveh. 18 And Ahikar, and Nasbas his brother's son, came: 19 and Tobias' wedding was kept seven days with great joy.

CHAPTER 12

1 Then Tobit called his son Tobias, and said unto him, My son, see that the man have his wages, which went with thee, and thou must give him more. 2 And Tobias said unto him, O father, it is no harm to me to give him half of those things which I have brought: 3 for he hath brought me again to thee in safety, and made whole my wife, and brought me the money, and likewise healed thee. 4 Then the old man said, It is due unto him. 5 So he called the angel, and he said unto him, Take half of all that ye have brought, and go away in safety.

6 Then he took them both apart, and said unto them, Bless God, praise him, and magnify him, and praise him for the things which he hath done unto you in the sight of all that live. It is good to

praise God, and exalt his name, and
honorably to show forth the works of
God; therefore be not slack to praise
him. 7 It is good to keep close the secret
of a king, but it is honorable to reveal
the works of God. Do that which is
good, and no evil shall touch you.
8 Prayer is good with fasting and alms
and righteousness. A little with
righteousness is better than much with
unrighteousness. It is better to give
alms than to lay up gold: 9 for alms doth
deliver from death, and shall purge
away all sin. Those that exercise alms
and righteousness shall be filled with
life: 10 but they that sin are enemies to
their own life. 11 Surely I will keep close
nothing from you. For I said, It was good
to keep close the secret of a king, but
that it was honorable to reveal the
works of God. 12 Now therefore, when
thou didst pray, and Sara thy daughter-
in-law, I did bring the remembrance of
your prayers before the Holy One: and
when thou didst bury the dead, I was
with thee likewise. 13 And when thou
didst not delay to rise up, and leave thy
dinner, to go and cover the dead, thy
good deed was not hid from me: but I
was with thee. 14 And now God hath sent
me to heal thee and Sara thy daughter-
in-law. 15 I am Raphael, one of the seven
holy angels, which present the prayers
of the saints, and which go in and out
before the glory of the Holy One.

16 Then they were both troubled, and
fell upon their faces: for they feared.
17 But he said unto them, Fear not, for
it shall go well with you; praise God
therefore. 18 For not of any favor of
mine, but by the will of our God I came;
wherefore praise him for ever. 19 All
these days I did appear unto you; but I
did neither eat nor drink, but ye did see
a vision. 20 Now therefore give God
thanks: for I go up to him that sent me;
but write all things which are done in a
book. 21 And when they arose, they saw
him no more. 22 Then they confessed the
great and wonderful works of God, and
how the angel of the Lord had appeared
unto them.

CHAPTER 13

1 Then Tobit wrote a prayer of rejoicing,
and said, Blessed be God that liveth for
ever, and blessed be his kingdom. 2 For
he doth scourge, and hath mercy: he
leadeth down to hell, and bringeth up
again: neither is there any that can
avoid his hand. 3 Confess him before the
Gentiles, ye children of Israel: for he
hath scattered us among them. 4 There
declare his greatness, and extol him
before all the living: for he is our Lord,
and he is the God our Father for ever.

5 And he will scourge us for our
iniquities, and will have mercy again,
and will gather us out of all nations,
among whom he hath scattered us. 6 If
ye turn to him with your whole heart,
and with your whole mind, and deal
uprightly before him, then will he turn
unto you, and will not hide his face
from you. Therefore see what he will do
with you, and confess him with your
whole mouth, and praise the Lord of
might, and extol the everlasting King.
In the land of my captivity do I praise
him, and declare his might and majesty
to a sinful nation. O ye sinners, turn and
do justice before him: who can tell if he
will accept you, and have mercy on you?
7 I will extol my God, and my soul shall
praise the King of heaven, and shall
rejoice in his greatness. 8 Let all men
speak, and let all praise him for his
righteousness.

9 O Jerusalem, the holy city, he will

scourge thee for thy children's works,
and will have mercy again on the sons
of the righteous. 10 Give praise to the
Lord, for he is good: and praise the
everlasting King, that his tabernacle
may be builded in thee again with joy,
and let him make joyful there in thee
those that are captives, and love in thee
for ever those that are miserable.
11 Many nations shall come from far to
the name of the Lord God with gifts in
their hands, even gifts to the King of
heaven; all generations shall praise thee
with great joy.
12 Cursed are all they which hate thee,
and blessed shall all be which love thee
for ever. 13 Rejoice and be glad for the
children of the just: for they shall be
gathered together, and shall bless the
Lord of the just. 14 O blessed are they
which love thee, for they shall rejoice
in thy peace: blessed are they which
have been sorrowful for all thy
scourges; for they shall rejoice for thee,
when they have seen all thy glory, and
shall be glad for ever.
15 Let my soul bless God the great King.
16 For Jerusalem shall be built up with
sapphires, and emeralds, and precious
stone: thy walls and towers and
battlements with pure gold. 17 And the
streets of Jerusalem shall be paved with
beryl and carbuncle and stones of
Ophir. 18 And all her streets shall say,
Alleluia; and they shall praise him,
saying, Blessed be God, which hath
extolled it for ever.

CHAPTER 14

1 So Tobit made an end of praising
God. 2 And he was eight and fifty years
old when he lost his sight, which was
restored to him after eight years: and he
gave alms, and he increased in the fear
of the Lord God, and praised him. 3 And
when he was very aged, he called his
son, and the six sons of his son, and said
to him, My son, take thy children; for,
behold, I am aged, and am ready to
depart out of this life. 4 Go into Me´di-a
my son, for I surely believe those things
which Jonah the prophet spake of
Nin´eveh, that it shall be overthrown;
and that for a time peace shall rather be
in Me´di-a; and that our brethren shall
lie scattered in the earth from that good
land: and Jerusalem shall be desolate,
and the house of God in it shall be
burned, and shall be desolate for a time;
5 and that again God will have mercy on
them, and bring them again into the
land, where they shall build a temple,
but not like to the first, until the time of that
age be fulfilled; and afterward they
shall return from all places of their
captivity, and build up Jerusalem
gloriously, and the house of God shall
be built in it for ever with a glorious
building, as the prophets have spoken
thereof. 6 And all nations shall turn, and
fear the Lord God truly, and shall bury
their idols. 7 So shall all nations praise
the Lord, and his people shall confess
God, and the Lord shall exalt his
people; and all those which love the
Lord God in truth and justice shall
rejoice, showing mercy to our brethren.
8 And now, my son, depart out of
Nin´eveh, because that those things
which the prophet Jonah spake shall
surely come to pass. 9 But keep thou the
law and the commandments, and
show thyself merciful and just, that it
may go well with thee. 10 And bury me
decently, and thy mother with me; but
tarry no longer at Nin´eveh.
Remember, my son, how Haman
handled Ahikar that brought him up,
how out of light he brought him into

darkness, and how he rewarded him
again: yet Ahikar was saved, but the
other had his reward: for he went down
into darkness. Manas´seh gave alms,
and escaped the snares of death which
they had set for him: but Haman fell
into the snare, and perished.
[11]Wherefore now, my son, consider
what alms doeth, and how
righteousness doth deliver. When he
had said these things, he gave up the
ghost in the bed, being an hundred
and eight and fifty years old; and he
buried him honorably. [12]And when
Anna his mother was dead, he buried
her with his father.
But Tobias departed with his wife and
children to Ecbatana to Ragu´el his
father- in-law, [13]where he became old
with honor, and he buried his father and
mother-in- law honorably, and he
inherited their substance, and his father
Tobit's. [14]And he died at Ecbatana in
Me´di-a, being an hundred and seven
and twenty years old. [15]But before he
died he heard of the destruction of
Nin´eveh, which was taken by
Nebuchadnez´zar and Ahasue´rus: and
before his death he rejoiced over
Nin´eveh.

JUDITH

CHAPTER 1

1 In the twelfth year of the reign of
Nebuchadnez′zar, who reigned in
Nin′eveh, the great city; in the days of
Arphax′ad, which reigned over the
Medes in Ecbatana, 2 and built in
Ecbatana walls round about of stones
hewn three cubits broad and six cubits
long, and made the height of the wall
seventy cubits, and the breadth thereof
fifty cubits: 3 and set the towers thereof
upon the gates of it, an hundred cubits
high, and the breadth thereof in the
foundation threescore cubits: 4 and he
made the gates thereof, even gates that
were raised to the height of seventy
cubits, and the breadth of them was forty
cubits, for the going forth of his mighty
armies, and for the setting in array of
his footmen: 5 even in those days king
Nebuchadnez′zar made war with king
Arphax′ad in the great plain, which is
the plain in the borders of Ragau. 6 And
there came unto him all they that dwelt
in the hill country, and all that dwelt by
Euphra′tes, and Tigris, and Hydas′pes,
and the plain of Ar′i-och the king of the
E′lamites, and very many nations of the
sons of Chalde′ans, assembled
themselves to the battle.

7 Then Nebuchadnez′zar king of
the Assyrians sent unto all that dwelt in
Persia, and to all that dwelt westward, and
to those that dwelt in Cili′cia, and
Damascus, and Lebanon, and
Antilebanon, and to all that dwelt upon
the sea coast, 8 and to those among the
nations that were of Carmel, and Gil′e-
ad, and the higher Galilee, and the
great plain of Esdra-e′lon, 9 and to all
that were in Samaria and the cities
thereof, and beyond Jordan unto
Jerusalem, and Bethany, and Chellus,
and Kadesh, and the river of Egypt,
and Tah′panhes, and Raam′ses, and
all the land of Goshen, 10 until ye come
beyond Tanis and Memphis, and to all
the inhabitants of Egypt, until ye come
to the borders of Ethiopia. 11 But all the
inhabitants of the land made light of the
commandment of Nebuchadnez′zar
king of the Assyrians, neither went they
with him to the battle; for they were not
afraid of him: yea, he was before them
as one man, and they sent away his
ambassadors from them without effect,
and with disgrace. 12 Therefore
Nebuchadnez′zar was very angry with
all this country, and sware by his throne
and kingdom, that he would surely be
avenged upon all those coasts of
Cili′cia, and Damascus, and Syria, and
that he would slay with the sword all
the inhabitants of the land of Moab, and
the children of Ammon, and all Judah,
and all that were in Egypt, till ye come
to the borders of the two seas.

13 Then he marched in battle array with
his power against king Arphax′ad in
the seventeenth year, and he prevailed
in his battle: for he overthrew all the
power of Arphax′ad, and all his
horsemen, and all his chariots, 14 and
became lord of his cities, and came
unto Ecbatana, and took the towers, and
spoiled the streets thereof, and turned
the beauty thereof into shame. 15 He
took also Arphax′ad in the mountains
of Ragau, and smote him through with
his darts, and destroyed him utterly that
day. 16 So he returned afterward to
Nin′eveh, both he and all his company
of sundry nations, being a very great
multitude of men of war, and there he
took his ease, and banqueted, both he
and his army, an hundred and twenty
days.

CHAPTER 2

[1]And in the eighteenth year, the two
and twentieth day of the first month,
there was talk in the house of
Nebuchadnez´zar king of the Assyrians,
that he should, as he said, avenge
himself on all the earth. [2]So he called
unto him all his officers, and all his
nobles, and communicated with them
his secret counsel, and concluded the
afflicting of the whole earth out of his
own mouth. [3]Then they decreed to
destroy all flesh, that did not obey the
commandment of his mouth. [4]And
when he had ended his counsel,
Nebuchadnez´zar king of the Assyrians
called Holofer´nes the chief captain of
his army, which was next unto him, and
said unto him,

[5]Thus saith the great king, the lord of
the whole earth, Behold, thou shalt go
forth from my presence, and take with
thee men that trust in their own
strength, of footmen an hundred and
twenty thousand; and the number of
horses with their riders twelve
thousand. [6]And thou shalt go against
all the west country, because they
disobeyed my commandment. [7]And
thou shalt declare unto them, that they
prepare for me earth and water: for I
will go forth in my wrath against them,
and will cover the whole face of the
earth with the feet of mine army, and
I will give them for a spoil unto them:
[8]so that their slain shall fill their valleys
and brooks, and the river shall be filled
with their dead, till it overflow: [9]and I
will lead them captives to the utmost
parts of all the earth. [10]Thou therefore
shalt go forth, and take beforehand for
me all their coasts: and if they will yield
themselves unto thee, thou shalt reserve
them for me till the day of their
punishment. [11]But concerning them
that rebel, let not thine eye spare them;
but put them to the slaughter, and spoil
them wheresoever thou goest. [12]For as
I live, and by the power of my
kingdom, whatsoever I have spoken, that
will I do by mine hand. [13]And take thou
heed that thou transgress none of the
commandments of thy lord, but
accomplish them fully, as I have
commanded thee, and defer not to do
them.

[14]Then Holofer´nes went forth from
the presence of his lord, and called all
the governors and captains, and the
officers of the army of Assyria; [15]and
he mustered the chosen men for the
battle, as his lord had commanded him,
unto an hundred and twenty thousand,
and twelve thousand archers on
horseback; [16]and he ranged them, as a
great army is ordered for the war. [17]And
he took camels and asses for their
carriages, a very great number; and
sheep and oxen and goats without
number for their provision: [18]and
plenty of victual for every man of the
army, and very much gold and silver
out of the king's house. [19]Then he went
forth and all his power to go before
king Nebuchadnez´zar in the voyage,
and to cover all the face of the earth
westward with their chariots, and
horsemen, and their chosen footmen.
[20]A great number also sundry countries
came with them like locusts, and like the
sand of the earth: for the multitude was
without number.

[21]And they went forth of Nin´eveh
three days' journey toward the plain of
Bec´tileth, and pitched from Bec´tileth
near the mountain which is at the left
hand of the upper Cili´cia. [22]Then he
took all his army, his footmen, and
horsemen, and chariots, and went from

thence into the hill country; 23 and
destroyed Put and Lud, and spoiled all
the children of Rasses, and the children
of Ish´ma-el, which were toward the
wilderness at the south of the land of the
Chel´lians. 24 Then he went over
Euphra´tes, and went through
Mesopota´mi-a, and destroyed all the
high cities that were upon the river
Arbon´ai, till ye come to the sea. 25 And
he took the borders of Cili´cia, and
killed all that resisted him, and came to
the borders of Japheth, which were
toward the south, over against Arabia.
26 He compassed also all the children of
Mid´i-an, and burned up their
tabernacles, and spoiled their
sheepcotes. 27 Then he went down into
the plain of Damascus in the time of
wheat harvest, and burnt up all their
fields, and destroyed their flocks and
herds, also he spoiled their cities, and
utterly wasted their countries, and
smote all their young men with the edge
of the sword.
28 Therefore the fear and dread of him
fell upon all the inhabitants of the sea
coasts, which were in Sidon and Tyre,
and them that dwelt in Sur and Oci´na,
and all that dwelt in Jabneh; and they
that dwelt in Ash´dod and Ash´kelon
feared him greatly.

CHAPTER 3

1 So they sent ambassadors unto him to
treat of peace, saying, 2 Behold, we the
servants of Nebuchadnez´zar the great
king lie before thee; use us as shall be
good in thy sight. 3 Behold, our houses,
and all our places, and all our fields of
wheat, and flocks, and herds, and all the
lodges of our tents, lie before thy face;
use them as it pleaseth thee. 4 Behold,
even our cities and the inhabitants
thereof are thy servants; come and deal
with them as seemeth good unto thee.
5 So the men came to Holofer´nes, and
declared unto him after this manner.
6 Then came he down toward the sea
coast, both he and his army, and set
garrisons in the high cities, and took out
of them chosen men for aid. 7 So they
and all the country round about received
them with garlands, with dances, and
with timbrels. 8 Yet he did cast down
their frontiers, and cut down their
groves: for he had decreed to destroy all
the gods of the land, that all nations
should worship Nebuchadnez´zar only,
and that all tongues and tribes should
call upon him as god. 9 Also he came
over against Esdra-e´lon near unto
Judah, over against the great strait of
Judah. 10 And he pitched between Geba
and Scythop´olis, and there he tarried a
whole month, that he might gather
together all the carriages of his army.

CHAPTER 4

1 Now the children of Israel, that
dwelt in Judah, heard all that
Holofer´nes the chief captain of
Nebuchadnez´zar king of the Assyrians
had done to the nations, and after what
manner he had spoiled all their
temples, and brought them to nought.
2 Therefore they were exceedingly
afraid of him, and were troubled for
Jerusalem, and for the temple of the
Lord their God: 3 for they were newly
returned from the captivity, and all the
people of Judah were lately gathered
together: and the vessels, and the altar,
and the house, were sanctified after the
profanation. 4 Therefore they sent into
all the coasts of Samaria, and the
villages, and to Beth–ho´ron, and
Belmen, and Jericho, and to Choba, and

Esor'a, and to the valley of Salem: 5and possessed themselves beforehand of all the tops of the high mountains, and fortified the villages that were in them, and laid up victuals for the provision of war: for their fields were of late reaped. 6Also Joi'akim the high priest, which was in those days in Jerusalem, wrote to them that dwelt in Bethu'lia, and Betomes'tham, which is over against Esdra-e'lon toward the open country, near to Dothan, 7charging them to keep the passages of the hill country: for by them there was an entrance into Judah, and it was easy to stop them that would come up, because the passage was strait, for two men at the most.

8And the children of Israel did as Joi'akim the high priest had commanded them, with the ancients of all the people of Israel, which dwelt at Jerusalem. 9Then every man of Israel cried to God with great fervency, and with great vehemency did they humble their souls: 10both they, and their wives, and their children, and their cattle, and every stranger and hireling, and their servants bought with money, put sackcloth upon their loins. 11Thus every man and women, and the little children, and the inhabitants of Jerusalem, fell before the temple, and cast ashes upon their heads, and spread out their sackcloth before the face of the Lord: also they put sackcloth about the altar, 12and cried to the God of Israel all with one consent earnestly, that he would not give their children for a prey, and their wives for a spoil, and the cities of their inheritance to destruction, and the sanctuary to profanation and reproach, and for the nations to rejoice at. 13So God heard their prayers, and looked upon their afflictions: for the people fasted many days in all Judah and Jerusalem before the sanctuary of the Lord Almighty. 14And Joi'akim the high priest, and all the priests that stood before the Lord, and they which ministered unto the Lord, had their loins girt with sackcloth, and offered the daily burnt offerings, with the vows and free gifts of the people, 15and had ashes on their mitres, and cried unto the Lord with all their power, that he would look upon all the house of Israel graciously.

CHAPTER 5

1Then was it declared to Holofer'nes, the chief captain of the army of Assyria, that the children of Israel had prepared for war, and had shut up the passages of the hill country, and had fortified all the tops of the high hills, and had laid impediments in the champaign countries: 2wherewith he was very angry, and called all the princes of Moab, and the captains of Ammon, and all the governors of the sea coast, 3and he said unto them, Tell me now, ye sons of Canaan, who this people is, that dwelleth in the hill country, and what are the cities that they inhabit, and what is the multitude of their army, and wherein is their power and strength, and what king is set over them, or captain of their army; 4and why have they determined not to come and meet me, more than all the inhabitants of the west.

5Then said A'chior, the captain of all the sons of Ammon, Let my lord now hear a word from the mouth of thy servant, and I will declare unto thee the truth concerning this people, which dwelleth near thee, and inhabiteth the hill countries: and there shall no lie come out of the mouth of thy servant.

6 This people are descended of the
Chalde´ans: 7 and they sojourned
heretofore in Mesopota´mi-a, because
they would not follow the gods of their
fathers, which were in the land of
Chalde´a. 8 For they left the way of their
ancestors, and worshipped the God of
heaven, the God whom they knew: so
they cast them out from the face of their
gods, and they fled into Mesopota´mi-
a, and sojourned there many days.
9 Then their God commanded them to
depart from the place where they
sojourned, and to go into the land of
Canaan: where they dwelt, and were
increased with gold and silver, and with
very much cattle. 10 But when a famine
covered all the land of Canaan, they
went down into Egypt, and sojourned
there, while they were nourished, and
became there a great multitude, so that
one could not number their nation.
11 Therefore the king of Egypt rose up
against them, and dealt subtly with
them, and brought them low with
laboring in brick, and made them slaves.
12 Then they cried unto their God, and
he smote all the land of Egypt with
incurable plagues: so the Egyptians
cast them out of their sight. 13 And God
dried the Red Sea before them, 14 and
brought them to mount Si´nai, and
Ka´desh– barne´a, and cast forth all
that dwelt in the wilderness. 15 So they
dwelt in the land of the Amorites, and
they destroyed by their strength all
them of Heshbon, and passing over
Jordan they possessed all the hill
country. 16 And they cast forth before
them the Canaanite, the Per´izzite, the
Jeb´usite, and the Shech´emite, and all
the Gir´gashites, and they dwelt in that
country many days. 17 And whilst they
sinned not before their God, they
prospered, because the God that hateth
iniquity was with them. 18 But when
they departed from the way which he
appointed them, they were
destroyed in many battles very sore,
and were led captives into a land that
was not theirs, and the temple of their
God was cast to the ground, and their
cities were taken by the enemies. 19 But
now are they returned to their God,
and are come up from the places
where they were scattered, and have
possessed Jerusalem, where their
sanctuary is, and are seated in the hill
country; for it was desolate. 20 Now,
therefore, my lord and governor, if
there be any error in this people, and
they sin against their God, let us
consider that this shall be their ruin, and
let us go up, and we shall overcome
them. 21 But if there be no iniquity in
their nation, let my lord now pass by, lest
their Lord defend them, and their God
be for them, and we become a reproach
before all the world.

22 And when A´chior had finished these
sayings, all the people standing round
about the tent murmured, and the chief
men of Holofer´nes, and all that dwelt
by the sea side, and in Moab, spake that
he should kill him. 23 For, say they, we
will not be afraid of the face of the
children of Israel: for, lo, it is a people
that have no strength nor power for a
strong battle. 24 Now therefore, lord
Holofer´nes, we will go up, and they
shall be a prey to be devoured of all
thine army.

CHAPTER 6

1 And when the tumult of men that
were about the council was ceased,
Holofer´nes the chief captain of the
army of Assyria said unto A´chior and
all the Moabites before all the company

of other nations, [2]And who art thou,
A´chior, and the hirelings of E´phra-im,
that thou hast prophesied among us as
today, and hast said, that we should not
make war with the people of Israel,
because their God will defend them?
and who is God but Nebuchadnez´zar?
[3]He will send his power, and will
destroy them from the face of the earth,
and their God shall not deliver them:
but we his servants will destroy them
as one man; for they are not able to
sustain the power of our horses. [4]For
with them we will tread them under foot,
and their mountains shall be drunken
with their blood, and their fields shall be
filled with their dead bodies, and their
footsteps shall not be able to stand
before us, for they shall utterly perish,
saith king Nebuchadnez´zar, lord of all
the earth: for he said, None of my
words shall be in vain.
[5]And thou, A´chior, an hireling of
Ammon, which hast spoken these
words in the day of thine iniquity, shalt
see my face no more from this day,
until I take vengeance of this nation that
came out of Egypt. [6]And then shall the
sword of mine army, and the multitude
of them that serve me, pass through thy
sides, and thou shalt fall among their
slain, when I return. [7]Now therefore my
servants shall bring thee back into the
hill country, and shall set thee in one of
the cities of the passages: [8]and thou
shalt not perish, till thou be destroyed
with them. [9]And if thou persuade thyself
in thy mind that they shall not be taken,
let not thy countenance fall: I have
spoken it, and none of my words shall
be in vain. [10]Then Holofer´nes
commanded his servants, that waited in
his tent, to take A´chior, and bring him
to Bethu´lia, and deliver him into the
hands of the children of Israel. [11]So his
servants took him, and brought him out
of the camp into the plain, and they went
from the midst of the plain into the hill
country, and came unto the fountains
that were under Bethu´lia. [12]And when
the men of the city saw them, they took
up their weapons, and went out of the
city to the top of the hill: and every man
that used a sling kept them from
coming up by casting of stones against
them. [13]Nevertheless having gotten
privily under the hill, they bound
A´chior, and cast him down, and left
him at the foot of the hill, and returned
to their lord.
[14]But the Israelites descended from
their city, and came unto him, and
loosed him, and brought him into
Bethu´lia, and presented him to the
governors of the city: [15]which were in
those days Ozi´as the son of Micha, of
the tribe of Simeon, and Chabris the
son of Gothon´iel, and Charmis the son
of Mel´chiel. [16]And they called together
all the ancients of the city, and all their
youth ran together, and their women, to
the assembly, and they set A´chior in
the midst of all their people. Then
Ozi´as asked him of that which was
done. [17]And he answered and declared
unto them the words of the council of
Holofer´nes, and all the words that he
had spoken in the midst of the princes
of Assyria, and whatsoever
Holofer´nes had spoken proudly
against the house of Israel. [18]Then the
people fell down and worshipped
God, and cried unto God, saying, [19]O
Lord God of heaven, behold their pride,
and pity the low estate of our nation,
and look upon the face of those that are
sanctified unto thee this day. [20]Then
they comforted A´chior, and praised
him greatly. [21]And Ozi´as took him out
of the assembly unto his house, and

made a feast to the elders; and they
called on the God of Israel all that night
for help.

CHAPTER 7

[1]The next day Holofer´nes commanded
all his army, and all his people which
were come to take his part, that they
should remove their camp against
Bethu´lia, to take aforehand the ascents
of the hill country, and to make war
against the children of Israel. [2]Then
their strong men removed their camps
in that day, and the army of the men of
war was an hundred and seventy
thousand footmen, and twelve thousand
horsemen, beside the baggage, and
other men that were afoot among them,
a very great multitude. [3]And they
camped in the valley near unto
Bethu´lia, by the fountain, and they
spread themselves in breadth over
Dothan even to Belmaim, and in length
from Bethu´lia unto Cyamon, which is
over against Esdra-e´lon.

[4]Now the children of Israel, when they
saw the multitude of them, were greatly
troubled, and said every one to his
neighbor, Now will these men lick up
the face of the earth; for neither the
high mountains, nor the valleys, nor the
hills, are able to bear their weight.
[5]Then every man took up his weapons
of war, and when they had kindled fires
upon their towers, they remained and
watched all that night.

[6]But in the second day Holofer´nes
brought forth all his horsemen in the
sight of the children of Israel which
were in Bethu´lia, [7]and viewed the
passages up to the city, and came to the
fountains of their waters, and took
them, and set garrisons of men of war
over them, and he himself removed
toward his people.

[8]Then came unto him all the chief of the
children of Esau, and all the governors
of the people of Moab, and the captains
of the sea coast, and said, [9]Let our lord
now hear a word, that there be not an
overthrow in thine army. [10]For this
people of the children of Israel do
not trust in their spears, but in the
height of the mountains wherein they
dwell, because it is not easy to come up
to the tops of their mountains. [11]Now
therefore, my lord, fight not against
them in battle array, and there shall not
so much as one man of thy people
perish. [12]Remain in thy camp, and keep
all the men of thine army, and let thy
servants get into their hands the
fountain of water, which issueth forth
of the foot of the mountain: [13]for all the
inhabitants of Bethu´lia have their
water thence; so shall thirst kill them,
and they shall give up their city, and we
and our people shall go up to the tops of
the mountains that are near, and will
camp upon them, to watch that none go
out of the city. [14]So they and their
wives and their children shall be
consumed with famine, and before
the sword come against them, they
shall be overthrown in the streets where
they dwell. [15]Thus shalt thou render
them an evil reward; because they
rebelled, and met not thy person
peaceably.

[16]And these words pleased Holofer´nes
and all his servants, and he appointed to
do as they had spoken. [17]So the camp of
the children of Ammon departed, and
with them five thousand of the
Assyrians, and they pitched in the
valley, and took the waters, and the
fountains of the waters of the children
of Israel. [18]Then the children of Esau
went up with the children of Ammon,

and camped in the hill country over
against Dothan: and they sent some of
them toward the south, and toward the
east, over against Ek´rebel, which is
near unto Chusi, that is upon the brook
Mochmur; and the rest of the army of
the Assyrians camped in the plain, and
covered the face of the whole land; and
their tents and carriages were pitched to
a very great multitude.
19 Then the children of Israel cried unto
the Lord their God, because their heart
failed, for all their enemies had
compassed them round about, and there
was no way to escape out from among
them. 20 Thus all the company of
Assyria remained about them, both
their footmen, chariots, and horsemen,
four and thirty days, so that all their
vessels of water failed all the
inhabitants of Bethu´lia. 21 And the
cisterns were emptied, and they had not
water to drink their fill for one day; for
they gave them drink by measure.
22 Therefore their young children were
out of heart, and their women and
young men fainted for thirst, and fell
down in the streets of the city, and by
the passages of the gates, and there was
no longer any strength in them. 23 Then
all the people assembled to Ozi´as, and
to the chief of the city, both young men,
and women, and children, and cried
with a loud voice, and said before all
the elders, 24 God be judge between us and
you: for ye have done us great injury, in
that ye have not required peace of the
children of Assyria. 25 For now we have
no helper: but God hath sold us into their
hands, that we should be thrown down
before them with thirst and great
destruction. 26 Now therefore call them
unto you, and deliver the whole city for
a spoil to the people of Holofer´nes,
and to all his army. 27 For it is better for
us to be made a spoil unto them, than to
die for thirst: for we will be his servants,
that our souls may live, and not see the
death of our infants before our eyes, nor
our wives nor our children to die. 28 We
take to witness against you the heaven
and the earth, and our God and Lord of
our fathers, which punisheth us
according to our sins and the sins of our
fathers, that he do not according as we
have said this day. 29 Then there was
great weeping with one consent in the
midst of the assembly; and they cried
unto the Lord God with a loud voice.
30 Then said Ozi´as to them, Brethren,
be of good courage, let us yet endure
five days, in the which space the Lord
our God may turn his mercy toward us;
for he will not forsake us utterly. 31 And
if these days pass, and there come no
help unto us, I will do according to
your word. 32 And he dispersed the
people, every one to their own charge;
and they went unto the walls and towers
of their city, and sent the women and
children into their houses: and they
were very low brought in the city.

CHAPTER 8

1 Now at that time Judith heard thereof,
which was the daughter of Mera´ri, the
son of Ox, the son of Joseph, the son of
O´ziel, the son of Elci´a, the son of
Anani´as, the son of Gedeon, the son of
Raph´aim, the son of Acitho, the son of
Eli´u, the son of Eli´ab, the son of
Nathan´a-el, the son of Samael, the son
of Salasad´ai, the son of Israel. 2 And
Manass´es was her husband, of her
tribe and kindred, who died in the
barley harvest. 3 For as he stood
overseeing them that bound sheaves in
the field, the heat came upon his head,
and he fell on his bed, and died in the

city of Bethu´lia: and they buried him
with his fathers in the field between
Dothan and Ba´lamo. 4 So Judith was a
widow in her house three years and four
months. 5 And she made her a tent upon
the top of her house, and put on
sackcloth upon her loins, and wore her
widow's apparel. 6 And she fasted all
the days of her widowhood, save the
eves of the sabbaths, and the sabbaths,
and the eves of the new moons, and the
new moons, and the feasts and solemn
days of the house of Israel. 7 She was
also of a goodly countenance, and very
beautiful to behold: and her husband
Manass´es had left her gold, and silver,
and menservants, and maidservants,
and cattle, and lands; and she remained
upon them. 8 And there was none that
gave her an ill word; for she feared God
greatly.
9 Now when she heard the evil words
of the people against the governor, that
they fainted for lack of water; for Judith
had heard all the words that Ozi´as had
spoken unto them, and that he had
sworn to deliver the city unto the
Assyrians after five days; 10 then she
sent her waitingwoman, that had the
government of all things that she had,
to call Ozi´as and Chabris and Charmis,
the ancients of the city. 11 And they
came unto her, and she said unto them,
Hear me now, O ye governors of the
inhabitants of Bethu´lia: for your words
that ye have spoken before the people
this day are not right, touching this oath
which ye made and pronounced
between God and you, and have
promised to deliver the city to our
enemies, unless within these days the
Lord turn to help you. 12 And now who
are ye that have tempted God this day,
and stand instead of God among the
children of men? 13 And now try the Lord
Almighty, but ye shall never know any
thing. 14 For ye cannot find the depth of
the heart of man, neither can ye
perceive the things that he thinketh:
then how can ye search out God, that
hath made all these things, and know
his mind, or comprehend his purpose?
Nay, my brethren, provoke not the Lord
our God to anger. 15 For if he will not
help us within these five days, he hath
power to defend us when he will, even
every day, or to destroy us before our
enemies. 16 Do not bind the counsels of
the Lord our God: for God is not as
man, that he may be threatened; neither
is he as the son of man, that he should
be wavering. 17 Therefore let us wait for
salvation of him, and call upon him to
help us, and he will hear our voice, if it
please him.
18 For there arose none in our age,
neither is there any now in these days,
neither tribe, nor family, nor people,
nor city, among us, which worship gods
made with hands, as hath been
aforetime. 19 For the which cause our
fathers were given to the sword, and for
a spoil, and had a great fall before our
enemies. 20 But we know none other
god, therefore we trust that he will not
despise us, nor any of our nation. 21 For
if we be taken so, all Judah shall lie
waste, and our sanctuary shall be
spoiled; and he will require the
profanation thereof at our mouth. 22 And
the slaughter of our brethren, and the
captivity of the country, and the
desolation of our inheritance, will he
turn upon our heads among the
Gentiles, wheresoever we shall be in
bondage; and we shall be an offense and
a reproach to all them that possess us.
23 For our servitude shall not be directed
to favor: but the Lord our God shall
turn it to dishonor. 24 Now therefore, O

brethren, let us show an example to our
brethren, because their hearts depend
upon us, and the sanctuary, and the
house, and the altar, rest upon us.
25 Moreover let us give thanks to the
Lord our God, which trieth us, even as
he did our fathers. 26 Remember what
things he did to Abraham, and how
he tried Isaac, and what happened to
Jacob in Mesopota'mi-a of Syria, when
he kept the sheep of Laban his mother's
brother. 27 For he hath not tried us in the
fire, as he did them, for the examination
of their hearts, neither hath he taken
vengeance on us: but the Lord doth
scourge them that come near unto him,
to admonish them.
28 Then said Ozi'as to her, All that thou
hast spoken hast thou spoken with a
good heart, and there is none that may
gainsay thy words. 29 For this is not the
first day wherein thy wisdom is
manifested; but from the beginning of
thy days all the people have known thy
understanding, because the disposition
of thine heart is good. 30 But the people
were very thirsty, and compelled us to
do unto them as we have spoken, and
to bring an oath upon ourselves, which
we will not break. 31 Therefore now
pray thou for us, because thou art a
godly woman, and the Lord will send
us rain to fill our cisterns, and we shall
faint no more.
32 Then said Judith unto them, Hear me,
and I will do a thing, which shall go
throughout all generations to the
children of our nation. 33 Ye shall stand
this night in the gate, and I will go forth
with my waitingwoman: and within the
days that ye have promised to deliver
the city to our enemies the Lord will
visit Israel by mine hand. 34 But inquire
not ye of mine act: for I will not declare
it unto you, till the things be finished
that I do. 35 Then said Ozi'as and the
princes unto her, Go in peace, and the
Lord God be before thee, to take
vengeance on our enemies. 36 So they
returned from the tent, and went to their
wards.

CHAPTER 9

1 Judith fell upon her face, and put
ashes upon her head, and uncovered the
sackcloth wherewith she was clothed;
and about the time that the incense of
that evening was offered in Jerusalem
in the house of the Lord Judith cried
with a loud voice, and said, 2 O Lord
God of my father Simeon, to whom thou
gavest a sword to take vengeance of the
strangers, who loosened the girdle of a
maid to defile her, and discovered the
thigh to her shame, and polluted her
virginity to her reproach; for thou
saidst, It shall not be so; and yet they
did so: 3 wherefore thou gavest their
rulers to be slain, so that they dyed their
bed in blood, being deceived, and
smotest the servants with their lords,
and the lords upon their thrones; 4 and
hast given their wives for a prey, and
their daughters to be captives, and all
their spoils to be divided among thy
dear children; which were moved with
thy zeal, and abhorred the pollution of
their blood, and called upon thee for
aid: O God, O my God, hear me also a
widow.
5 For thou hast wrought not only those
things, but also the things which fell out
before, and which ensued after; thou
hast thought upon the things which are
now, and which are to come. 6 Yea, what
things thou didst determine were ready
at hand, and said, Lo, we are here: for all
thy ways are prepared, and thy
judgments are in thy foreknowledge.

7For, behold, the Assyrians are
multiplied in their power; they are
exalted with horse and man; they glory in
the strength of their footmen; they trust
in shield, and spear, and bow, and sling;
and know not that thou art the Lord that
breakest the battles: the Lord is thy
name. 8Throw down their strength in
thy power, and bring down their force
in thy wrath: for they have purposed to
defile thy sanctuary, and to pollute the
tabernacle where thy glorious name
resteth, and to cast down with sword the
horn of thy altar. 9Behold their pride,
and send thy wrath upon their heads:
give into mine hand, which am a
widow, the power that I have
conceived. 10Smite by the deceit of my
lips the servant with the prince, and the
prince with the servant: break down
their stateliness by the hand of a
woman. 11For thy power standeth not
in multitude, nor thy might in strong
men: for thou art a God of the afflicted,
an helper of the oppressed, an upholder
of the weak, a protector of the forlorn,
a Saviour of them that are without
hope.
12I pray thee, I pray thee, O God of my
father, and God of the inheritance of
Israel, Lord of the heavens and earth,
Creator of the waters, King of every
creature, hear thou my prayer: 13and
make my speech and deceit to be their
wound and stripe, who have purposed
cruel things against thy covenant, and
thy hallowed house, and against the top
of Zion, and against the house of the
possession of thy children. 14And make
every nation and tribe to acknowledge
that thou art the God of all power and
might, and that there is none other that
protecteth the people of Israel but thou.

CHAPTER 10

1Now after that she had ceased to cry
unto the God of Israel, and had made an
end of all these words, 2she rose where
she had fallen down, and called her
maid, and went down into the house, in
the which she abode in the sabbath
days, and in her feast days, 3and pulled
off the sackcloth which she had on, and
put off the garments of her widowhood,
and washed her body all over with
water, and anointed herself with
precious ointment, and braided the hair
of her head, and put on a tire upon it,
and put on her garments of gladness,
wherewith she was clad during the
life of Manass′es her husband. 4And she
took sandals upon her feet, and put
about her her bracelets, and her
chains, and her rings, and her
earrings, and all her ornaments, and
decked herself bravely, to allure the
eyes of all men that should see her.
5Then she gave her maid a bottle of
wine, and a cruse of oil, and filled a bag
with parched corn, and lumps of figs,
and with fine bread; so she folded all
these things together, and laid them
upon her. 6Thus they went forth to the
gate of the city of Bethu′lia, and
found standing there Ozi′as, and the
ancients of the city, Chabris and
Charmis. 7And when they saw her, that
her countenance was altered, and her
apparel was changed, they wondered at
her beauty very greatly, and said unto
her. 8The God, the God of our
fathers, give thee favor, and
accomplish thine enterprises to the
glory of the children of Israel, and to the
exaltation of Jerusalem. Then they
worshipped God. 9And she said unto
them, Command the gates of the city
to be opened unto me, that I may go

forth to accomplish the things whereof
ye have spoken with me. So they
commanded the young men to open
unto her, as she had spoken. [10]And
when they had done so, Judith went out,
she, and her maid with her; and the men
of the city looked after her, until she was
gone down the mountain, and till she
had passed the valley, and could see her
no more.
[11]Thus they went straight forth in the
valley: and the first watch of the
Assyrians met her, [12]and took her, and
asked her, Of what people art thou? and
whence comest thou? and whither goest
thou? And she said, I am a woman of
the Hebrews, and am fled from them: for
they shall be given you to be consumed:
[13]and I am coming before Holofer′nes
the chief captain of your army, to
declare words of truth; and I will show
him a way, whereby he shall go, and
win all the hill country, without losing
the body or life of any one of his
men. [14]Now when the men heard her
words, and beheld her countenance,
they wondered greatly at her beauty,
and said unto her, [15]Thou hast saved thy
life, in that thou hast hasted to come
down to the presence of our lord: now
therefore come to his tent, and some of
us shall conduct thee, until they have
delivered thee to his hands. [16]And when
thou standest before him, be not afraid
in thine heart, but show unto him
according to thy word; and he will treat
thee well.
[17]Then they chose out of them an
hundred men to accompany her and her
maid; and they brought her to the tent
of Holofer′nes. [18]Then was there a
concourse throughout all the camp: for
her coming was noised among the
tents, and they came about her, as she
stood without the tent of Holofer′nes,
till they told him of her. [19]And they
wondered at her beauty, and admired the
children of Israel because of her, and
every one said to his neighbor, Who
would despise this people, that have
among them such women? surely it is
not good that one man of them be left,
who being let go might deceive the
whole earth.
[20]And they that lay near Holofer′nes
went out, and all his servants, and they
brought her into the tent. [21]Now
Holofer′nes rested upon his bed under
a canopy, which was woven with
purple, and gold, and emeralds, and
precious stones. [22]So they showed him
of her; and he came out before his tent
with silver lamps going before him.
[23]And when Judith was come before
him and his servants they all marveled
at the beauty of her countenance; and
she fell down upon her face, and did
reverence unto him: and his servants
took her up.

CHAPTER 11

[1]Then said Holofer′nes unto her,
Woman, be of good comfort, fear not in
thine heart: for I never hurt any that was
willing to serve Nebuchadnez′zar, the
king of all the earth. [2]Now therefore, if
thy people that dwelleth in the
mountains had not set light by me, I
would not have lifted up my spear
against them: but they have done
these things to themselves. [3]But now
tell me wherefore thou art fled from
them, and art come unto us: for thou art
come for safeguard; be of good
comfort, thou shalt live this night, and
hereafter: [4]for none shall hurt thee, but
treat thee well, as they do the servants
of king Nebuchadnez′zar my lord.
[5]Then Judith said unto him, Receive the

words of thy servant, and suffer thine
handmaid to speak in thy presence,
and I will declare no lie to my lord this
night. 6And if thou wilt follow the
words of thine handmaid, God will
bring the thing perfectly to pass by
thee; and my lord shall not fail of his
purposes. 7As Nebuchadnez′zar king of
all the earth liveth, and as his power
liveth, who hath sent thee for the
upholding of every living thing: for not
only men shall serve him by thee, but
also the beasts of the field, and the
cattle, and the fowls of the air, shall live
by thy power under Nebuchadnez′zar
and all his house. 8For we have heard of
thy wisdom and thy policies, and it is
reported in all the earth, that thou only
art excellent in all the kingdom, and
mighty in knowledge, and wonderful in
feats of war.
9Now as concerning the matter, which
A′chior did speak in thy council, we
have heard his words; for the men of
Bethu′lia saved him, and he declared
unto them all that he had spoken unto
thee. 10Therefore, O lord and governor,
reject not his word; but lay it up in thine
heart, for it is true: for our nation shall
not be punished, neither can sword
prevail against them, except they sin
against their God. 11And now, that my
lord be not defeated and frustrate of his
purpose, even death is now fallen upon
them, and their sin hath overtaken
them, wherewith they will provoke
their God to anger, whensoever they
shall do that which is not fit to be done:
12for their victuals fail them, and all
their water is scant, and they have
determined to lay hands upon their
cattle, and purposed to consume all
those things, that God hath forbidden
them to eat by his laws: 13and are
resolved to spend the firstfruits of the
corn, and the tenths of wine and oil,
which they had sanctified, and reserved
for the priests that serve in Jerusalem
before the face of our God; the which
things it is not lawful for any of the
people so much as to touch with their
hands. 14For they have sent some to
Jerusalem, because they also that dwell
there have done the like, to bring them
a licence from the senate. 15Now when
they shall bring them word, they will
forthwith do it, and they shall be given
to thee to be destroyed the same day.
16Wherefore I thine handmaid,
knowing all this, am fled from their
presence; and God hath sent me to work
things with thee, whereat all the earth
shall be astonished, and whosoever
shall hear it. 17For thy servant is
religious, and serveth the God of
heaven day and night: now therefore,
my lord, I will remain with thee, and
thy servant will go out by night into the
valley, and I will pray unto God, and he
will tell me when they have committed
their sins: 18and I will come and show
it unto thee: then thou shalt go forth
with all thine army, and there shall be
none of them that shall resist thee.
19And I will lead thee through the midst
of Judah, until thou come before
Jerusalem; and I will set thy throne in
the midst thereof; and thou shalt drive
them as sheep that have no shepherd,
and a dog shall not so much as open his
mouth at thee: for these things were told
me according to my foreknowledge,
and they were declared unto me, and I
am sent to tell thee.
20Then her words pleased Holofer′nes
and all his servants; and they marveled
at her wisdom, and said, 21There is not
such a woman from one end of the earth
to the other, both for beauty of face, and
wisdom of words. 22Likewise

Holofer´nes said unto her, God hath
done well to send thee before the
people, that strength might be in our
hands, and destruction upon them that
lightly regard my lord. 23And now thou
art both beautiful in thy countenance,
and witty in thy words: surely if thou
do as thou hast spoken, thy God shall be
my God, and thou shalt dwell in the
house of king Nebuchadnez´zar, and
shalt be renowned through the whole
earth.

CHAPTER 12

1Then he commanded to bring her in
where his plate was set; and bade that they
should prepare for her of his own meats,
and that she should drink of his own
wine. 2And Judith said, I will not eat
thereof, lest there be an offense: but
provision shall be made for me of the
things that I have brought. 3Then
Holofer´nes said unto her, If thy
provision should fail, how should we
give thee the like? for there be none
with us of thy nation. 4Then said Judith
unto him, As thy soul liveth, my lord,
thine handmaid shall not spend those
things that I have, before the Lord work
by mine hand the things that he hath
determined.
5Then the servants of Holofer´nes
brought her into the tent, and she slept till
midnight, and she arose when it was
toward the morning watch, 6and sent to
Holofer´nes, saying, Let my lord now
command that thine handmaid may go
forth unto prayer. 7Then Holofer´nes
commanded his guard that they should
not stay her: thus she abode in the camp
three days, and went out in the night
into the valley of Bethu´lia, and washed
herself in a fountain of water by the
camp. 8And when she came out, she
besought the Lord God of Israel to
direct her way to the raising up of the
children of her people. 9So she came in
clean, and remained in the tent, until
she did eat her meat at evening.
10And in the fourth day Holofer´nes
made a feast to his own servants only,
and called none of the officers to the
banquet. 11Then said he to Bagoas the
eunuch, who had charge over all that he
had, Go now, and persuade this Hebrew
woman which is with thee, that she
come unto us, and eat and drink with
us. 12For, lo, it will be a shame for our
person, if we shall let such a woman go,
not having had her company; for if we
draw her not unto us, she will laugh us
to scorn. 13Then went Bagoas from the
presence of Holofer´nes, and came to
her, and he said, Let not this fair damsel
fear to come to my lord, and to be
honored in his presence, and drink
wine, and be merry with us, and be
made this day as one of the daughters
of the Assyrians, which serve in the
house of Nebuchadnez´zar. 14Then said
Judith unto him, Who am I now, that I
should gainsay my lord? surely
whatsoever pleaseth him I will do
speedily, and it shall be my joy unto the
day of my death. 15So she arose, and
decked herself with her apparel and all
her woman's attire, and her maid went
and laid soft skins on the ground for her
over against Holofer´nes, which she
had received of Bagoas for her daily
use, that she might sit and eat upon
them.
16Now when Judith came in and sat
down, Holofer´nes his heart was
ravished with her, and his mind was
moved, and he desired greatly her
company; for he waited a time to
deceive her, from the day that he had
seen her. 17Then said Holofer´nes unto

her, Drink now, and be merry with us. 18 So Judith said, I will drink now, my lord, because my life is magnified in me this day more than all the days since I was born. 19 Then she took and ate and drank before him what her maid had prepared. 20 And Holofer´nes took great delight in her, and drank more wine than he had drunk at any time in one day since he was born.

CHAPTER 13

1 Now when the evening was come, his servants made haste to depart, and Bagoas shut his tent without, and dismissed the waiters from the presence of his lord; and they went to their beds: for they were all weary, because the feast had been long. 2 And Judith was left alone in the tent, and Holofer´nes lying along upon his bed: for he was filled with wine. 3 Now Judith had commanded her maid to stand without her bedchamber, and to wait for her coming forth, as she did daily: for she said she would go forth to her prayers, and she spake to Bagoas according to the same purpose. 4 So all went forth, and none was left in the bedchamber, neither little nor great.
Then Judith, standing by his bed, said in her heart, O Lord God of all power, look at this present upon the works of mine hands for the exaltation of Jerusalem. 5 For now is the time to help thine inheritance, and to execute mine enterprises to the destruction of the enemies which are risen against us. 6 Then she came to the pillar of the bed, which was at Holofer´nes' head, and took down his falchion from thence, 7 and approached to his bed, and took hold of the hair of his head, and said, Strengthen me, O Lord God of Israel, this day. 8 And she smote twice upon his neck with all her might, and she took away his head from him, 9 and tumbled his body down from the bed, and pulled down the canopy from the pillars.
And anon after she went forth, and gave Holofer´nes his head to her maid; 10 and she put it in her bag of meat: so they twain went together according to their custom unto prayer: and when they passed the camp, they compassed the valley, and went up the mountain of Bethu´lia, and came to the gates thereof. 11 Then said Judith afar off to the watchmen at the gate, Open, open now the gate: God, even our God, is with us, to show his power yet in Jerusalem, and his forces against the enemy, as he hath even done this day. 12 Now when the men of her city heard her voice, they made haste to go down to the gate of their city, and they called the elders of the city. 13 And then they ran all together, both small and great, for it was strange unto them that she was come: so they opened the gate, and received them, and made a fire for a light, and stood round about them. 14 Then she said to them with a loud voice, Praise, praise God, praise God, I say, for he hath not taken away his mercy from the house of Israel, but hath destroyed our enemies by mine hands this night.

15 So she took the head out of the bag, and showed it, and said unto them, Behold the head of Holofer´nes, the chief captain of the army of Assyria, and behold the canopy, wherein he did lie in his drunkenness; and the Lord hath smitten him by the hand of a woman. 16 As the Lord liveth, who hath kept me in my way that I went, my countenance hath deceived him to his destruction, and yet hath he not committed sin with me, to defile and

shame me.
17 Then all the people were wonderfully
astonished, and bowed themselves, and
worshipped God, and said with one
accord, Blessed be thou, O our God,
which hast this day brought to nought
the enemies of thy people. 18 Then said
Ozi´as unto her, O daughter, blessed
art thou of the most high God above all
the women upon the earth; and blessed
be the Lord God, which hath created
the heavens and the earth, which hath
directed thee to the cutting off of the
head of the chief of our enemies. 19 For
this thy confidence shall not depart
from the heart of men, which remember
the power of God for ever. 20 And God
turn these things to thee for a perpetual
praise, to visit thee in good things,
because thou hast not spared thy life for
the affliction of our nation, but hast
revenged our ruin, walking a straight
way before our God. And all the people
said, So be it, so be it.

CHAPTER 14

1 Then said Judith unto them, Hear me
now, my brethren, and take this head,
and hang it upon the highest place of
your walls. 2 And so soon as the
morning shall appear, and the sun shall
come forth upon the earth, take ye every
one his weapons, and go forth every
valiant man out of the city, and set ye a
captain over them, as though ye would
go down into the field toward the
watch of the Assyrians; but go not
down. 3 Then they shall take their
armor, and shall go into their camp,
and raise up the captains of the army
of Assyria, and shall run to the tent
of Holofer´nes, but shall not find him:
then fear shall fall upon them, and they
shall flee before your face. 4 So ye, and
all that inhabit the coast of Israel,
shall pursue them, and overthrow them
as they go. 5 But before ye do these
things, call me A´chior the Ammonite,
that he may see and know him that
despised the house of Israel, and that
sent him to us, as it were to his death.
6 Then they called A´chior out of the
house of Ozi´as; and when he was
come, and saw the head of Holofer´nes
in a man's hand in the assembly of the
people, he fell down on his face, and
his spirit failed. 7 But when they had
recovered him, he fell at Judith's feet,
and reverenced her, and said, Blessed
art thou in all the tabernacle of Judah,
and in all nations, which hearing thy
name shall be astonished. 8 Now
therefore tell me all the things that thou
hast done in these days. Then Judith
declared unto him in the midst of the
people all that she had done, from the
day that she went forth until that hour
she spake unto them. 9 And when she
had left off speaking, the people
shouted with a loud voice, and made a
joyful noise in their city. 10 And when
A´chior had seen all that the God of
Israel had done, he believed in God
greatly, and circumcised the flesh of his
foreskin, and was joined unto the house
of Israel unto this day.
11 And as soon as the morning arose,
they hanged the head of Holofer´nes
upon the wall, and every man took his
weapons, and they went forth by bands
unto the straits of the mountain. 12 But
when the Assyrians saw them, they sent
to their leaders, which came to their
captains and tribunes, and to every one
of their rulers. 13 So they came to
Holofer´nes' tent, and said to him that
had the charge of all his things, Waken
now our lord: for the slaves have been
bold to come down against us to battle,

that they may be utterly destroyed.
14 Then went in Bagoas, and knocked
at the door of the tent; for he thought that
he had slept with Judith. 15 But because
none answered, he opened it, and went
into the bedchamber, and found him cast
upon the floor dead, and his head was
taken from him. 16 Therefore he cried
with a loud voice, with weeping, and
sighing, and a mighty cry, and rent his
garments. 17 After he went into the tent
where Judith lodged: and when he
found her not, he leaped out to the
people, and cried, 18 These slaves have
dealt treacherously; one woman of the
Hebrews hath brought shame upon the
house of king Nebuchadnez′zar: for,
behold, Holofer′nes lieth upon the
ground without a head. 19 When the
captains of the Assyrians' army heard
these words, they rent their coats, and
their minds were wonderfully troubled,
and there was a cry and a very great
noise throughout the camp.

CHAPTER 15

1 And when they that were in the tents
heard, they were astonished at the thing
that was done. 2 And fear and trembling
fell upon them, so that there was no man
that durst abide in the sight of his
neighbor, but rushing out all together,
they fled into every way of the plain,
and of the hill country. 3 They also that
had camped in the mountains round
about Bethu′lia fled away. Then the
children of Israel, every one that was a
warrior among them, rushed out upon
them. 4 Then sent Ozi′as to
Betomas′them, and to Be′bai, and
Choba, and Cola, and to all the coasts
of Israel, such as should tell the things
that were done, and that all should rush
forth upon their enemies to destroy
them. 5 Now when the children of Israel
heard it, they all fell upon them with
one consent, and slew them unto
Choba: likewise also they that came
from Jerusalem, and from all the hill
country, (for men had told them what
things were done in the camp of their
enemies,) and they that were in Gil′e-
ad, and in Galilee, chased them with a
great slaughter, until they were past
Damascus and the borders thereof.
6 And the residue, that dwelt at
Bethu′lia, fell upon the camp of
Assyria, and spoiled them, and were
greatly enriched. 7 And the children of
Israel that returned from the slaughter
had that which remained; and the
villages and the cities, that were in the
mountains and in the plain, got many
spoils: for the multitude was very great.
8 Then Joi′akim the high priest, and the
ancients of the children of Israel that
dwelt in Jerusalem, came to behold the
good things that God had showed to
Israel, and to see Judith, and to salute
her. 9 And when they came unto her,
they blessed her with one accord, and
said unto her, Thou art the exaltation of
Jerusalem, thou art the great glory of
Israel, thou art the great rejoicing of our
nation: 10 thou hast done all these things
by thine hand: thou hast done much
good to Israel, and God is pleased
therewith: blessed be thou of the
Almighty Lord for evermore. And all
the people said, So be it. 11 And the
people spoiled the camp the space of
thirty days: and they gave unto Judith
Holofer′nes his tent, and all his plate,
and beds, and vessels, and all his stuff:
and she took it, and laid it on her mule;
and made ready her carts, and laid them
thereon. 12 Then all the women of
Israel ran together to see her, and
blessed her, and made a dance among
them for her: and she took branches in

her hand, and gave also to the women
that were with her. 13 And they put a
garland of olive upon her and her maid
that was with her, and she went before
all the people in the dance, leading all
the women: and all the men of Israel
followed in their armor with garlands,
and with songs in their mouths.

CHAPTER 16

1 Then Judith began to sing this
thanksgiving in all Israel, and all the
people sang after her this song of
praise. 2 And Judith said, Begin unto my
God with timbrels, sing unto my Lord
with cymbals: tune unto him a new
psalm: exalt him, and call upon his
name. 3 For God breaketh the battles:
for among the camps in the midst of the
people he hath delivered me out of the
hands of them that persecuted me.
4 Asshur came out of the mountains
from the north, he came with ten
thousands of his army, the multitude
whereof stopped the torrents, and their
horsemen have covered the hills. 5 He
bragged that he would burn up my
borders, and kill my young men with
the sword, and dash the sucking
children against the ground, and make
mine infants as a prey, and my virgins
as a spoil.
6 But the Almighty Lord hath
disappointed them by the hand of a
woman. 7 For the mighty one did not fall
by the young men, neither did the sons
of the Titans smite him, nor high
giants set upon him: but Judith the
daughter of Mera´ri weakened him
with the beauty of her countenance.
8 For she put off the garment of her
widowhood for the exaltation of those
that were oppressed in Israel, and
anointed her face with ointment, and
bound her hair in a tire, and took a linen
garment to deceive him. 9 Her sandals
ravished his eyes, her beauty took his
mind prisoner, and the falchion passed
through his neck. 10 The Persians
quaked at her boldness, and the Medes
were daunted at her hardiness. 11 Then
my afflicted shouted for joy, and my
weak ones cried aloud; but they were
astonished: these lifted up their
voices, but they were overthrown.
12 The sons of the damsels have pierced
them through, and wounded them as
fugatives' children: they perished by
the battle of the Lord.
13 I will sing unto the Lord a new song:
O Lord, thou art great and glorious,
wonderful in strength, and invincible.
14 Let all creatures serve thee: for thou
spakest, and they were made, thou didst
send forth thy spirit, and it created
them, and there is none that can resist
thy voice. 15 For the mountains shall be
moved from their foundations with the
waters, the rocks shall melt as wax at thy
presence: yet thou art merciful to them
that fear thee. 16 For all sacrifice is too
little for a sweet savor unto thee, and all
the fat is not sufficient for thy burnt
offering: but he that feareth the Lord is
great at all times.
17 Woe to the nations that rise up against
my kindred! the Lord Almighty will
take vengeance of them in the day of
judgment, in putting fire and worms in
their flesh; and they shall feel them, and
weep for ever.
18 Now as soon as they entered into
Jerusalem, they worshipped the Lord;
and as soon as the people were purified,
they offered their burnt offerings, and
their free offerings, and their gifts.
19 Judith also dedicated all the stuff of
Holofer´nes, which the people had
given her, and gave the canopy, which
she had taken out of his bedchamber,

for a gift unto the Lord. [20]So the people
continued feasting in Jerusalem before
the sanctuary for the space of three
months, and Judith remained with them.
[21]After this time every one returned to
his own inheritance, and Judith went to
Bethu´lia, and remained in her own
possession, and was in her time
honorable in all the country. [22]And
many desired her, but none knew her all
the days of her life, after that Manass´es
her husband was dead, and was gathered
to his people. [23]But she increased more
and more in honor, and waxed old in her
husband's house, being an hundred and
five years old, and made her maid free;
so she died in Bethu´lia: and they
buried her in the cave of her husband
Manass´es. [24]And the house of Israel
lamented her seven days: and before
she died, she did distribute her goods to
all them that were nearest of kindred to
Manass´es her husband, and to them
that were the nearest of her kindred.
[25]And there was none that made the
children of Israel any more afraid in the
days of Judith, nor a long time after her
death.

ESTHER

CHAPTER 10

4Then Mor′decai said, God hath done these things. 5For I remember a dream which I saw concerning these matters, and nothing thereof hath failed. 6A little fountain became a river, and there was light, and the sun, and much water: this river is Esther, whom the king married, and made queen: 7and the two dragons are I and Haman. 8And the nations were those that were assembled to destroy the name of the Jews: 9and my nation is this Israel, which cried to God, and were saved: for the Lord hath saved his people, and the Lord hath delivered us from all those evils, and God hath wrought signs and great wonders, which have not been done among the Gentiles.

10Therefore hath he made two lots, one for the people of God, and another for all the Gentiles. 11And these two lots came at the hour, and time, and day of judgment, before God among all nations. 12So God remembered his people, and justified his inheritance.

13Therefore those days shall be unto them in the month Adar, the fourteenth and fifteenth day of the same month, with an assembly, and joy, and with gladness before God, according to the generations for ever among his people.

CHAPTER 11

1In the fourth year of the reign of Ptolemy and Cleopatra, Dosith′eus, who said he was a priest and Levite, and Ptolemy, his son, brought this epistle of Purim, which they said was the same, and that Lysim′achus the son of Ptolemy, that was in Jerusalem, had translated it.

2In the second year of the reign of Artaxerx′es the great, in the first day of the month Nisan, Mor′decai the son of Ja′ir, the son of Shim′e-i, the son of Kish, of the tribe of Benjamin, had a dream; 3who was a Jew, and dwelt in the city of Shushan, a great man, being a servitor in the king's court. 4He was also one of the captives, which Nebuchadnez′zar the king of Babylon carried from Jerusalem with Jeconi′ah king of Judah; and this was his dream:

5Behold a noise of a tumult, with thunder, and earthquakes, and uproar in the land: 6and, behold, two great dragons came forth ready to fight, and their cry was great. 7And at their cry all nations were prepared to battle, that they might fight against the righteous people. 8And lo a day of darkness and obscurity, tribulation and anguish, affliction and great uproar, upon earth.

9And the whole righteous nation was troubled, fearing their own evils, and were ready to perish. 10Then they cried unto God, and upon their cry, as it were from a little fountain, was made a great flood, even much water. 11The light and the sun rose up, and the lowly were exalted, and devoured the glorious.

12Now when Mor′decai, who had seen this dream, and what God had determined to do, was awake, he bare this dream in mind, and until night by all means was desirous to know it.

CHAPTER 12

1And Mor′decai took his rest in the court with Bigthan and Teresh, the two eunuchs of the king, and keepers of the palace. 2And he heard their devices, and searched out their purposes, and learned that they were about to lay

hands upon Artaxerx´es the king; and
so he certified the king of them. 3 Then
the king examined the two eunuchs, and
after that they had confessed it, they
were strangled. 4 And the king made a
record of these things, and Mor´decai
also wrote thereof. 5 So the king
commanded Mor´decai to serve in the
court, and for this he rewarded him.
6 Howbeit Haman the son of
Hammeda´tha the A´gagite, who was
in great honor with the king, sought to
molest Mor´decai and his people
because of the two eunuchs of the king.

CHAPTER 13

1 The copy of the letters was this: The
great king Artaxerx´es writeth these
things to the princes and governors that
are under him from India unto Ethiopia
in an hundred and seven and twenty
provinces.
2 After that I became lord over many
nations, and had dominion over the
whole world, not lifted up with
presumption of my authority, but
carrying myself alway with equity and
mildness, I purposed to settle my
subjects continually in a quiet life, and
making my kingdom peaceable, and
open for passage to the utmost coasts, to
renew peace, which is desired of all
men.
3 Now when I asked my counselors how
this might be brought to pass, Haman,
that excelled in wisdom among us, and
was approved for his constant good will
and steadfast fidelity, and had the honor
of the second place in the kingdom,
4 declared unto us, that in all nations
throughout the world there was
scattered a certain malicious people,
that had laws contrary to all nations, and
continually despised the commandments
of kings, so as the uniting of our
kingdoms, honorably intended by us,
cannot go forward. 5 Seeing then we
understand that this people alone is
continually in opposition unto all men,
differing in the strange manner of their
laws, and evil affected to our state, working
all the mischief they can, that our
kingdom may not be firmly established:
6 therefore have we commanded, that all
they that are signified in writing unto
you by Haman, who is ordained over
the affairs, and is next unto us, shall all,
with their wives and children, be utterly
destroyed by the sword of their
enemies, without all mercy and pity, the
fourteenth day of the twelfth month
Adar of this present year: 7 that they, who
of old and now also are malicious, may
in one day with violence go into the
grave, and so ever hereafter cause our
affairs to be well settled, and without
trouble.
8 Then Mor´decai thought upon all the
works of the Lord, and made his prayer
unto him, 9 saying, O Lord, Lord, the
King Almighty: for the whole world is
in thy power, and if thou hast appointed
to save Israel, there is no man that can
gainsay thee: 10 for thou hast made
heaven and earth, and all the wondrous
things under the heaven. 11 Thou art
Lord of all things, and there is no man
that can resist thee, which art the Lord.
12 Thou knowest all things, and thou
knowest, Lord, that it was neither in
contempt nor pride, nor for any desire
of glory, that I did not bow down to
proud Haman. 13 For I could have been
content with good will for the salvation
of Israel to kiss the soles of his feet.
14 But I did this, that I might not prefer
the glory of man above the glory of God:
neither will I worship any but thee, O
God, neither will I do it in pride. 15 And
now, O Lord God and King, spare thy

people: for their eyes are upon us to
bring us to nought; yea, they desire to
destroy the inheritance, that hath been
thine from the beginning. 16Despise not
the portion, which thou hast delivered
out of Egypt for thine own self. 17Hear
my prayer, and be merciful unto thine
inheritance: turn our sorrow into joy,
that we may live, O Lord, and praise
thy name: and destroy not the mouths
of them that praise thee, O Lord.
18All Israel in like manner cried most
earnestly unto the Lord, because their
death was before their eyes.

CHAPTER 14

1Queen Esther also, being in fear of
death, resorted unto the Lord: 2and laid
away her glorious apparel, and put on
the garments of anguish and mourning:
and instead of precious ointments, she
covered her head with ashes and dung,
and she humbled her body greatly, and
all the places of her joy she filled with
her torn hair. 3And she prayed unto the
Lord God of Israel, saying,
O my Lord, thou only art our King: help
me, desolate woman, which have no
helper but thee: 4for my danger is in
mine hand.
5From my youth up I have heard in the
tribe of my family, that thou, O Lord,
tookest Israel from among all people,
and our fathers from all their
predecessors, for a perpetual
inheritance, and thou hast performed
whatsoever thou didst promise them.
6And now we have sinned before thee:
therefore hast thou given us into the
hands of our enemies, 7because we
worshipped their gods: O Lord, thou art
righteous.
8Nevertheless it satisfieth them not, that
we are in bitter captivity: but they have
stricken hands with their idols, 9that
they will abolish the thing that thou
with thy mouth hast ordained, and
destroy thine inheritance, and stop the
mouth of them that praise thee, and
quench the glory of thy house, and of
thine altar, 10and open the mouths of the
heathen to set forth the praises of the
idols, and to magnify a fleshly king for
ever.
11O Lord, give not thy scepter unto
them that be nothing, and let them not
laugh at our fall; but turn their device
upon themselves, and make him an
example, that hath begun this against
us. 12Remember, O Lord, make thyself
known in time of our affliction, and
give me boldness, O King of the
nations, and Lord of all power. 13Give
me eloquent speech in my mouth
before the lion: turn his heart to hate
him that fighteth against us, that there
may be an end of him, and of all that
are likeminded to him: 14but deliver us
with thine hand, and help me that am
desolate, and which have no other help
but thee.
15Thou knowest all things, O Lord;
thou knowest that I hate the glory of
the unrighteous, and abhor the bed
of the uncircumcised, and of all the
heathen. 16Thou knowest my necessity:
for I abhor the sign of my high estate,
which is upon mine head in the days
wherein I show myself, and that I abhor
it as a menstruous rag, and that I wear
it not when I am private by myself,
17and that thine handmaid hath not
eaten at Haman's table, and that I have
not greatly esteemed the king's feast,
nor drunk the wine of the drink
offerings. 18Neither had thine handmaid
any joy since the day that I was brought
hither to this present, but in thee, O Lord
God of Abraham.

19 O thou mighty God above all, hear the
voice of the forlorn and deliver us out
of the hands of the mischievous, and
deliver me out of my fear.

CHAPTER 15

1 And upon the third day, when she had
ended her prayer, she laid away her
mourning garments, and put on her
glorious apparel. 2 And being gloriously
adorned, after she had called upon God,
who is the beholder and Saviour of all
things, she took two maids with her:
3 and upon the one she leaned, as
carrying herself daintily; 4 and the other
followed, bearing up her train. 5 And
she was ruddy through the perfection of
her beauty, and her countenance was
cheerful and very amiable: but her heart
was in anguish for fear. 6 Then having
passed through all the doors, she stood
before the king, who sat upon his royal
throne, and was clothed with all his
robes of majesty, all glittering with
gold and precious stones; and he was
very dreadful. 7 Then lifting up his
countenance that shone with majesty,
he looked very fiercely upon her: and
the queen fell down, and was pale, and
fainted, and bowed herself upon the
head of the maid that went before her.
8 Then God changed the spirit of the
king into mildness, who in a fear leaped
from his throne, and took her in his
arms, till she came to herself again, and
comforted her with loving words, and
said unto her, 9 Esther, what is the
matter? I am thy brother, be of good
cheer: 10 thou shalt not die, though our
commandment be general: come near.
11 And so he held up his golden scepter,
and laid it upon her neck, 12 and
embraced her, and said, Speak unto me.
13 Then said she unto him, I saw thee,
my lord, as an angel of God, and my
heart was troubled for fear of thy
majesty. 14 For wonderful art thou, lord,
and thy countenance is full of grace.
15 And as she was speaking, she fell
down for faintness.
16 Then the king was troubled, and all
his servants comforted her.

CHAPTER 16

1 The great king Artaxerx′es unto the
princes and governors of an hundred
and seven and twenty provinces from
India unto Ethiopia, and unto all our
faithful subjects, greeting.
2 Many, the more often they are honored
with the great bounty of their
gracious princes, the more proud they
are waxen, 3 and endeavor to hurt not
our subjects only, but not being able to
bear abundance, do take in hand to
practice also against those that do them
good: 4 and take not only thankfulness
away from among men, but also lifted
up with the glorious words of lewd
persons, that were never good, they
think to escape the justice of God, that
seeth all things, and hateth evil.
5 Oftentimes also fair speech of those,
that are put in trust to manage their
friends' affairs, hath caused many that
are in authority to be partakers of
innocent blood, and hath enwrapped
them in remediless calamities:
6 beguiling with the falsehood and
deceit of their lewd disposition the
innocency and goodness of princes.
7 Now ye may see this, as we have
declared, not so much by ancient
histories, as ye may, if ye search what
hath been wickedly done of late
through the pestilent behavior of them
that are unworthily placed in authority.
8 And we must take care for the time to

come, that our kingdom may be quiet
and peaceable for all men, [9]both by
changing our purposes, and always
judging things that are evident with
more equal proceeding. [10]For Haman, a
Macedo´nian, the son of Hammeda´tha,
being indeed a stranger from the
Persian blood, and far distant from
our goodness, and as a stranger
received of us, [11]had so far forth
obtained the favor that we show toward
every nation, as that he was called our
father, and was continually honored of
all men, as the next person unto the
king. [12]But he, not bearing his great
dignity, went about to deprive us of our
kingdom and life: [13]having by manifold
and cunning deceits sought of us the
destruction, as well of Mor´decai, who
saved our life, and continually procured
our good, as also of blameless Esther,
partaker of our kingdom, with their
whole nation. [14]For by these means he
thought, finding us destitute of friends,
to have translated the kingdom of the
Persians to the Macedo´nians.

[15]But we find that the Jews, whom this
wicked wretch hath delivered to utter
destruction, are no evildoers, but live
by most just laws: [16]and that they be
children of the most high and most
mighty living God, who hath ordered
the kingdom both unto us and to our
progenitors in the most excellent
manner. [17]Wherefore ye shall do well
not to put in execution the letters sent
unto you by Haman the son of
Hammeda´tha. [18]For he, that was the
worker of these things, is hanged at the
gates of Shushan with all his family:
God, who ruleth all things, speedily
rendering vengeance to him according
to his deserts.

[19]Therefore ye shall publish the copy of
this letter in all places, that the Jews
may freely live after their own laws.
[20]And ye shall aid them, that even the
same day, being the thirteenth day of
the twelfth month Adar, they may be
avenged on them, who in the time of
their affliction shall set upon them.
[21]For Almighty God hath turned to joy
unto them the day, wherein the chosen
people should have perished. [22]Ye shall
therefore among your solemn feasts
keep it an high day with all feasting:
[23]that both now and hereafter there may
be safety to us, and the well affected
Persians; but to those which do
conspire against us a memorial of
destruction.

[24]Therefore every city and country
whatsoever, which shall not do
according to these things, shall be
destroyed without mercy with fire and
sword, and shall be made not only
unpassable for men, but also most
hateful to wild beasts and fowls for ever.

WISDOM OF SOLOMON

CHAPTER 1

1Love righteousness, ye that be judges
of the earth: think of the Lord with a
good heart, and in simplicity of heart
seek him. 2For he will be found of them
that tempt him not; and showeth
himself unto such as do not distrust
him. 3For froward thoughts separate
from God: and his power, when it is
tried, reproveth the unwise. 4For into a
malicious soul wisdom shall not enter;
nor dwell in the body that is subject unto
sin. 5For the holy spirit of discipline will
flee deceit, and remove from thoughts
that are without understanding, and will
not abide when unrighteousness
cometh in.
6For wisdom is a loving spirit; and will
not acquit a blasphemer of his words:
for God is witness of his reins, and a
true beholder of his heart, and a hearer
of his tongue. 7For the Spirit of the Lord
filleth the world: and that which
containeth all things hath knowledge of
the voice.
8Therefore he that speaketh
unrighteous things cannot be hid:
neither shall vengeance, when it
punisheth, pass by him. 9For inquisition
shall be made into the counsels of the
ungodly: and the sound of his words
shall come unto the Lord for the
manifestation of his wicked deeds.
10For the ear of jealousy heareth all
things: and the noise of murmurings
is not hid. 11Therefore beware of
murmuring, which is unprofitable; and
refrain your tongue from backbiting:
for there is no word so secret, that shall
go for nought: and the mouth that
belieth slayeth the soul. 12Seek not
death in the error of your life: and pull
not upon yourselves destruction with
the works of your hands.
13For God made not death: neither hath
he pleasure in the destruction of the
living.
14For he created all things, that they
might have their being: and the
generations of the world were
healthful; and there is no poison of
destruction in them, nor the kingdom of
death upon the earth: 15(for
righteousness is immortal:) 16but
ungodly men with their works and
words called it to them: for when they
thought to have it their friend, they
consumed to nought, and made a
covenant with it, because they are
worthy to take part with it.

CHAPTER 2

1For the ungodly said, reasoning with
themselves, but not aright, Our life is
short and tedious, and in the death of a
man there is no remedy: neither was
there any man known to have returned
from the grave. 2For we are born at all
adventure: and we shall be hereafter as
though we had never been: for the
breath in our nostrils is as smoke, and a
little spark in the moving of our heart:
3which being extinguished, our body
shall be turned into ashes, and our spirit
shall vanish as the soft air, 4and our
name shall be forgotten in time, and no
man shall have our works in
remembrance, and our life shall pass
away as the trace of a cloud, and shall
be dispersed as a mist, that is driven
away with the beams of the sun, and
overcome with the heat thereof. 5For
our time is a very shadow that passeth

away; and after our end there is no
returning: for it is fast sealed, so that no
man cometh again.
6 Come on therefore, let us enjoy the
good things that are present: and let us
speedily use the creatures like as in
youth. 7 Let us fill ourselves with costly
wine and ointments: and let no flower of
the spring pass by us: 8 let us crown
ourselves with rosebuds, before they be
withered: 9 let none of us go without his
part of our voluptuousness: let us leave
tokens of our joyfulness in every place:
for this is our portion, and our lot is this.
10 Let us oppress the poor righteous
man, let us not spare the widow, nor
reverence the ancient gray hairs of the
aged. 11 Let our strength be the law of
justice: for that which is feeble is found
to be nothing worth. 12 Therefore let us
lie in wait for the righteous; because he
is not for our turn, and he is clean
contrary to our doings: he upbraideth
us with our offending the law, and
objecteth to our infamy the
transgressings of our education. 13 He
professeth to have the knowledge of
God: and he calleth himself the child of
the Lord. 14 He was made to reprove our
thoughts. 15 He is grievous unto us even
to behold: for his life is not like other
men's, his ways are of another fashion.
16 We are esteemed of him as
counterfeits: he abstaineth from our
ways as from filthiness: he
pronounceth the end of the just to be
blessed, and maketh his boast that God
is his father. 17 Let us see if his words be
true: and let us prove what shall happen
in the end of him. 18 For if the just man
be the son of God, he will help him, and
deliver him from the hand of his
enemies. 19 Let us examine him with
despitefulness and torture, that we may
know his meekness, and prove his
patience. 20 Let us condemn him with a
shameful death: for by his own saying
he shall be respected.
21 Such things they did imagine, and
were deceived: for their own
wickedness hath blinded them. 22 As for
the mysteries of God, they knew them
not: neither hoped they for the wages
of righteousness, nor discerned a
reward for blameless souls. 23 For God
created man to be immortal, and made
him to be an image of his own eternity.
24 Nevertheless through envy of the
devil came death into the world: and
they that do hold of his side do find it.

CHAPTER 3

1 But the souls of the righteous are in the
hand of God, and there shall no torment
touch them. 2 In the sight of the
unwise they seemed to die: and their
departure is taken for misery, 3 and their
going from us to be utter destruction:
but they are in peace. 4 For though
they be punished in the sight of men,
yet is their hope full of immortality.
5 And having been a little chastised,
they shall be greatly rewarded: for God
proved them, and found them worthy
for himself. 6 As gold in the furnace
hath he tried them, and received them
as a burnt offering. 7 And in the time
of their visitation they shall shine, and
run to and fro like sparks among the
stubble. 8 They shall judge the nations,
and have dominion over the people,
and their Lord shall reign for ever.
9 They that put their trust in him shall
understand the truth: and such as be
faithful in love shall abide with him: for
grace and mercy is to his saints, and he
hath care for his elect. 10 But the ungodly
shall be punished according to their own
imaginations, which have neglected the

righteous, and forsaken the Lord. 11For
whoso despiseth wisdom and nurture,
he is miserable, and their hope is vain,
their labors unfruitful, and their works
unprofitable: 12their wives are foolish,
and their children wicked: 13their
offspring is cursed. Wherefore blessed
is the barren that is undefiled, which
hath not known the sinful bed: she shall
have fruit in the visitation of souls.
14And blessed is the eunuch, which
with his hands hath wrought no
iniquity, nor imagined wicked things
against God: for unto him shall be
given the special gift of faith, and an
inheritance in the temple of the Lord
more acceptable to his mind. 15For
glorious is the fruit of good labors: and
the root of wisdom shall never fall
away.

16As for the children of adulterers, they
shall not come to their perfection, and
the seed of an unrighteous bed shall be
rooted out. 17For though they live long,
yet shall they be nothing regarded: and
their last age shall be without honor,
18or, if they die quickly, they have no
hope, neither comfort in the day of trial.
19For horrible is the end of the
unrighteous generation.

CHAPTER 4

1Better it is to have no children, and to
have virtue: for the memorial thereof is
immortal: because it is known with
God, and with men. 2When it is present,
men take example at it; and when it is
gone, they desire it: it weareth a crown,
and triumpheth for ever, having gotten
the victory, striving for undefiled
rewards.

3But the multiplying brood of the
ungodly shall not thrive, nor take deep
rooting from bastard slips, nor lay any
fast foundation. 4For though they
flourish in branches for a time; yet
standing not fast, they shall be shaken
with the wind, and through the force of
winds they shall be rooted out. 5The
imperfect branches shall be broken off,
their fruit unprofitable, not ripe to eat,
yea, meet for nothing. 6For children
begotten of unlawful beds are
witnesses of wickedness against their
parents in their trial.

7But though the righteous be prevented
with death, yet shall he be in rest. 8For
honorable age is not that which
standeth in length of time, nor that is
measured by number of years. 9But
wisdom is the gray hair unto men, and
an unspotted life is old age.

10He pleased God, and was beloved of
him: so that living among sinners he
was translated. 11Yea, speedily was he
taken away, lest that wickedness should
alter his understanding, or deceit
beguile his soul. 12For the bewitching
of naughtiness doth obscure things that
are honest; and the wandering of
concupiscence doth undermine the
simple mind. 13He, being made perfect
in a short time, fulfilled a long time:
14for his soul pleased the Lord:
therefore hasted he to take him away
from among the wicked. 15This the
people saw, and understood it not,
neither laid they up this in their minds,
That his grace and mercy is with his
saints, and that he hath respect unto his
chosen.

16Thus the righteous that is dead shall
condemn the ungodly which are living;
and youth that is soon perfected the
many years and old age of the
unrighteous. 17For they shall see the
end of the wise, and shall not
understand what God in his counsel
hath decreed of him, and to what end

the Lord hath set him in safety. 18They
shall see him, and despise him; but God
shall laugh them to scorn: and they
shall hereafter be a vile carcase, and a
reproach among the dead for evermore.
19For he shall rend them, and cast them
down headlong, that they shall be
speechless; and he shall shake them
from the foundation; and they shall
be utterly laid waste, and be in sorrow;
and their memorial shall perish. 20And
when they cast up the accounts of their
sins, they shall come with fear: and
their own iniquities shall convince
them to their face.

CHAPTER 5

1Then shall the righteous man stand in
great boldness before the face of such
as have afflicted him, and made no
account of his labors. 2When they see it,
they shall be troubled with terrible fear,
and shall be amazed at the strangeness of
his salvation, so far beyond all that they
looked for. 3And they repenting and
groaning for anguish of spirit shall say
within themselves, This was he, whom
we had sometimes in derision, and a
proverb of reproach: 4we fools
accounted his life madness, and his
end to be without honor: 5how is he
numbered among the children of God,
and his lot is among the saints!
6Therefore have we erred from the way
of truth, and the light of righteousness
hath not shone unto us, and the sun of
righteousness rose not upon us. 7We
wearied ourselves in the way of
wickedness and destruction: yea, we
have gone through deserts, where there
lay no way: but as for the way of the
Lord, we have not known it. 8What hath
pride profited us? or what good hath
riches with our vaunting brought us?
9All those things are passed away like a
shadow, and as a post that hasted by;
10and as a ship that passeth over the
waves of the water, which when it is
gone by, the trace thereof cannot be
found, neither the pathway of the keel
in the waves; 11or as when a bird hath
flown through the air, there is no token
of her way to be found, but the light air
being beaten with the stroke of her
wings, and parted with the violent noise
and motion of them, is passed through,
and therein afterwards no sign where
she went is to be found; 12or like as when
an arrow is shot at a mark, it parteth the
air, which immediately cometh together
again, so that a man cannot know where
it went through: 13even so we in like
manner, as soon as we were born,
began to draw to our end, and had no
sign of virtue to show; but were
consumed in our own wickedness.
14For the hope of the ungodly is like
dust that is blown away with the wind;
like a thin froth that is driven away with
the storm; like as the smoke which is
dispersed here and there with a
tempest, and passeth away as the
remembrance of a guest that tarrieth but
a day.

15But the righteous live for evermore;
their reward also is with the Lord,
and the care of them is with the most
High. 16Therefore shall they receive a
glorious kingdom, and a beautiful
crown from the Lord's hand: for with
his right hand shall he cover them, and
with his arm shall he protect them.

17He shall take to him his jealousy
for complete armor, and make the
creature his weapon for the revenge
of his enemies. 18He shall put on
righteousness as a breastplate, and
true judgment instead of an helmet.
19He shall take holiness for an invincible

shield. [20]His severe wrath shall he
sharpen for a sword, and the world shall
fight with him against the unwise.
[21]Then shall the right aiming
thunderbolts go abroad; and from the
clouds, as from a well-drawn bow, shall
they fly to the mark. [22]And hailstones
full of wrath shall be cast as out of a
stone bow, and the water of the sea
shall rage against them, and the floods
shall cruelly drown them. [23]Yea, a
mighty wind shall stand up against
them, and like a storm shall blow them
away: thus iniquity shall lay waste the
whole earth, and ill-dealing shall
overthrow the thrones of the mighty.

CHAPTER 6

[1]Hear therefore, O ye kings, and
understand; learn, ye that be judges of
the ends of the earth. [2]Give ear, ye that
rule the people, and glory in the
multitude of nations. [3]For power is
given you of the Lord, and sovereignty
from the Highest, who shall try your
works, and search out your counsels.
[4]Because, being ministers of his
kingdom, ye have not judged aright,
nor kept the law, nor walked after the
counsel of God; [5]horribly and speedily
shall he come upon you: for a sharp
judgment shall be to them that be in
high places. [6]For mercy will soon
pardon the meanest: but mighty men
shall be mightily tormented. [7]For he
which is Lord over all shall fear no
man's person, neither shall he stand in
awe of any man's greatness: for he hath
made the small and great, and careth for
all alike. [8]But a sore trial shall come
upon the mighty. [9]Unto you therefore,
O kings, do I speak, that ye may learn
wisdom, and not fall away. [10]For they
that keep holiness holily shall be judged
holy: and they that have learned such
things shall find what to answer.
[11]Wherefore set your affection upon my
words; desire them, and ye shall be
instructed.

[12]Wisdom is glorious, and never fadeth
away: yea, she is easily seen of them
that love her, and found of such as seek
her. [13]She preventeth them that desire
her, in making herself first known unto
them. [14]Whoso seeketh her early shall
have no great travail: for he shall find
her sitting at his doors. [15]To think
therefore upon her is perfection of
wisdom: and whoso watcheth for her
shall quickly be without care. [16]For she
goeth about seeking such as are worthy
of her, showeth herself favorably unto
them in the ways, and meeteth them in
every thought.

[17]For the very true beginning of her is
the desire of discipline; and the care
of discipline is love; [18]and love is the
keeping of her laws; and the giving
heed unto her laws is the assurance of
incorruption; [19]and incorruption
maketh us near unto God: [20]therefore
the desire of wisdom bringeth to a
kingdom. [21]If your delight be then in
thrones and scepters, O ye kings of the
people, honor wisdom, that ye may
reign for evermore.

[22]As for wisdom, what she is, and how
she came up, I will tell you, and will not
hide mysteries from you: but will seek
her out from the beginning of her
nativity, and bring the knowledge of her
into light, and will not pass over the
truth. [23]Neither will I go with
consuming envy; for such a man shall
have no fellowship with wisdom. [24]But
the multitude of the wise is the welfare
of the world: and a wise king is the
upholding of the people. [25]Receive
therefore instruction through my

words, and it shall do you good.

CHAPTER 7

1 I myself also am a mortal man, like to
all, and the offspring of him that was
first made of the earth, 2 and in my
mother's womb was fashioned to be flesh
in the time of ten months, being
compacted in blood, of the seed of man,
and the pleasure that came with sleep.
3 And when I was born, I drew in the
common air, and fell upon the earth,
which is of like nature, and the first
voice which I uttered was crying, as all
others do. 4 I was nursed in swaddling
clothes, and that with cares. 5 For there
is no king that had any other beginning
of birth. 6 For all men have one entrance
into life, and the like going out.
7 Wherefore I prayed, and
understanding was given me: I called
upon God, and the spirit of wisdom
came to me. 8 I preferred her before
scepters and thrones, and esteemed
riches nothing in comparison of her.
9 Neither compared I unto her any
precious stone, because all gold in
respect of her is as a little sand, and
silver shall be counted as clay before
her. 10 I loved her above health and
beauty, and chose to have her instead of
light: for the light that cometh from her
never goeth out. 11 All good things
together came to me with her, and
innumerable riches in her hands. 12 And
I rejoiced in them all, because wisdom
goeth before them: and I knew not that
she was the mother of them. 13 I learned
diligently, and do communicate her
liberally: I do not hide her riches. 14 For
she is a treasure unto men that never
faileth: which they that use become the
friends of God, being commended for
the gifts that come from learning.
15 God hath granted me to speak as I
would, and to conceive as is meet for
the things that are given me: because
it is he that leadeth unto wisdom, and
directeth the wise. 16 For in his hand are
both we and our words; all wisdom
also, and knowledge of workmanship.
17 For he hath given me certain
knowledge of the things that are,
namely, to know how the world was
made, and the operation of the
elements: 18 the beginning, ending, and
midst of the times: the alterations of the
turning of the sun, and the change of
seasons: 19 the circuits of years, and the
positions of stars: 20 the natures of living
creatures, and the furies of wild beasts:
the violence of winds, and the
reasonings of men: the diversities of
plants, and the virtues of roots: 21 and
all such things as are either secret or
manifest, them I know. 22 For wisdom,
which is the worker of all things, taught
me.
For in her is an understanding spirit,
holy, one only, manifold, subtle, lively,
clear, undefiled, plain, not subject to
hurt, loving the thing that is good, quick,
which cannot be letted, ready to do
good, 23 kind to man, steadfast, sure,
free from care, having all power,
overseeing all things, and going
through all understanding, pure, and
most subtle, spirits. 24 For wisdom is
more moving than any motion: she
passeth and goeth through all things by
reason of her pureness. 25 For she is the
breath of the power of God, and a pure
influence flowing from the glory of the
Almighty: therefore can no defiled
thing fall into her. 26 For she is the
brightness of the everlasting light, the
unspotted mirror of the power of God,
and the image of his goodness. 27 And
being but one, she can do all things: and

remaining in herself, she maketh all
things new: and in all ages entering into
holy souls, she maketh them friends of
God, and prophets. 28 For God loveth
none but him that dwelleth with
wisdom. 29 For she is more beautiful
than the sun, and above all the order of
stars: being compared with the light,
she is found before it. 30 For after this
cometh night: but vice shall not prevail
against wisdom.

CHAPTER 8

1 Wisdom reacheth from one end to
another mightily: and sweetly doth she
order all things.
2 I loved her, and sought her out from my
youth, I desired to make her my spouse,
and I was a lover of her beauty. 3 In that
she is conversant with God, she
magnifieth her nobility: yea, the Lord
of all things himself loved her. 4 For she
is privy to the mysteries of the
knowledge of God, and a lover of his
works. 5 If riches be a possession to be
desired in this life; what is richer than
wisdom, that worketh all things? 6 And
if prudence work; who of all that are is a
more cunning workman than she? 7 And
if a man love righteousness, her labors
are virtues: for she teacheth temperance
and prudence, justice and fortitude:
which are such things, as men can
have nothing more profitable in their
life. 8 If a man desire much experience,
she knoweth things of old, and
conjectureth aright what is to come: she
knoweth the subtleties of speeches, and
can expound dark sentences: she
foreseeth signs and wonders, and the
events of seasons and times.
9 Therefore I purposed to take her to me
to live with me, knowing that she would
be a counselor of good things, and a
comfort in cares and grief. 10 For her
sake I shall have estimation among the
multitude, and honor with the elders,
though I be young. 11 I shall be found of
a quick conceit in judgment, and shall
be admired in the sight of great men.
12 When I hold my tongue, they shall
bide my leisure, and when I speak, they
shall give good ear unto me: if I talk
much, they shall lay their hands upon
their mouth. 13 Moreover by the means
of her I shall obtain immortality, and
leave behind me an everlasting
memorial to them that come after me.
14 I shall set the people in order, and the
nations shall be subject unto me.
15 Horrible tyrants shall be afraid, when
they do but hear of me; I shall be found
good among the multitude, and valiant
in war. 16 After I am come into mine
house, I will repose myself with her: for
her conversation hath no bitterness; and
to live with her hath no sorrow, but
mirth and joy.
17 Now when I considered these things
in myself, and pondered them in my
heart, how that to be allied unto
wisdom is immortality; 18 and great
pleasure it is to have her friendship; and
in the works of her hands are infinite
riches; and in the exercise of conference
with her, prudence; and in talking with
her, a good report; I went about seeking
how to take her to me. 19 For I was a witty
child, and had a good spirit. 20 Yea rather,
being good, I came into a body
undefiled. 21 Nevertheless, when I
perceived that I could not otherwise
obtain her, except God gave her me;
and that was a point of wisdom also to
know whose gift she was; I prayed unto
the Lord, and besought him, and with
my whole heart I said,

CHAPTER 9

1 O God of my fathers, and Lord of
mercy, who hast made all things with
thy word, 2 and ordained man through
thy wisdom, that he should have
dominion over the creatures which thou
hast made, 3 and order the world
according to equity and righteousness,
and execute judgment with an upright
heart: 4 give me wisdom, that sitteth
by thy throne; and reject me not from
among thy children: 5 for I thy servant
and son of thine handmaid am a feeble
person, and of a short time, and too
young for the understanding of
judgment and laws. 6 For though a man
be never so perfect among the
children of men, yet if thy wisdom be
not with him, he shall be nothing
regarded. 7 Thou hast chosen me to be a
king of thy people, and a judge of thy
sons and daughters: 8 thou hast
commanded me to build a temple upon
thy holy mount, and an altar in the city
wherein thou dwellest, a resemblance
of the holy tabernacle, which thou hast
prepared from the beginning. 9 And
wisdom was with thee: which knoweth
thy works, and was present when thou
madest the world, and knew what was
acceptable in thy sight, and right in thy
commandments. 10 O send her out of thy
holy heavens, and from the throne of
thy glory, that being present she may
labor with me, that I may know what is
pleasing unto thee. 11 For she knoweth
and understandeth all things, and she
shall lead me soberly in my doings, and
preserve me in her power. 12 So shall my
works be acceptable, and then shall I
judge thy people righteously, and be
worthy to sit in my father's seat.
13 For what man is he that can know the
counsel of God? or who can think what
the will of the Lord is? 14 For the
thoughts of mortal men are miserable,
and our devices are but uncertain. 15 For
the corruptible body presseth down the
soul, and the earthy tabernacle
weigheth down the mind that museth
upon many things. 16 And hardly do we
guess aright at things that are upon
earth, and with labor do we find the
things that are before us: but the things
that are in heaven who hath searched
out? 17 And thy counsel who hath
known, except thou give wisdom, and
send thy Holy Spirit from above? 18 For
so the ways of them which lived on the
earth were reformed, and men were
taught the things that are pleasing unto
thee, and were saved through wisdom.

CHAPTER 10

1 She preserved the first formed father
of the world, that was created alone,
and brought him out of his fall, 2 and
gave him power to rule all things.
3 But when the unrighteous went away
from her in his anger, he perished also
in the fury wherewith he murdered his
brother.
4 For whose cause the earth being
drowned with the flood, wisdom again
preserved it, and directed the course of
the righteous in a piece of wood of
small value.
5 Moreover, the nations in their wicked
conspiracy being confounded, she
found out the righteous, and preserved
him blameless unto God, and kept him
strong against his tender compassion
toward his son.
6 When the ungodly perished, she
delivered the righteous man, who fled
from the fire which fell down upon the
five cities. 7 Of whose wickedness even
to this day the waste land that smoketh

is a testimony, and plants bearing fruit
that never come to ripeness: and a
standing pillar of salt is a monument of
an unbelieving soul. 8 For regarding not
wisdom, they got not only this hurt, that
they knew not the things which were
good; but also left behind them to the
world a memorial of their foolishness:
so that in the things wherein they
offended they could not so much as be
hid.
9 But wisdom delivered from pain
those that attended upon her. 10 When
the righteous fled from his brother's
wrath, she guided him in right paths,
showed him the kingdom of God, and
gave him knowledge of holy things,
made him rich in his travails, and
multiplied the fruit of his labors. 11 In
the covetousness of such as oppressed
him she stood by him, and made him
rich. 12 She defended him from his
enemies, and kept him safe from those
that lay in wait, and in a sore conflict
she gave him the victory; that he might
know that godliness is stronger than all.
13 When the righteous was sold, she
forsook him not, but delivered him
from sin: she went down with him into
the pit, 14 and left him not in bonds, till
she brought him the scepter of the
kingdom, and power against those that
oppressed him: as for them that had
accused him, she shewed them to be
liars, and gave him perpetual glory.
15 She delivered the righteous people
and blameless seed from the nation
that oppressed them. 16 She entered into
the soul of the servant of the Lord, and
withstood dreadful kings in wonders
and signs; 17 rendered to the righteous a
reward of their labors, guided them in a
marvelous way, and was unto them for
a cover by day, and a light of stars in
the night season; 18 brought them
through the Red Sea, and led them
through much water: 19 but she drowned
their enemies, and cast them up out of
the bottom of the deep. 20 Therefore the
righteous spoiled the ungodly, and
praised thy holy name, O Lord, and
magnified with one accord thine hand,
that fought for them. 21 For wisdom
opened the mouth of the dumb, and
made the tongues of them that cannot
speak eloquent.

CHAPTER 11

1 She prospered their works in the hand
of the holy prophet. 2 They went
through the wilderness that was not
inhabited, and pitched tents in places
where there lay no way. 3 They stood
against their enemies, and were
avenged of their adversaries. 4 When
they were thirsty, they called upon thee,
and water was given them out of the
flinty rock, and their thirst was
quenched out of the hard stone.
5 For by what things their enemies were
punished, by the same they in their
need were benefited. 6 For instead of a
fountain of a perpetual running river
troubled with foul blood, 7 for a manifest
reproof of that commandment, whereby
the infants were slain, thou gavest unto
them abundance of water by a means
which they hoped not for: 8 declaring by
that thirst then how thou hadst punished
their adversaries. 9 For when they were
tried, albeit but in mercy chastised, they
knew how the ungodly were judged in
wrath and tormented, thirsting in
another manner than the just. 10 For
these thou didst admonish and try, as a
father: but the other, as a severe king,
thou didst condemn and punish.
11 Whether they were absent or present,
they were vexed alike. 12 For a

double grief came upon them, and a
groaning for the remembrance of things
past. 13 For when they heard by their
own punishments the other to be
benefited, they had some feeling of the
Lord. 14 For whom they rejected with
scorn, when he was long before thrown
out at the casting forth of the infants,
him in the end, when they saw what
came to pass, they admired.
15 But for the foolish devices of their
wickedness, wherewith being deceived
they worshipped serpents void of
reason, and vile beasts, thou didst send
a multitude of unreasonable beasts
upon them for vengeance; 16 that they
might know, that wherewithal a man
sinneth, by the same also shall he be
punished. 17 For thy Almighty hand,
that made the world of matter without
form, wanted not means to send among
them a multitude of bears, or fierce
lions, 18 or unknown wild beasts, full of
rage, newly created, breathing out
either a fiery vapor, or filthy scents of
scattered smoke, or shooting horrible
sparkles out of their eyes: 19 whereof not
only the harm might dispatch them at
once, but also the terrible sight utterly
destroy them. 20 Yea, and without these
might they have fallen down with one
blast, being persecuted of vengeance,
and scattered abroad through the breath
of thy power: but thou hast ordered all
things in measure and number and
weight.
21 For thou canst show thy great strength
at all times when thou wilt; and who
may withstand the power of thine arm?
22 For the whole world before thee is as
a little grain of the balance, yea, as a
drop of the morning dew that falleth
down upon the earth. 23 But thou hast
mercy upon all; for thou canst do all
things, and winkest at the sins of men,
because they should amend. 24 For thou
lovest all the things that are, and
abhorrest nothing which thou hast made:
for never wouldest thou have made any
thing, if thou hadst hated it. 25 And how
could any thing have endured, if it had
not been thy will? or been preserved, if
not called by thee? 26 But thou sparest
all: for they are thine, O Lord, thou
lover of souls.

CHAPTER 12

1 For thine incorruptible Spirit is in all
things. 2 Therefore chastenest thou them
by little and little that offend, and
warnest them by putting them in
remembrance wherein they have
offended, that leaving their wickedness
they may believe on thee, O Lord. 3 For it
was thy will to destroy by the hands of
our fathers both those old inhabitants of
thy holy land, 4 whom thou hatedst for
doing most odious works of
witchcrafts, and wicked sacrifices; 5 and
also those merciless murderers of
children, and devourers of man's flesh,
and the feasts of blood, 6 with their
priests out of the midst of their
idolatrous crew, and the parents, that
killed with their own hands souls
destitute of help: 7 that the land, which
thou esteemedst above all other, might
receive a worthy colony of God's
children. 8 Nevertheless even those thou
sparedst as men, and didst send wasps,
forerunners of thine host, to destroy
them by little and little. 9 Not that thou
wast unable to bring the ungodly under
the hand of the righteous in battle, or to
destroy them at once with cruel beasts,
or with one rough word: 10 but
executing thy judgments upon them by
little and little, thou gavest them place
of repentance, not being ignorant that

they were a naughty generation, and
that their malice was bred in them, and
that their cogitation would never be
changed. 11 For it was a cursed seed
from the beginning; neither didst thou
for fear of any man give them pardon for
those things wherein they sinned.
12 For who shall say, What hast thou
done? or who shall withstand thy
judgment? or who shall accuse thee for
the nations that perish, whom thou hast
made? or who shall come to stand
against thee, to be revenged for the
unrighteous men? 13 For neither is there
any God but thou that careth for all, to
whom thou mightest show that thy
judgment is not unright. 14 Neither shall
king or tyrant be able to set his face
against thee for any whom thou hast
punished. 15 Forsomuch then as thou art
righteous thyself, thou orderest all
things righteously: thinking it not
agreeable with thy power to condemn
him that hath not deserved to be
punished. 16 For thy power is the
beginning of righteousness, and
because thou art the Lord of all, it
maketh thee to be gracious unto all.
17 For when men will not believe that
thou art of a full power, thou showest
thy strength, and among them that know
it thou makest their boldness manifest.
18 But thou, mastering thy power,
judgest with equity, and orderest us
with great favor: for thou mayest use
power when thou wilt.
19 But by such works hast thou taught
thy people that the just man should be
merciful, and hast made thy children
to be of a good hope that thou givest
repentance for sins. 20 For if thou didst
punish the enemies of thy children, and
the condemned to death, with such
deliberation, giving them time and
place, whereby they might be delivered
from their malice: 21 with how great
circumspection didst thou judge thine
own sons, unto whose fathers thou hast
sworn, and made covenants of good
promises? 22 Therefore, whereas thou
dost chasten us, thou scourgest our
enemies a thousand times more, to the
intent that, when we judge, we should
carefully think of thy goodness, and
when we ourselves are judged, we
should look for mercy.
23 Wherefore, whereas men have lived
dissolutely and unrighteously, thou
hast tormented them with their own
abominations. 24 For they went astray
very far in the ways of error, and held
them for gods, which even among the
beasts of their enemies were despised,
being deceived, as children of no
understanding. 25 Therefore unto them,
as to children without the use of reason,
thou didst send a judgment to mock
them. 26 But they that would not be
reformed by that correction, wherein he
dallied with them, shall feel a judgment
worthy of God. 27 For, look, for what
things they grudged, when they were
punished, that is, for them whom they
thought to be gods; [now] being
punished in them, when they saw it,
they acknowledged him to be the true
God, whom before they denied to
know; and therefore came extreme
damnation upon them.

CHAPTER 13

1 Surely vain are all men by nature, who
are ignorant of God, and could not out
of the good things that are seen know
him that is: neither by considering the
works did they acknowledge the
workmaster; 2 but deemed either fire, or
wind, or the swift air, or the circle of the
stars, or the violent water, or the lights

of heaven, to be the gods which govern
the world. 3With whose beauty if they
being delighted took them to be gods;
let them know how much better the
Lord of them is: for the first author of
beauty hath created them. 4But if they
were astonished at their power and
virtue, let them understand by them,
how much mightier he is that made
them. 5For by the greatness and beauty
of the creatures proportionably the
maker of them is seen. 6But yet for this
they are the less to be blamed: for they
peradventure err, seeking God, and
desirous to find him. 7For being
conversant in his works they search
him diligently, and believe their sight:
because the things are beautiful that are
seen. 8Howbeit neither are they to be
pardoned. 9For if they were able to
know so much, that they could aim at
the world; how did they not sooner find
out the Lord thereof?
10But miserable are they, and in dead
things is their hope, who called them
gods, which are the works of men's
hands, gold and silver, to show art in,
and resemblances of beasts, or a stone
good for nothing, the work of an
ancient hand. 11Now a carpenter that
felleth timber, after he hath sawn down
a tree meet for the purpose, and taken
off all the bark skilfully round about,
and hath wrought it handsomely, and
made a vessel thereof fit for the service of
man's life; 12and after spending the
refuse of his work to dress his meat,
hath filled himself; 13and taking the very
refuse among those which served to no
use, being a crooked piece of wood, and
full of knots, hath carved it diligently,
when he had nothing else to do, and
formed it by the skill of his
understanding, and fashioned it to the
image of a man; 14or made it like some
vile beast, laying it over with vermilion,
and with paint coloring it red, and
covering every spot therein; 15and when
he had made a convenient room for it,
set it in a wall, and made it fast with
iron: 16for he provided for it that it
might not fall, knowing that it was
unable to help itself; for it is an image,
and hath need of help: 17then maketh he
prayer for his goods, for his wife and
children, and is not ashamed to speak to
that which hath no life. 18For health he
calleth upon that which is weak: for life
prayeth to that which is dead: for aid
humbly beseecheth that which hath
least means to help: and for a good
journey he asketh of that which cannot
set a foot forward: 19and for gaining and
getting, and for good success of his
hands, asketh ability to do of him, that
is most unable to do any thing.

CHAPTER 14

1Again, one preparing himself to sail,
and about to pass through the raging
waves, calleth upon a piece of wood
more rotten than the vessel that carrieth
him. 2For verily desire of gain devised
that, and the workman built it by his
skill. 3But thy providence, O Father,
governeth it: for thou hast made a way
in the sea, and a safe path in the waves;
4showing that thou canst save from all
danger: yea, though a man went to sea
without art. 5Nevertheless thou
wouldest not that the works of thy
wisdom should be idle, and therefore
do men commit their lives to a small
piece of wood, and passing the rough
sea in a weak vessel are saved. 6For in
the old time also, when the proud giants
perished, the hope of the world
governed by thy hand escaped in a
weak vessel, and left to all ages a seed
of generation. 7For blessed is the wood

whereby righteousness cometh.
8 But that which is made with hands
is cursed, as well it, as he that made it:
he, because he made it; and it, because,
being corruptible, it was called god.
9 For the ungodly and his ungodliness
are both alike hateful unto God. 10 For
that which is made shall be punished
together with him that made it.
11 Therefore even upon the idols of the
Gentiles shall there be a visitation:
because in the creature of God they are
become an abomination, and
stumbling-blocks to the souls of men,
and a snare to the feet of the unwise.
12 For the devising of idols was the
beginning of spiritual fornication, and
the invention of them the corruption
of life. 13 For neither were they from the
beginning, neither shall they be for
ever. 14 For by the vain glory of men
they entered into the world, and
therefore shall they come shortly to an
end. 15 For a father afflicted with
untimely mourning, when he hath made
an image of his child soon taken away,
now honored him as a god, which was
then a dead man, and delivered to those
that were under him ceremonies and
sacrifices. 16 Thus in process of time an
ungodly custom grown strong was kept
as a law, and graven images were
worshipped by the commandments of
kings. 17 Whom men could not honor in
presence, because they dwelt far off,
they took the counterfeit of his visage
from far, and made an express image of a
king whom they honored, to the end that
by this their forwardness they might
flatter him that was absent, as if he were
present. 18 Also the singular diligence
of the artificer did help to set forward
the ignorant to more superstition. 19 For
he, peradventure willing to please one
in authority, forced all his skill to make
the resemblance of the best fashion.
20 And so the multitude, allured by the
grace of the work, took him now for a
god, which a little before was but
honored as a man. 21 And this was an
occasion to deceive the world: for men,
serving either calamity or tyranny, did
ascribe unto stones and stocks the
incommunicable name.
22 Moreover this was not enough for
them, that they erred in the knowledge
of God; but whereas they lived in the
great war of ignorance, those so great
plagues called they peace. 23 For whilst
they slew their children in sacrifices, or
used secret ceremonies, or made
revelings of strange rites; 24 they kept
neither lives nor marriages any longer
undefiled: but either one slew another
traiterously, or grieved him by
adultery. 25 So that there reigned in all
men without exception blood,
manslaughter, theft, and dissimulation,
corruption, unfaithfulness, tumults,
perjury, 26 disquieting of good men,
forgetfulness of good turns, defiling
of souls, changing of kind, disorder
in marriages, adultery, and shameless
uncleanness. 27 For the worshipping of
idols not to be named is the beginning,
the cause, and the end, of all evil. 28 For
either they are mad when they be
merry, or prophesy lies, or live
unjustly, or else lightly forswear
themselves. 29 For insomuch as their
trust is in idols, which have no life;
though they swear falsely, yet they look
not to be hurt. 30 Howbeit for both
causes shall they be justly punished:
both because they thought not well of
God, giving heed unto idols, and also
unjustly swore in deceit, despising
holiness. 31 For it is not the power of
them by whom they swear: but it is the
just vengeance of sinners, that

punisheth always the offense of the
ungodly.

CHAPTER 15

1 But thou, O God, art gracious and true,
longsuffering, and in mercy ordering
all things. 2 For if we sin, we are thine,
knowing thy power: but we will not sin,
knowing that we are counted thine.
3 For to know thee is perfect
righteousness: yea, to know thy power is
the root of immortality. 4 For neither did
the mischievous invention of men
deceive us, nor an image spotted with
divers colors, the painter's fruitless
labor; 5 the sight whereof enticeth fools
to lust after it, and so they desire the
form of a dead image, that hath no
breath. 6 Both they that make them,
they that desire them, and they that
worship them, are lovers of evil things,
and are worthy to have such things to
trust upon.
7 For the potter, tempering soft earth,
fashioneth every vessel with much
labor for our service: yea, of the same
clay he maketh both the vessels that serve
for clean uses, and likewise also all such
as serve to the contrary: but what is the
use of either sort, the potter himself is
the judge. 8 And employing his labors
lewdly, he maketh a vain god of the
same clay, even he which a little before
was made of earth himself, and within a
little while after returneth to the same,
out of the which he was taken, when his
life which was lent him shall be
demanded. 9 Notwithstanding his care
is, not that he shall have much labor,
nor that his life is short: but striveth to
excel goldsmiths and silversmiths, and
endeavoreth to do like the workers in
brass, and counteth it his glory to make
counterfeit things. 10 His heart is ashes,
his hope is more vile than earth, and his
life of less value than clay: 11 forasmuch
as he knew not his Maker, and him that
inspired into him an active soul, and
breathed in a living spirit. 12 But they
counted our life a pastime, and our time
here a market for gain: for, say they, we
must be getting every way, though it be by
evil means. 13 For this man, that of
earthly matter maketh brittle vessels
and graven images, knoweth himself to
offend above all others.
14 And all the enemies of thy people,
that hold them in subjection, are most
foolish, and are more miserable than
very babes. 15 For they counted all the
idols of the heathen to be gods: which
neither have the use of eyes to see, nor
noses to draw breath, nor ears to hear,
nor fingers of hands to handle; and as
for their feet, they are slow to go. 16 For
man made them, and he that borrowed
his own spirit fashioned them: but no
man can make a god like unto himself.
17 For being mortal, he worketh a dead
thing with wicked hands: for he himself
is better than the things which he
worshippeth: whereas he lived once,
but they never. 18 Yea, they worshipped
those beasts also that are most hateful:
for being compared together, some are
worse than others. 19 Neither are they
beautiful, so much as to be desired in
respect of beasts: but they went without
the praise of God and his blessing.

CHAPTER 16

1 Therefore by the like were they
punished worthily, and by the
multitude of beasts tormented. 2 Instead
of which punishment, dealing
graciously with thine own people, thou
preparedst for them meat of a strange
taste, even quails to stir up their

appetite: 3to the end that they, desiring
food, might for the ugly sight of the
beasts sent among them loathe even
that, which they must needs desire; but
these, suffering penury for a short
space, might be made partakers of a
strange taste. 4For it was requisite, that
upon them exercising tyranny should
come penury, which they could not
avoid: but to these it should only be
showed how their enemies were
tormented.

5For when the horrible fierceness of
beasts came upon these, and they
perished with the stings of crooked
serpents, thy wrath endured not for
ever: 6but they were troubled for a
small season, that they might be
admonished, having a sign of salvation,
to put them in remembrance of the
commandment of thy law. 7For he that
turned himself toward it was not saved
by the thing that he saw, but by thee,
that art the Saviour of all. 8And in this
thou madest thine enemies confess, that
it is thou who deliverest from all evil:
9for them the bitings of grasshoppers
and flies killed, neither was there found
any remedy for their life: for they were
worthy to be punished by such. 10But
thy sons not the very teeth of venomous
dragons overcame: for thy mercy was
ever by them, and healed them. 11For
they were pricked, that they should
remember thy words; and were
quickly saved, that not falling into
deep forgetfulness, they might be
continually mindful of thy goodness.
12For it was neither herb, nor
mollifying plaster, that restored them
to health: but thy word, O Lord, which
healeth all things. 13For thou hast
power of life and death: thou leadest to
the gates of hell, and bringest up again.
14A man indeed killeth through his
malice: and the spirit, when it is gone
forth, returneth not; neither the soul
received up cometh again.

15But it is not possible to escape thine
hand. 16For the ungodly, that denied to
know thee, were scourged by the
strength of thine arm: with strange
rains, hails, and showers, were they
persecuted, that they could not avoid,
and through fire were they consumed.
17For, which is most to be wondered at,
the fire had more force in the water, that
quencheth all things: for the world
fighteth for the righteous. 18For
sometime the flame was mitigated, that
it might not burn up the beasts that were
sent against the ungodly; but
themselves might see and perceive that
they were persecuted with the
judgment of God. 19And at another time
it burneth even in the midst of water
above the power of fire, that it might
destroy the fruits of an unjust land.

20Instead whereof thou feddest thine
own people with angels' food, and didst
send them from heaven bread prepared
without their labor, able to content
every man's delight, and agreeing to
every taste. 21For thy sustenance
declared thy sweetness unto thy
children, and serving to the appetite of
the eater, tempered itself to every
man's liking. 22But snow and ice
endured the fire, and melted not, that
they might know that fire burning in the
hail, and sparkling in the rain, did
destroy the fruits of the enemies. 23But
this again did even forget his own
strength, that the righteous might be
nourished. 24For the creature that
serveth thee, who art the Maker
increaseth his strength against the
unrighteous for their punishment, and
abateth his strength for the benefit of
such as put their trust in thee.
25Therefore even then was it altered

into all fashions, and was obedient to
thy grace, that nourisheth all things,
according to the desire of them that
had need: 26 that thy children, O Lord,
whom thou lovest, might know, that it
is not the growing of fruits that
nourisheth man: but that it is thy word,
which preserveth them that put their
trust in thee. 27 For that which was not
destroyed of the fire, being warmed
with a little sunbeam, soon melted
away: 28 that it might be known, that we
must prevent the sun to give thee
thanks, and at the dayspring pray unto
thee. 29 For the hope of the unthankful
shall melt away as the winter's hoar
frost, and shall run away as unprofitable
water.

CHAPTER 17

1 For great are thy judgments, and
cannot be expressed: therefore
unnurtured souls have erred. 2 For when
unrighteous men thought to oppress
the holy nation; they being shut up in
their houses, the prisoners of darkness,
and fettered with the bonds of a long
night, lay [there] exiled from the
eternal providence. 3 For while they
supposed to lie hid in their secret sins,
they were scattered under a dark veil of
forgetfulness, being horribly
astonished, and troubled with [strange]
apparitions. 4 For neither might the
corner that held them keep them from
fear: but noises [as of waters] falling
down sounded about them, and sad
visions appeared unto them with heavy
countenances. 5 No power of the fire
might give them light: neither could the
bright flames of the stars endure to
lighten that horrible night. 6 Only there
appeared unto them a fire kindled of
itself, very dreadful: for being much
terrified, they thought the things which
they saw to be worse than the sight they
saw not. 7 As for the illusions of art
magic, they were put down, and their
vaunting in wisdom was reproved with
disgrace. 8 For they, that promised to
drive away terrors and troubles from a
sick soul, were sick themselves of fear,
worthy to be laughed at. 9 For though no
terrible thing did fear them; yet being
scared with beasts that passed by, and
hissing of serpents, 10 they died for fear,
denying that they saw the air, which
could of no side be avoided. 11 For
wickedness, condemned by her own
witness, is very timorous, and being
pressed with conscience, always
forecasteth grievous things. 12 For fear
is nothing else but a betraying of the
succors which reason offereth. 13 And
the expectation from within, being less,
counteth the ignorance more than the
cause which bringeth the torment. 14 But
they sleeping the same sleep that night,
which was indeed intolerable, and
which came upon them out of the
bottoms of inevitable hell, 15 were partly
vexed with monstrous apparitions, and
partly fainted, their heart failing them:
for a sudden fear, and not looked for,
came upon them.
16 So then whosoever there fell down
was straitly kept, shut up in a prison
without iron bars. 17 For whether he
were husbandman, or shepherd, or a
laborer in the field, he was overtaken,
and endured that necessity, which could
not be avoided: for they were all bound
with one chain of darkness. 18 Whether
it were a whistling wind, or a melodious
noise of birds among the spreading
branches, or a pleasing fall of water
running violently, 19 or a terrible sound
of stones cast down, or a running that
could not be seen of skipping beasts, or

a roaring voice of most savage wild
beasts, or a rebounding echo from the
hollow mountain; these things made
them to swoon for fear. 20 For the whole
world shone with clear light, and none
were hindered in their labor: 21 over
them only was spread a heavy night, an
image of that darkness which should
afterward receive them: but yet were
they unto themselves more grievous
than the darkness.

CHAPTER 18

1 Nevertheless thy saints had a very
great light, whose voice they hearing,
and not seeing their shape, because
they also had not suffered the same
things, they counted them happy. 2 But
for that they did not hurt them now, of
whom they had been wronged before,
they thanked them, and besought them
pardon for that they had been enemies.
3 Instead whereof thou gavest them a
burning pillar of fire, both to be a
guide of the unknown journey, and an
harmless sun to entertain them
honorably. 4 For they were worthy to be
deprived of light and imprisoned in
darkness, who had kept thy sons shut
up, by whom the uncorrupt light of the
law was to be given unto the world.
5 And when they had determined to slay
the babes of the saints, one child being
cast forth, and saved, to reprove them,
thou tookest away the multitude of
their children, and destroyedst them
altogether in a mighty water. 6 Of that
night were our fathers certified afore,
that assuredly knowing unto what
oaths they had given credence, they
might afterwards be of good cheer. 7 So
of thy people was accepted both the
salvation of the righteous, and
destruction of the enemies. 8 For
wherewith thou didst punish our
adversaries, by the same thou didst
glorify us, whom thou hadst called.
9 For the righteous children of good men
did sacrifice secretly, and with one
consent made a holy law, that the saints
should be like partakers of the same
good and evil, the fathers now singing
out the songs of praise. 10 But on the other
side there sounded an ill according cry of
the enemies, and a lamentable noise
was carried abroad for children that
were bewailed. 11 The master and the
servant were punished after one
manner; and like as the king, so
suffered the common person. 12 So they
all together had innumerable dead with
one kind of death; neither were the
living sufficient to bury them: for in one
moment the noblest offspring of them
was destroyed. 13 For whereas they
would not believe any thing by reason
of the enchantments; upon the
destruction of the firstborn, they
acknowledged this people to be the
sons of God. 14 For while all things were
in quiet silence, and that night was in the
midst of her swift course, 15 thine
Almighty word leaped down from
heaven out of thy royal throne, as a
fierce man of war into the midst of a
land of destruction, 16 and brought thine
unfeigned commandment as a sharp
sword, and standing up filled all things
with death; and it touched the heaven,
but it stood upon the earth. 17 Then
suddenly visions of horrible dreams
troubled them sore, and terrors came
upon them unlooked for. 18 And one
thrown here, and another there, half
dead, showed the cause of his death.
19 For the dreams that troubled them did
foreshow this, lest they should perish,
and not know why they were afflicted.
20 Yea, the tasting of death touched the

righteous also, and there was a
destruction of the multitude in the
wilderness: but the wrath endured not
long.
21For then the blameless man made
haste, and stood forth to defend them;
and bringing the shield of his proper
ministry, even prayer, and the
propitiation of incense, set himself
against the wrath, and so brought the
calamity to an end, declaring that he
was thy servant. 22So he overcame the
destroyer, not with strength of body, nor
force of arms, but with a word subdued he
him that punished, alleging the oaths
and covenants made with the fathers.
23For when the dead were now fallen
down by heaps one upon another,
standing between, he stayed the wrath,
and parted the way to the living.
24For in the long garment was the whole
world, and in the four rows of the
stones was the glory of the fathers
graven, and thy Majesty upon the
diadem of his head.
25Unto these the destroyer gave place,
and was afraid of them: for it was
enough that they only tasted of the
wrath.

CHAPTER 19

1As for the ungodly, wrath came upon
them without mercy unto the end: for
he knew before what they would do;
2how that having given them leave to
depart, and sent them hastily away,
they would repent and pursue them.
3For whilst they were yet mourning
and making lamentation at the graves
of the dead, they added another foolish
device, and pursued them as fugitives,
whom they had intreated to be gone.
4For the destiny, whereof they were
worthy, drew them unto this end, and
made them forget the things that had
already happened, that they might fulfil
the punishment which was wanting to
their torments: 5and that thy people
might pass a wonderful way: but they
might find a strange death.
6For the whole creature in his proper
kind was fashioned again anew, serving
the peculiar commandments that were
given unto them, that thy children
might be kept without hurt: 7as namely,
a cloud shadowing the camp; and
where water stood before, dry land
appeared; and out of the Red Sea a way
without impediment; and out of the
violent stream a green field:
8wherethrough all the people went that
were defended with thy hand, seeing
thy marvelous strange wonders. 9For
they went at large like horses, and
leaped like lambs, praising thee, O
Lord, who hadst delivered them.
10For they were yet mindful of the
things that were done while they
sojourned in the strange land, how the
ground brought forth flies instead of
cattle, and how the river cast up a
multitude of frogs instead of fishes.
11But afterwards they saw a new
generation of fowls, when, being led
with their appetite, they asked
delicate meats. 12For quails came up
unto them from the sea for their
contentment.
13And punishments came upon the
sinners not without former signs by
the force of thunders: for they suffered
justly according to their own
wickedness, insomuch as they used a
more hard and hateful behavior toward
strangers. 14For the Sodomites did not
receive those, whom they knew not
when they came: but these brought
friends into bondage, that had well
deserved of them. 15And not only so,

but peradventure some respect shall be
had of those, because they used
strangers not friendly: [16]but these very
grievously afflicted them, whom they
had received with feastings, and were
already made partakers of the same
laws with them. [17]Therefore even with
blindness were these stricken, as those
were at the doors of the righteous man:
when, being compassed about with
horrible great darkness, every one
sought the passage of his own doors.
[18]For the elements were changed in
themselves by a kind of harmony, like
as in a psaltery notes change the name
of the tune, and yet are always sounds;
which may well be perceived by the
sight of the things that have been done.
[19]For earthly things were turned into
watery, and the things, that before
swam in the water, now went upon the
ground. [20]The fire had power in the
water, forgetting his own virtue: and
the water forgot his own quenching
nature. [21]On the other side, the flames
wasted not the flesh of the corruptible
living things, though they walked
therein; neither melted they the icy kind
of heavenly meat, that was of nature apt
to melt. [22]For in all things, O Lord, thou
didst magnify thy people, and glorify
them, neither didst thou lightly regard
them: but didst assist them in every time
and place.

ECCLESIASTICUS (SIRACH)

CHAPTER 1

1 All wisdom cometh from the Lord,
and is with him for ever. 2 Who can
number the sand of the sea, and the
drops of rain, and the days of eternity?
3 Who can find out the height of heaven,
and the breadth of the earth, and the
deep, and wisdom? 4 Wisdom hath been
created before all things, and the
understanding of prudence from
everlasting. 5 The word of God most
high is the fountain of wisdom; and her
ways are everlasting commandments.
6 To whom hath the root of wisdom
been revealed? or who hath known her
wise counsels? 7 [Unto whom hath the
knowledge of wisdom been made
manifest? and who hath understood her
great experience?] 8 There is one wise
and greatly to be feared, the Lord sitting
upon his throne. 9 He created her, and
saw her, and numbered her, and poured
her out upon all his works. 10 She is with
all flesh according to his gift, and he
hath given her to them that love him.

11 The fear of the Lord is honor, and
glory, and gladness, and a crown of
rejoicing. 12 The fear of the Lord maketh
a merry heart, and giveth joy, and
gladness, and a long life. 13 Whoso
feareth the Lord, it shall go well with
him at the last, and he shall find favor
in the day of his death. 14 To fear the
Lord is the beginning of wisdom: and it
was created with the faithful in the
womb. 15 She hath built an everlasting
foundation with men, and she shall
continue with their seed. 16 To fear the
Lord is fulness of wisdom, and filleth
men with her fruits. 17 She filleth all
their house with things desirable, and
the garners with her increase. 18 The
fear of the Lord is a crown of wisdom,
making peace and perfect health to
flourish; both which are the gifts of
God: and it enlargeth their rejoicing
that love him. 19 Wisdom raineth down
skill and knowledge of understanding,
and exalteth them to honor that hold her
fast. 20 The root of wisdom is to fear the
Lord, and the branches thereof are long
life. 21 The fear of the Lord driveth away
sins: and where it is present, it turneth
away wrath.

22 A furious man cannot be justified; for
the sway of his fury shall be his
destruction. 23 A patient man will bear
for a time, and afterward joy shall
spring up unto him. 24 He will hide his
words for a time, and the lips of many
shall declare his wisdom. 25 The parables
of knowledge are in the treasures of
wisdom: but godliness is an
abomination to a sinner. 26 If thou desire
wisdom, keep the commandments, and
the Lord shall give her unto thee.
27 For the fear of the Lord is wisdom and
instruction: and faith and meekness are
his delight. 28 Distrust not the fear of
the Lord when thou art poor: and come
not unto him with a double heart. 29 Be
not an hypocrite in the sight of men, and
take good heed what thou speakest.
30 Exalt not thyself, lest thou fall, and
bring dishonor upon thy soul, and so
God discover thy secrets, and cast thee
down in the midst of the congregation,
because thou camest not in truth to the
fear of the Lord, but thy heart is full of
deceit.

CHAPTER 2

1My son, if thou come to serve the Lord,
prepare thy soul for temptation. 2Set
thy heart aright, and constantly endure,
and make not haste in time of trouble.
3Cleave unto him, and depart not
away, that thou mayest be increased
at thy last end. 4Whatsoever is brought
upon thee take cheerfully, and be
patient when thou art changed to a low
estate. 5For gold is tried in the fire, and
acceptable men in the furnace of
adversity. 6Believe in him, and he will
help thee; order thy way aright, and
trust in him.

7Ye that fear the Lord, wait for his
mercy; and go not aside, lest ye fall. 8Ye
that fear the Lord, believe him; and
your reward shall not fail. 9Ye that fear
the Lord, hope for good, and for
everlasting joy and mercy. 10Look at
the generations of old, and see; did ever
any trust in the Lord, and was
confounded? or did any abide in his
fear, and was forsaken? or whom did he
ever despise, that called upon him?
11For the Lord is full of compassion and
mercy, longsuffering, and very pitiful,
and forgiveth sins, and saveth in time
of affliction. 12Woe be to fearful hearts,
and faint hands, and the sinner that goeth
two ways! 13Woe unto him that is
fainthearted! for he believeth not;
therefore shall he not be defended.
14Woe unto you that have lost patience!
and what will ye do when the Lord shall
visit you?

15They that fear the Lord will not
disobey his word; and they that love
him will keep his ways. 16They that fear
the Lord will seek that which is well-
pleasing unto him; and they that love
him shall be filled with the law. 17They
that fear the Lord will prepare their
hearts, and humble their souls in his
sight, 18saying, We will fall into the
hands of the Lord, and not into the
hands of men: for as his majesty is, so is
his mercy.

CHAPTER 3

1Hear me your father, O children, and
do thereafter, that ye may be safe. 2For
the Lord hath given the father honor
over the children, and hath confirmed
the authority of the mother over the
sons. 3Whoso honoreth his father
maketh an atonement for his sins: 4and
he that honoreth his mother is as one
that layeth up treasure. 5Whoso
honoreth his father shall have joy of his
own children; and when he maketh his
prayer, he shall be heard. 6He that
honoreth his father shall have a long
life; and he that is obedient unto the
Lord shall be a comfort to his mother.
7He that feareth the Lord will honor his
father, and will do service unto his
parents, as to his masters. 8Honor thy
father and mother both in word and
deed, that a blessing may come
upon thee from them. 9For the blessing
of the father establisheth the houses of
children; but the curse of the mother
rooteth out foundations. 10Glory not in
the dishonor of thy father; for thy
father's dishonor is no glory unto
thee. 11For the glory of a man is from
the honor of his father; and a mother in
dishonor is a reproach to the children.
12My son, help thy father in his age, and
grieve him not as long as he liveth.
13And if his understanding fail, have
patience with him; and despise him not
when thou art in thy full strength. 14For
the relieving of thy father shall not be
forgotten: and instead of sins it shall be
added to build thee up. 15In the day of

thine affliction it shall be remembered;
thy sins also shall melt away, as the ice
in the fair warm weather. 16He that
forsaketh his father is as a blasphemer;
and he that angereth his mother is
cursed of God.
17My son, go on with thy business in
meekness; so shalt thou be beloved of
him that is approved. 18The greater thou
art, the more humble thyself, and thou
shalt find favor before the Lord. 19Many
are in high place, and of renown: but
mysteries are revealed unto the meek.
20For the power of the Lord is great, and
he is honored of the lowly. 21Seek not
out things that are too hard for thee,
neither search the things that are above
thy strength. 22But what is commanded
thee, think thereupon with reverence;
for it is not needful for thee to see with
thine eyes the things that are in secret.
23Be not curious in unnecessary
matters: for more things are showed
unto thee than men understand. 24For
many are deceived by their own vain
opinion; and an evil suspicion hath
overthrown their judgment. 25Without
eyes thou shalt want light: profess not
the knowledge therefore that thou hast
not.
26A stubborn heart shall fare evil at the
last; and he that loveth danger shall
perish therein. 27An obstinate heart shall
be laden with sorrows; and the wicked
man shall heap sin upon sin. 28In the
punishment of the proud there is no
remedy; for the plant of wickedness
hath taken root in him. 29The heart of
the prudent will understand a parable;
and an attentive ear is the desire of a
wise man.
30Water will quench a flaming fire; and
alms maketh an atonement for sins.
31And he that requiteth good turns is
mindful of that which may come
hereafter; and when he falleth, he shall
find a stay.

CHAPTER 4

1My son, defraud not the poor of his
living, and make not the needy eyes to
wait long. 2Make not an hungry soul
sorrowful; neither provoke a man in his
distress. 3Add not more trouble to an
heart that is vexed; and defer not to give
to him that is in need. 4Reject not the
supplication of the afflicted; neither
turn away thy face from a poor man.
5Turn not away thine eye from the
needy, and give him none occasion to
curse thee: 6for if he curse thee in the
bitterness of his soul, his prayer shall be
heard of him that made him. 7Get
thyself the love of the congregation,
and bow thy head to a great man. 8Let
it not grieve thee to bow down thine ear
to the poor, and give him a friendly
answer with meekness. 9Deliver him
that suffereth wrong from the hand of
the oppressor; and be not fainthearted
when thou sittest in judgment. 10Be as a
father unto the fatherless, and instead
of an husband unto their mother: so
shalt thou be as the son of the most
High, and he shall love thee more than
thy mother doth.
11Wisdom exalteth her children, and
layeth hold of them that seek her. 12He
that loveth her loveth life; and they that
seek to her early shall be filled with joy.
13He that holdeth her fast shall inherit
glory; and wheresoever she entereth,
the Lord will bless. 14They that serve
her shall minister to the Holy One: and
them that love her the Lord doth love.
15Whoso giveth ear unto her shall
judge the nations: and he that
attendeth unto her shall dwell securely.
16If a man commit himself unto her, he

shall inherit her; and his generation shall
hold her in possession. 17 For at the first
she will walk with him by crooked
ways, and bring fear and dread upon
him, and torment him with her
discipline, until she may trust his soul,
and try him by her laws. 18 Then will she
return the straight way unto him, and
comfort him, and show him her secrets.
19 But if he go wrong, she will forsake
him, and give him over to his own ruin.
20 Observe the opportunity, and beware
of evil; and be not ashamed when it
concerneth thy soul. 21 For there is a
shame that bringeth sin; and there is a
shame which is glory and grace.
22 Accept no person against thy soul,
and let not the reverence of any man
cause thee to fall. 23 And refrain not to
speak, when there is occasion to do
good, and hide not thy wisdom in her
beauty. 24 For by speech wisdom shall
be known: and learning by the word of
the tongue. 25 In no wise speak against
the truth; but be abashed of the error of
thine ignorance. 26 Be not ashamed to
confess thy sins; and force not the
course of the river. 27 Make not thyself
an underling to a foolish man; neither
accept the person of the mighty.
28 Strive for the truth unto death, and the
Lord shall fight for thee. 29 Be not hasty
in thy tongue, and in thy deeds slack
and remiss. 30 Be not as a lion in thy
house, nor frantic among thy servants.
31 Let not thine hand be stretched out to
receive, and shut when thou shouldest
repay.

CHAPTER 5

1 Set not thy heart upon thy goods; and
say not, I have enough for my life.
2 Follow not thine own mind and thy
strength, to walk in the ways of thy
heart: 3 and say not, Who shall control
me for my works? for the Lord will
surely revenge thy pride. 4 Say not, I
have sinned, and what harm hath
happened unto me? for the Lord is
longsuffering, he will in no wise let
thee go. 5 Concerning propitiation, be
not without fear to add sin unto sin:
6 and say not, His mercy is great; he will
be pacified for the multitude of my
sins: for mercy and wrath come from
him, and his indignation resteth upon
sinners. 7 Make no tarrying to turn to the
Lord, and put not off from day to day: for
suddenly shall the wrath of the Lord
come forth, and in thy security thou
shalt be destroyed, and perish in the day
of vengeance.
8 Set not thine heart upon goods unjustly
gotten; for they shall not profit thee in
the day of calamity. 9 Winnow not with
every wind, and go not into every way: for
so doth the sinner that hath a double
tongue. 10 Be steadfast in thy
understanding; and let thy word be the
same. 11 Be swift to hear; and let thy life
be sincere; and with patience give
answer. 12 If thou hast understanding,
answer thy neighbor; if not, lay thy
hand upon thy mouth. 13 Honor and
shame is in talk: and the tongue of man
is his fall. 14 Be not called a whisperer,
and lie not in wait with thy tongue: for
a foul shame is upon the thief, and an
evil condemnation upon the double
tongue. 15 Be not ignorant of any thing
in a great matter or a small.

CHAPTER 6

1 Instead of a friend become not an
enemy; for [thereby] thou shalt inherit
an ill name, shame, and reproach: even
so shall a sinner that hath a double
tongue.

2 Extol not thyself in the counsel of
thine own heart; that thy soul be not
torn in pieces as a bull [straying alone.]
3 Thou shalt eat up thy leaves, and lose
thy fruit, and leave thyself as a dry tree.
4 A wicked soul shall destroy him that
hath it, and shall make him to be
laughed to scorn of his enemies.

5 Sweet language will multiply friends:
and a fairspeaking tongue will increase
kind greetings. 6 Be in peace with many:
nevertheless have but one counselor
of a thousand. 7 If thou wouldest get a
friend, prove him first, and be not
hasty to credit him. 8 For some man is a
friend for his own occasion, and will
not abide in the day of thy trouble. 9 And
there is a friend, who being turned to
enmity and strife will discover thy
reproach. 10 Again, some friend is a
companion at the table, and will not
continue in the day of thy affliction.
11 But in thy prosperity he will be as
thyself, and will be bold over thy
servants. 12 If thou be brought low, he
will be against thee, and will hide himself
from thy face. 13 Separate thyself from
thine enemies, and take heed of thy
friends. 14 A faithful friend is a strong
defense: and he that hath found such an
one hath found a treasure. 15 Nothing
doth countervail a faithful friend,
and his excellency is invaluable. 16 A
faithful friend is the medicine of life;
and they that fear the Lord shall find
him. 17 Whoso feareth the Lord shall
direct his friendship aright: for as he is,
so shall his neighbor be also.

18 My son, gather instruction from thy
youth up: so shalt thou find wisdom till
thine old age. 19 Come unto her as one
that ploweth and soweth, and wait for
her good fruits: for thou shalt not toil
much in laboring about her, but thou
shalt eat of her fruits right soon.
20 She is very unpleasant to the
unlearned: he that is without
understanding will not remain with her.
21 She will lie upon him as a mighty
stone of trial; and he will cast her from
him ere it be long. 22 For wisdom is
according to her name, and she is not
manifest unto many. 23 Give ear, my
son, receive my advice, and refuse not
my counsel, 24 and put thy feet into her
fetters, and thy neck into her chain.
25 Bow down thy shoulder, and bear her,
and be not grieved with her bonds.
26 Come unto her with thy whole heart,
and keep her ways with all thy power.
27 Search, and seek, and she shall be
made known unto thee: and when thou
hast got hold of her, let her not go. 28 For
at the last thou shalt find her rest, and
that shall be turned to thy joy. 29 Then
shall her fetters be a strong defense for
thee, and her chains a robe of glory.
30 For there is a golden ornament upon
her, and her bands are purple lace.
31 Thou shalt put her on as a robe of
honor, and shalt put her about thee as a
crown of joy. 32 My son, if thou wilt,
thou shalt be taught: and if thou wilt
apply thy mind, thou shalt be prudent.
33 If thou love to hear, thou shalt receive
understanding: and if thou bow thine
ear, thou shalt be wise. 34 Stand in the
multitude of the elders; and cleave unto
him that is wise. 35 Be willing to hear
every godly discourse; and let not the
parables of understanding escape thee.
36 And if thou seest a man of
understanding, get thee betimes unto
him, and let thy foot wear the steps of his
door. 37 Let thy mind be upon the
ordinances of the Lord, and meditate
continually in his commandments: he
shall establish thine heart, and give thee
wisdom at thine own desire.

CHAPTER 7

[1]Do no evil, so shall no harm come unto
thee. [2]Depart from the unjust, and
iniquity shall turn away from thee. [3]My
son, sow not upon the furrows of
unrighteousness, and thou shalt not
reap them sevenfold.
[4]Seek not of the Lord pre-eminence,
neither of the king the seat of
honor. [5]Justify not thyself before the
Lord; and boast not of thy wisdom
before the king. [6]Seek not to be judge,
being not able to take away iniquity;
lest at any time thou fear the person of
the mighty, and lay a stumbling-block
in the way of thy uprightness. [7]Offend
not against the multitude of a city, and
then thou shalt not cast thyself down
among the people. [8]Bind not one sin
upon another; for in one thou shalt not
be unpunished. [9]Say not, God will look
upon the multitude of my oblations,
and when I offer to the most high God,
he will accept it. [10]Be not fainthearted
when thou makest thy prayer, and
neglect not to give alms.
[11]Laugh no man to scorn in the
bitterness of his soul: for there is one
which humbleth and exalteth.
[12]Devise not a lie against thy brother;
neither do the like to thy friend. [13]Use
not to make any manner of lie: for the
custom thereof is not good. [14]Use not
many words in a multitude of elders,
and make not much babbling when
thou prayest.
[15]Hate not laborious work, neither
husbandry, which the most High hath
ordained. [16]Number not thyself among
the multitude of sinners, but remember
that wrath will not tarry long. [17]Humble
thy soul greatly: for the vengeance of
the ungodly is fire and worms.
[18]Change not a friend for any good by
no means; neither a faithful brother for
the gold of Ophir. [19]Forego not a wise
and good woman: for her grace is above
gold. [20]Whereas thy servant worketh
truly, treat him not evil, nor the hireling
that bestoweth himself wholly for thee.
[21]Let thy soul love a good servant, and
defraud him not of liberty.
[22]Hast thou cattle? have an eye to them:
and if they be for thy profit, keep them
with thee. [23]Hast thou children? instruct
them, and bow down their neck from
their youth. [24]Hast thou daughters?
have a care of their body, and show not
thyself cheerful toward them. [25]Marry
thy daughter, and so shalt thou have
performed a weighty matter: but give
her to a man of understanding.
[26]Hast thou a wife after thy mind?
forsake her not: but give not thyself
over to a light woman. [27]Honor thy
father with thy whole heart, and forget
not the sorrows of thy mother.
[28]Remember that thou wast begotten of
them; and how canst thou recompense
them the things that they have done for
thee?
[29]Fear the Lord with all thy soul, and
reverence his priests. [30]Love him that
made thee with all thy strength, and
forsake not his ministers. [31]Fear the
Lord, and honor the priest; and give
him his portion, as it is commanded
thee; the firstfruits, and the trespass
offering, and the gift of the shoulders,
and the sacrifice of sanctification, and
the firstfruits of the holy things.
[32]And stretch thine hand unto the poor,
that thy blessing may be perfected. [33]A
gift hath grace in the sight of every man
living; and for the dead detain it not.
[34]Fail not to be with them that weep, and
mourn with them that mourn. [35]Be not
slow to visit the sick: for that shall
make thee to be beloved. [36]Whatsoever
thou takest in hand, remember the end,

and thou shalt never do amiss.

CHAPTER 8

1 Strive not with a mighty man, lest thou
fall into his hands. 2 Be not at variance
with a rich man, lest he overweigh thee:
for gold hath destroyed many, and
perverted the hearts of kings. 3 Strive not
with a man that is full of tongue, and
heap not wood upon his fire. 4 Jest not
with a rude man, lest thy ancestors be
disgraced.
5 Reproach not a man that turneth from
sin, but remember that we are all
worthy of punishment. 6 Dishonor not a
man in his old age: for even some of us
wax old. 7 Rejoice not over thy greatest
enemy being dead, but remember that
we die all. 8 Despise not the discourse of
the wise, but acquaint thyself with their
proverbs: for of them thou shalt learn
instruction, and how to serve great men
with ease. 9 Miss not the discourse of the
elders: for they also learned of their
fathers, and of them thou shalt learn
understanding, and to give answer as
need requireth.
10 Kindle not the coals of a sinner, lest
thou be burnt with the flame of his fire.
11 Rise not up [in anger] at the presence
of an injurious person, lest he lie in wait
to entrap thee in thy words. 12 Lend not
unto him that is mightier than thyself;
for if thou lendest him, count it but lost.
13 Be not surety above thy power: for if
thou be surety, take care to pay it. 14 Go
not to law with a judge; for they will
judge for him according to his honor.
15 Travel not by the way with a bold
fellow, lest he become grievous unto
thee: for he will do according to his own
will, and thou shalt perish with him
through his folly. 16 Strive not with an
angry man, and go not with him into a
solitary place: for blood is as nothing in
his sight, and where there is no help, he
will overthrow thee. 17 Consult not with
a fool; for he cannot keep counsel. 18 Do
no secret thing before a stranger; for
thou knowest not what he will bring
forth. 19 Open not thine heart to every
man, lest he requite thee with a shrewd
turn.

CHAPTER 9

1 Be not jealous over the wife of thy
bosom, and teach her not an evil lesson
against thyself. 2 Give not thy soul unto
a woman to set her foot upon thy
substance. 3 Meet not with an harlot, lest
thou fall into her snares. 4 Use not
much the company of a woman that is
a singer, lest thou be taken with her
attempts. 5 Gaze not on a maid, that thou
fall not by those things that are precious
in her. 6 Give not thy soul unto harlots,
that thou lose not thine inheritance.
7 Look not round about thee in the
streets of the city, neither wander thou
in the solitary places thereof. 8 Turn
away thine eye from a beautiful
woman, and look not upon another's
beauty; for many have been deceived
by the beauty of a woman; for herewith
love is kindled as a fire. 9 Sit not at all
with another man's wife, nor sit down
with her in thine arms, and spend not
thy money with her at the wine; lest
thine heart incline unto her, and so
through thy desire thou fall into
destruction.
10 Forsake not an old friend; for the new
is not comparable to him: a new friend
is as new wine; when it is old, thou shalt
drink it with pleasure. 11 Envy not the
glory of a sinner: for thou knowest not
what shall be his end. 12 Delight not in
the thing that the ungodly have pleasure

in; but remember they shall not go
unpunished unto their grave. 13Keep
thee far from the man that hath power
to kill; so shalt thou not doubt the fear
of death: and if thou come unto him,
make no fault, lest he take away thy life
presently: remember that thou goest in
the midst of snares, and that thou
walkest upon the battlements of the
city. 14As near as thou canst, try to
understand thy neighbor, and consult
with the wise. 15Let thy talk be with the
wise, and all thy communication in the
law of the most High. 16And let just
men eat and drink with thee; and let thy
glorying be in the fear of the Lord.
17For the hand of the artificer the work
shall be commended: and the wise ruler
of the people for his speech. 18A man of
an ill tongue is dangerous in his city;
and he that is rash in his talk shall be
hated.

CHAPTER 10

1A wise judge will instruct his people;
and the government of a prudent man is
well ordered. 2As the judge of the
people is himself, so are his officers;
and what manner of man the ruler of the
city is, such are all they that dwell
therein. 3An unwise king destroyeth his
people; but through the prudence of them
which are in authority the city shall be
inhabited. 4The power of the earth is in
the hand of the Lord, and in due time he
will set over it one that is profitable. 5In
the hand of God is the prosperity of
man: and upon the person of the scribe
shall he lay his honor.

6Bear not hatred to thy neighbor for
every wrong; and do nothing at all by
injurious practices. 7Pride is hateful
before God and man: and by both doth
one commit iniquity. 8Because of
unrighteous dealings, injuries, and
riches got by deceit, the kingdom is
translated from one people to another.
9Why is earth and ashes proud? There
is not a more wicked thing than a
covetous man: for such an one setteth
his own soul to sale; because while he
liveth he casteth away his bowels.
10The physician cutteth off a long
disease; and he that is today a king
tomorrow shall die. 11For when a man
is dead, he shall inherit creeping things,
beasts, and worms. 12The beginning of
pride is when one departeth from God,
and his heart is turned away from his
Maker. 13For pride is the beginning of
sin, and he that hath it shall pour out
abomination: and therefore the Lord
brought upon them strange calamities,
and overthrew them utterly. 14The Lord
hath cast down the thrones of proud
princes, and set up the meek in their
stead. 15The Lord hath plucked up the
roots of the proud nations, and planted
the lowly in their place. 16The Lord
overthrew countries of the heathen, and
destroyed them to the foundations of
the earth. 17He took some of them
away, and destroyed them, and hath
made their memorial to cease from the
earth. 18Pride was not made for men,
nor furious anger for them that are born
of a woman.

19They that fear the Lord are a sure
seed, and they that love him an
honorable plant: they that regard not
the law are a dishonorable seed; they
that transgress the commandments are
a deceivable seed. 20Among brethren he
that is chief is honorable; so are they that
fear the Lord in his eyes. 21The fear of the
Lord goeth before the obtaining of
authority: but roughness and pride is
the losing thereof. 22Whether he be rich,
noble, or poor, their glory is the fear of

the Lord. 23 It is not meet to despise the
poor man that hath understanding;
neither is it convenient to magnify a
sinful man. 24 Great men, and judges,
and potentates, shall be honored; yet is
there none of them greater than he that
feareth the Lord. 25 Unto the servant that
is wise shall they that are free do
service: and he that hath knowledge
will not grudge when he is reformed.
26 Be not overwise in doing thy
business; and boast not thyself in the
time of thy distress. 27 Better is he that
laboreth, and aboundeth in all things,
than he that boasteth himself, and
wanteth bread. 28 My son, glorify thy
soul in meekness, and give it honor
according to the dignity thereof. 29 Who
will justify him that sinneth against his
own soul? and who will honor him that
dishonoreth his own life? 30 The poor
man is honored for his skill, and the
rich man is honored for his riches. 31 He
that is honored in poverty, how much
more in riches? and he that is
dishonorable in riches, how much
more in poverty?

CHAPTER 11

1 Wisdom lifteth up the head of him that
is of low degree, and maketh him to sit
among great men. 2 Commend not a
man for his beauty; neither abhor a man
for his outward appearance. 3 The bee is
little among such as fly; but her fruit is the
chief of sweet things. 4 Boast not of thy
clothing and raiment, and exalt not
thyself in the day of honor: for the
works of the Lord are wonderful, and
his works among men are hidden.
5 Many kings have sat down upon the
ground; and one that was never thought
of hath worn the crown. 6 Many mighty
men have been greatly disgraced; and
the honorable delivered into other
men's hands. 7 Blame not before thou
hast examined the truth: understand
first, and then rebuke. 8 Answer not
before thou hast heard the cause:
neither interrupt men in the midst of
their talk. 9 Strive not in a matter that
concerneth thee not; and sit not in
judgment with sinners. 10 My son,
meddle not with many matters: for if
thou meddle much, thou shalt not be
innocent; and if thou follow after, thou
shalt not obtain, neither shalt thou
escape by fleeing. 11 There is one that
laboreth, and taketh pains, and maketh
haste, and is so much the more behind.
12 Again, there is another that is slow,
and hath need of help, wanting ability,
and full of poverty; yet the eye of the
Lord looked upon him for good, and
set him up from his low estate, 13 and
lifted up his head from misery; so that
many that saw it marveled at him.
14 Prosperity and adversity, life and
death, poverty and riches, come of
the Lord. 15 Wisdom, knowledge, and
understanding of the law, are of the
Lord: love, and the way of good works,
are from him. 16 Error and darkness had
their beginning together with sinners:
and evil shall wax old with them that
glory therein. 17 The gift of the Lord
remaineth with the godly, and his favor
bringeth prosperity for ever. 18 There is
that waxeth rich by his wariness and
pinching, and this is the portion of his
reward: 19 whereas he saith, I have
found rest, and now will eat continually
of my goods; and yet he knoweth not
what time shall come upon him, and
that he must leave those things to
others, and die. 20 Be steadfast in thy
covenant, and be conversant therein,
and wax old in thy work. 21 Marvel not
at the works of sinners; but trust in the

Lord, and abide in thy labor: for it is an
easy thing in the sight of the Lord on
the sudden to make a poor man rich.
22 The blessing of the Lord is in the
reward of the godly, and suddenly he
maketh his blessing flourish. 23 Say not,
What profit is there of my service? and
what good things shall I have hereafter?
24 Again, say not, I have enough, and
possess many things, and what evil can
come to me hereafter? 25 In the day of
prosperity there is a forgetfulness of
affliction: and in the day of affliction
there is no more remembrance of
prosperity. 26 For it is an easy thing unto
the Lord in the day of death to reward a
man according to his ways. 27 The
affliction of an hour maketh a man
forget pleasure: and in his end his deeds
shall be discovered. 28 Judge none
blessed before his death: for a man shall
be known in his children.
29 Bring not every man into thine house:
for the deceitful man hath many trains.
30 Like as a partridge taken [and kept] in
a cage, so is the heart of the proud; and
like as a spy, watcheth he for thy fall:
31 for he lieth in wait, and turneth good
into evil, and in things worthy praise
will lay blame upon thee. 32 Of a spark
of fire a heap of coals is kindled: and a
sinful man layeth wait for blood. 33 Take
heed of a mischievous man, for he
worketh wickedness; lest he bring upon
thee a perpetual blot. 34 Receive a
stranger into thine house, and he will
disturb thee, and turn thee out of thine
own.

CHAPTER 12

1 When thou wilt do good, know to
whom thou doest it; so shalt thou be
thanked for thy benefits. 2 Do good to
the godly man, and thou shalt find a
recompense; and if not from him, yet
from the most High. 3 There can no good
come to him that is always occupied in
evil, nor to him that giveth no alms.
4 Give to the godly man, and help not a
sinner. 5 Do well unto him that is lowly,
but give not to the ungodly: hold back
thy bread, and give it not unto him, lest
he overmaster thee thereby: for [else]
thou shalt receive twice as much evil
for all the good thou shalt have done
unto him. 6 For the most High hateth
sinners, and will repay vengeance unto
the ungodly, and keepeth them against
the mighty day of their punishment.
7 Give unto the good, and help not the
sinner.
8 A friend cannot be known in
prosperity: and an enemy cannot be
hidden in adversity. 9 In the prosperity
of a man enemies will be grieved: but
in his adversity even a friend will depart.
10 Never trust thine enemy: for like as
iron rusteth, so is his wickedness.
11 Though he humble himself, and go
crouching, yet take good heed and
beware of him, and thou shalt be unto
him as if thou hadst wiped a looking-
glass, and thou shalt know that his rust
hath not been altogether wiped away.
12 Set him not by thee, lest, when he
hath overthrown thee, he stand up in
thy place; neither let him sit at thy right
hand, lest he seek to take thy seat, and
thou at the last remember my words,
and be pricked therewith. 13 Who will
pity a charmer that is bitten with a
serpent, or any such as come nigh wild
beasts? 14 So one that goeth to a sinner,
and is defiled with him in his sins, who
will pity? 15 For a while he will abide
with thee, but if thou begin to fall, he
will not tarry. 16 An enemy speaketh
sweetly with his lips, but in his heart he
imagineth how to throw thee into a pit:

he will weep with his eyes, but if he find
opportunity, he will not be satisfied
with blood. 17If adversity come upon
thee, thou shalt find him there first; and
though he pretend to help thee, yet shall
he undermine thee. 18He will shake his
head, and clap his hands, and whisper
much, and change his countenance.

CHAPTER 13

1He that toucheth pitch shall be defiled
therewith; and he that hath
fellowship with a proud man shall be
like unto him. 2Burden not thyself
above thy power while thou livest; and
have no fellowship with one that is
mightier and richer than thyself: for
how agree the kettle and the earthen
pot together? for if the one be smitten
against the other, it shall be broken.
3The rich man hath done wrong, and yet
he threateneth withal: the poor is
wronged, and he must intreat also. 4If
thou be for his profit, he will use thee:
but if thou have nothing, he will forsake
thee. 5If thou have any thing, he will
live with thee: yea, he will make thee
bare, and will not be sorry for it. 6If he
have need of thee, he will deceive thee,
and smile upon thee, and put thee in
hope; he will speak thee fair, and say,
What wantest thou? 7And he will
shame thee by his meats, until he have
drawn thee dry twice or thrice, and at
the last he will laugh thee to scorn:
afterward, when he seeth thee, he will
forsake thee, and shake his head at thee.
8Beware that thou be not deceived, and
brought down in thy jollity. 9If thou be
invited of a mighty man, withdraw
thyself, and so much the more will he
invite thee. 10Press thou not upon him,
lest thou be put back; stand not far off,
lest thou be forgotten. 11Affect not to be
made equal unto him in talk, and believe
not his many words: for with much
communication will he tempt thee, and
smiling upon thee will get out thy
secrets: 12but cruelly he will lay up thy
words, and will not spare to do thee
hurt, and to put thee in prison.
13Observe, and take good heed, for thou
walkest in peril of thy overthrowing:
when thou hearest these things, awake
in thy sleep. 14Love the Lord all thy life,
and call upon him for thy salvation.
15Every beast loveth his like, and every
man loveth his neighbor. 16All flesh
consorteth according to kind, and a
man will cleave to his like. 17What
fellowship hath the wolf with the lamb?
so the sinner with the godly. 18What
agreement is there between the hyena
and a dog? and what peace between the
rich and the poor? 19As the wild ass is
the lion's prey in the wilderness: so the
rich eat up the poor. 20As the proud hate
humility: so doth the rich abhor the
poor. 21A rich man beginning to fall is
held up of his friends: but a poor man
being down is thrust away by his
friends.
22When a rich man is fallen, he hath
many helpers: he speaketh things not to
be spoken, and yet men justify him: the
poor man slipped, and yet they rebuked
him too; he spake wisely, and could
have no place. 23When a rich man
speaketh, every man holdeth his
tongue, and, look, what he saith, they
extol it to the clouds: but if the poor
man speak, they say, What fellow is
this? and if he stumble, they will help
to overthrow him.
24Riches are good unto him that hath no
sin, and poverty is evil in the mouth of
the ungodly. 25The heart of a man
changeth his countenance, whether it be
for good or evil: and a merry heart

maketh a cheerful countenance.
26 A cheerful countenance is a token of
a heart that is in prosperity; and the
finding out of parables is a wearisome
labor of the mind.

CHAPTER 14

1 Blessed is the man that hath not slipped
with his mouth, and is not pricked with
the multitude of sins. 2 Blessed is he
whose conscience hath not condemned
him, and who is not fallen from his
hope in the Lord.
3 Riches are not comely for a niggard:
and what should an envious man do
with money? 4 He that gathereth by
defrauding his own soul gathereth for
others, that shall spend his goods
riotously. 5 He that is evil to himself, to
whom will he be good? he shall not
take pleasure in his goods. 6 There is
none worse than he that envieth
himself; and this is a recompense of his
wickedness. 7 And if he doeth good, he
doeth it unwillingly; and at the last he
will declare his wickedness. 8 The
envious man hath a wicked eye; he
turneth away his face, and despiseth
men. 9 A covetous man's eye is not
satisfied with his portion; and the
iniquity of the wicked drieth up his
soul. 10 A wicked eye envieth [his]
bread, and he is a niggard at his table.
11 My son, according to thy ability do
good to thyself, and give the Lord his
due offering. 12 Remember that death
will not be long in coming, and that the
covenant of the grave is not showed
unto thee. 13 Do good unto thy friend
before thou die, and according to thy
ability stretch out thy hand and give to
him. 14 Defraud not thyself of the good
day, and let not the part of a good desire
overpass thee. 15 Shalt thou not leave thy
travails unto another? and thy labors
to be divided by lot? 16 Give, and take,
and sanctify thy soul; for there is no
seeking of dainties in the grave. 17 All
flesh waxeth old as a garment: for the
covenant from the beginning is, Thou
shalt die the death. 18 As of the green
leaves on a thick tree, some fall, and
some grow; so is the generation of flesh
and blood, one cometh to an end, and
another is born. 19 Every work rotteth
and consumeth away, and the worker
thereof shall go withal.
20 Blessed is the man that doth meditate
good things in wisdom, and that
reasoneth of holy things by his
understanding. 21 He that considereth
her ways in his heart shall also have
understanding in her secrets. 22 Go after
her as one that traceth, and lie in wait in
her ways. 23 He that prieth in at her
windows shall also hearken at her
doors. 24 He that doth lodge near her
house shall also fasten a pin in her
walls. 25 He shall pitch his tent nigh unto
her, and shall lodge in a lodging where
good things are. 26 He shall set his
children under her shelter, and shall
lodge under her branches. 27 By her he
shall be covered from heat, and in her
glory shall he dwell.

CHAPTER 15

1 He that feareth the Lord will do good,
and he that hath the knowledge of the
law shall obtain her. 2 And as a mother
shall she meet him, and receive him
as a wife married of a virgin. 3 With the
bread of understanding shall she feed
him, and give him the water of wisdom
to drink. 4 He shall be stayed upon her,
and shall not be moved; and shall rely
upon her, and shall not be
confounded. 5 She shall exalt him above

his neighbors, and in the midst of the
congregation shall she open his mouth.
6He shall find joy and a crown of
gladness, and she shall cause him to
inherit an everlasting name. 7But
foolish men shall not attain unto her,
and sinners shall not see her. 8For she is
far from pride, and men that are liars
cannot remember her.

9Praise is not seemly in the mouth
of a sinner, for it was not sent him of
the Lord. 10For praise shall be uttered in
wisdom, and the Lord will prosper it.

11Say not thou, It is through the Lord
that I fell away: for thou oughtest not to
do the things that he hateth. 12Say not
thou, He hath caused me to err: for
he hath no need of the sinful man.
13The Lord hateth all abomination: and
they that fear God love it not. 14He
himself made man from the beginning,
and left him in the hand of his counsel;
15if thou wilt, to keep the
commandments, and to perform
acceptable faithfulness. 16He hath set
fire and water before thee: stretch forth
thy hand unto whether thou wilt.
17Before man is life and death; and
whether him liketh shall be given him.
18For the wisdom of the Lord is great,
and he is mighty in power, and
beholdeth all things: 19and his eyes are
upon them that fear him, and he
knoweth every work of man.

20He hath commanded no man to do
wickedly, neither hath he given any
man license to sin.

CHAPTER 16

1Desire not a multitude of unprofitable
children, neither delight in ungodly
sons. 2Though they multiply, rejoice
not in them, except the fear of the Lord
be with them. 3Trust not thou in their
life, neither respect their multitude: for
one that is just is better than a thousand;
and better it is to die without children,
than to have them that are ungodly. 4For
by one that hath understanding shall the
city be replenished: but the kindred of
the wicked shall speedily become
desolate. 5Many such things have I seen
with mine eyes, and mine ear hath
heard greater things than these.

6In the congregation of the ungodly shall
a fire be kindled; and in a rebellious
nation wrath is set on fire. 7He was not
pacified toward the old giants, who fell
away in the strength of their
foolishness. 8Neither spared he the
place where Lot sojourned, but
abhorred them for their pride. 9He
pitied not the people of perdition, who
were taken away in their sins: 10nor the
six hundred thousand footmen, who
were gathered together in the hardness
of their hearts. 11And if there be one
stiffnecked among the people, it is
marvel if he escape unpunished: for
mercy and wrath are with him; he is
mighty to forgive, and to pour out
displeasure. 12As his mercy is great, so
is his correction also: he judgeth a man
according to his works 13The sinner
shall not escape with his spoils: and
the patience of the godly shall not be
frustrate. 14Make way for every work of
mercy: for every man shall find
according to his works. 15The Lord
hardened Pharaoh, that he should not
know him, that his powerful works
might be known to the world. 16His
mercy is manifest to every creature;
and he hath separated his light from the
darkness with an adamant. 17Say not
thou, I will hide myself from the Lord:
shall any remember me from above? I
shall not be remembered among so
many people: for what is my soul

among such an infinite number of
creatures? [18]Behold, the heaven, and the
heaven of heavens, the deep, and the
earth, and all that therein is, shall be
moved when he shall visit. [19]The
mountains also and foundations of the
earth be shaken with trembling, when
the Lord looketh upon them. [20]No heart
can think upon these things worthily:
and who is able to conceive his ways?
[21]It is a tempest which no man can see:
for the most part of his works are hid.
[22]Who can declare the works of his
justice? or who can endure them? for
his covenant is afar off, and the trial of
all things is in the end. [23]He that
wanteth understanding will think upon
vain things: and a foolish man erring
imagineth follies.

[24]My son, hearken unto me, and learn
knowledge, and mark my words with
thy heart. [25]I will show forth doctrine in
weight, and declare his knowledge
exactly. [26]The works of the Lord are
done in judgment from the beginning:
and from the time he made them he
disposed the parts thereof. [27]He
garnished his works for ever, and in his
hand are the chief of them unto all
generations: they neither labor, nor are
weary, nor cease from their works.
[28]None of them hindereth another, and
they shall never disobey his word.
[29]After this the Lord looked upon the
earth, and filled it with his blessings.
[30]With all manner of living things hath
he covered the face thereof; and they
shall return into it again.

CHAPTER 17

[1]The Lord created man of the earth, and
turned him into it again. [2]He gave them
few days, and a short time, and power
also over the things therein. [3]He endued
them with strength by themselves, and
made them according to his image, [4]and
put the fear of man upon all flesh, and
gave him dominion over beasts and
fowls. [5][They received the use of the
five operations of the Lord, and in the
sixth place he imparted them
understanding, and in the seventh
speech, an interpreter of the cogitations
thereof.] [6]Counsel, and a tongue, and
eyes, ears, and a heart, gave he them to
understand. [7]Withal he filled them with
the knowledge of understanding, and
showed them good and evil. [8]He set his
eye upon their hearts, that he might
show them the greatness of his works.
[9]He gave them to glory in his
marvelous acts for ever, that they might
declare his works with understanding.
[10]And the elect shall praise his holy
name. [11]Beside this he gave them
knowledge, and the law of life for an
heritage. [12]He made an everlasting
covenant with them, and showed them
his judgments. [13]Their eyes saw the
majesty of his glory, and their ears
heard his glorious voice. [14]And he said
unto them, Beware of all
unrighteousness; and he gave every
man commandment concerning his
neighbor.

[15]Their ways are ever before him, and
shall not be hid from his eyes.
[16]Every man from his youth is given to
evil; neither could they make to
themselves fleshy hearts for stony.
[17]For in the division of the nations of
the whole earth he set a ruler over
every people; but Israel is the Lord's
portion: [18]whom, being his firstborn, he
nourisheth with discipline, and giving
him the light of his love doth not forsake
him. [19]Therefore all their works are as the
sun before him, and his eyes are
continually upon their ways. [20]None of

their unrighteous deeds are hid from
him, but all their sins are before the
Lord. 21 But the Lord being gracious
and knowing his workmanship, neither
left nor forsook them, but spared them.
22 The alms of a man is as a signet with
him, and he will keep the good deeds of
man as the apple of the eye, and give
repentance to his sons and daughters.
23 Afterwards he will rise up and reward
them, and render their recompense
upon their heads. 24 But unto them that
repent, he granted them return, and
comforted those that failed in patience.
25 Return unto the Lord, and forsake thy
sins, make thy prayer before his face,
and offend less. 26 Turn again to the
most High, and turn away from
iniquity: for he will lead thee out of
darkness into the light of health, and
hate thou abomination vehemently.
27 Who shall praise the most High in the
grave, instead of them which live and
give thanks? 28 Thanksgiving perisheth
from the dead, as from one that is not:
the living and sound in heart shall
praise the Lord. 29 How great is the
loving-kindness of the Lord our God,
and his compassion unto such as turn
unto him in holiness! 30 For all things
cannot be in men, because the son of
man is not immortal. 31 What is brighter
than the sun? yet the light thereof
faileth: and flesh and blood will
imagine evil. 32 He vieweth the power
of the height of heaven; and all men are
but earth and ashes.

CHAPTER 18

1 He that liveth for ever created all things
in general. 2 The Lord only is righteous,
and there is none other but he, 3 who
governeth the world with the palm of
his hand, and all things obey his will: for
he is the King of all, by his power dividing
holy things among them from profane.
4 To whom hath he given power to
declare his works? and who shall find
out his noble acts? 5 Who shall number
the strength of his majesty? and who
shall also tell out his mercies? 6 As for
the wondrous works of the Lord, there
may nothing be taken from them,
neither may any thing be put unto them,
neither can the ground of them be found
out. 7 When a man hath done, then he
beginneth; and when he leaveth off,
then he shall be doubtful.

8 What is man, and whereto serveth he?
what is his good, and what is his evil?
9 The number of a man's days at the most
are an hundred years. 10 As a drop of
water unto the sea, and a gravelstone in
comparison of the sand; so are a
thousand years to the days of eternity.
11 Therefore is God patient with them,
and poureth forth his mercy upon them.
12 He saw and perceived their end to be
evil; therefore he multiplied his
compassion. 13 The mercy of man is
toward his neighbor; but the mercy of
the Lord is upon all flesh: he reproveth,
and nurtureth, and teacheth, and
bringeth again, as a shepherd his flock.
14 He hath mercy on them that receive
discipline, and that diligently seek after
his judgments.

15 My son, blemish not thy good deeds,
neither use uncomfortable words when
thou givest any thing. 16 Shall not the
dew assuage the heat? so is a word
better than a gift. 17 Lo, is not a word
better than a gift? but both are with a
gracious man. 18 A fool will upbraid
churlishly, and a gift of the envious
consumeth the eyes.

19 Learn before thou speak, and use
physic or ever thou be sick. 20 Before
judgment examine thyself, and in the

day of visitation thou shalt find mercy.
21 Humble thyself before thou be sick,
and in the time of sins show repentance.
22 Let nothing hinder thee to pay thy
vow in due time, and defer not until
death to be justified. 23 Before thou
prayest, prepare thyself; and be not as
one that tempteth the Lord. 24 Think
upon the wrath that shall be at the end,
and the time of vengeance, when he
shall turn away his face. 25 When thou
hast enough, remember the time of
hunger: and when thou art rich, think
upon poverty and need. 26 From the
morning until the evening the time is
changed, and all things are soon done
before the Lord. 27 A wise man will fear
in every thing, and in the day of sinning
he will beware of offense: but a fool
will not observe time. 28 Every man of
understanding knoweth wisdom, and
will give praise unto him that found
her. 29 They that were of understanding
in sayings became also wise
themselves, and poured forth exquisite
parables.
30 Go not after thy lusts, but refrain
thyself from thine appetites. 31 If thou
givest thy soul the desires that please
her, she will make thee a laughingstock
to thine enemies that malign thee.
32 Take not pleasure in much good
cheer, neither be tied to the expense
thereof. 33 Be not made a beggar by
banqueting upon borrowing, when thou
hast nothing in thy purse: for thou shalt
lie in wait for thine own life, and be
talked on.

CHAPTER 19

1 A laboring man that is given to
drunkenness shall not be rich: and he
that contemneth small things shall fall by
little and little. 2 Wine and women will
make men of understanding to fall
away: and he that cleaveth to harlots
will become impudent. 3 Moths and
worms shall have him to heritage, and
a bold man shall be taken away.
4 He that is hasty to give credit is
lightminded; and he that sinneth shall
offend against his own soul. 5 Whoso
taketh pleasure in wickedness shall
be condemned: but he that resisteth
pleasures crowneth his life. 6 He that
can rule his tongue shall live without
strife; and he that hateth babbling shall
have less evil. 7 Rehearse not unto
another that which is told unto thee, and
thou shalt fare never the worse.
8 Whether it be to friend or foe, talk not
of other men's lives; and if thou canst
without offense, reveal them not. 9 For
he heard and observed thee, and when
time cometh he will hate thee. 10 If thou
hast heard a word, let it die with thee;
and be bold, it will not burst thee. 11 A
fool travaileth with a word, as a woman
in labor of a child. 12 As an arrow that
sticketh in a man's thigh, so is a word
within a fool's belly.
13 Admonish a friend, it may be he hath
not done it: and if he have done it, that
he do it no more. 14 Admonish thy
friend, it may be he hath not said it: and
if he have, that he speak it not again.
15 Admonish a friend: for many times it
is a slander, and believe not every tale.
16 There is one that slippeth in his
speech, but not from his heart; and who
is he that hath not offended with his
tongue? 17 Admonish thy neighbor
before thou threaten him; and not being
angry, give place to the law of the most
High. 18 The fear of the Lord is the first
step to be accepted [of him,] and
wisdom obtaineth his love. 19 The
knowledge of the commandments of
the Lord is the doctrine of life: and they

that do things that please him shall receive the fruit of the tree of immortality.

20 The fear of the Lord is all wisdom; and in all wisdom is the performance of the law, and the knowledge of his omnipotency. 21 If a servant say to his master, I will not do as it pleaseth thee; though afterward he do it, he angereth him that nourisheth him. 22 The knowledge of wickedness is not wisdom, neither at any time the counsel of sinners prudence. 23 There is a wickedness, and the same an abomination; and there is a fool wanting in wisdom. 24 He that hath small understanding, and feareth God, is better than one that hath much wisdom, and transgresseth the law of the most High. 25 There is an exquisite subtlety, and the same is unjust; and there is one that turneth aside to make judgment appear; and there is a wise man that justifieth in judgment. 26 There is a wicked man that hangeth down his head sadly; but inwardly he is full of deceit, 27 casting down his countenance, and making as if he heard not: where he is not known, he will do thee a mischief before thou be aware. 28 And if for want of power he be hindered from sinning, yet when he findeth opportunity he will do evil. 29 A man may be known by his look, and one that hath understanding by his countenance, when thou meetest him. 30 A man's attire, and excessive laughter, and gait, show what he is.

CHAPTER 20

1 There is a reproof that is not comely: again, some man holdeth his tongue, and he is wise. 2 It is much better to reprove, than to be angry secretly: and he that confesseth his fault shall be preserved from hurt. 3 How good is it, when thou art reproved, to show repentance! for so shalt thou escape wilful sin. 4 As is the lust of an eunuch to deflower a virgin; so is he that executeth judgment with violence. 5 There is one that keepeth silence, and is found wise: and another by much babbling becometh hateful. 6 Some man holdeth his tongue, because he hath not to answer: and some keepeth silence, knowing his time. 7 A wise man will hold his tongue till he see opportunity: but a babbler and a fool will regard no time. 8 He that useth many words shall be abhorred; and he that taketh to himself authority therein shall be hated. 9 There is a sinner that hath good success in evil things; and there is a gain that turneth to loss. 10 There is a gift that shall not profit thee; and there is a gift whose recompense is double. 11 There is an abasement because of glory; and there is that lifteth up his head from a low estate. 12 There is that buyeth much for a little, and repayeth it sevenfold. 13 A wise man by his words maketh him beloved: but the graces of fools shall be poured out. 14 The gift of a fool shall do thee no good when thou hast it; neither yet of the envious for his necessity: for he looketh to receive many things for one. 15 He giveth little, and upbraideth much; he openeth his mouth like a crier; today he lendeth, and tomorrow will he ask it again: such an one is to be hated of God and man. 16 The fool saith, I have no friends, I have no thank for all my good deeds, and they that eat my bread speak evil of me. 17 How oft, and of how many shall he be laughed to scorn! for he knoweth not aright what it is to have; and it is all one unto him as if he had it not.

18 To slip upon a pavement is better than to slip with the tongue: so the fall of

the wicked shall come speedily. [19]An
unseasonable tale will always be in the
mouth of the unwise. [20]A wise sentence
shall be rejected when it cometh out of
a fool's mouth; for he will not speak it
in due season. [21]There is that is hindered
from sinning through want: and when he
taketh rest, he shall not be troubled.
[22]There is that destroyeth his own soul
through bashfulness, and by accepting
of persons overthroweth himself.
[23]There is that for bashfulness
promiseth to his friend, and maketh
him his enemy for nothing.
[24]A lie is a foul blot in a man, yet
it is continually in the mouth of the
untaught. [25]A thief is better than a man
that is accustomed to lie: but they both
shall have destruction to heritage. [26]The
disposition of a liar is dishonorable,
and his shame is ever with him.
[27]A wise man shall promote himself to
honor with his words: and he that hath
understanding will please great men.
[28]He that tilleth his land shall increase his
heap: and he that pleaseth great men
shall get pardon for iniquity. [29]Presents
and gifts blind the eyes of the wise, and
stop up his mouth that he cannot
reprove. [30]Wisdom that is hid, and
treasure that is hoarded up, what profit
is in them both? [31]Better is he that
hideth his folly than a man that hideth
his wisdom. [32]Necessary patience in
seeking the Lord is better than he that
leadeth his life without a guide.

CHAPTER 21

[1]My son, hast thou sinned? do so no
more, but ask pardon for thy former
sins. [2]Flee from sin as from the face of a
serpent: for if thou comest too near it, it
will bite thee: the teeth thereof are as the
teeth of a lion, slaying the souls of men.
[3]All iniquity is as a two-edged sword,
the wounds whereof cannot be healed.
[4]To terrify and do wrong will waste
riches: thus the house of proud men
shall be made desolate. [5]A prayer out
of a poor man's mouth reacheth to the
ears of God, and his judgment cometh
speedily. [6]He that hateth to be reproved
is in the way of sinners: but he that
feareth the Lord will repent from his
heart. [7]An eloquent man is known far
and near; but a man of understanding
knoweth when he slippeth. [8]He that
buildeth his house with other men's
money is like one that gathereth
himself stones for the tomb of his
burial. [9]The congregation of the wicked
is like tow wrapped together: and the
end of them is a flame of fire to destroy
them. [10]The way of sinners is made
plain with stones, but at the end thereof
is the pit of hell. [11]He that keepeth the
law of the Lord getteth the
understanding thereof: and the
perfection of the fear of the Lord is
wisdom. [12]He that is not wise will not
be taught: but there is a wisdom which
multiplieth bitterness. [13]The
knowledge of a wise man shall abound
like a flood: and his counsel is like a
pure fountain of life. [14]The inner
parts of a fool are like a broken
vessel, and he will hold no knowledge
as long as he liveth. [15]If a skilful man
hear a wise word, he will commend it,
and add unto it: but as soon as one of
no understanding heareth it, it
displeaseth him, and he casteth it
behind his back. [16]The talking of a
fool is like a burden in the way: but
grace shall be found in the lips of the
wise. [17]They inquire at the mouth of the
wise man in the congregation, and they
shall ponder his words in their heart.
[18]As is a house that is destroyed, so is

wisdom to a fool: and the knowledge of
the unwise is as talk without sense.
19Doctrine unto fools is as fetters on the
feet, and like manacles on the right
hand. 20A fool lifteth up his voice with
laughter, but a wise man doth scarce
smile a little. 21Learning is unto a wise
man as an ornament of gold, and like a
bracelet upon his right arm. 22A foolish
man's foot is soon in his [neighbor's]
house: but a man of experience is
ashamed of him. 23A fool will peep in at
the door into the house: but he that is
well nurtured will stand without. 24It is
the rudeness of a man to hearken at the
door: but a wise man will be grieved
with the disgrace. 25The lips of talkers
will be telling such things as pertain not
unto them: but the words of such as have
understanding are weighed in the
balance. 26The heart of fools is in their
mouth: but the mouth of the wise is in
their heart. 27When the ungodly curseth
Satan, he curseth his own soul. 28A
whisperer defileth his own soul, and is
hated wheresoever he dwelleth.

CHAPTER 22

1A slothful man is compared to a filthy
stone, and every one will hiss him out
to his disgrace. 2A slothful man is
compared to the filth of a dunghill:
every man that takes it up will shake his
hand.
3An evil-nurtured son is the dishonor of
his father that begat him: and a [foolish]
daughter is born to his loss. 4A wise
daughter shall bring an inheritance to
her husband: but she that liveth
dishonestly is her father's heaviness.
5She that is bold dishonored both her
father and her husband, but they both
shall despise her. 6A tale out of
season [is as] music in mourning: but
stripes and correction of wisdom are
never out of time.
7Whoso teacheth a fool is as one that
glueth a potsherd together, and as he
that waketh one from a sound sleep.
8He that telleth a tale to a fool speaketh
to one in a slumber: when he hath told his
tale, he will say, What is the matter? 9If
children live honestly, and have
wherewithal, they shall cover the
baseness of their parents. 10But
children, being haughty, through
disdain and want of nurture do stain the
nobility of their kindred. 11Weep for the
dead, for he hath lost the light: and
weep for the fool, for he wanteth
understanding: make little weeping for
the dead, for he is at rest: but the life of
the fool is worse than death. 12Seven
days do men mourn for him that is
dead; but for a fool and an ungodly man
all the days of his life. 13Talk not much
with a fool, and go not to him that hath
no understanding: beware of him, lest
thou have trouble, and thou shalt never
be defiled with his fooleries: depart
from him, and thou shalt find rest, and
never be disquieted with madness.
14What is heavier than lead? and what is
the name thereof, but a fool? 15Sand,
and salt, and a mass of iron, is easier to
bear, than a man without
understanding. 16As timber girt and
bound together in a building cannot be
loosed with shaking: so the heart that is
stablished by advised counsel shall fear
at no time. 17A heart settled upon a
thought of understanding is as a fair
plastering on the wall of a gallery.
18Pales set on an high place will never
stand against the wind: so a fearful
heart in the imagination of a fool
cannot stand against any fear. 19He that
pricketh the eye will make tears to fall:
and he that pricketh the heart maketh it

to show her knowledge. 20 Whoso casteth
a stone at the birds frayeth them away:
and he that upbraideth his friend
breaketh friendship. 21 Though thou
drewest a sword at thy friend, yet
despair not: for there may be a
returning [to favor.] 22 If thou hast
opened thy mouth against thy friend,
fear not; for there may be a
reconciliation: except for upbraiding, or
pride, or disclosing of secrets, or a
treacherous wound: for, for these things
every friend will depart. 23 Be faithful to
thy neighbor in his poverty, that thou
mayest rejoice in his prosperity: abide
steadfast unto him in the time of his
trouble, that thou mayest be heir with
him in his heritage: for a mean estate is
not always to be contemned: nor the
rich that is foolish to be had in
admiration. 24 As the vapor and smoke
of a furnace goeth before the fire; so
reviling before blood. 25 I will not be
ashamed to defend a friend; neither will
I hide myself from him. 26 And if any
evil happen unto me by him, every one
that heareth it will beware of him.

27 Who shall set a watch before my
mouth, and a seal of wisdom upon my
lips, that I fall not suddenly by them,
and that my tongue destroy me not?

CHAPTER 23

1 O Lord, Father and Governor of all my
whole life, leave me not to their
counsels, and let me not fall by them.
2 Who will set scourges over my
thoughts, and the discipline of wisdom
over mine heart? That they spare me not
for mine ignorances, and it pass not by
my sins: 3 Lest mine ignorances
increase, and my sins abound to my
destruction, and I fall before mine
adversaries, and mine enemy rejoice
over me, whose hope is far from thy
mercy. 4 O Lord, Father and God of my
life, give me not a proud look, but turn
away from thy servants always a
haughty mind. 5 Turn away from me
vain hopes and concupiscence, and
thou shalt hold him up that is desirous
always to serve thee. 6 Let not the
greediness of the belly nor lust of the
flesh take hold of me; and give not
over me thy servant into an impudent
mind.

7 Hear, O ye children, the discipline of
the mouth: he that keepeth it shall never
be taken in his lips. 8 The sinner shall be
left in his foolishness: both the evil
speaker and the proud shall fall thereby.
9 Accustom not thy mouth to
swearing; neither use thyself to the
naming of the Holy One. 10 For as a
servant that is continually beaten shall
not be without a blue mark: so he that
sweareth and nameth God continually
shall not be faultless. 11 A man that
useth much swearing shall be filled
with iniquity, and the plague shall
never depart from his house: if he shall
offend, his sin shall be upon him: and if
he acknowledge not his sin, he maketh
a double offense: and if he swear in
vain, he shall not be innocent, but his
house shall be full of calamities.
12 There is a word that is clothed about
with death: God grant that it be not
found in the heritage of Jacob; for all
such things shall be far from the godly,
and they shall not wallow in their sins.
13 Use not thy mouth to intemperate
swearing, for therein is the word of sin.
14 Remember thy father and thy mother,
when thou sittest among great men. Be
not forgetful before them, and so thou
by thy custom become a fool, and wish
that thou hadst not been born, and curse
the day of thy nativity. 15 The man that

is accustomed to opprobrious words
will never be reformed all the days of
his life. 16 Two sorts of men multiply
sin, and the third will bring wrath: a hot
mind is as a burning fire, it will never
be quenched till it be consumed: a
fornicator in the body of his flesh will
never cease till he hath kindled a fire.
17 All bread is sweet to a whoremonger,
he will not leave off till he die. 18 A man
that breaketh wedlock, saying thus in
his heart, Who seeth me? I am
compassed about with darkness, the
walls cover me, and no body seeth me;
what need I to fear? the most High will
not remember my sins: 19 such a man
only feareth the eyes of men, and
knoweth not that the eyes of the Lord
are ten thousand times brighter than the
sun, beholding all the ways of men,
and considering the most secret parts.
20 He knew all things ere ever they were
created; so also after they were
perfected he looked upon them all.
21 This man shall be punished in the
streets of the city, and where he
suspecteth not he shall be taken. 22 Thus
shall it go also with the wife that
leaveth her husband, and bringeth in an
heir by another. 23 For first, she hath
disobeyed the law of the most High;
and secondly, she hath trespassed
against her own husband; and thirdly,
she hath played the whore in adultery,
and brought children by another man.
24 She shall be brought out into the
congregation, and inquisition shall be
made of her children. 25 Her children
shall not take root, and her branches
shall bring forth no fruit. 26 She shall
leave her memory to be cursed, and her
reproach shall not be blotted out. 27 And
they that remain shall know that there
is nothing better than the fear of the
Lord, and that there is nothing sweeter
than to take heed unto the
commandments of the Lord. 28 It is
great glory to follow the Lord, and to
be received of him is long life.

CHAPTER 24

1 Wisdom shall praise herself, and shall
glory in the midst of her people. 2 In the
congregation of the most High shall she
open her mouth, and triumph before
his power. 3 I came out of the mouth of
the most High, and covered the earth
as a cloud. 4 I dwelt in high places, and
my throne is in a cloudy pillar. 5 I alone
compassed the circuit of heaven, and
walked in the bottom of the deep. 6 In
the waves of the sea, and in all the
earth, and in every people and nation, I
got a possession. 7 With all these I
sought rest: and in whose inheritance
shall I abide?
8 So the Creator of all things gave me
a commandment, and he that made me
caused my tabernacle to rest, and said,
Let thy dwelling be in Jacob, and thine
inheritance in Israel. 9 He created me
from the beginning before the world, and
I shall never fail. 10 In the holy tabernacle
I served before him; and so was I
established in Zion. 11 Likewise in the
beloved city he gave me rest, and in
Jerusalem was my power. 12 And I took
root in an honorable people, even in the
portion of the Lord's inheritance.
13 I was exalted like a cedar in Lebanon,
and as a cypress tree upon the
mountains of Hermon. 14 I was exalted
like a palm tree in En–ge´di, and as a rose
plant in Jericho, as a fair olive tree in a
pleasant field, and grew up as a plane
tree by the water. 15 I gave a sweet smell
like cinnamon and aspalathus, and I
yielded a pleasant odor like the best
myrrh, as galbanum, and onyx, and

sweet storax, and as the fume of
frankincense in the tabernacle. 16 As the
turpentine tree I stretched out my
branches, and my branches are the
branches of honor and grace. 17 As the
vine brought I forth pleasant savor, and
my flowers are the fruit of honor and
riches. 18 I am the mother of fair love,
and fear, and knowledge, and holy
hope: I therefore, being eternal, am
given to all my children which are
named of him.
19 Come unto me, all ye that be desirous
of me, and fill yourselves with my
fruits. 20 For my memorial is sweeter
than honey, and mine inheritance than
the honeycomb. 21 They that eat me
shall yet be hungry, and they that drink
me shall yet be thirsty. 22 He that
obeyeth me shall never be confounded,
and they that work by me shall not do
amiss.
23 All these things are the book of the
covenant of the most high God, even
the law which Moses commanded
for an heritage unto the congregations
of Jacob. 24 Faint not to be strong in the
Lord; that he may confirm you, cleave
unto him: for the Lord Almighty is God
alone, and beside him there is no other
Saviour. 25 He filleth all things with his
wisdom, as Phison and as Tigris in the
time of the new fruits. 26 He maketh the
understanding to abound like
Euphra´tes, and as Jordan in the time of
the harvest. 27 He maketh the doctrine of
knowledge appear as the light, and as
Gihon in the time of vintage. 28 The first
man knew her not perfectly: no more
shall the last find her out. 29 For her
thoughts are more than the sea, and her
counsels profounder than the great
deep. 30 I also came out as a brook from
a river, and as a conduit into a garden.
31 I said, I will water my best garden,
and will water abundantly my garden
bed: and, lo, my brook became a river,
and my river became a sea. 32 I will yet
make doctrine to shine as the morning,
and will send forth her light afar off. 33 I
will yet pour out doctrine as prophecy,
and leave it to all ages for ever.
34 Behold that I have not labored for
myself only, but for all them that seek
wisdom.

CHAPTER 25

1 In three things I was beautified, and
stood up beautiful both before God and
men: the unity of brethren, the love of
neighbors, a man and a wife that agree
together. 2 Three sorts of men my soul
hateth, and I am greatly offended at
their life: a poor man that is proud, a
rich man that is a liar, and an old
adulterer that doteth. 3 If thou hast
gathered nothing in thy youth, how canst
thou find any thing in thine age? 4 O
how comely a thing is judgment for
gray hairs, and for ancient men to know
counsel! 5 O how comely is the wisdom
of old men, and understanding and
counsel to men of honor. 6 Much
experience is the crown of old men, and
the fear of God is their glory. 7 There be
nine things which I have judged in
mine heart to be happy, and the tenth I
will utter with my tongue: A man that
hath joy of his children; and he that
liveth to see the fall of his enemy: 8 well
is him that dwelleth with a wife of
understanding, and that hath not slipped
with his tongue, and that hath not
served a man more unworthy than
himself: 9 well is him that hath found
prudence, and he that speaketh in the
ears of them that will hear: 10 O how
great is he that findeth wisdom! yet is
there none above him that feareth the

Lord. 11 But the love of the Lord passeth
all things for illumination: he that
holdeth it, whereto shall he be likened?
12 The fear of the Lord is the beginning
of his love: and faith is the beginning of
cleaving unto him. 13 [Give me] any
plague, but the plague of the heart: and
any wickedness, but the wickedness of
a woman: 14 and any affliction, but the
affliction from them that hate me: and
any revenge, but the revenge of enemies.
15 There is no head above the head of a
serpent; and there is no wrath above the
wrath of an enemy. 16 I had rather dwell
with a lion and a dragon, than to keep
house with a wicked woman. 17 The
wickedness of a woman changeth
her face, and darkeneth her
countenance like sackcloth. 18 Her
husband shall sit among his neighbors;
and when he heareth it shall sigh
bitterly. 19 All wickedness is but little
to the wickedness of a woman: let the
portion of a sinner fall upon her. 20 As
the climbing up a sandy way is to the
feet of the aged, so is a wife full of
words to a quiet man. 21 Stumble not at
the beauty of a woman, and desire her
not for pleasure. 22 A woman, if she
maintain her husband, is full of anger,
impudence, and much reproach. 23 A
wicked woman abateth the courage,
maketh an heavy countenance and a
wounded heart: a woman that will not
comfort her husband in distress maketh
weak hands and feeble knees. 24 Of the
woman came the beginning of sin, and
through her we all die. 25 Give the water
no passage; neither a wicked woman
liberty to gad abroad. 26 If she go not as
thou wouldest have her, cut her off
from thy flesh, and give her a bill of
divorce, and let her go.

CHAPTER 26

1 Blessed is the man that hath a virtuous
wife, for the number of his days shall
be double. 2 A virtuous woman rejoiceth
her husband, and he shall fulfil the
years of his life in peace. 3 A good wife
is a good portion, which shall be given in
the portion of them that fear the Lord.
4 Whether a man be rich or poor, if he
have a good heart toward the Lord, he
shall at all times rejoice with a cheerful
countenance. 5 There be three things
that mine heart feareth; and for the
fourth I was sore afraid: the slander
of a city, the gathering together of an
unruly multitude, and a false
accusation: all these are worse than
death. 6 But a grief of heart and
sorrow is a woman that is jealous over
another woman, and a scourge of the
tongue which communicateth with all.
7 An evil wife is a yoke shaken to and
fro: he that hath hold of her is as
though he held a scorpion. 8 A drunken
woman and a gadder abroad causeth
great anger, and she will not cover her
own shame. 9 The whoredom of a
woman may be known in her haughty
looks and eyelids. 10 If thy daughter be
shameless, keep her in straitly, lest she
abuse herself through overmuch
liberty. 11 Watch over an impudent eye:
and marvel not if she trespass against
thee. 12 She will open her mouth, as a
thirsty traveler when he hath found a
fountain, and drink of every water near
her: by every hedge will she sit down,
and open her quiver against every
arrow. 13 The grace of a wife delighteth
her husband, and her discretion will
fatten his bones. 14 A silent and loving
woman is a gift of the Lord; and there
is nothing so much worth as a mind well
instructed. 15 A shamefaced and faithful

woman is a double grace, and her
continent mind cannot be valued.
16 As the sun when it ariseth in the
high heaven; so is the beauty of a good
wife in the ordering of her house. 17 As
the clear light is upon the holy
candlestick; so is the beauty of the face
in ripe age. 18 As the golden pillars are
upon the sockets of silver; so are the
fair feet with a constant heart.
19 My son, keep the flower of thine
age sound; and give not thy strength
to strangers. 20 When thou hast gotten a
fruitful possession through all the field,
sow it with thine own seed, trusting in
the goodness of thy stock. 21 So thy race
which thou leavest shall be magnified,
having the confidence of their good
descent. 22 An harlot shall be accounted
as spittle; but a married woman is a
tower against death to her husband. 23 A
wicked woman is given as a portion to
a wicked man: but a godly woman is
given to him that feareth the Lord. 24 A
dishonest woman contemneth shame:
but an honest woman will reverence her
husband. 25 A shameless woman shall be
counted as a dog; but she that is
shamefaced will fear the Lord. 26 A
woman that honoreth her husband shall
be judged wise of all; but she that
dishonoreth him in her pride shall be
counted ungodly of all. 27 A loud crying
woman and a scold shall be sought out
to drive away the enemies. 28 There be
two things that grieve my heart; and the
third maketh me angry: a man of war
that suffereth poverty; and men of
understanding that are not set by; and
one that returneth from righteousness to
sin; the Lord prepareth such an one for
the sword. 29 A merchant shall hardly
keep himself from doing wrong; and an
huckster shall not be freed from sin.

CHAPTER 27

1 Many have sinned for a small matter;
and he that seeketh for abundance will
turn his eyes away. 2 As a nail sticketh
fast between the joinings of the stones;
so doth sin stick close between buying
and selling. 3 Unless a man hold
himself diligently in the fear of the
Lord, his house shall soon be
overthrown.
4 As when one sifteth with a sieve, the
refuse remaineth; so the filth of man in
his talk. 5 The furnace proveth the
potter's vessels; so the trial of man is in
his reasoning. 6 The fruit declareth if the
tree have been dressed; so is the
utterance of a conceit in the heart of
man. 7 Praise no man before thou
hearest him speak; for this is the trial of
men.
8 If thou followest righteousness, thou
shalt obtain her, and put her on, as a
glorious long robe. 9 The birds will
resort unto their like; so will truth
return unto them that practice in her.
10 As the lion lieth in wait for the prey;
so sin for them that work iniquity.
11 The discourse of a godly man is
always with wisdom; but a fool
changeth as the moon. 12 If thou be
among the indiscreet, observe the time;
but be continually among men of
understanding. 13 The discourse of fools
is irksome, and their sport is the
wantonness of sin. 14 The talk of him
that sweareth much maketh the hair
stand upright; and their brawls make
one stop his ears. 15 The strife of the
proud is bloodshedding, and their
revilings are grievous to the ear.
16 Whoso discovereth secrets loseth his
credit; and shall never find friend to his
mind. 17 Love thy friend, and be faithful
unto him: but if thou betrayest his

secrets, follow no more after him. 18For
as a man hath destroyed his enemy; so
hast thou lost the love of thy neighbor.
19As one that letteth a bird go out of
his hand, so hast thou let thy neighbor
go, and shalt not get him again. 20Follow
after him no more, for he is too far off;
he is as a roe escaped out of the snare.
21As for a wound, it may be bound up;
and after reviling there may be
reconciliation: but he that betrayeth
secrets is without hope.
22He that winketh with the eyes
worketh evil: and he that knoweth him
will depart from him. 23When thou art
present, he will speak sweetly, and will
admire thy words: but at the last he will
writhe his mouth, and slander thy
sayings. 24I have hated many things, but
nothing like him; for the Lord will hate
him.
25Whoso casteth a stone on high casteth
it on his own head; and a deceitful
stroke shall make wounds. 26Whoso
diggeth a pit shall fall therein: and he
that setteth a trap shall be taken
therein. 27He that worketh mischief, it
shall fall upon him, and he shall not
know whence it cometh. 28Mockery and
reproach are from the proud; but
vengeance, as a lion, shall lie in wait for
them. 29They that rejoice at the fall of
the righteous shall be taken in the snare;
and anguish shall consume them before
they die.
30Malice and wrath, even these are
abominations; and the sinful man shall
have them both.

CHAPTER 28

1He that revengeth shall find vengeance
from the Lord, and he will surely keep
his sins [in remembrance.] 2Forgive thy
neighbor the hurt that he hath done unto
thee, so shall thy sins also be forgiven when
thou prayest. 3One man beareth
hatred against another, and doth he seek
pardon from the Lord? 4He showeth no
mercy to a man, which is like himself:
and doth he ask forgiveness of his own
sins? 5If he that is but flesh nourish
hatred, who will intreat for pardon of
his sins? 6Remember thy end, and let
enmity cease; [remember] corruption
and death, and abide in the
commandments. 7Remember the
commandments, and bear no malice to
thy neighbor: [remember] the covenant
of the Highest, and wink at ignorance.
8Abstain from strife, and thou shalt
diminish thy sins: for a furious man
will kindle strife. 9A sinful man
disquieteth friends, and maketh debate
among them that be at peace. 10As the
matter of the fire is, so it burneth: and as
a man's strength is, so is his wrath; and
according to his riches his anger riseth;
and the stronger they are which
contend, the more they will be
inflamed. 11An hasty contention
kindleth a fire: and an hasty fighting
sheddeth blood. 12If thou blow the
spark, it shall burn: if thou spit upon it,
it shall be quenched: and both these
come out of thy mouth.
13Curse the whisperer and double-
tongued: for such have destroyed many
that were at peace. 14A backbiting
tongue hath disquieted many, and
driven them from nation to nation:
strong cities hath it pulled down, and
overthrown the houses of great men.
15A backbiting tongue hath cast out
virtuous women, and deprived them of
their labors. 16Whoso hearkeneth unto it
shall never find rest, and never dwell
quietly. 17The stroke of the whip
maketh marks in the flesh: but the
stroke of the tongue breaketh the bones.

[18]Many have fallen by the edge of the
sword: but not so many as have fallen by
the tongue. [19]Well is he that is defended
from it, and hath not passed through the
venom thereof; who hath not drawn the
yoke thereof, nor hath been bound in
her bands. [20]For the yoke thereof is a
yoke of iron, and the bands thereof are
bands of brass. [21]The death thereof is an
evil death, the grave were better than it.
[22]It shall not have rule over them that
fear God, neither shall they be burned
with the flame thereof. [23]Such as
forsake the Lord shall fall into it; and it
shall burn in them, and not be
quenched; it shall be sent upon them as
a lion, and devour them as a leopard.
[24]Look that thou hedge thy possession
about with thorns, and bind up thy
silver and gold, [25]and weigh thy words
in a balance, and make a door and bar for
thy mouth. [26]Beware thou slide not by
it, lest thou fall before him that lieth in
wait.

CHAPTER 29

[1]He that is merciful will lend unto his
neighbor; and he that strengtheneth his
hand keepeth the commandments.
[2]Lend to thy neighbor in time of his
need, and pay thou thy neighbor again
in due season. [3]Keep thy word, and
deal faithfully with him, and thou shalt
always find the thing that is necessary
for thee. [4]Many, when a thing was lent
them, reckoned it to be found, and put
them to trouble that helped them. [5]Till
he hath received, he will kiss a man's
hand; and for his neighbor's money
he will speak submissively: but when
he should repay, he will prolong the
time, and return words of grief, and
complain of the time. [6]If he prevail, he
shall hardly receive the half, and he will
count as if he had found it: if not, he
hath deprived him of his money, and he
hath gotten him an enemy without
cause: he payeth him with cursings and
railings; and for honor he will pay him
disgrace. [7]Many therefore have refused
to lend for other men's ill-dealing,
fearing to be defrauded. [8]Yet have thou
patience with a man in poor estate, and
delay not to show him mercy. [9]Help the
poor for the commandment's sake, and
turn him not away because of his
poverty. [10]Lose thy money for thy
brother and thy friend, and let it not rust
under a stone to be lost. [11]Lay up thy
treasure according to the
commandments of the most High, and
it shall bring thee more profit than gold.
[12]Shut up alms in thy storehouses: and it
shall deliver thee from all affliction. [13]It
shall fight for thee against thine
enemies better than a mighty shield and
strong spear. [14]An honest man is surety
for his neighbor: but he that is
impudent will forsake him. [15]Forget not
the friendship of thy surety, for he hath
given his life for thee. [16]A sinner will
overthrow the good estate of his surety:
[17]and he that is of an unthankful mind
will leave him [in danger] that
delivered him. [18]Suretyship hath
undone many of good estate, and
shaken them as a wave of the sea:
mighty men hath it driven from their
houses, so that they wandered among
strange nations. [19]A wicked man
transgressing the commandments of the
Lord shall fall into suretyship: and he
that undertaketh and followeth other
men's business for gain shall fall into
suits. [20]Help thy neighbor according to
thy power, and beware that thou thyself
fall not into the same. [21]The chief thing
for life is water, and bread, and
clothing, and an house to cover shame.

22 Better is the life of a poor man in a
mean cottage, than delicate fare in
another man's house. 23 Be it little or
much, hold thee contented, that thou
hear not the reproach of thy house.
24 For it is a miserable life to go from
house to house: for where thou art a
stranger, thou darest not open thy
mouth. 25 Thou shalt entertain, and feast,
and have no thanks: moreover thou
shalt hear bitter words: 26 Come, thou
stranger, and furnish a table, and feed
me of that thou hast ready. 27 Give
place, thou stranger, to an honorable
man; my brother cometh to be lodged,
and I have need of mine house. 28 These
things are grievous to a man of
understanding; the upbraiding of
houseroom, and reproaching of the
lender.

CHAPTER 30

1 He that loveth his son causeth him oft to
feel the rod, that he may have joy of
him in the end. 2 He that chastiseth his son
shall have joy in him, and shall rejoice
of him among his acquaintance. 3 He that
teacheth his son grieveth the enemy: and
before his friends he shall rejoice of
him. 4 Though his father die, yet he is as
though he were not dead: for he hath
left one behind him that is like himself.
5 While he lived, he saw and rejoiced in
him: and when he died, he was not
sorrowful. 6 He left behind him an
avenger against his enemies, and one
that shall requite kindness to his
friends. 7 He that maketh too much of
his son shall bind up his wounds; and
his bowels will be troubled at every cry.
8 An horse not broken becometh
headstrong: and a child left to himself
will be wilful. 9 Cocker thy child, and
he shall make thee afraid: play with
him, and he will bring thee to
heaviness. 10 Laugh not with him, lest
thou have sorrow with him, and lest
thou gnash thy teeth in the end. 11 Give
him no liberty in his youth, and wink
not at his follies. 12 Bow down his neck
while he is young, and beat him on the
sides while he is a child, lest he wax
stubborn, and be disobedient unto thee,
and so bring sorrow to thine heart.
13 Chastise thy son, and hold him to
labor, lest his lewd behavior be an
offense unto thee.

14 Better is the poor, being sound and
strong of constitution, than a rich man
that is afflicted in his body. 15 Health
and good estate of body are above all
gold, and a strong body above infinite
wealth. 16 There is no riches above a
sound body, and no joy above the joy
of the heart. 17 Death is better than a
bitter life or continual sickness.
18 Delicates poured upon a mouth shut
up are as messes of meat set upon a
grave. 19 What good doeth the offering
unto an idol? for neither can it eat nor
smell: so is he that is persecuted of the
Lord. 20 He seeth with his eyes and
groaneth, as an eunuch that embraceth
a virgin and sigheth.

21 Give not over thy mind to
heaviness, and afflict not thyself in
thine own counsel. 22 The gladness of
the heart is the life of man, and the
joyfulness of a man prolongeth his days.
23 Love thine own soul, and comfort thy
heart, remove sorrow far from thee: for
sorrow hath killed many, and there is
no profit therein. 24 Envy and wrath
shorten the life, and carefulness
bringeth age before the time. 25 A
cheerful and good heart will have a care
of his meat and diet.

CHAPTER 31

1 Watching for riches consumeth the
flesh, and the care thereof driveth away
sleep. 2 Watching care will not let a man
slumber, as a sore disease breaketh
sleep. 3 The rich hath great labor in
gathering riches together; and when he
resteth, he is filled with his delicates.
4 The poor laboreth in his poor estate;
and when he leaveth off, he is still
needy. 5 He that loveth gold shall not
be justified, and he that followeth
corruption shall have enough thereof.
6 Gold hath been the ruin of many, and
their destruction was present. 7 It is a
stumbling-block unto them that sacrifice
unto it, and every fool shall be taken
therewith. 8 Blessed is the rich that is
found without blemish, and hath not
gone after gold. 9 Who is he? and we
will call him blessed: for wonderful
things hath he done among his people.
10 Who hath been tried thereby, and
found perfect? then let him glory. Who
might offend, and hath not offended? or
done evil, and hath not done it? 11 His
goods shall be established, and the
congregation shall declare his alms. 12 If
thou sit at a bountiful table, be not
greedy upon it, and say not, There is
much meat on it. 13 Remember that a
wicked eye is an evil thing: and what is
created more wicked than an eye?
therefore it weepeth upon every
occasion. 14 Stretch not thine hand
whithersoever it looketh, and thrust it
not with him into the dish. 15 Judge of
thy neighbor by thyself: and be discreet
in every point. 16 Eat, as it becometh a
man, those things which are set before
thee; and devour not, lest thou be hated.
17 Leave off first for manners' sake; and
be not unsatiable, lest thou offend.
18 When thou sittest among many, reach
not thine hand out first of all. 19 A very
little is sufficient for a man well
nurtured, and he fetcheth not his wind
short upon his bed. 20 Sound sleep
cometh of moderate eating: he riseth
early, and his wits are with him: but the
pain of watching, and choler, and pangs
of the belly, are with an unsatiable man.
21 And if thou hast been forced to eat,
arise, go forth, vomit, and thou shalt
have rest. 22 My son, hear me, and
despise me not, and at the last thou shalt
find as I told thee: in all thy works be
quick, so shall there no sickness come
unto thee. 23 Whoso is liberal of his
meat, men shall speak well of him; and
the report of his good housekeeping
will be believed. 24 But against him that
is a niggard of his meat the whole city
shall murmur; and the testimonies of
his niggardness shall not be doubted of.
25 Show not thy valiantness in wine; for
wine hath destroyed many. 26 The
furnace proveth the edge by
dipping: so doth wine the hearts of the
proud by drunkenness. 27 Wine is as
good as life to a man, if it be drunk
moderately: what life is then to a man
that is without wine? for it was made to
make men glad. 28 Wine measurably
drunk and in season bringeth gladness
of the heart, and cheerfulness of the
mind: 29 but wine drunken with excess
maketh bitterness of the mind, with
brawling and quarrelling.
30 Drunkenness increaseth the rage of a
fool till he offend: it diminisheth
strength, and maketh wounds.
31 Rebuke not thy neighbor at the wine,
and despise him not in his mirth: give
him no despiteful words, and press not
upon him with urging him [to drink.]

CHAPTER 32

1 If thou be made the master [of a feast,]
lift not thyself up, but be among them
as one of the rest; take diligent care for
them, and so sit down. 2 And when thou
hast done all thy office, take thy place,
that thou mayest be merry with them,
and receive a crown for thy well
ordering of the feast. 3 Speak, thou that
art the elder, for it becometh thee, but
with sound judgment; and hinder not
music. 4 Pour not out words where there
is a musician, and show not forth
wisdom out of time. 5 A concert of music
in a banquet of wine is as a signet of
carbuncle set in gold. 6 As a signet of an
emerald set in a work of gold, so is the
melody of music with pleasant wine.
7 Speak, young man, if there be need of
thee: and yet scarcely when thou art
twice asked. 8 Let thy speech be short,
comprehending much in few words; be
as one that knoweth and yet holdeth
his tongue. 9 If thou be among great
men, make not thyself equal with them;
and when ancient men are in place, use
not many words. 10 Before the thunder
goeth lightning; and before a
shamefaced man shall go favor. 11 Rise
up betimes, and be not the last; but get
thee home without delay. 12 There take
thy pastime, and do what thou wilt: but
sin not by proud speech. 13 And for
these things bless him that made thee,
and hath replenished thee with his good
things.
14 Whoso feareth the Lord will receive
his discipline; and they that seek him
early shall find favor. 15 He that seeketh
the law shall be filled therewith: but the
hypocrite will be offended thereat.
16 They that fear the Lord shall find
judgment, and shall kindle justice as a
light. 17 A sinful man will not be
reproved, but findeth an excuse
according to his will. 18 A man of
counsel will be considerate; but a
strange and proud man is not daunted
with fear, even when of himself he hath
done without counsel. 19 Do nothing
without advice; and when thou hast once
done, repent not. 20 Go not in a way
wherein thou mayest fall, and stumble
not among the stones. 21 Be not
confident in a plain way. 22 And beware
of thine own children. 23 In every good
work trust thy own soul; for this is the
keeping of the commandments. 24 He
that believeth in the Lord taketh heed to
the commandment; and he that trusteth
in him shall fare never the worse.

CHAPTER 33

1 There shall no evil happen unto him
that feareth the Lord; but in
temptation even again he will deliver
him. 2 A wise man hateth not the law;
but he that is an hypocrite therein is as
a ship in a storm. 3 A man of
understanding trusteth in the law; and
the law is faithful unto him, as an
oracle. 4 Prepare what to say, and so
thou shalt be heard: and bind up
instruction, and then make answer.
5 The heart of the foolish is like a
cartwheel; and his thoughts are like a
rolling axletree. 6 A stallion horse is as a
mocking friend, he neigheth under
every one that sitteth upon him.
7 Why doth one day excel another, when
as all the light of every day in the year
is of the sun? 8 By the knowledge of the
Lord they were distinguished: and he
altered seasons and feasts. 9 Some of
them hath he made high days, and
hallowed them, and some of them hath
he made ordinary days. 10 And all men
are from the ground, and Adam was

created of earth. 11 In much knowledge
the Lord hath divided them, and made
their ways diverse. 12 Some of them
hath he blessed and exalted, and some
of them hath he sanctified, and set near
himself: but some of them hath he
cursed and brought low, and turned out
of their places. 13 As the clay is in the
potter's hand, to fashion it at his
pleasure: so man is in the hand of him
that made him, to render to them as
liketh him best. 14 Good is set against
evil, and life against death: so is the
godly against the sinner, and the sinner
against the godly. 15 So look upon all the
works of the most High; and there are
two and two, one against another.
16 I awaked up last of all, as one
that gathereth after the grapegatherers:
by the blessing of the Lord I profited,
and filled my winepress like a gatherer
of grapes. 17 Consider that I labored not
for myself only, but for all them that
seek learning. 18 Hear me, O ye great
men of the people, and hearken with
your ears, ye rulers of the congregation.
19 Give not thy son and wife, thy brother
and friend, power over thee while thou
livest, and give not thy goods to
another: lest it repent thee, and thou
intreat for the same again. 20 As long as
thou livest and hast breath in thee, give
not thyself over to any. 21 For better it is
that thy children should seek to thee,
than that thou shouldest stand to their
courtesy. 22 In all thy works keep to
thyself the pre- eminence; leave not a
stain in thine honor. 23 At the time when
thou shalt end thy days, and finish thy
life, distribute thine inheritance.
24 Fodder, a wand, and burdens, are for
the ass; and bread, correction, and
work, for a servant. 25 If thou set thy
servant to labor, thou shalt find rest: but
if thou let him go idle, he shall seek
liberty. 26 A yoke and a collar do bow the
neck: so are tortures and torments for an
evil servant. 27 Send him to labor, that
he be not idle; for idleness teacheth
much evil. 28 Set him to work, as is fit
for him: if he be not obedient, put on
more heavy fetters. 29 But be not
excessive toward any; and without
discretion do nothing. 30 If thou have a
servant, let him be unto thee as thyself,
because thou hast bought him with a
price. 31 If thou have a servant, entreat
him as a brother: for thou hast need of
him, as of thine own soul: if thou
entreat him evil, and he run from thee,
which way wilt thou go to seek him?

CHAPTER 34

1 The hopes of a man void of
understanding are vain and false: and
dreams lift up fools. 2 Whoso regardeth
dreams is like him that catcheth at a
shadow, and followeth after the wind.
3 The vision of dreams is the
resemblance of one thing to another,
even as the likeness of a face to a face.
4 Of an unclean thing what can be
cleansed? and from that thing which is
false what truth can come?
5 Divinations, and soothsayings, and
dreams, are vain: and the heart fancieth,
as a woman's heart in travail. 6 If they
be not sent from the most High in thy
visitation, set not thy heart upon them.
7 For dreams have deceived many, and
they have failed that put their trust in
them. 8 The law shall be found perfect
without lies: and wisdom is perfection
to a faithful mouth.
9 A man that hath traveled knoweth
many things; and he that hath much
experience will declare wisdom. 10 He
that hath no experience knoweth little:
but he that hath traveled is full of

prudence. 11 When I traveled, I saw many things; and I understand more than I can express. 12 I was ofttimes in danger of death: yet I was delivered because of these things.

13 The spirit of those that fear the Lord shall live; for their hope is in him that saveth them. 14 Whoso feareth the Lord shall not fear nor be afraid; for he is his hope. 15 Blessed is the soul of him that feareth the Lord: to whom doth he look? and who is his strength? 16 For the eyes of the Lord are upon them that love him, he is their mighty protection and strong stay, a defense from heat, and a cover from the sun at noon, a preservation from stumbling, and an help from falling. 17 He raiseth up the soul, and lighteneth the eyes: he giveth health, life, and blessing. 18 He that sacrificeth of a thing wrongfully gotten, his offering is ridiculous; and the gifts of unjust men are not accepted. 19 The most High is not pleased with the offerings of the wicked; neither is he pacified for sin by the multitude of sacrifices. 20 Whoso bringeth an offering of the goods of the poor doeth as one that killeth the son before his father's eyes. 21 The bread of the needy is their life: he that defraudeth him thereof is a man of blood. 22 He that taketh away his neighbor's living slayeth him; and he that defraudeth the laborer of his hire is a bloodshedder. 23 When one buildeth, and another pulleth down, what profit have they then but labor? 24 When one prayeth, and another curseth, whose voice will the Lord hear? 25 He that washeth himself after the touching of a dead body, if he touch it again, what availeth his washing? 26 So is it with a man that fasteth for his sins, and goeth again, and doeth the same: who will hear his prayer? or what doth his humbling profit him?

CHAPTER 35

1 He that keepeth the law bringeth offerings enough: he that taketh heed to the commandment offereth a peace offering. 2 He that requiteth a good turn offereth fine flour; and he that giveth alms sacrificeth praise. 3 To depart from wickedness is a thing pleasing to the Lord; and to forsake unrighteousness is a propitiation. 4 Thou shalt not appear empty before the Lord. 5 For all these things [are to be done] because of the commandment. 6 The offering of the righteous maketh the altar fat, and the sweet savor thereof is before the most High. 7 The sacrifice of a just man is acceptable. and the memorial thereof shall never be forgotten. 8 Give the Lord his honor with a good eye, and diminish not the firstfruits of thine hands. 9 In all thy gifts show a cheerful countenance, and dedicate thy tithes with gladness. 10 Give unto the most High according as he hath enriched thee; and as thou hast gotten, give with a cheerful eye. 11 For the Lord recompenseth, and will give thee seven times as much.

12 Do not think to corrupt with gifts; for such he will not receive: and trust not to unrighteous sacrifices; for the Lord is judge, and with him is no respect of persons. 13 He will not accept any person against a poor man, but will hear the prayer of the oppressed. 14 He will not despise the supplication of the fatherless; nor the widow, when she poureth out her complaint. 15 Do not the tears run down the widow's cheeks? and is not her cry against him that causeth them to fall? 16 He that serveth the Lord shall be accepted with favor, and his

prayer shall reach unto the clouds. 17 The
prayer of the humble pierceth the clouds:
and till it come nigh, he will not be
comforted; and will not depart, till
the most High shall behold to judge
righteously, and execute judgment.
18 For the Lord will not be slack, neither
will the Mighty be patient toward them,
till he have smitten in sunder the loins
of the unmerciful, and repaid
vengeance to the heathen; till he have
taken away the multitude of the proud,
and broken the sceptre of the
unrighteous; 19 till he have rendered to
every man according to his deeds, and
to the works of men according to their
devices; till he have judged the cause of
his people, and made them to rejoice in
his mercy. 20 Mercy is seasonable in the
time of affliction, as clouds of rain in
the time of drought.

CHAPTER 36

1 Have mercy upon us, O Lord God of
all, and behold us: 2 and send thy fear
upon all the nations that seek not after
thee. 3 Lift up thy hand against the
strange nations, and let them see thy
power. 4 As thou wast sanctified in us
before them: so be thou magnified
among them before us. 5 And let them
know thee, as we have known thee, that
there is no God but only thou, O God.
6 Show new signs, and make other
strange wonders: glorify thy hand and
thy right arm, that they may set forth
thy wondrous works. 7 Raise up
indignation, and pour out wrath: take
away the adversary, and destroy the
enemy. 8 Make the time short,
remember the covenant, and let them
declare thy wonderful works. 9 Let him
that escapeth be consumed by the rage of
the fire; and let them perish that oppress
the people. 10 Smite in sunder the heads
of the rulers of the heathen, that say,
There is none other but we. 11 Gather all
the tribes of Jacob together, and inherit
thou them, as from the beginning. 12 O
Lord, have mercy upon the people that
is called by thy name, and upon Israel,
whom thou hast named thy firstborn.
13 O be merciful unto Jerusalem, thy
holy city, the place of thy rest. 14 Fill
Zion with thine unspeakable oracles,
and thy people with thy glory: 15 Give
testimony unto those that thou hast
possessed from the beginning, and raise
up prophets that have been in thy name.
16 Reward them that wait for thee, and
let thy prophets be found faithful. 17 O
Lord, hear the prayer of thy servants,
according to the blessing of Aaron over
thy people, that all they which dwell
upon the earth may know that thou art
the Lord, the eternal God.
18 The belly devoureth all meats, yet is
one meat better than another. 19 As the
palate tasteth divers kinds of venison: so
doth an heart of understanding false
speeches. 20 A froward heart causeth
heaviness: but a man of experience will
recompense him.
21 A woman will receive every man, yet
is one daughter better than another.
22 The beauty of a woman cheereth the
countenance, and a man loveth nothing
better. 23 If there be kindness, meekness,
and comfort, in her tongue, then is not
her husband like other men. 24 He that
getteth a wife beginneth a possession, a
help like unto himself, and a pillar of
rest. 25 Where no hedge is, there the
possession is spoiled: and he that hath
no wife will wander up and down
mourning. 26 Who will trust a thief well-
appointed, that skippeth from city to
city? so [who will believe] a man that
hath no house, and lodgeth wheresoever

the night taketh him?

CHAPTER 37

1 Every friend saith, I am his friend also:
but there is a friend, which is only a
friend in name. 2 Is it not a grief unto
death, when a companion and friend is
turned to an enemy? 3 O wicked
imagination, whence camest thou in to
cover the earth with deceit? 4 There is a
companion, which rejoiceth in the
prosperity of a friend, but in the time of
trouble will be against him. 5 There is a
companion, which helpeth his friend for
the belly, and taketh up the buckler
against the enemy. 6 Forget not thy friend
in thy mind, and be not unmindful of
him in thy riches.
7 Every counselor extolleth counsel;
but there is some that counseleth for
himself. 8 Beware of a counselor, and
know before what need he hath; for he
will counsel for himself; lest he cast the
lot upon thee, 9 and say unto thee, Thy
way is good: and afterward he stand
on the other side, to see what shall
befall thee. 10 Consult not with one that
suspecteth thee: and hide thy counsel
from such as envy thee. 11 Neither
consult with a woman touching her of
whom she is jealous; neither with a
coward in matters of war; nor with a
merchant concerning exchange; nor
with a buyer of selling; nor with an
envious man of thankfulness; nor with
an unmerciful man touching kindness;
nor with the slothful for any work; nor
with an hireling for a year of finishing
work; nor with an idle servant of much
business: hearken not unto these in any
matter of counsel. 12 But be continually
with a godly man, whom thou knowest
to keep the commandments of the Lord,
whose mind is according to thy mind,
and will sorrow with thee, if thou shalt
miscarry. 13 And let the counsel of thine
own heart stand: for there is no man
more faithful unto thee than it. 14 For a
man's mind is sometime wont to tell
him more than seven watchmen, that sit
above in an high tower. 15 And above all
this pray to the most High, that he will
direct thy way in truth.
16 Let reason go before every
enterprise, and counsel before every
action. 17 The countenance is a sign of
changing of the heart. 18 Four manner of
things appear: good and evil, life and
death: but the tongue ruleth over them
continually. 19 There is one that is wise
and teacheth many, and yet is
unprofitable to himself. 20 There is
one that showeth wisdom in words,
and is hated: he shall be destitute of all
food. 21 For grace is not given him
from the Lord; because he is deprived
of all wisdom. 22 Another is wise to
himself; and the fruits of understanding
are commendable in his mouth. 23 A
wise man instructeth his people; and
the fruits of his understanding fail not.
24 A wise man shall be filled with
blessing; and all they that see him shall
count him happy. 25 The days of the life
of man may be numbered: but the days
of Israel are innumerable. 26 A wise man
shall inherit glory among his people,
and his name shall be perpetual. 27 My
son, prove thy soul in thy life, and
see what is evil for it, and give not
that unto it. 28 For all things are not
profitable for all men, neither hath
every soul pleasure in every thing. 29 Be
not unsatiable in any dainty thing, nor
too greedy upon meats: 30 for excess of
meats bringeth sickness, and surfeiting
will turn into choler. 31 By surfeiting
have many perished; but he that taketh
heed prolongeth his life.

CHAPTER 38

1 Honor a physician with the honor due
unto him for the uses which ye may
have of him: for the Lord hath created
him. 2 For of the most High cometh
healing, and he shall receive honor of
the king. 3 The skill of the physician
shall lift up his head: and in the sight of
great men he shall be in admiration.
4 The Lord hath created medicines out
of the earth; and he that is wise will not
abhor them. 5 Was not the water made
sweet with wood, that the virtue thereof
might be known? 6 And he hath given
men skill, that he might be honored in
his marvelous works. 7 With such doth
he heal [men,] and taketh away their
pains. 8 Of such doth the apothecary
make a confection; and of his works
there is no end; and from him is peace
over all the earth. 9 My son, in thy
sickness be not negligent: but pray unto
the Lord, and he will make thee
whole. 10 Leave off from sin, and order
thine hands aright, and cleanse thy
heart from all wickedness. 11 Give a
sweet savor, and a memorial of fine
flour; and make a fat offering, as not
being. 12 Then give place to the
physician, for the Lord hath created
him: let him not go from thee, for thou
hast need of him. 13 There is a time
when in their hands there is good
success. 14 For they shall also pray unto
the Lord, that he would prosper that,
which they give for ease and remedy to
prolong life. 15 He that sinneth before his
Maker, let him fall into the hand of the
physician.

16 My son, let tears fall down over the
dead, and begin to lament, as if thou
hadst suffered great harm thyself; and
then cover his body according to the
custom, and neglect not his burial.
17 Weep bitterly, and make great moan,
and use lamentation, as he is worthy,
and that a day or two, lest thou be evil
spoken of: and then comfort thyself for
thy heaviness. 18 For of heaviness cometh
death, and the heaviness of the heart
breaketh strength. 19 In affliction also
sorrow remaineth: and the life of the
poor is the curse of the heart. 20 Take no
heaviness to heart: drive it away, and
remember the last end. 21 Forget it not,
for there is no turning again: thou shalt
not do him good, but hurt thyself.
22 Remember my judgment: for thine
also shall be so; yesterday for me, and
today for thee. 23 When the dead is at
rest, let his remembrance rest; and be
comforted for him, when his spirit is
departed from him. 24 The wisdom of a
learned man cometh by opportunity of
leisure: and he that hath little business
shall become wise. 25 How can he get
wisdom that holdeth the plow, and that
glorieth in the goad, that driveth oxen,
and is occupied in their labors, and
whose talk is of bullocks? 26 He giveth
his mind to make furrows; and is
diligent to give the kine fodder. 27 So
every carpenter and workmaster, that
laboreth night and day: and they that
cut and grave seals, and are diligent to
make great variety, and give themselves
to counterfeit imagery, and watch to
finish a work: 28 the smith also sitting by
the anvil, and considering the iron
work, the vapor of the fire wasteth his
flesh, and he fighteth with the heat of
the furnace: the noise of the hammer
and the anvil is ever in his ears, and his
eyes look still upon the pattern of the
thing that he maketh; he setteth his
mind to finish his work, and watcheth
to polish it perfectly: 29 so doth the
potter sitting at his work, and turning
the wheel about with his feet, who is

always carefully set at his work, and
maketh all his work by number; 30 he
fashioneth the clay with his arm, and
boweth down his strength before his
feet; he applieth himself to lead it over;
and he is diligent to make clean the
furnace: 31 all these trust to their hands:
and every one is wise in his work.
32 Without these cannot a city be
inhabited: and they shall not dwell
where they will, nor go up and down:
33 they shall not be sought for in public
counsel, nor sit high in the
congregation: they shall not sit on the
judges' seat, nor understand the
sentence of judgment: they cannot
declare justice and judgment; and they
shall not be found where parables are
spoken. 34 But they will maintain the
state of the world, and [all] their desire
is in the work of their craft.

CHAPTER 39

1 But he that giveth his mind to the law
of the most High, and is occupied
in the meditation thereof, will seek
out the wisdom of all the ancient, and
be occupied in prophecies. 2 He will
keep the sayings of the renowned men:
and where subtle parables are, he will
be there also. 3 He will seek out the
secrets of grave sentences, and be
conversant in dark parables. 4 He shall
serve among great men, and appear
before princes: he will travel through
strange countries; for he hath tried the
good and the evil among men. 5 He will
give his heart to resort early to the Lord
that made him, and will pray before the
most High, and will open his mouth in
prayer, and make supplication for his
sins. 6 When the great Lord will, he shall
be filled with the spirit of
understanding: he shall pour out wise
sentences, and give thanks unto the
Lord in his prayer. 7 He shall direct his
counsel and knowledge, and in his
secrets shall he meditate. 8 He shall
show forth that which he hath learned,
and shall glory in the law of the
covenant of the Lord. 9 Many shall
commend his understanding; and so
long as the world endureth, it shall not be
blotted out; his memorial shall not
depart away, and his name shall live
from generation to generation.
10 Nations shall show forth his wisdom,
and the congregation shall declare his
praise. 11 If he die, he shall leave a
greater name than a thousand: and if he
live, he shall increase it.

12 Yet have I more to say, which I have
thought upon; for I am filled as the
moon at the full. 13 Hearken unto me, ye
holy children, and bud forth as a rose
growing by the brook of the field:
14 and give ye a sweet savor as
frankincense, and flourish as a lily,
send forth a smell, and sing a song of
praise, bless the Lord in all his works.
15 Magnify his name, and show forth his
praise with the songs of your lips, and
with harps, and in praising him ye shall
say after this manner: 16 All the works
of the Lord are exceeding good, and
whatsoever he commandeth shall be
accomplished in due season. 17 And
none may say, What is this? wherefore
is that? for at time convenient they shall
all be sought out: at his commandment
the waters stood as an heap, and at the
words of his mouth the receptacles of
waters. 18 At his commandment is done
whatsoever pleaseth him; and none can
hinder, when he will save. 19 The works
of all flesh are before him, and nothing
can be hid from his eyes. 20 He seeth
from everlasting to everlasting; and
there is nothing wonderful before him.

21 A man need not to say, What is this?
wherefore is that? for he hath made all
things for their uses. 22 His blessing
covered the dry land as a river, and
watered it as a flood. 23 As he hath
turned the waters into saltness: so shall
the heathen inherit his wrath. 24 As his
ways are plain unto the holy; so are
they stumbling-blocks unto the wicked.
25 For the good are good things created
from the beginning: so evil things for
sinners. 26 The principal things for the
whole use of man's life are water, fire,
iron, and salt, flour of wheat, honey,
milk, and the blood of the grape, and
oil, and clothing. 27 All these things are
for good to the godly: so to the sinners
they are turned into evil. 28 There be
spirits that are created for vengeance,
which in their fury lay on sore strokes;
in the time of destruction they pour out
their force, and appease the wrath of
him that made them. 29 Fire, and hail,
and famine, and death, all these were
created for vengeance; 30 teeth of wild
beasts, and scorpions, serpents, and
the sword, punishing the wicked to
destruction. 31 They shall rejoice in his
commandment, and they shall be ready
upon earth, when need is; and when
their time is come, they shall not
transgress his word. 32 Therefore from
the beginning I was resolved, and
thought upon these things, and have left
them in writing. 33 All the works of the
Lord are good: and he will give every
needful thing in due season. 34 So that a
man cannot say, This is worse than that:
for in time they shall all be well
approved. 35 And therefore praise ye the
Lord with the whole heart and mouth,
and bless the name of the Lord.

CHAPTER 40

1 Great travail is created for every man,
and an heavy yoke is upon the sons of
Adam, from the day that they go out of
their mother's womb, till the day that
they return to the mother of all things.
2 Their imagination of things to come,
and the day of death, [trouble] their
thoughts, and [cause] fear of heart;
3 from him that sitteth on a throne of
glory, unto him that is humbled in earth
and ashes; 4 from him that weareth
purple and a crown, unto him that is
clothed with a linen frock. 5 Wrath, and
envy, trouble, and unquietness, fear of
death, and anger, and strife, and in the
time of rest upon his bed his night
sleep, do change his knowledge. 6 A
little or nothing is his rest, and
afterward he is in his sleep, as in a day
of keeping watch, troubled in the vision
of his heart, as if he were escaped out
of a battle. 7 When all is safe, he
awaketh, and marveleth that the fear
was nothing. 8 [Such things happen]
unto all flesh, both man and beast, and
that is sevenfold more upon sinners.
9 Death, and bloodshed, strife, and
sword, calamities, famine, tribulation,
and the scourge; 10 these things are
created for the wicked, and for their
sakes came the flood. 11 All things that
are of the earth shall turn to the earth
again: and that which is of the waters
doth return into the sea.
12 All bribery and injustice shall be
blotted out: but true dealing shall
endure for ever. 13 The goods of the
unjust shall be dried up like a river, and
shall vanish with noise, like a great
thunder in rain. 14 While he openeth his
hand he shall rejoice: so shall
transgressors come to nought. 15 The
children of the ungodly shall not bring

forth many branches: but are as unclean roots upon a hard rock. 16The weed growing upon every water and bank of a river shall be pulled up before all grass. 17Bountifulness is as a most fruitful garden, and mercifulness endureth for ever.

18To labor, and to be content with that a man hath, is a sweet life: but he that findeth a treasure is above them both. 19Children and the building of a city continue a man's name: but a blameless wife is counted above them both. 20Wine and music rejoice the heart: but the love of wisdom is above them both. 21The pipe and the psaltery make sweet melody: but a pleasant tongue is above them both. 22Thine eye desireth favor and beauty: but more than both corn while it is green. 23A friend and companion never meet amiss: but above both is a wife with her husband. 24Brethren and help are against time of trouble: but alms shall deliver more than them both. 25Gold and silver make the foot stand sure: but counsel is esteemed above them both. 26Riches and strength lift up the heart: but the fear of the Lord is above them both: there is no want in the fear of the Lord, and it needeth not to seek help. 27The fear of the Lord is a fruitful garden, and covereth him above all glory.

28My son, lead not a beggar's life; for better it is to die than to beg. 29The life of him that dependeth on another man's table is not to be counted for a life; for he polluteth himself with other men's meat: but a wise man well nurtured will beware thereof. 30Begging is sweet in the mouth of the shameless: but in his belly there shall burn a fire.

CHAPTER 41

1O death, how bitter is the remembrance of thee to a man that liveth at rest in his possessions, unto the man that hath nothing to vex him, and that hath prosperity in all things; yea, unto him that is yet able to receive meat! 2O death, acceptable is thy sentence unto the needy, and unto him whose strength faileth, that is now in the last age, and is vexed with all things, and to him that despaireth, and hath lost patience! 3Fear not the sentence of death, remember them that have been before thee, and that come after; for this is the sentence of the Lord over all flesh. 4And why art thou against the pleasure of the most High? there is no inquisition in the grave, whether thou have lived ten, or an hundred, or a thousand years.

5The children of sinners are abominable children, and they that are conversant in the dwelling of the ungodly. 6The inheritance of sinners' children shall perish, and their posterity shall have a perpetual reproach. 7The children will complain of an ungodly father, because they shall be reproached for his sake. 8Woe be unto you, ungodly men, which have forsaken the law of the most high God! for if ye increase, it shall be to your destruction: 9and if ye be born, ye shall be born to a curse: and if ye die, a curse shall be your portion. 10All that are of the earth shall turn to earth again: so the ungodly shall go from a curse to destruction. 11The mourning of men is about their bodies: but an ill name of sinners shall be blotted out. 12Have regard to thy name; for that shall continue with thee above a thousand great treasures of gold. 13A good life hath but few days: but a good name

endureth for ever.
14My children, keep discipline in peace:
for wisdom that is hid, and a treasure that is
not seen, what profit is in them both? 15A
man that hideth his foolishness is better
than a man that hideth his wisdom.
16Therefore be shamefaced according to
my word: for it is not good to retain all
shamefacedness; neither is it altogether
approved in every thing. 17Be ashamed
of whoredom before father and mother:
and of a lie before a prince and a mighty
man; 18of an offense before a judge and
ruler; of iniquity before a congregation
and people; of unjust dealing before thy
partner and friend; 19and of theft in
regard of the place where thou
sojournest, and in regard of the truth of
God and his covenant; and to lean with
thine elbow upon the meat; and of
scorning to give and take; 20and of
silence before them that salute thee;
and to look upon an harlot; 21and to
turn away thy face from thy kinsman;
or to take away a portion or a gift; or to
gaze upon another man's wife; 22or to
be overbusy with his maid, and come
not near her bed; or of upbraiding
speeches before friends; and after thou
hast given, upbraid not; 23or of iterating
and speaking again that which thou hast
heard; and of revealing of secrets. 24So
shalt thou be truly shamefaced, and
find favor before all men.

CHAPTER 42

1Of these things be not thou ashamed,
and accept no person to sin thereby: 2of
the law of the most High, and his
covenant; and of judgment to justify the
ungodly; 3of reckoning with thy
partners and travelers; or of the gift of
the heritage of friends; 4of exactness of
balance and weights; or of getting much
or little; 5and of merchants' indifferent
selling; of much correction of children;
and to make the side of an evil servant
to bleed. 6Sure keeping is good, where an
evil wife is; and shut up, where many
hands are. 7Deliver all things in number
and weight; and put all in writing that
thou givest out, or receivest in. 8Be not
ashamed to inform the unwise and
foolish, and the extreme aged that
contendeth with those that are young:
thus shalt thou be truly learned, and
approved of all men living.
9The father waketh for the daughter,
when no man knoweth; and the care for
her taketh away sleep: when she is
young, lest she pass away the flower of
her age; and being married, lest she
should be hated: 10in her virginity, lest
she should be defiled and gotten with
child in her father's house; and having
an husband, lest she should misbehave
herself; and when she is married, lest
she should be barren. 11Keep a sure
watch over a shameless daughter, lest
she make thee a laughingstock to thine
enemies, and a byword in the city, and a
reproach among the people, and make
thee ashamed before the multitude.
12Behold not every body's beauty, and
sit not in the midst of women. 13For
from garments cometh a moth, and
from women wickedness. 14Better is
the churlishness of a man than a
courteous woman, a woman, I say,
which bringeth shame and reproach.
15I will now remember the works of
the Lord, and declare the things that
I have seen: In the words of the Lord
are his works. 16The sun that giveth
light looketh upon all things, and
the work thereof is full of the glory of
the Lord. 17The Lord hath not given
power to the saints to declare all his
marvelous works, which the Almighty

Lord firmly settled, that whatsoever is might be established for his glory. 18He seeketh out the deep, and the heart, and considereth their crafty devices; for the Lord knoweth all that may be known, and he beholdeth the signs of the world. 19He declareth the things that are past, and for to come, and revealeth the steps of hidden things. 20No thought escapeth him, neither any word is hidden from him. 21He hath garnished the excellent works of his wisdom, and he is from everlasting to everlasting: unto him may nothing be added, neither can he be diminished, and he hath no need of any counselor. 22Oh how desirable are all his works! and that a man may see even to a spark. 23All these things live and remain for ever for all uses, and they are all obedient. 24All things are double one against another: and he hath made nothing imperfect. 25One thing establisheth the good of another: and who shall be filled with beholding his glory?

CHAPTER 43

1The pride of the height, the clear firmament, the beauty of heaven, with his glorious show; 2the sun when it appeareth, declaring at his rising a marvelous instrument, the work of the most High: 3at noon it parcheth the country, and who can abide the burning heat thereof? 4A man blowing a furnace is in works of heat, but the sun burneth the mountains three times more; breathing out fiery vapors, and sending forth bright beams, it dimmeth the eyes. 5Great is the Lord that made it; and at his commandment it runneth hastily.

6He made the moon also to serve in her season for a declaration of times, and a sign of the world. 7From the moon is the sign of feasts, a light that decreaseth in her perfection. 8The month is called after her name, increasing wonderfully in her changing, being an instrument of the armies above, shining in the firmament of heaven; 9the beauty of heaven, the glory of the stars, an ornament giving light in the highest places of the Lord. 10At the commandment of the Holy One they will stand in their order, and never faint in their watches.

11Look upon the rainbow, and praise him that made it; very beautiful it is in the brightness thereof. 12It compasseth the heaven about with a glorious circle, and the hands of the most High have bended it.

13By his commandment he maketh the snow to fall apace, and sendeth swiftly the lightnings of his judgment. 14Through this the treasures are opened: and clouds fly forth as fowls. 15By his great power he maketh the clouds firm, and the hailstones are broken small. 16At his sight the mountains are shaken, and at his will the south wind bloweth. 17The noise of the thunder maketh the earth to tremble: so doth the northern storm and the whirlwind: as birds flying he scattereth the snow, and the falling down thereof is as the lighting of grasshoppers: 18the eye marveleth at the beauty of the whiteness thereof, and the heart is astonished at the raining of it. 19The hoarfrost also as salt he poureth on the earth, and being congealed, it lieth on the top of sharp stakes. 20When the cold north wind bloweth, and the water is congealed into ice, it abideth upon every gathering together of water, and clotheth the water as with a breastplate. 21It devoureth the

mountains, and burneth the wilderness,
and consumeth the grass as fire. 22A
present remedy of all is a mist coming
speedily: a dew coming after heat
refresheth.
23By his counsel he appeaseth the deep,
and planteth islands therein. 24They that
sail on the sea tell of the danger thereof;
and when we hear it with our ears, we
marvel thereat. 25For therein be strange
and wondrous works, variety of all
kinds of beasts and whales created.
26By him the end of them hath
prosperous success, and by his word all
things consist.
27We may speak much, and yet come
short: wherefore in sum, he is all.
28How shall we be able to magnify him?
for he is great above all his works. 29The
Lord is terrible and very great, and
marvelous is his power. 30When ye
glorify the Lord, exalt him as much as
ye can; for even yet will he far exceed:
and when ye exalt him, put forth all your
strength, and be not weary; for ye can
never go far enough. 31Who hath seen
him, that he might tell us? and who can
magnify him as he is?
32There are yet hid greater things than
these be, for we have seen but a few of
his works.
33For the Lord hath made all things; and
to the godly hath he given wisdom.

CHAPTER 44

1Let us now praise famous men, and
our fathers that begot us. 2The Lord
hath wrought great glory by them
through his great power from the
beginning. 3Such as did bear rule in
their kingdoms, men renowned for their
power, giving counsel by their
understanding, and declaring
prophecies: 4leaders of the people by
their counsels, and by their knowledge
of learning meet for the people, wise
and eloquent in their instructions: 5such
as found out musical tunes, and recited
verses in writing: 6rich men furnished with
ability, living peaceably in their
habitations: 7all these were honored in
their generations, and were the glory of
their times. 8There be of them, that
have left a name behind them, that
their praises might be reported. 9And
some there be, which have no memorial;
who are perished, as though they had
never been; and are become as though
they had never been born; and their
children after them. 10But these were
merciful men, whose righteousness
hath not been forgotten. 11With their
seed shall continually remain a good
inheritance, and their children are
within the covenant. 12Their seed
standeth fast, and their children for
their sakes. 13Their seed shall remain for
ever, and their glory shall not be blotted
out. 14Their bodies are buried in peace;
but their name liveth for evermore.
15The people will tell of their wisdom,
and the congregation will show forth
their praise.
16Enoch pleased the Lord, and was
translated, being an example of
repentance to all generations.
17Noah was found perfect and
righteous; in the time of wrath he was
taken in exchange [for the world;]
therefore was he left as a remnant unto
the earth, when the flood came. 18An
everlasting covenant was made with
him, that all flesh should perish no
more by the flood.
19Abraham was a great father of many
people: in glory was there none like
unto him; 20who kept the law of the
most High, and was in covenant with
him: he established the covenant in his

flesh; and when he was proved, he was
found faithful. [21]Therefore he assured
him by an oath, that he would bless the
nations in his seed, and that he would
multiply him as the dust of the earth,
and exalt his seed as the stars, and cause
them to inherit from sea to sea, and
from the river unto the utmost part of
the land.
[22]With Isaac did he establish likewise
[for Abraham his father's sake] the
blessing of all men, and the covenant,
[23]and made it rest upon the head of
Jacob. He acknowledged him in his
blessing, and gave him an heritage, and
divided his portions; among the twelve
tribes did he part them.

CHAPTER 45

[1]And he brought out of him a merciful
man, which found favor in the sight of
all flesh, even Moses, beloved of God
and men, whose memorial is blessed.
[2]He made him like to the glorious
saints, and magnified him, so that his
enemies stood in fear of him. [3]By his
words he caused the wonders to cease,
and he made him glorious in the sight
of kings, and gave him a
commandment for his people, and
showed him part of his glory. [4]He
sanctified him in his faithfulness and
meekness, and chose him out of all
men. [5]He made him to hear his voice,
and brought him into the dark cloud,
and gave him commandments before his
face, even the law of life and
knowledge, that he might teach Jacob
his covenants, and Israel his judgments.
[6]He exalted Aaron, an holy man like
unto him, even his brother, of the tribe
of Levi. [7]An everlasting covenant he
made with him, and gave him the
priesthood among the people; he
beautified him with comely ornaments,
and clothed him with a robe of glory,
[8]he put upon him perfect glory; and
strengthened him with rich garments,
with breeches, with a long robe, and
the ephod. [9]And he compassed him
with pomegranates, and with many
golden bells round about, that as he
went there might be a sound, and a
noise made that might be heard in the
temple, for a memorial to the children
of his people; [10]with an holy garment,
with gold, and blue silk, and purple,
the work of the embroiderer, with a
breastplate of judgment, and with Urim
and Thummim; [11]with twisted scarlet,
the work of the cunning workman, with
precious stones graven like seals, and
set in gold, the work of the jeweller,
with a writing engraved for a memorial,
after the number of the tribes of Israel.
[12]He set a crown of gold upon the
mitre, wherein was engraved Holiness,
an ornament of honor, a costly work,
the desires of the eyes, goodly and
beautiful. [13]Before him there were none
such, neither did ever any stranger put
them on, but only his children and his
children's children perpetually.
[14]Their sacrifices shall be wholly
consumed every day twice continually.
[15]Moses consecrated him, and anointed
him with holy oil: this was appointed
unto him by an everlasting covenant,
and to his seed, so long as the heavens
should remain, that they should
minister unto him, and execute the
office of the priesthood, and bless the
people in his name. [16]He chose him out
of all men living to offer sacrifices to
the Lord, incense, and a sweet savor, for a
memorial, to make reconciliation for his
people. [17] He gave unto him his
commandments, and authority in the
statutes of judgments, that he should

teach Jacob the testimonies, and inform
Israel in his laws. 18 Strangers conspired
together against him, and maligned him
in the wilderness, even the men that
were of Dathan's and Abi´ram's side,
and the congregation of Korah, with
fury and wrath. 19 This the Lord saw,
and it displeased him, and in his
wrathful indignation were they
consumed: he did wonders upon them,
to consume them with the fiery flame.
20 But he made Aaron more honorable,
and gave him an heritage, and divided
unto him the firstfruits of the increase;
especially he prepared bread in
abundance: 21 for they eat of the
sacrifices of the Lord, which he gave
unto him and his seed. 22 Howbeit in
the land of the people he had no
inheritance, neither had he any portion
among the people: for the Lord himself
is his portion and inheritance.
23 The third in glory is Phin´ehas the son
of Ele-a´zar, because he had zeal in the
fear of the Lord, and stood up with
good courage of heart when the people
were turned back, and made
reconciliation for Israel. 24 Therefore
was there a covenant of peace made
with him, that he should be the chief of
the sanctuary and of his people, and
that he and his posterity should have the
dignity of the priesthood for ever:
25 according to the covenant made with
David son of Jesse, of the tribe of Judah,
that the inheritance of the king should
be to his posterity alone: so the
inheritance of Aaron should also be
unto his seed. 26 God give you wisdom
in your heart to judge his people in
righteousness, that their good things be
not abolished, and that their glory may
endure for ever.

CHAPTER 46

1 Joshua the son of Nun was valiant in
the wars, and was the successor of
Moses in prophecies, who according to
his name was made great for the saving
of the elect of God, and taking
vengeance of the enemies that rose up
against them, that he might set Israel in
their inheritance. 2 How great glory got
he, when he did lift up his hands, and
stretched out his sword against the
cities! 3 Who before him so stood to it?
for the Lord himself brought his
enemies unto him. 4 Did not the sun go
back by his means? and was not one
day as long as two? 5 He called upon the
most high Lord, when the enemies
pressed upon him on every side; and
the great Lord heard him. 6 And with
hailstones of mighty power he made the
battle to fall violently upon the nations,
and in the descent [of Beth–ho´ron] he
destroyed them that resisted, that the
nations might know all their strength,
because he fought in the sight of the
Lord, and he followed the Mighty One.
7 In the time of Moses also he did a work
of mercy, he and Caleb the son of
Jephun´neh, in that they withstood the
congregation, and withheld the people
from sin, and appeased the wicked
murmuring. 8 And of six hundred
thousand people on foot, they two were
preserved to bring them into the
heritage, even unto the land that
floweth with milk and honey. 9 The
Lord gave strength also unto Caleb,
which remained with him unto his old
age: so that he entered upon the high
places of the land, and his seed
obtained it for an heritage: 10 that all the
children of Israel might see that it is
good to follow the Lord.
11 And concerning the judges, every one

by name, whose heart went not a
whoring, nor departed from the Lord,
let their memory be blessed. 12 Let their
bones flourish out of their place, and let
the name of them that were honored be
continued upon their children.
13 Samuel, the prophet of the Lord,
beloved of his Lord, established a
kingdom, and anointed princes over his
people. 14 By the law of the Lord he
judged the congregation, and the Lord
had respect unto Jacob. 15 By his
faithfulness he was found a true
prophet, and by his word he was known
to be faithful in vision. 16 He called
upon the mighty Lord, when his
enemies pressed upon him on every
side, when he offered the sucking lamb.
17 And the Lord thundered from heaven,
and with a great noise made his voice
to be heard. 18 And he destroyed the
rulers of the Tyrians, and all the princes
of the Philistines. 19 And before his long
sleep he made protestations in the sight
of the Lord and his anointed, I have not
taken any man's goods, so much as a
shoe: and no man did accuse him. 20 And
after his death he prophesied, and
showed the king his end, and lifted up
his voice from the earth in prophecy, to
blot out the wickedness of the people.

CHAPTER 47

1 And after him rose up Nathan to
prophesy in the time of David. 2 As is
the fat taken away from the peace
offering, so was David chosen out of the
children of Israel. 3 He played with lions
as with kids, and with bears as with
lambs. 4 Slew he not a giant, when he
was yet but young? and did he not take
away reproach from the people, when
he lifted up his hand with the stone in
the sling, and beat down the boasting of
Goli'ath? 5 For he called upon the most
high Lord; and he gave him strength in
his right hand to slay that mighty
warrior, and set up the horn of his
people. 6 So the people honored him
with ten thousands, and praised him in
the blessings of the Lord, in that he
gave him a crown of glory. 7 For he
destroyed the enemies on every side,
and brought to nought the Philistines
his adversaries, and brake their horn in
sunder unto this day. 8 In all his works
he praised the Holy One most high with
words of glory; with his whole heart he
sang songs, and loved him that made
him. 9 He set singers also before the
altar, that by their voices they might
make sweet melody, and daily sing
praises in their songs. 10 He beautified
their feasts, and set in order the solemn
times until the end, that they might
praise his holy name, and that the
temple might sound from morning.
11 The Lord took away his sins, and
exalted his horn for ever: he gave him a
covenant of kings, and a throne of glory
in Israel.
12 After him rose up a wise son, and for
his sake he dwelt at large. 13 Solomon
reigned in a peaceable time, and was
honored; for God made all quiet round
about him, that he might build an house
in his name, and prepare his sanctuary
for ever. 14 How wise wast thou in thy
youth, and, as a flood, filled with
understanding! 15 Thy soul covered the
whole earth, and thou filledst it with
dark parables. 16 Thy name went far
unto the islands; and for thy peace thou
wast beloved. 17 The countries marveled
at thee for thy songs, and proverbs, and
parables, and interpretations. 18 By the
name of the Lord God, which is called
the Lord God of Israel, thou didst gather
gold as tin, and didst multiply silver as

lead. 19 Thou didst bow thy loins unto
women, and by thy body thou wast
brought into subjection. 20 Thou didst
stain thy honor, and pollute thy seed: so
that thou broughtest wrath upon thy
children, and wast grieved for thy folly.
21 So the kingdom was divided, and out
of E´phrai-m ruled a rebellious
kingdom. 22 But the Lord will never
leave off his mercy, neither shall any of
his works perish, neither will he abolish
the posterity of his elect, and the seed of
him that loveth him he will not take
away: wherefore he gave a remnant
unto Jacob, and out of him a root unto
David.
23 Thus rested Solomon with his fathers,
and of his seed he left behind him
Rehobo´am, even the foolishness of the
people, and one that had no
understanding, who turned away the
people through his counsel. There was
also Jerobo´am the son of Nebat, who
caused Israel to sin, and showed E´phra-
im the way of sin: 24 and their sins were
multiplied exceedingly, that they were
driven out of the land. 25 For they sought
out all wickedness, till the vengeance
came upon them.

CHAPTER 48

1 Then stood up Eli´jah the prophet as
fire, and his word burned like a lamp.
2 He brought a sore famine upon them,
and by his zeal he diminished their
number. 3 By the word of the Lord he
shut up the heaven, and also three times
brought down fire. 4 O Eli´jah, how
wast thou honored in thy wondrous
deeds! and who may glory like unto
thee! 5 Who didst raise up a dead man
from death, and his soul from the place
of the dead, by the word of the most
High: 6 who broughtest kings to
destruction, and honorable men from
their bed: 7 who heardest the rebuke of
the Lord in Si´nai, and in Horeb the
judgment of vengeance: 8 who
anointedst kings to take revenge, and
prophets to succeed after him: 9 who
wast taken up in a whirlwind of fire,
and in a chariot of fiery horses: 10 who
wast ordained for reproofs in their
times, to pacify the wrath of the Lord's
judgment, before it brake forth into
fury, and to turn the heart of the father
unto the son, and to restore the tribes of
Jacob. 11 Blessed are they that saw thee,
and slept in love; for we shall surely
live.
12 Eli´jah it was, who was covered with
a whirlwind: and Eli´sha was filled
with his spirit: whilst he lived, he was
not moved with the presence of any
prince, neither could any bring him into
subjection. 13 No word could overcome
him; and after his death his body
prophesied. 14 He did wonders in his
life, and at his death were his works
marvelous.
15 For all this the people repented not,
neither departed they from their sins,
till they were spoiled and carried out of
their land, and were scattered through
all the earth: yet there remained a small
people, and a ruler in the house of David:
16 of whom some did that which was
pleasing to God, and some multiplied
sins.
17 Hezeki´ah fortified his city, and
brought in water into the midst thereof:
he digged the hard rock with iron, and
made wells for waters. 18 In his time
Sennach´erib came up, and sent Rab–
sha´keh, and lifted up his hand against
Zion, and boasted proudly. 19 Then
trembled their hearts and hands, and
they were in pain, as women in
travail. 20 But they called upon the

Lord which is merciful, and stretched
out their hands toward him: and
immediately the Holy One heard them
out of heaven, and delivered them by
the ministry of Isaiah. 21 He smote the
host of the Assyrians, and his angel
destroyed them. 22 For Hezeki'ah had
done the thing that pleased the Lord,
and was strong in the ways of David his
father, as Isaiah the prophet, who was
great and faithful in his vision, had
commanded him. 23 In his time the sun
went backward, and he lengthened the
king's life. 24 He saw by an excellent
spirit what should come to pass at the
last, and he comforted them that
mourned in Zion. 25 He showed what
should come to pass for ever, and secret
things or ever they came.

CHAPTER 49

1 The remembrance of Josi'ah is like the
composition of the perfume that is
made by the art of the apothecary: it is
sweet as honey in all mouths, and as
music at a banquet of wine. 2 He
behaved himself uprightly in the
conversion of the people, and took
away the abominations of iniquity. 3 He
directed his heart unto the Lord, and in
the time of the ungodly he established
the worship of God.
4 All, except David and Hezeki'ah and
Josi'ah, were defective: for they
forsook the law of the most High, even
the kings of Judah failed. 5 Therefore he
gave their power unto others, and their
glory to a strange nation. 6 They burnt
the chosen city of the sanctuary, and
made the streets desolate, according to
the prophecy of Jeremiah. 7 For they
treated him evil, who nevertheless was
a prophet, sanctified in his mother's
womb, that he might root out, and
afflict, and destroy; and that he might
build up also, and plant.
8 It was Ezekiel who saw the glorious
vision, which was shown him upon the
chariot of the cherubim. 9 For he made
mention of the enemies under the figure
of the rain, and directed them that went
right. 10 And of the twelve prophets let
the memorial be blessed, and let their
bones flourish again out of their place:
for they comforted Jacob, and delivered
them by assured hope.
11 How shall we magnify Zerub'babel?
even he was as a signet on the right
hand: 12 so was Jesh'u-a the son of
Joz'adak: who in their time builded the
house, and set up an holy temple to the
Lord, which was prepared for
everlasting glory. 13 And among the
elect was Nehemi'ah, whose renown is
great, who raised up for us the walls
that were fallen, and set up the gates
and the bars, and raised up our ruins
again.
14 But upon the earth was no man
created like Enoch; for he was taken
from the earth. 15 Neither was there a
man born like unto Joseph, a governor
of his brethren, a stay of the people,
whose bones were regarded of the
Lord. 16 Shem and Seth were in great
honor among men, and so was Adam
above every living thing in the creation.

CHAPTER 50

1 Simon the high priest, the son of
Oni'as, who in his life repaired the
house again, and in his days fortified
the temple: 2 and by him was built from
the foundation the double height, the
high fortress of the wall about the
temple: 3 in his days the cistern to
receive water, being in compass as the
sea, was covered with plates of brass:

[4]he took care of the temple that it should not fall, and fortified the city against besieging: [5]how was he honored in the midst of the people in his coming out of the sanctuary! [6]he was as the morning star in the midst of a cloud, and as the moon at the full: [7]as the sun shining upon the temple of the most High, and as the rainbow giving light in the bright clouds: [8]and as the flower of roses in the spring of the year, as lilies by the rivers of waters, and as the branches of the frankincense tree in the time of summer: [9]as fire and incense in the censer, and as a vessel of beaten gold set with all manner of precious stones: [10]and as a fair olive tree budding forth fruit, and as a cypress tree which groweth up to the clouds. [11]When he put on the robe of honor, and was clothed with the perfection of glory, when he went up to the holy altar, he made the garment of holiness honorable. [12]When he took the portions out of the priests' hands, he himself stood by the hearth of the altar, compassed with his brethren round about, as a young cedar in Lebanon; and as palm trees compassed they him round about. [13]So were all the sons of Aaron in their glory, and the oblations of the Lord in their hands, before all the congregation of Israel. [14]And finishing the service at the altar, that he might adorn the offering of the most high Almighty, [15]he stretched out his hand to the cup, and poured of the blood of the grape, he poured out at the foot of the altar a sweetsmelling savor unto the most high King of all. [16]Then shouted the sons of Aaron, and sounded the silver trumpets, and made a great noise to be heard, for a remembrance before the most High. [17]Then all the people together hasted, and fell down to the earth upon their faces to worship their Lord God Almighty, the most High. [18]The singers also sang praises with their voices, with great variety of sounds was there made sweet melody. [19]And the people besought the Lord, the most High, by prayer before him that is merciful, till the solemnity of the Lord was ended, and they had finished his service. [20]Then he went down, and lifted up his hands over the whole congregation of the children of Israel, to give the blessing of the Lord with his lips, and to rejoice in his name. [21]And they bowed themselves down to worship the second time, that they might receive a blessing from the most High.

[22]Now therefore bless ye the God of all, which only doeth wondrous things every where, which exalteth our days from the womb, and dealeth with us according to his mercy. [23]He grant us joyfulness of heart, and that peace may be in our days in Israel for ever: [24]that he would confirm his mercy with us, and deliver us at his time!

[25]There be two manner of nations which my heart abhorreth, and the third is no nation: [26]they that sit upon the mountain of Samaria, and they that dwell among the Philistines, and that foolish people that dwell in Shechem.

[27]Jesus the son of Sirach of Jerusalem hath written in this book the instruction of understanding and knowledge, who out of his heart poured forth wisdom.

[28]Blessed is he that shall be exercised in these things; and he that layeth them up in his heart shall become wise. [29]For if he do them, he shall be strong to all things: for the light of the Lord leadeth him, who giveth wisdom to the godly. Blessed be the Lord for ever. Amen, Amen.

CHAPTER 51

1 I will thank thee, O Lord and King, and
praise thee, O God my Saviour: I do
give praise unto thy name: 2 for thou art
my defender and helper, and hast
preserved my body from destruction,
and from the snare of the slanderous
tongue, and from the lips that forge lies,
and has been mine helper against mine
adversaries: 3 and hast delivered me,
according to the multitude of thy
mercies and greatness of thy name,
from the teeth of them that were ready
to devour me, and out of the hands of
such as sought after my life, and from
the manifold afflictions which I had;
4 from the choking of fire on every side,
and from the midst of the fire which I
kindled not; 5 from the depth of the belly
of hell, from an unclean tongue, and
from lying words. 6 By an accusation to
the king from an unrighteous tongue
my soul drew near even unto death, my
life was near to the hell beneath. 7 They
compassed me on every side, and
there was no man to help me: I looked
for the succor of men, but there was
none. 8 Then thought I upon thy mercy,
O Lord, and upon thy acts of old, how
thou deliverest such as wait for thee,
and savest them out of the hands of the
enemies. 9 Then lifted I up my
supplication from the earth, and prayed
for deliverance from death. 10 I called
upon the Lord, the Father of my Lord,
that he would not leave me in the days
of my trouble, and in the time of the
proud, when there was no help. 11 I will
praise thy name continually, and will
sing praise with thanksgiving; and so
my prayer was heard: 12 for thou savedst
me from destruction, and deliveredst
me from the evil time: therefore will I
give thanks, and praise thee, and bless
thy name, O Lord.
13 When I was yet young, or ever I went
abroad, I desired wisdom openly in
my prayer. 14 I prayed for her before the
temple, and will seek her out even to
the end. 15 Even from the flower till the
grape was ripe hath my heart delighted
in her: my foot went the right way, from
my youth up sought I after her. 16 I bowed
down mine ear a little, and received her,
and got much learning. 17 I profited
therein, therefore will I ascribe the glory
unto him that giveth me wisdom. 18 For
I purposed to do after her, and earnestly
I followed that which is good; so shall I
not be confounded. 19 My soul hath
wrestled with her, and in my doings I
was exact: I stretched forth my hands to
the heaven above, and bewailed my
ignorances of her. 20 I directed my soul
unto her, and I found her in pureness:
I have had my heart joined with her
from the beginning, therefore shall I
not be foresaken. 21 My heart was
troubled in seeking her: therefore have
I gotten a good possession. 22 The Lord
hath given me a tongue for my reward,
and I will praise him therewith.
23 Draw near unto me, ye unlearned, and
dwell in the house of learning.
24 Wherefore are ye slow, and what say ye
of these things, seeing your souls are very
thirsty? 25 I opened my mouth, and said,
Buy her for yourselves without money.
26 Put your neck under the yoke, and let
your soul receive instruction: she is
hard at hand to find. 27 Behold with your
eyes, how that I have had but little
labor, and have gotten unto me much
rest. 28 Get learning with a great sum of
money, and get much gold by her. 29 Let
your soul rejoice in his mercy, and be not
ashamed of his praise. 30 Work your
work betimes, and in his time he will
give you your reward.

BARUCH

CHAPTER 1

1 And these are the words of the book,
which Baruch the son of Neri´ah, the
son of Ma-asei´ah, the son of
Zedeki´ah, the son of Hasadi´ah, the
son of Hilki´ah, wrote in Babylon, 2 in
the fifth year, and in the seventh day of
the month, what time as the Chalde´ans
took Jerusalem, and burnt it with fire.
3 And Baruch did read the words of this
book in the hearing of Jeconi´ah the son
of Jehoi´akim king of Judah, and in the
ears of all the people that came to hear
the book, 4 and in the hearing of the
nobles, and of the king's sons, and in
the hearing of the elders, and of all the
people, from the lowest unto the
highest, even of all them that dwelt at
Babylon by the river Sud. 5 Whereupon
they wept, fasted, and prayed before the
Lord.
6 They made also a collection of money
according to every man's power: 7 and
they sent it to Jerusalem unto
Jehoi´akim the high priest, the son of
Hilki´ah, son of Shallum, and to the
priests, and to all the people which
were found with him at Jerusalem, 8 at
the same time when he received the
vessels of the house of the Lord, that
were carried out of the temple, to return
them into the land of Judah, the tenth
day of the month Sivan, namely, silver
vessels, which Zedeki´ah the son of
Josi´ah king of Judah had made, 9 after
that Nebuchadnez´zar king of Babylon
had carried away Jeconi´ah, and the
princes, and the captives, and the
mighty men, and the people of the land,
from Jerusalem, and brought them unto
Babylon. 10 And they said, Behold, we
have sent you money to buy you burnt
offerings, and sin offerings, and
incense, and prepare ye manna, and
offer upon the altar of the Lord our
God; 11 and pray for the life of
Nebuchadnez´zar king of Babylon, and
for the life of Belshaz´zar his son, that
their days may be upon earth as the days
of heaven: 12 and the Lord will give us
strength, and lighten our eyes, and we
shall live under the shadow of
Nebuchadnez´zar king of Babylon,
and under the shadow of Belshaz´zar his
son, and we shall serve them many
days, and find favor in their sight.
13 Pray for us also unto the Lord our God,
for we have sinned against the Lord our
God; and unto this day the fury of the
Lord and his wrath is not turned from
us. 14 And ye shall read this book which
we have sent unto you, to make
confession in the house of the Lord,
upon the feasts and solemn days.
15 And ye shall say, To the Lord our God
belongeth righteousness, but unto us
the confusion of faces, as it is come to
pass this day, unto them of Judah, and
to the inhabitants of Jerusalem, 16 and to
our kings, and to our princes, and to our
priests, and to our prophets, and to our
fathers: 17 for we have sinned before the
Lord, 18 and disobeyed him, and have
not hearkened unto the voice of the
Lord our God, to walk in the
commandments that he gave us openly:
19 since the day that the Lord brought our
forefathers out of the land of Egypt,
unto this present day, we have been
disobedient unto the Lord our God, and
we have been negligent in not hearing
his voice. 20 Wherefore the evils cleaved
unto us, and the curse, which the Lord
appointed by Moses his servant at the
time that he brought our fathers out of

the land of Egypt, to give us a land that
floweth with milk and honey, like as it
is to see this day. 21 Nevertheless we
have not hearkened unto the voice of
the Lord our God, according unto all
the words of the prophets, whom he
sent unto us: 22 but every man followed
the imagination of his own wicked
heart, to serve strange gods, and to
do evil in the sight of the Lord our
God.

CHAPTER 2

1 Therefore the Lord hath made good his
word, which he pronounced against us,
and against our judges that judged
Israel, and against our kings, and
against our princes, and against the men
of Israel and Judah, 2 to bring upon us
great plagues, such as never happened
under the whole heaven, as it came to
pass in Jerusalem, according to the
things that were written in the law of
Moses; 3 that a man should eat the flesh
of his own son, and the flesh of his own
daughter. 4 Moreover he hath delivered
them to be in subjection to all the
kingdoms that are round about us, to be
as a reproach and desolation among all
the people round about, where the Lord
hath scattered them. 5 Thus we were
cast down, and not exalted, because we
have sinned against the Lord our God,
and have not been obedient unto his
voice.

6 To the Lord our God appertaineth
righteousness: but unto us and to our
fathers open shame, as appeareth this
day. 7 For all these plagues are come
upon us, which the Lord hath
pronounced against us. 8 Yet have we
not prayed before the Lord, that we
might turn every one from the
imaginations of his wicked heart.
9 Wherefore the Lord watched over us
for evil, and the Lord hath brought it
upon us: for the Lord is righteous in all
his works which he hath commanded
us. 10 Yet we have not hearkened unto
his voice, to walk in the
commandments of the Lord, that he
hath set before us. The Exiles Pray for
Restoration

11 And now, O Lord God of Israel,
that hast brought thy people out of the
land of Egypt with a mighty hand, and
high arm, and with signs, and with
wonders, and with great power, and
hast gotten thyself a name, as appeareth
this day: 12 O Lord our God, we have
sinned, we have done ungodly, we have
dealt unrighteously in all thine
ordinances. 13 Let thy wrath turn from
us: for we are but a few left among the
heathen, where thou hast scattered us.
14 Hear our prayers, O Lord, and our
petitions, and deliver us for thine own
sake, and give us favor in the sight of
them which have led us away: 15 that all
the earth may know that thou art the
Lord our God, because Israel and his
posterity is called by thy name. 16 O
Lord, look down from thine holy
house, and consider us: bow down
thine ear, O Lord, to hear us. 17 Open
thine eyes, and behold; for the dead that
are in the graves, whose souls are taken
from their bodies, will give unto the
Lord neither praise nor righteousness:
18 but the soul that is greatly vexed,
which goeth stooping and feeble, and
the eyes that fail, and the hungry soul,
will give thee praise and righteousness,
O Lord. 19 Therefore we do not make
our humble supplication before thee,
O Lord our God, for the righteousness
of our fathers, and of our kings. 20 For
thou hast sent out thy wrath and
indignation upon us, as thou hast

spoken by thy servants the prophets,
saying, 21Thus saith the Lord, Bow
down your shoulders to serve the king
of Babylon: so shall ye remain in the
land that I gave unto your fathers. 22But
if ye will not hear the voice of the Lord,
to serve the king of Babylon, 23I will
cause to cease out of the cites of Judah,
and from without Jerusalem, the voice
of mirth, and the voice of joy, the voice
of the bridegroom, and the voice of
the bride: and the whole land shall be
desolate of inhabitants. 24But we would
not hearken unto thy voice, to serve the
king of Babylon: therefore hast thou
made good the words that thou spakest
by thy servants the prophets, namely,
that the bones of our kings, and the
bones of our fathers, should be taken
out of their places. 25And, lo, they are
cast out to the heat of the day, and to the
frost of the night, and they died in great
miseries by famine, by sword, and by
pestilence. 26And the house which is
called by thy name hast thou laid waste,
as it is to be seen this day, for the
wickedness of the house of Israel and
the house of Judah.
27O Lord our God, thou hast dealt with
us after all thy goodness, and according
to all that great mercy of thine, 28as thou
spakest by thy servant Moses in the day
when thou didst command him to write
thy law before the children of Israel,
saying, 29If ye will not hear my voice,
surely this very great multitude shall be
turned into a small number among the
nations, where I will scatter them. 30For
I knew that they would not hear me,
because it is a stiffnecked people: but
in the land of their captivities they shall
remember themselves, 31and shall
know that I am the Lord their God:
for I will give them an heart, and ears
to hear: 32and they shall praise me in the
land of their captivity, and think upon
my name, 33and return from their stiff
neck, and from their wicked deeds: for
they shall remember the way of their
fathers, which sinned before the Lord.
34And I will bring them again into the
land which I promised with an oath
unto their fathers, Abraham, Isaac, and
Jacob, and they shall be lords of it: and
I will increase them, and they shall not
be diminished. 35And I will make an
everlasting covenant with them to be
their God, and they shall be my people:
and I will no more drive my people of
Israel out of the land that I have given
them.

CHAPTER 3

1O Lord Almighty, God of Israel, the
soul in anguish, the troubled spirit,
crieth unto thee. 2Hear, O Lord, and
have mercy; for thou art merciful: and
have pity upon us, because we have
sinned before thee. 3For thou endurest
for ever, and we perish utterly. 4O Lord
Almighty, thou God of Israel, hear now
the prayers of the dead Israelites, and of
their children, which have sinned
before thee, and not hearkened unto the
voice of thee their God: for the which
cause these plagues cleave unto us.
5Remember not the iniquities of our
forefathers: but think upon thy power
and thy name now at this time. 6For thou
art the Lord our God, and thee, O Lord,
will we praise. 7And for this cause thou
hast put thy fear in our hearts, to the
intent that we should call upon thy
name, and praise thee in our captivity:
for we have called to mind all the
iniquity of our forefathers, that sinned
before thee. 8Behold, we are yet this
day in our captivity, where thou hast
scattered us, for a reproach and a curse,

and to be subject to payments,
according to all the iniquities of our
fathers, which departed from the Lord
our God. [9]Hear, Israel, the
commandments of life: give ear to
understand wisdom. [10]How happeneth
it, Israel, that thou art in thine enemies'
land, that thou art waxen old in a
strange country, that thou art defiled
with the dead, [11]that thou art counted
with them that go down into the grave?
[12]Thou hast forsaken the fountain of
wisdom. [13]For if thou hadst walked in
the way of God, thou shouldest have
dwelled in peace for ever. [14]Learn
where is wisdom, where is strength,
where is understanding; that thou
mayest know also where is length of
days, and life, where is the light of the
eyes, and peace. [15]Who hath found out
her place? or who hath come into her
treasures?
[16]Where are the princes of the heathen
become, and such as ruled the beasts
upon the earth; [17]they that had their
pastime with the fowls of the air, and
they that hoarded up silver and gold,
wherein men trust, and made no end of
their getting? [18]For they that wrought in
silver, and were so careful, and whose
works are unsearchable, [19]they are
vanished and gone down to the grave,
and others are come up in their steads.
[20]Young men have seen light, and
dwelt upon the earth: but the way of
knowledge have they not known, [21]nor
understood the paths thereof, nor laid
hold of it: their children were far off
from that way. [22]It hath not been heard of
in Canaan, neither hath it been seen in
Teman. [23]The Hag´arenes that seek
wisdom upon earth, the merchants of
Meran and of Teman, the authors of
fables, and searchers out of
understanding; none of these have
known the way of wisdom, or
remember her paths. [24]O Israel, how
great is the house of God! and how
large is the place of his possession!
[25]Great, and hath none end; high, and
unmeasurable. [26]There were the giants
famous from the beginning, that were
of so great stature, and so expert in
war. [27]Those did not the Lord choose,
neither gave he the way of knowledge
unto them: [28]But they were destroyed,
because they had no wisdom, and
perished through their own foolishness.
[29]Who hath gone up into heaven, and
taken her, and brought her down from
the clouds? [30]Who hath gone over the
sea, and found her, and will bring her
for pure gold? [31]No man knoweth her
way, nor thinketh of her path. [32]But he
that knoweth all things knoweth her,
and hath found her out with his
understanding: he that prepared the
earth for evermore hath filled it with
fourfooted beasts: [33]he that sendeth
forth light, and it goeth, calleth it again,
and it obeyeth him with fear. [34]The stars
shone in their watches, and rejoiced:
when he calleth them, they say, Here
we be; and so with cheerfulness they
showed light unto him that made them.
[35]This is our God, and there shall none
other be accounted of in comparison of
him. [36]He hath found out all the way of
knowledge, and hath given it unto
Jacob his servant, and to Israel his
beloved. [37]Afterward did he show
himself upon earth, and conversed with
men.

CHAPTER 4

[1]This is the book of the commandments
of God, and the law that endureth for
ever: all they that keep it shall come to
life; but such as leave it shall die. [2]Turn

thee, O Jacob, and take hold of it: walk
in the presence of the light thereof, that
thou mayest be illuminated. 3 Give not
thine honor to another, nor the things
that are profitable unto thee to a strange
nation. 4 O Israel, happy are we: for
things that are pleasing to God are made
known unto us. 5 Be of good cheer, my
people, the memorial of Israel. 6 Ye were
sold to the nations, not for [your]
destruction: but because ye moved God
to wrath, ye were delivered unto the
enemies. 7 For ye provoked him that
made you by sacrificing unto devils,
and not to God. 8 Ye have forgotten the
everlasting God, that brought you up;
and ye have grieved Jerusalem, that
nursed you. 9 For when she saw the
wrath of God coming upon you, she
said, Hearken, O ye that dwell about
Zion: God hath brought upon me great
mourning; 10 for I saw the captivity of
my sons and daughters, which the
Everlasting brought upon them. 11 With
joy did I nourish them; but sent them
away with weeping and mourning. 12 Let
no man rejoice over me, a widow, and
forsaken of many, who for the sins of
my children am left desolate; because
they departed from the law of God.
13 They knew not his statutes, nor
walked in the ways of his
commandments, nor trod in the paths of
discipline in his righteousness. 14 Let
them that dwell about Zion come, and
remember ye the captivity of my sons
and daughters, which the Everlasting
hath brought upon them. 15 For he hath
brought a nation upon them from far, a
shameless nation, and of a strange
language, who neither reverenced old
man, nor pitied child. 16 These have
carried away the dear beloved children
of the widow, and left her that was
alone desolate without daughters. 17 But
what can I help you? 18 For he that
brought these plagues upon you will
deliver you from the hands of your
enemies. 19 Go your way, O my
children, go your way: for I am left
desolate. 20 I have put off the clothing of
peace, and put upon me the sackcloth of
my prayer: I will cry unto the
Everlasting in my days. 21 Be of good
cheer, O my children, cry unto the Lord,
and he shall deliver you from the power
and hand of the enemies. 22 For my hope
is in the Everlasting, that he will save
you; and joy is come unto me from the
Holy One, because of the mercy which
shall soon come unto you from the
Everlasting our Saviour. 23 For I sent
you out with mourning and weeping:
but God will give you to me again with
joy and gladness for ever. 24 Like as
now the neighbors of Zion have seen
your captivity: so shall they see shortly
your salvation from our God, which shall
come upon you with great glory, and
brightness of the Everlasting. 25 My
children, suffer patiently the wrath that
is come upon you from God: for
thine enemy hath persecuted thee; but
shortly thou shalt see his destruction,
and shalt tread upon his neck. 26 My
delicate ones have gone rough ways,
and were taken away as a flock caught
of the enemies.

27 Be of good comfort, O my children,
and cry unto God: for ye shall be
remembered of him that brought these
things upon you. 28 For as it was your
mind to go astray from God: so, being
returned, seek him ten times more. 29 For
he that hath brought these plagues upon
you shall bring you everlasting joy
again with your salvation.

30 Take a good heart, O Jerusalem: for
he that gave thee that name will
comfort thee. 31 Miserable are they that

afflicted thee, and rejoiced at thy fall.
32 Miserable are the cities which thy
children served: miserable is she that
received thy sons. 33 For as she rejoiced
at thy ruin, and was glad of thy fall: so
shall she be grieved for her own
desolation. 34 For I will take away the
rejoicing of her great multitude, and her
pride shall be turned into mourning.
35 For fire shall come upon her from the
Everlasting, long to endure; and she
shall be inhabited of devils for a great
time.
36 O Jerusalem, look about thee toward
the east, and behold the joy that cometh
unto thee from God. 37 Lo, thy sons come,
whom thou sentest away, they come
gathered together from the east to the
west by the word of the Holy One,
rejoicing in the glory of God.

CHAPTER 5

1 Put off, O Jerusalem, the garment of
thy mourning and affliction, and put
on the comeliness of the glory that
cometh from God for ever. 2 Cast about
thee a double garment of the
righteousness which cometh from God;
and set a diadem on thine head of the
glory of the Everlasting. 3 For God will
show thy brightness unto every country
under heaven. 4 For thy name shall be
called of God for ever The peace of
righteousness, and The glory of God's
worship. 5 Arise, O Jerusalem, and
stand on high, and look about toward
the east, and behold thy children
gathered from the west unto the east by
the word of the Holy One, rejoicing in
the remembrance of God. 6 For they
departed from thee on foot, and were led
away of their enemies: but God
bringeth them unto thee exalted with
glory, as children of the kingdom. 7 For
God hath appointed that every high hill,
and banks of long continuance, should
be cast down, and valleys filled up, to
make even the ground, that Israel may
go safely in the glory of God.
8 Moreover even the woods and every
sweetsmelling tree shall overshadow
Israel by the commandment of God.
9 For God shall lead Israel with joy in the
light of his glory with the mercy and
righteousness that cometh from him.

CHAPTER 6

1 A copy of an epistle, which Jeremiah
sent unto them which were to be led
captives into Babylon by the king of the
Babylonians, to certify them, as it was
commanded him of God.
2 Because of the sins which ye have
committed before God, ye shall be
led away captives into Babylon by
Nebuchadnez´zar king of the
Babylonians. 3 So when ye be come
unto Babylon, ye shall remain there
many years, and for a long season,
namely, seven generations: and after that
I will bring you away peaceably from
thence. 4 Now shall ye see in Babylon
gods of silver, and of gold, and of wood,
borne upon shoulders, which cause the
nations to fear. 5 Beware therefore that
ye in no wise be like to strangers,
neither be ye afraid of them, when ye
see the multitude before them and
behind them, worshipping them. 6 But
say ye in your hearts, O Lord, we must
worship thee. 7 For mine angel is with
you, and I myself caring for your souls.
8 As for their tongue, it is polished by the
workman, and they themselves are
gilded and laid over with silver; yet are
they but false, and cannot speak. 9 And
taking gold, as it were for a virgin that
loveth to go gay, they make crowns for

the heads of their gods. 10Sometimes
also the priests convey from their gods
gold and silver, and bestow it upon
themselves. 11Yea, they will give
thereof to the common harlots, and
deck them as men with garments,
[being] gods of silver, and gods of
gold, and wood. 12Yet cannot these
gods save themselves from rust and
moths, though they be covered with
purple raiment. 13They wipe their faces
because of the dust of the temple, when
there is much upon them. 14And he that
cannot put to death one that offendeth
him holdeth a scepter, as though he
were a judge of the country. 15He hath
also in his right hand a dagger and an
ax: but cannot deliver himself from
war and thieves. 16Whereby they are
known not to be gods: therefore fear
them not.

17For like as a vessel that a man useth is
nothing worth when it is broken; even
so it is with their gods: when they be
set up in the temple, their eyes be full
of dust through the feet of them that
come in. 18And as the doors are made
sure on every side upon him that
offendeth the king, as being committed
to suffer death: even so the priests make
fast their temples with doors, with locks,
and bars, lest their gods be spoiled with
robbers. 19They light them candles,
yea, more than for themselves, whereof
they cannot see one. 20They are as one
of the beams of the temple, yet they say
their hearts are gnawed upon by things
creeping out of the earth; and when they
eat them and their clothes, they feel it
not. 21Their faces are blacked through
the smoke that cometh out of the
temple. 22Upon their bodies and heads
sit bats, swallows, and birds, and the
cats also. 23By this ye may know that
they are no gods: therefore fear them
not. 24Notwithstanding the gold that is
about them to make them beautiful,
except they wipe off the rust, they will
not shine: for neither when they were
molten did they feel it. 25The things
wherein there is no breath are bought
for a most high price. 26They are borne
upon shoulders, having no feet, whereby
they declare unto men that they be
nothing worth. 27They also that serve
them are ashamed: for if they fall to
the ground at any time, they cannot rise
up again of themselves: neither, if one
set them upright, can they move of
themselves: neither, if they be bowed
down, can they make themselves
straight: but they set gifts before them,
as unto dead men. 28As for the things
that are sacrificed unto them, their
priests sell and abuse; in like manner
their wives lay up part thereof in salt;
but unto the poor and impotent they
give nothing of it. 29Menstruous
women and women in childbed eat
their sacrifices: by these things ye may
know that they are no gods: fear them
not.

30For how can they be called gods?
because women set meat before the gods
of silver, gold, and wood. 31And the
priests sit in their temples, having their
clothes rent, and their heads and beards
shaven, and nothing upon their heads.
32They roar and cry before their gods,
as men do at the feast when one is dead.
33The priests also take off their
garments, and clothe their wives and
children. 34Whether it be evil that one
doeth unto them, or good, they are not
able to recompense it: they can neither
set up a king, nor put him down. 35In
like manner, they can neither give
riches nor money: though a man make
a vow unto them, and keep it not, they
will not require it. 36They can save no

man from death, neither deliver the
weak from the mighty. 37They cannot
restore a blind man to his sight, nor help
any man in his distress. 38They can
show no mercy to the widow, nor do
good to the fatherless. 39Their gods of
wood, and which are overlaid with gold
and silver, are like the stones that be
hewn out of the mountain: they that
worship them shall be confounded.
40How should a man then think and say
that they are gods, when even the
Chalde´ans themselves dishonor them?
41Who if they shall see one dumb that
cannot speak, they bring him, and
intreat Bel that he may speak, as though
he were able to understand. 42Yet they
cannot understand this themselves, and
leave them: for they have no
knowledge. 43The women also with
cords about them, sitting in the ways,
burn bran for perfume: but if any of
them, drawn by some that passeth by,
lie with him, she reproacheth her
fellow, that she was not thought worthy
as herself, nor her cord broken.
44Whatsoever is done among them is
false: how may it then be thought or said
that they are gods?
45They are made of carpenters and
goldsmiths: they can be nothing else
than the workmen will have them to be.
46And they themselves that made them
can never continue long; how should
then the things that are made of them be
gods? 47For they left lies and reproaches
to them that come after. 48For when
there cometh any war or plague upon
them, the priests consult with
themselves, where they may be hidden
with them. 49How then cannot men
perceive that they be no gods, which
can neither save themselves from war,
nor from plague? 50For seeing they be
but of wood, and overlaid with silver
and gold, it shall be known hereafter
that they are false: 51and it shall
manifestly appear to all nations and
kings that they are no gods, but the
works of men's hands, and that there
is no work of God in them. 52Who then
may not know that they are no gods?
53For neither can they set up a king in
the land, nor give rain unto men.
54Neither can they judge their own
cause, nor redress a wrong, being
unable: for they are as crows between
heaven and earth. 55Whereupon when
fire falleth upon the house of gods of
wood, or laid over with gold or silver,
their priests will flee away, and escape;
but they themselves shall be burned
asunder like beams. 56Moreover they
cannot withstand any king or enemies:
how can it then be thought or said that
they be gods? 57Neither are those gods
of wood, and laid over with silver or
gold, able to escape either from thieves
or robbers. 58Whose gold, and silver,
and garments wherewith they are
clothed, they that are strong do take,
and go away withal: neither are they
able to help themselves. 59Therefore it
is better to be a king that showeth his
power, or else a profitable vessel in an
house, which the owner shall have use
of, than such false gods; or to be a door
in an house, to keep such things safe as
be therein, than such false gods; or a
pillar of wood in a palace, than such
false gods.
60For sun, moon, and stars, being
bright, and sent to do their offices, are
obedient. 61In like manner the lightning
when it breaketh forth is easy to be
seen; and after the same manner the
wind bloweth in every country. 62And
when God commandeth the clouds to
go over the whole world, they do as
they are bidden. 63And the fire sent

from above to consume hills and woods
doeth as it is commanded: but these are
like unto them neither in show nor
power.
64Wherefore it is neither to be supposed
nor said that they are gods, seeing they
are able neither to judge causes, nor to
do good unto men.
65Knowing therefore that they are no
gods, fear them not.
66For they can neither curse nor bless
kings: 67neither can they show signs in
the heavens among the heathen, nor
shine as the sun, nor give light as the
moon.
68The beasts are better than they: for
they can get under a covert, and help
themselves. 69It is then by no means
manifest unto us that they are gods:
therefore fear them not.
70For as a scarecrow in a garden of
cucumbers keepeth nothing: so are
their gods of wood, and laid over with
silver and gold.
71And likewise their gods of wood, and
laid over with silver and gold, are like
to a white thorn in an orchard, that
every bird sitteth upon; as also to a dead
body, that is cast into the dark.
72And ye shall know them to be no gods
by the bright purple that rotteth upon
them: and they themselves afterward
shall be eaten, and shall be a reproach
in the country.
73Better therefore is the just man that
hath none idols: for he shall be far from
reproach.

THE SONG OF THE THREE HOLY CHILDREN

CHAPTER 1

1 And they walked in the midst of the
fire, praising God, and blessing the
Lord. 2 Then Azari´ah stood up, and
prayed on this manner; and opening his
mouth in the midst of the fire said,
3 Blessed art thou, O Lord God of our
fathers: thy name is worthy to be
praised and glorified for evermore: 4 for
thou art righteous in all the things that
thou hast done to us: yea, true are all
thy works, thy ways are right, and all
thy judgments truth. 5 In all the things
that thou hast brought upon us, and
upon the holy city of our fathers, even
Jerusalem, thou hast executed true
judgment: for according to truth and
judgment didst thou bring all these
things upon us because of our sins. 6 For
we have sinned and committed iniquity,
departing from thee. 7 In all things have
we trespassed, and not obeyed thy
commandments, nor kept them, neither
done as thou hast commanded us, that
it might go well with us. 8 Wherefore all
that thou hast brought upon us, and every
thing that thou hast done to us, thou hast
done in true judgment. 9 And thou didst
deliver us into the hands of lawless
enemies, most hateful forsakers of
God, and to an unjust king, and the
most wicked in all the world. 10 And
now we cannot open our mouths, we
are become a shame and reproach to thy
servants, and to them that worship
thee. 11 Yet deliver us not up wholly,
for thy name's sake, neither disannul
thou thy covenant: 12 and cause not thy
mercy to depart from us, for thy
beloved Abraham's sake, for thy
servant Isaac's sake, and for thy holy
Israel's sake; 13 to whom thou hast
spoken and promised, that thou
wouldest multiply their seed as the stars
of heaven, and as the sand that lieth upon
the seashore. 14 For we, O Lord, are
become less than any nation, and be
kept under this day in all the world
because of our sins. 15 Neither is there at
this time prince, or prophet, or leader,
or burnt offering, or sacrifice, or
oblation, or incense, or place to
sacrifice before thee, and to find mercy.
16 Nevertheless in a contrite heart and
an humble spirit let us be accepted.
17 Like as in the burnt offerings of rams
and bullocks, and like as in ten
thousands of fat lambs: so let our
sacrifice be in thy sight this day, and
grant that we may wholly go after thee:
for they shall not be confounded that
put their trust in thee. 18 And now we
follow thee with all our heart, we fear
thee, and seek thy face. 19 Put us not to
shame: but deal with us after thy
loving-kindness, and according to the
multitude of thy mercies. 20 Deliver us
also according to thy marvelous works,
and give glory to thy name, O Lord: and
let all them that do thy servants hurt be
ashamed; 21 and let them be confounded
in all their power and might, and let
their strength be broken; 22 and let them
know that thou art Lord, the only God,
and glorious over the whole world.
23 And the king's servants, that put
them in, ceased not to make the oven
hot with rosin, pitch, tow, and small
wood; 24 so that the flame streamed forth
above the furnace forty and nine cubits.
25 And it passed through, and burned
those Chalde´ans it found about the
furnace. 26 But the angel of the Lord

came down into the oven together with
Azari′ah and his fellows, and smote the
flame of the fire out of the oven; 27 and
made the midst of the furnace as it had
been a moist whistling wind, so that
the fire touched them not at all, neither
hurt nor troubled them.
28 Then the three, as out of one mouth,
praised, glorified, and blessed, God in
the furnace, saying, 29 Blessed art thou,
O Lord God of our fathers: and to be
praised and exalted above all for ever.
30 And blessed is thy glorious and holy
name: and to be praised and exalted
above all for ever. 31 Blessed art thou in
the temple of thine holy glory: and to be
praised and glorified above all for ever.
32 Blessed art thou that beholdest the
depths, and sittest upon the cherubim:
and to be praised and exalted above all
for ever. 33 Blessed art thou on the
glorious throne of thy kingdom: and to
be praised and glorified above all for
ever. 34 Blessed art thou in the
firmament of heaven: and above all to
be praised and glorified for ever.
35 O all ye works of the Lord, bless ye
the Lord: praise and exalt him above all
for ever. 36 O ye heavens, bless ye the
Lord: praise and exalt him above all for
ever. 37 O ye angels of the Lord, bless ye
the Lord: praise and exalt him above all
for ever. 38 O all ye waters that be
above the heaven, bless ye the Lord:
praise and exalt him above all for
ever. 39 O all ye powers of the Lord,
bless ye the Lord: praise and exalt him
above all for ever. 40 O ye sun and
moon, bless ye the Lord: praise and
exalt him above all for ever. 41 O ye
stars of heaven, bless ye the Lord:
praise and exalt him above all for ever.
42 O every shower and dew, bless ye the
Lord: praise and exalt him above all for
ever. 43 O all ye winds, bless ye the
Lord: praise and exalt him above all for
ever. 44 O ye fire and heat, bless ye the
Lord: praise and exalt him above all for
ever. 45 O ye winter and summer,
bless ye the Lord: praise and exalt him
above all for ever. 46 O ye dews and
storms of snow, bless ye the Lord:
praise and exalt him above all for ever.
47 O ye nights and days, bless ye the
Lord: praise and exalt him above all for
ever. 48 O ye light and darkness, bless ye
the Lord: praise and exalt him above all
for ever. 49 O ye ice and cold, bless ye the
Lord: praise and exalt him above all for
ever. 50 O ye frost and snow, bless ye the
Lord: praise and exalt him above all for
ever. 51 O ye lightnings and clouds,
bless ye the Lord: praise and exalt him
above all for ever. 52 O let the earth bless
the Lord: praise and exalt him above all
for ever. 53 O ye mountains and little
hills, bless ye the Lord: praise and exalt
him above all for ever. 54 O all ye things
that grow on the earth, bless ye the
Lord: praise and exalt him above all for
ever. 55 O ye fountains, bless ye the
Lord: praise and exalt him above all for
ever. 56 O ye seas and rivers, bless ye
the Lord: praise and exalt him above all
for ever. 57 O ye whales, and all that
move in the waters, bless ye the Lord:
praise and exalt him above all for ever.
58 O all ye fowls of the air, bless ye the
Lord: praise and exalt him above all for
ever.
59 O all ye beasts and cattle, bless ye the
Lord: praise and exalt him above all for
ever.
60 O ye children of men, bless ye the
Lord: praise and exalt him above all for
ever.
61 O Israel, bless ye the Lord: praise and
exalt him above all for ever.
62 O ye priests of the Lord, bless ye the
Lord: praise and exalt him above all for

ever. [63]O ye servants of the Lord, bless
ye the Lord: praise and exalt him above
all for ever.
[64]O ye spirits and souls of the righteous,
bless ye the Lord: praise and exalt him
above all for ever.
[65]O ye holy and humble men of heart,
bless ye the Lord: praise and exalt him
above all for ever.
[66]O Hanani´ah, Azari´ah, and Mish´a-
el, bless ye the Lord: praise and exalt
him above all for ever: for he hath
delivered us from hell, and saved us
from the hand of death, and delivered
us out of the midst of the furnace and
burning flame: even out of the midst of
the fire hath he delivered us.
[67]O give thanks unto the Lord, because
he is gracious: for his mercy endureth
for ever.
[68]O all ye that worship the Lord, bless
the God of gods, praise him, and give
him thanks: for his mercy endureth for
ever.

THE HISTORY OF SUSANNA

CHAPTER 1

1 There dwelt a man in Babylon, called
Joakim: 2 and he took a wife, whose
name was Susanna, the daughter of
Hilki´ah, a very fair woman, and one
that feared the Lord. 3 Her parents also
were righteous, and taught their
daughter according to the law of Moses.
4 Now Joakim was a great rich man, and
had a fair garden joining unto his
house: and to him resorted the Jews;
because he was more honorable than all
the others.
5 The same year were appointed two of
the ancients of the people to be judges,
such as the Lord spake of, that
wickedness came from Babylon from
ancient judges, who seemed to govern
the people. 6 These kept much at
Joakim's house: and all that had any
suits in law came unto them. 7 Now
when the people departed away at
noon, Susanna went into her husband's
garden to walk. 8 And the two elders
saw her going in every day, and
walking; so that their lust was inflamed
toward her. 9 And they perverted their
own mind, and turned away their eyes,
that they might not look unto heaven,
nor remember just judgments. 10 And
albeit they both were wounded with her
love, yet durst not one show another his
grief. 11 For they were ashamed to
declare their lust, that they desired to
have to do with her. 12 Yet they watched
diligently from day to day to see her.
13 And the one said to the other, Let us
now go home: for it is dinner time. 14 So
when they were gone out, they parted
the one from the other, and turning
back again they came to the same place;
and after that they had asked one
another the cause, they acknowledged
their lust: then appointed they a time
both together, when they might find her
alone.
15 And it fell out, as they watched a fit
time, she went in as before with two
maids only, and she was desirous to
wash herself in the garden: for it was
hot. 16 And there was nobody there save
the two elders, that had hid themselves,
and watched her. 17 Then she said to her
maids, Bring me oil and washing balls,
and shut the garden doors, that I may
wash me. 18 And they did as she bade
them, and shut the garden doors, and
went out themselves at privy doors to
fetch the things that she had
commanded them: but they saw not the
elders, because they were hid. 19 Now
when the maids were gone forth, the two
elders rose up, and ran unto her, saying,
20 Behold, the garden doors are shut,
that no man can see us, and we are in
love with thee; therefore consent unto
us, and lie with us. 21 If thou wilt not, we
will bear witness against thee, that a
young man was with thee: and therefore
thou didst send away thy maids from
thee. 22 Then Susanna sighed, and said,
I am straitened on every side: for if I do
this thing, it is death unto me: and if I
do it not, I cannot escape your hands.
23 It is better for me to fall into your
hands, and not do it, than to sin in the
sight of the Lord. 24 With that Susanna
cried with a loud voice: and the two
elders cried out against her. 25 Then ran
the one, and opened the garden door.
26 So when the servants of the house
heard the cry in the garden, they rushed
in at the privy door, to see what was
done unto her. 27 But when the elders

had declared their matter, the servants
were greatly ashamed: for there was
never such a report made of Susanna.
28 And it came to pass the next day,
when the people were assembled to her
husband Joakim, the two elders came
also full of mischievous imagination
against Susanna to put her to death;
29 and said before the people, Send for
Susanna, the daughter of Hilki′ah,
Joakim's wife. And so they sent. 30 So
she came with her father and mother,
her children, and all her kindred. 31 Now
Susanna was a very delicate woman,
and beauteous to behold. 32 And these
wicked men commanded to uncover
her face, (for she was covered) that they
might be filled with her beauty.
33 Therefore her friends and all that saw
her wept. 34 Then the two elders stood
up in the midst of the people, and laid
their hands upon her head. 35 And she
weeping looked up toward heaven: for
her heart trusted in the Lord. 36 And the
elders said, As we walked in the garden
alone, this woman came in with two
maids, and shut the garden doors, and
sent the maids away. 37 Then a young
man, who there was hid, came unto her,
and lay with her. 38 Then we that stood
in a corner of the garden, seeing this
wickedness, ran unto them. 39 And
when we saw them together, the man
we could not hold: for he was stronger
than we, and opened the door, and
leaped out. 40 But having taken this
woman, we asked who the young man
was, but she would not tell us: these
things do we testify. 41 Then the
assembly believed them, as those that
were the elders and judges of the
people: so they condemned her to
death.
42 Then Susanna cried out with a loud
voice, and said, O everlasting God, that
knowest the secrets, and knowest all
things before they be: 43 thou knowest
that they have borne false witness
against me, and, behold, I must die;
whereas I never did such things as these
men have maliciously invented against
me.
44 And the Lord heard her voice.
45 Therefore when she was led to be put
to death, the Lord raised up the holy
spirit of a young youth, whose name
was Daniel: 46 who cried with a loud
voice, I am clear from the blood of this
woman. 47 Then all the people turned
them toward him, and said, What mean
these words that thou hast spoken? 48 So
he standing in the midst of them said,
Are ye such fools, ye sons of Israel, that
without examination or knowledge of
the truth ye have condemned a daughter
of Israel? 49 Return again to the place of
judgment: for they have borne false
witness against her. 50 Wherefore all
the people turned again in haste, and
the elders said unto him, Come, sit
down among us, and show it us, seeing
God hath given thee the honor of an
elder. 51 Then said Daniel unto them,
Put these two aside one far from
another, and I will examine them. 52 So
when they were put asunder one from
another, he called one of them, and said
unto him, O thou that art waxen old in
wickedness, now thy sins which thou
hast committed aforetime are come to
light: 53 for thou hast pronounced false
judgment, and hast condemned the
innocent, and hast let the guilty go free;
albeit the Lord saith, The innocent and
righteous shalt thou not slay. 54 Now
then, if thou hast seen her, tell me,
under what tree sawest thou them
companying together? Who answered,
Under a mastick tree. 55 And Daniel
said, Very well; thou hast lied against

thine own head; for even now the angel
of God hath received the sentence of
God to cut thee in two. 56 So he put him
aside, and commanded to bring the
other, and said unto him, O thou seed
of Canaan, and not of Judah, beauty
hath deceived thee, and lust hath
perverted thine heart. 57 Thus have ye
dealt with the daughters of Israel, and
they for fear companied with you: but the
daughter of Judah would not abide your
wickedness. 58 Now therefore tell me,
under what tree didst thou take them
companying together? Who answered,
Under an holm tree. 59 Then said Daniel
unto him, Well; thou hast also lied
against thine own head: for the angel of
God waiteth with the sword to cut thee
in two, that he may destroy you.
60 With that all the assembly cried out
with a loud voice, and praised God,
who saveth them that trust in him.
61 And they arose against the two elders,
for Daniel had convicted them of false
witness by their own mouth: 62 and
according to the law of Moses they did
unto them in such sort as they
maliciously intended to do to their
neighbor: and they put them to death.
Thus the innocent blood was saved the
same day. 63 Therefore Hilki′ah and his
wife praised God for their daughter
Susanna, with Joakim her husband, and
all the kindred, because there was no
dishonesty found in her. 64 From that
day forth was Daniel had in great
reputation in the sight of the people.

THE HISTORY OF BEL AND THE DRAGON

CHAPTER 1

1 And king Asty´ages was gathered to
his fathers, and Cyrus of Persia
received his kingdom. 2 And Daniel
conversed with the king, and was
honored above all his friends.
3 Now the Babylonians had an idol,
called Bel, and there were spent upon
him every day twelve great measures of
fine flour, and forty sheep, and six
vessels of wine. 4 And the king
worshipped it and went daily to adore
it: but Daniel worshipped his own
God. And the king said unto him,
Why dost not thou worship Bel? 5 Who
answered and said, Because I may not
worship idols made with hands, but the
living God, who hath created the
heaven and the earth, and hath
sovereignty over all flesh. 6 Then said
the king unto him, Thinkest thou not
that Bel is a living God? seest thou not
how much he eateth and drinketh every
day? 7 Then Daniel smiled, and said, O
king, be not deceived: for this is but
clay within, and brass without, and did
never eat or drink anything. 8 So the
king was wroth, and called for his
priests, and said unto them, If ye tell me
not who this is that devoureth these
expenses, ye shall die. 9 But if ye can
certify me that Bel devoureth them,
then Daniel shall die: for he hath
spoken blasphemy against Bel. And
Daniel said unto the king, Let it be
according to thy word.
10 Now the priests of Bel were
threescore and ten, beside their wives
and children. And the king went with
Daniel into the temple of Bel. 11 So
Bel's priests said, Lo, we go out: but
thou, O king, set on the meat, and make
ready the wine, and shut the door fast,
and seal it with thine own signet; 12 and
tomorrow when thou comest in, if thou
findest not that Bel hath eaten up all, we
will suffer death: or else Daniel, that
speaketh falsely against us. 13 And they
little regarded it: for under the table
they had made a privy entrance,
whereby they entered in continually,
and consumed those things. 14 So when
they were gone forth, the king set meats
before Bel. Now Daniel had
commanded his servants to bring ashes,
and those they strewed throughout all
the temple in the presence of the king
alone: then went they out, and shut the
door, and sealed it with the king's
signet, and so departed. 15 Now in the
night came the priests with their wives
and children, as they were wont to do,
and did eat and drink up all.
16 In the morning betime the king arose,
and Daniel with him. 17 And the
king said, Daniel, are the seals whole?
And he said, Yea, O king, they be
whole. 18 And as soon as he had opened
the door, the king looked upon the
table, and cried with a loud voice, Great
art thou, O Bel, and with thee is no
deceit at all. 19 Then laughed Daniel,
and held the king that he should not go
in, and said, Behold now the pavement,
and mark well whose footsteps are these.
20 And the king said, I see the footsteps
of men, women, and children. And then
the king was angry, 21 and took the
priests with their wives and children,
who showed him the privy doors,
where they came in, and consumed
such things as were upon the table.
22 Therefore the king slew them, and

delivered Bel into Daniel's power, who destroyed him and his temple.

23 And in that same place there was a great dragon, which they of Babylon worshipped. 24 And the king said unto Daniel, Wilt thou also say that this is of brass? lo, he liveth, he eateth and drinketh; thou canst not say that he is no living god: therefore worship him. 25 Then said Daniel unto the king, I will worship the Lord my God: for he is the living God. 26 But give me leave, O king, and I shall slay this dragon without sword or staff. The king said, I give thee leave. 27 Then Daniel took pitch, and fat, and hair, and did seethe them together, and made lumps thereof: this he put in the dragon's mouth, and so the dragon burst in sunder: and Daniel said, Lo, these are the gods ye worship. 28 When they of Babylon heard that, they took great indignation, and conspired against the king, saying, The king is become a Jew, and he hath destroyed Bel, he hath slain the dragon, and put the priests to death. 29 So they came to the king, and said, Deliver us Daniel, or else we will destroy thee and thine house.

30 Now when the king saw that they pressed him sore, being constrained, he delivered Daniel unto them: 31 who cast him into the lions' den: where he was six days. 32 And in the den there were seven lions, and they had given them every day two carcases, and two sheep: which then were not given to them, to the intent they might devour Daniel.

33 Now there was in Judea a prophet, called Habak΄kuk, who had made pottage, and had broken bread in a bowl, and was going into the field, for to bring it to the reapers. 34 But the angel of the Lord said unto Habak΄kuk, Go, carry the dinner that thou hast into Babylon unto Daniel, who is in the lions' den. 35 And Habak΄kuk said, Lord, I never saw Babylon: neither do I know where the den is. 36 Then the angel of the Lord took him by the crown, and bare him by the hair of his head, and through the vehemency of his spirit set him in Babylon over the den. 37 And Habak΄kuk cried, saying, O Daniel, Daniel, take the dinner which God hath sent thee. 38 And Daniel said, Thou hast remembered me, O God: neither hast thou forsaken them that seek thee and love thee. 39 So Daniel arose, and did eat: and the angel of the Lord set Habak΄kuk in his own place again immediately.

40 Upon the seventh day the king went to bewail Daniel: and when he came to the den, he looked in, and, behold, Daniel was sitting. 41 Then cried the king with a loud voice, saying, Great art thou, O Lord God of Daniel, and there is none other beside thee. 42 And he drew him out, and cast those that were the cause of his destruction into the den: and they were devoured in a moment before his face.

I MACCABEES

CHAPTER 1

1 And it happened, after that Alexander
son of Philip, the Macedo´nian, who
came out of the land of Kittim, had
smitten Dari´us king of the Persians
and Medes, that he reigned in his stead,
the first over Greece, 2 and made many
wars, and won many strong-holds, and
slew the kings of the earth, 3 and went
through to the ends of the earth, and
took spoils of many nations, insomuch
that the earth was quiet before him;
whereupon he was exalted, and his
heart was lifted up. 4 And he gathered a
mighty strong host, and ruled over
countries, and nations, and kings, who
became tributaries unto him. 5 And after
these things he fell sick, and perceived
that he should die. 6 Wherefore he called
his servants, such as were honorable, and
had been brought up with him from his
youth, and parted his kingdom among
them, while he was yet alive. 7 So
Alexander reigned twelve years, and
then died. 8 And his servants bare rule
every one in his place. 9 And after his
death they all put crowns upon
themselves; so did their sons after them
many years: and evils were multiplied
in the earth.
10 And there came out of them a wicked
root, An-ti´ochus surnamed E-
piph´anes, son of An-ti´ochus the king,
who had been an hostage at Rome, and
he reigned in the hundred and thirty and
seventh year of the kingdom of the
Greeks. 11 In those days went there out of
Israel wicked men, who persuaded
many, saying, Let us go and make a
covenant with the heathen that are round
about us: for since we departed from them
we have had much sorrow. 12 So this
device pleased them well. 13 Then
certain of the people were so forward
herein, that they went to the king, who
gave them license to do after the
ordinances of the heathen: 14 whereupon
they built a place of exercise at
Jerusalem according to the customs of
the heathen: 15 and made themselves
uncircumcised, and forsook the holy
covenant, and joined themselves to the
heathen, and were sold to do mischief.
16 Now when the kingdom was
established before An-ti´ochus, he
thought to reign over Egypt that he
might have the dominion of two
realms. 17 Wherefore he entered into
Egypt with a great multitude, with
chariots, and elephants, and horsemen,
and a great navy, 18 and made war
against Ptol´emy king of Egypt: but
Ptol´emy was afraid of him, and fled;
and many were wounded to death.
19 Thus they got the strong cities in the
land of Egypt and he took the spoils
thereof.
20 And after that An-ti´ochus had
smitten Egypt, he returned again in the
hundred forty and third year, and went
up against Israel and Jerusalem with a
great multitude, 21 and entered proudly
into the sanctuary, and took away the
golden altar, and the candlestick of
light, and all the vessels thereof, 22 and
the table of the showbread, and the
pouring vessels, and the vials, and the
censers of gold, and the veil, and the
crowns, and the golden ornaments that
were before the temple, all which he
pulled off. 23 He took also the silver and
the gold, and the precious vessels: also
he took the hidden treasures which he
found. 24 And when he had taken all
away, he went into his own land, having

made a great massacre, and spoken
very proudly.
25 Therefore there was a great mourning
in Israel, in every place where they
were; 26 so that the princes and elders
mourned, the virgins and young men
were made feeble, and the beauty of
women was changed. 27 Every
bridegroom took up lamentation, and
she that sat in the marriage chamber
was in heaviness. 28 The land also was
moved for the inhabitants thereof, and
all the house of Jacob was covered with
confusion.
29 And after two years fully expired the
king sent his chief collector of tribute
unto the cities of Judah, who came unto
Jerusalem with a great multitude, 30 and
spake peaceable words unto them, but
all was deceit: for when they had given
him credence, he fell suddenly upon the
city, and smote it very sore, and
destroyed much people of Israel.
31 And when he had taken the spoils of
the city, he set it on fire, and pulled
down the houses and walls thereof on
every side. 32 But the women and
children took they captive, and
possessed the cattle. 33 Then builded
they the city of David with a great and
strong wall, and with mighty towers,
and made it a stronghold for them.
34 And they put therein a sinful nation,
wicked men, and fortified themselves
therein. 35 They stored it also with
armor and victuals, and when they had
gathered together the spoils of
Jerusalem, they laid them up there,
and so they became a sore snare: 36 for
it was a place to lie in wait against the
sanctuary, and an evil adversary to
Israel. 37 Thus they shed innocent blood
on every side of the sanctuary, and
defiled it: 38 insomuch that the
inhabitants ofJerusalem fled because of
them: whereupon the city was made an
habitation of strangers, and became
strange to those that were born in her;
and her own children left her. 39 Her
sanctuary was laid waste like a
wilderness, her feasts were turned into
mourning, her sabbaths into reproach,
her honor into contempt. 40 As had
been her glory, so was her dishonor
increased, and her excellency was
turned into mourning.
41 Moreover king An-ti′ochus wrote to
his whole kingdom, that all should be
one people, 42 and every one should
leave his laws: so all the heathen agreed
according to the commandment of the
king. 43 Yea, many also of the Israelites
consented to his religion, and sacrificed
unto idols, and profaned the sabbath.
44 For the king had sent letters by
messengers unto Jerusalem and the
cities of Judah, that they should follow
the strange laws of the land, 45 and
forbid burnt offerings, and sacrifice,
and drink offerings, in the temple; and
that they should profane the sabbaths
and festival days: 46 and pollute the
sanctuary and holy people: 47 set up
altars, and groves, and chapels of idols,
and sacrifice swine's flesh, and unclean
beasts: 48 that they should also leave
their children uncircumcised, and make
their souls abominable with all manner
of uncleanness and profanation: 49 to the
end they might forget the law, and
change all the ordinances. 50 And
whosoever would not do according to
the commandment of the king, he said,
he should die. 51 In the selfsame manner
wrote he to his whole kingdom, and
appointed overseers over all the people,
commanding the cities of Judah to
sacrifice, city by city.
52 Then many of the people were
gathered unto them, to wit, every one

that forsook the law; and so they
committed evils in the land; 53 and
drove the Israelites into secret places,
even wheresoever they could flee for
succor. 54 Now the fifteenth day of the
month Chislev, in the hundred forty and
fifth year, they set up the abomination
of desolation upon the altar, and
builded idol altars throughout the cities
of Judah on every side; 55 and burned
incense at the doors of their houses, and
in the streets. 56 And when they had rent
in pieces the books of the law which
they found, they burned them with fire.
57 And wheresoever was found with any
the book of the testament, or if any
consented to the law, the king's
commandment was, that they should
put him to death. 58 Thus did they by
their authority unto the Israelites every
month, to as many as were found in the
cities. 59 Now the five and twentieth day
of the month they did sacrifice upon the
idol altar, which was upon the altar of
God. 60 At which time according to the
commandment they put to death certain
women, that had caused their children
to be circumcised. 61 And they hanged
the infants about their necks, and rifled
their houses, and slew them that had
circumcised them.
62 Howbeit many in Israel were fully
resolved and confirmed in themselves
not to eat any unclean thing.
63 Wherefore they chose rather to die,
that they might not be defiled with
meats, and that they might not profane
the holy covenant: so then they died.
64 And there was very great wrath upon
Israel.

CHAPTER 2

1 In those days arose Mattathi´as the
son of John, the son of Simeon, a priest
of the sons of Joi´arib, from Jerusalem,
and dwelt in Modin. 2 And he had five
sons, Joan´nan, called Caddis: 3 Simon,
called Thassi: 4 Judas, who was called
Maccabe´us: 5 Ele-a´zar, called Avaran:
and Jonathan, whose surname was
Apphus.
6 And when he saw the blasphemies
that were committed in Judah and
Jerusalem, 7 he said, Woe is me!
wherefore was I born to see this misery of
my people, and of the holy city, and to
dwell there, when it was delivered into
the hand of the enemy, and the
sanctuary into the hand of strangers?
8 Her temple is become as a man
without glory. 9 Her glorious vessels are
carried away into captivity, her infants
are slain in the streets, her young men
with the sword of the enemy. 10 What
nation hath not had a part in her
kingdom and gotten of her spoils? 11 All
her ornaments are taken away; of a
free woman she is become a
bondslave. 12 And, behold, our
sanctuary, even our beauty and our
glory, is laid waste, and the Gentiles
have profaned it. 13 To what end
therefore shall we live any longer?
14 Then Mattathi´as and his sons rent
their clothes, and put on sackcloth, and
mourned very sore.
15 In the meanwhile the king's officers,
such as compelled the people to revolt,
came into the city Modin, to make them
sacrifice. 16 And when many of Israel
came unto them, Mattathi´as also and
his sons came together. 17 Then
answered the king's officers, and said to
Mattathi´as on this wise, Thou art a
ruler, and an honorable and great man in
this city, and strengthened with sons and
brethren: 18 now therefore come thou
first, and fulfil the king's
commandment, like as all the heathen

have done, yea, and the men of Judah
also, and such as remain at Jerusalem:
so shalt thou and thy house be in the
number of the king's friends, and thou
and thy children shall be honored with
silver and gold, and many rewards.
[19]Then Mattathi´as answered and spake
with a loud voice, Though all the
nations that are under the king's
dominion obey him, and fall away
every one from the religion of their
fathers, and give consent to his
commandments: [20]yet will I and my
sons and my brethren walk in the
covenant of our fathers. [21]God forbid
that we should forsake the law and the
ordinances. [22]We will not hearken to
the king's words, to go from our
religion, either on the right hand, or the
left. [23]Now when he had left speaking
these words, there came one of the Jews
in the sight of all to sacrifice on the altar
which was at Modin, according to the
king's commandment. [24]Which thing
when Mattathi´as saw, he was inflamed
with zeal, and his reins trembled,
neither could he forbear to show his
anger according to judgment:
wherefore he ran, and slew him upon
the altar. [25]Also the king's
commissioner, who compelled men to
sacrifice, he killed at that time, and the
altar he pulled down. [26]Thus dealt he
zealously for the law of God, like as
Phin´ehas did unto Zimri the son of
Salu. [27]And Mattathi´as cried
throughout the city with a loud voice,
saying, Whosoever is zealous of the
law, and maintaineth the covenant, let
him follow me. [28]So he and his sons
fled into the mountains, and left all that
ever they had in the city.

[29]Then many that sought after justice
and judgment went down into the
wilderness, to dwell there: [30]both they,
and their children, and their wives, and
their cattle; because afflictions
increased sore upon them. [31]Now when
it was told the king's servants, and the
host that was at Jerusalem, in the city
of David, that certain men, who had
broken the king's commandment, were
gone down into the secret places in the
wilderness, [32]they pursued after them a
great number, and having overtaken
them, they camped against them, and
made war against them on the sabbath
day. [33]And they said unto them, Let
that which ye have done hitherto
suffice; come forth, and do according to
the commandment of the king, and ye
shall live. [34]But they said, We will not
come forth, neither will we do the
king's commandment, to profane the
sabbath day. [35]So then they gave them
the battle with all speed. [36]Howbeit
they answered them not, neither cast
they a stone at them, nor stopped the
places where they lay hid; [37]but said,
Let us die all in our innocency: heaven
and earth will testify for us, that ye put
us to death wrongfully. [38]So they rose up
against them in battle on the sabbath,
and they slew them, with their wives
and children, and their cattle, to the
number of a thousand people.

[39]Now when Mattathi´as and his
friends understood hereof, they
mourned for them right sore. [40]And one
of them said to another, If we all do as
our brethren have done, and fight not
for our lives and laws against the
heathen, they will now quickly root us
out of the earth. [41]At that time therefore
they decreed, saying, Whosoever shall
come to make battle with us on the
sabbath day, we will fight against him;
neither will we die all, as our brethren
that were murdered in the secret places.
[42]Then came there unto him a company

of Hasideans, who were mighty men of Israel, even all such as were voluntarily devoted unto the law. 43Also all they that fled for persecution joined themselves unto them, and were a stay unto them. 44So they joined their forces, and smote sinful men in their anger, and wicked men in their wrath: but the rest fled to the heathen for succor. 45Then Mattathi′as and his friends went round about, and pulled down the altars: 46and what children soever they found within the coast of Israel uncircumcised, those they circumcised valiantly. 47They pursued also after the proud men, and the work prospered in their hand. 48So they recovered the law out of the hand of the Gentiles, and out of the hand of kings, neither suffered they the sinner to triumph.

49Now when the time drew near that Mattathi′as should die, he said unto his sons, Now hath pride and rebuke gotten strength, and the time of destruction, and the wrath of indignation: 50now therefore, my sons, be ye zealous for the law, and give your lives for the covenant of your fathers. 51Call to remembrance what acts our fathers did in their time; so shall ye receive great honor and an everlasting name. 52Was not Abraham found faithful in temptation, and it was imputed unto him for righteousness? 53Joseph in the time of his distress kept the commandment, and was made lord of Egypt. 54Phin′ehas our father in being zealous and fervent obtained the covenant of an everlasting priesthood. 55Joshua for fulfilling the word was made a judge in Israel. 56Caleb for bearing witness before the congregation received the heritage of the land. 57David for being merciful possessed the throne of an everlasting kingdom. 58Eli′jah for being zealous and fervent for the law was taken up into heaven. 59Hanani′ah, Azari′ah, and Mish′a-el, by believing were saved out of the flame. 60Daniel for his innocency was delivered from the mouth of lions. 61And thus consider ye throughout all ages, that none that put their trust in him shall be overcome. 62Fear not then the words of a sinful man: for his glory shall be dung and worms. 63Today he shall be lifted up and tomorrow he shall not be found, because he is returned into his dust, and his thought is come to nothing. 64Wherefore, ye my sons, be valiant, and show yourselves men in the behalf of the law; for by it shall ye obtain glory. 65And behold, I know that your brother Simon is a man of counsel, give ear unto him alway: he shall be a father unto you. 66As for Judas Maccabe′us, he hath been mighty and strong, even from his youth up: let him be your captain, and fight the battle of the people. 67Take also unto you all those that observe the law, and avenge ye the wrong of your people. 68Recompense fully the heathen, and take heed to the commandments of the law. 69So he blessed them, and was gathered to his fathers. 70And he died in the hundred forty and sixth year, and his sons buried him in the sepulchres of his fathers at Modin, and all Israel made great lamentation for him.

CHAPTER 3

1Then his son Judas, called Maccabe′us, rose up in his stead. 2And all his brethren helped him, and so did all they that held with his father, and they fought with cheerfulness the battle of Israel. 3So he got his people great honor, and put on a breastplate as a

giant, and girt his warlike harness about
him, and he made battles, protecting the
host with his sword. [4]In his acts he was
like a lion, and like a lion's whelp
roaring for his prey. [5]For he pursued
the wicked, and sought them out, and
burnt up those that vexed his people.
[6]Wherefore the wicked shrunk for fear
of him, and all the workers of iniquity
were troubled, because salvation
prospered in his hand. [7]He grieved also
many kings, and made Jacob glad with
his acts, and his memorial is blessed for
ever. [8]Moreover he went through the
cities of Judah, destroying the ungodly
out of them, and turning away wrath
from Israel: [9]so that he was renowned
unto the utmost part of the earth, and he
received unto him such as were ready
to perish.

[10]Then Apol-lo´nius gathered the
Gentiles together, and a great host out
of Samaria, to fight against Israel.
[11]Which thing when Judas perceived,
he went forth to meet him, and so he
smote him, and slew him: many also
fell down slain, but the rest fled.
[12]Wherefore Judas took their spoils,
and Apol-lo´nius' sword also, and
therewith he fought all his life long.
[13]Now when Seron, a prince of the army
of Syria, heard say that Judas had
gathered unto him a multitude and
company of the faithful to go out with
him to war; [14]he said, I will get me a
name and honor in the kingdom; for I
will go fight with Judas and them that
are with him, who despise the king's
commandment. [15]So he made him
ready to go up, and there went with him
a mighty host of the ungodly to help
him, and to be avenged of the children
of Israel. [16]And when he came near to
the going up of Beth–ho´ron, Judas went
forth to meet him with a small company:
[17]who, when they saw the host coming
to meet them, said unto Judas, How
shall we be able, being so few, to fight
against so great a multitude and so
strong, seeing we are ready to faint with
fasting all this day? [18]Unto whom Judas
answered, It is no hard matter for
many to be shut up in the hands of a
few; and with the God of heaven it is all
one, to deliver with a great multitude,
or a small company: [19]for the victory of
battle standeth not in the multitude of
an host; but strength cometh from
heaven. [20]They come against us in
much pride and iniquity to destroy us,
and our wives and children, and to spoil
us: [21]but we fight for our lives and our
laws. [22]Wherefore the Lord himself
will overthrow them before our face:
and as for you, be ye not afraid of them.
[23]Now as soon as he had left off
speaking, he leapt suddenly upon them,
and so Seron and his host was
overthrown before him. [24]And they
pursued them from the going down of
Beth–ho´ron unto the plain, where were
slain about eight hundred men of them;
and the residue fled into the land of the
Philistines. [25]Then began the fear of
Judas and his brethren, and an
exceeding great dread, to fall upon the
nations round about them. [26]Insomuch
as his fame came unto the king, and all
nations talked of the battles of Judas.

[27]Now when king An-ti´ochus heard
these things, he was full of indignation:
wherefore he sent and gathered
together all the forces of his realm,
even a very strong army. [28]He
opened also his treasure, and gave
his soldiers pay for a year,
commanding them to be ready
whensoever he should need them.
[29]Nevertheless, when he saw that the
money of his treasures failed and that

the tributes in the country were small,
because of the dissension and plague,
which he had brought upon the land in
taking away the laws which had been of
old time; 30he feared that he should not
be able to bear the charges any longer,
nor to have such gifts to give so
liberally as he did before: for he had
abounded above the kings that were
before him. 31Wherefore, being greatly
perplexed in his mind, he determined to
go into Persia, there to take the tributes
of the countries, and to gather much
money.
32So he left Lys´i-as, a nobleman, and
one of the blood royal, to oversee the
affairs of the king from the river
Euphra´tes unto the borders of Egypt:
33and to bring up his son An-ti´ochus,
until he came again. 34Moreover he
delivered unto him the half of his
forces, and the elephants, and gave him
charge of all things that he would have
done, as also concerning them that dwelt
in Judah and Jerusalem: 35to wit, that
he should send an army against them,
to destroy and root out the strength of
Israel, and the remnant of Jerusalem,
and to take away their memorial from
that place; 36and that he should place
strangers in all their quarters, and
divide their land by lot. 37So the king
took the half of the forces that
remained, and departed from An´ti-
och, his royal city, the hundred forty
and seventh year; and having passed the
river Euphra´tes, he went through the
high countries.
38Then Lys´i-as chose Ptol´emy the son
of Dorym´enes, and Nica´nor, and
Gorgias, mighty men of the king's
friends: 39and with them he sent forty
thousand footmen, and seven thousand
horsemen, to go into the land of Judah,
and to destroy it, as the king
commanded. 40So they went forth with
all their power, and came and pitched by
Emma´us in the plain country. 41And
the merchants of the country, hearing
the fame of them, took silver and gold
very much, with servants, and came
into the camp to buy the children of
Israel for slaves: a power also of Syria
and of the land of the Philistines joined
themselves unto them.
42Now when Judas and his brethren
saw that miseries were multiplied, and
that the forces did encamp themselves
in their borders; for they knew how
the king had given commandment to
destroy the people, and utterly abolish
them; 43they said one to another, Let us
restore the decayed estate of our
people, and let us fight for our people
and the sanctuary. 44Then was the
congregation gathered together, that
they might be ready for battle, and that
they might pray, and ask mercy and
compassion. 45Now Jerusalem lay void
as a wilderness, there was none of her
children that went in or out: the
sanctuary also was trodden down, and
aliens kept the stronghold; the heathen
had their habitation in that place; and
joy was taken from Jacob, and the pipe
with the harp ceased.
46Wherefore the Israelites assembled
themselves together, and came to
Mizpah, over against Jerusalem; for in
Mizpah was the place where they
prayed aforetime in Israel. 47Then they
fasted that day, and put on sackcloth,
and cast ashes upon their heads, and
rent their clothes, 48and laid open the
book of the law, wherein the heathen
had sought to paint the likeness of their
images. 49They brought also the priests'
garments, and the firstfruits, and the
tithes: and the Nazarites they stirred up,
who had accomplished their days.

50 Then cried they with a loud voice
toward heaven, saying, What shall we
do with these, and whither shall we
carry them away? 51 For thy sanctuary is
trodden down and profaned, and thy
priests are in heaviness, and brought
low. 52 And lo, the heathen are
assembled together against us to destroy
us: what things they imagine against us,
thou knowest. 53 How shall we be able
to stand against them, except thou, O
God, be our help?
54 Then sounded they with trumpets,
and cried with a loud voice. 55 And after
this Judas ordained captains over the
people, even captains over thousands,
and over hundreds, and over fifties, and
over tens. 56 But as for such as were
building houses, or had betrothed
wives, or were planting vineyards, or
were fearful, those he commanded that
they should return, every man to his
own house, according to the law. 57 So
the camp removed, and pitched upon
the south side of Emma′us. 58 And Judas
said, Arm yourselves, and be valiant
men, and see that ye be in readiness
against the morning, that ye may fight
with these nations, that are assembled
together against us to destroy us and
our sanctuary: 59 for it is better for us to
die in battle, than to behold the
calamities of our people and our
sanctuary. 60 Nevertheless, as the will of
God is in heaven, so let him do.

CHAPTER 4

1 Then took Gorgias five thousand
footmen, and a thousand of the best
horsemen, and removed out of the
camp by night; 2 to the end he might
rush in upon the camp of the Jews, and
smite them suddenly. And the men of
the fortress were his guides. 3 Now
when Judas heard thereof, he himself
removed, and the valiant men with him,
that he might smite the king's army
which was at Emma′us, 4 while as yet
the forces were dispersed from the
camp. 5 In the mean season came
Gorgias by night into the camp of Judas:
and when he found no man there, he
sought them in the mountains: for said
he, These fellows flee from us.
6 But as soon as it was day, Judas
showed himself in the plain with three
thousand men, who nevertheless had
neither armor nor swords to their
minds. 7 And they saw the camp of the
heathen, that it was strong and well
harnessed, and compassed round about
with horsemen; and these were expert
of war. 8 Then said Judas to the men that
were with him, Fear ye not their
multitude, neither be ye afraid of their
assault. 9 Remember how our fathers
were delivered in the Red Sea, when
Pharaoh pursued them with an army.
10 Now therefore let us cry unto heaven,
if peradventure the Lord will have
mercy upon us, and remember the
covenant of our fathers, and destroy
this host before our face this day: 11 that
so all the heathen may know that there
is one who delivereth and saveth Israel.
12 Then the strangers lifted up their
eyes, and saw them coming over
against them. 13 Wherefore they went
out of the camp to battle; but they that
were with Judas sounded their
trumpets. 14 So they joined battle, and
the heathen being discomfited fled into
the plain. 15 Howbeit all the hindmost of
them were slain with the sword: for
they pursued them unto Gezer, and
unto the plains of Idume′a, and
Ashdod, and Jabneh, so that there were
slain of them upon a three thousand
men. 16 This done, Judas returned again

with his host from pursuing them, 17 and
said to the people, Be not greedy of
the spoils, inasmuch as there is a battle
before us, 18 and Gorgias and his host
are here by us in the mountain: but
stand ye now against our enemies, and
overcome them, and after this ye may
boldly take the spoils. 19 As Judas was
yet speaking these words, there
appeared a part of them looking out of
the mountain: 20 who when they
perceived that the Jews had put their
host to flight and were burning the
tents; for the smoke that was seen
declared what was done: 21 when
therefore they perceived these things,
they were sore afraid, and seeing also
the host of Judas in the plain ready to
fight, 22 they fled every one into the land
of strangers. 23 Then Judas returned to
spoil the tents, where they got much
gold, and silver, and blue silk, and
purple of the sea, and great riches.
24 After this they went home, and sung a
song of thanksgiving, and praised the
Lord in heaven: because it is good,
because his mercy endureth for ever.
25 Thus Israel had a great deliverance
that day.

26 Now all the strangers that had
escaped came and told Lys´i-as what
had happened: 27 who, when he heard
thereof, was confounded and
discouraged, because neither such
things as he would were done unto
Israel, nor such things as the king
commanded him were come to pass.
28 The next year therefore following
Lys´i-as gathered together threescore
thousand choice men of foot, and five
thousand horsemen, that he might
subdue them. 29 So they came into
Idume´a, and pitched their tents at
Beth–zur, and Judas met them with ten
thousand men. 30 And when he saw that
mighty army, he prayed and said,
Blessed art thou, O Saviour of Israel,
who didst quell the violence of the
mighty man by the hand of thy servant
David, and gavest the host of
strangers into the hands of Jonathan the
son of Saul, and his armor-bearer;
31 shut up this army in the hand of thy
people Israel, and let them be
confounded in their power and
horsemen: 32 make them to be of no
courage, and cause the boldness of their
strength to fall away, and let them
quake at their destruction: 33 cast them
down with the sword of them that love
thee, and let all those that know thy
name praise thee with thanksgiving.

34 So they joined battle; and there were
slain of the host of Lys´i-as about five
thousand men, even before them were
they slain. 35 Now when Lys´i-as saw
his army put to flight, and the
manliness of Judas' soldiers, and how
they were ready either to live or die
valiantly, he went into An´ti-och, and
gathered together a company of
strangers, and having made his army
greater than it was, he purposed to come
again into Judea.

36 Then said Judas and his brethren,
Behold, our enemies are discomfited:
let us go up to cleanse and dedicate
the sanctuary. 37 Upon this all the host
assembled themselves together, and
went up into Mount Zion. 38 And when
they saw the sanctuary desolate, and
the altar profaned, and the gates burned
up, and shrubs growing in the courts as
in a forest, or in one of the mountains,
yea, and the priests' chambers pulled
down; 39 they rent their clothes, and
made great lamentation, and cast ashes
upon their heads, 40 and fell down flat to
the ground upon their faces, and blew
an alarm with the trumpets, and cried

toward heaven. 41Then Judas
appointed certain men to fight against
those that were in the fortress, until he
had cleansed the sanctuary.
42So he chose priests of blameless
conversation, such as had pleasure in
the law: 43who cleansed the sanctuary,
and bare out the defiled stones into an
unclean place. 44And when as they
consulted what to do with the altar of
burnt offerings, which was profaned;
45they thought it best to pull it down, lest
it should be a reproach to them, because
the heathen had defiled it: wherefore
they pulled it down, 46and laid up the
stones in the mountain of the temple in
a convenient place, until there should
come a prophet to show what should be
done with them. 47Then they took
whole stones according to the law, and
built a new altar according to the
former; 48and made up the sanctuary,
and the things that were within the
temple, and hallowed the courts.
49They made also new holy vessels, and
into the temple they brought the
candlestick, and the altar of burnt
offerings, and of incense, and the table.
50And upon the altar they burned
incense, and the lamps that were upon
the candlestick they lighted, that they
might give light in the temple.
51Furthermore they set the loaves upon
the table, and spread out the veils, and
finished all the works which they had
begun to make.
52Now on the five and twentieth day of
the ninth month, which is called the
month Chislev, in the hundred forty
and eighth year, they rose up betimes in
the morning, 53and offered sacrifice
according to the law upon the new
altar of burnt offerings, which they had
made. 54Look, at what time and what
day the heathen had profaned it, even in
that was it dedicated with songs, and
citherns, and harps, and cymbals.
55Then all the people fell upon their
faces, worshipping and praising the
God of heaven, who had given them
good success. 56And so they kept the
dedication of the altar eight days and
offered burnt offerings with gladness,
and sacrificed the sacrifice of
deliverance and praise. 57They decked
also the forefront of the temple with
crowns of gold, and with shields; and
the gates and the chambers they
renewed, and hanged doors upon them.
58Thus was there very great gladness
among the people, for that the reproach
of the heathen was put away.
59Moreover Judas and his brethren with
the whole congregation of Israel
ordained, that the days of the dedication
of the altar should be kept in their
season from year to year by the space
of eight days, from the five and
twentieth day of the month Chislev,
with mirth and gladness.
60At that time also they builded up the
Mount Zion with high walls and strong
towers round about, lest the Gentiles
should come and tread it down, as they
had done before. 61And they set there a
garrison to keep it, and fortified Beth–
zur to preserve it; that the people might
have a defense against Idume´a.

CHAPTER 5

1Now when the nations round about
heard that the altar was built and the
sanctuary renewed as before, it
displeased them very much.
2Wherefore they thought to destroy
the generation of Jacob that was among
them, and thereupon they began to slay
and destroy the people. 3Then Judas
fought against the children of Esau in

Idume´a at Akrab´bin, because they besieged Israel: and he gave them a great overthrow, and abated their courage, and took their spoils. [4]Also he remembered the injury of the children of Be´on, who had been a snare and an offense unto the people, in that they lay in wait for them in the ways. [5]He shut them up therefore in the towers, and encamped against them, and destroyed them utterly, and burned the towers of that place with fire, and all that were therein. [6]Afterward he passed over to the children of Ammon, where he found a mighty power, and much people, with Timo´theus their captain. [7]So he fought many battles with them, till at length they were discomfited before him; and he smote them. [8]And when he had taken Jazer, with the towns belonging thereto, he returned into Judea.

[9]Then the heathen that were at Gil´e-ad assembled themselves together against the Israelites that were in their quarters, to destroy them; but they fled to the fortress of Dath´ema. [10]And sent letters unto Judas and his brethren, The heathen that are round about us are assembled together against us to destroy us: [11]and they are preparing to come and take the fortress whereunto we are fled, Timo´theus being captain of their host. [12]Come now therefore, and deliver us from their hands, for many of us are slain: [13]yea, all our brethren that were in the places of Tob are put to death: their wives and their children also they have carried away captives, and borne away their stuff; and they have destroyed there about a thousand men.

[14]While these letters were yet reading, behold, there came other messengers from Galilee with their clothes rent, who reported on this wise, [15]and said, They of Ptolema´is, and of Tyre, and Sidon, and all Galilee of the Gentiles, are assembled together against us to consume us. [16]Now when Judas and the people heard these words, there assembled a great congregation together, to consult what they should do for their brethren, that were in trouble, and assaulted of them. [17]Then said Judas unto Simon his brother, Choose thee out men, and go and deliver thy brethren that are in Galilee, for I and Jonathan my brother will go into the country of Gil´e-ad. [18]So he left Joseph the son of Zachari´as, and Azari´as, captains of the people, with the remnant of the host in Judea to keep it. [19]Unto whom he gave commandment, saying, Take ye the charge of this people, and see that ye make not war against the heathen until the time that we come again. [20]Now unto Simon were given three thousand men to go into Galilee, and unto Judas eight thousand men for the country of Gil´e-ad.

[21]Then went Simon into Galilee, where he fought many battles with the heathen, so that the heathen were discomfited by him. [22]And he pursued them unto the gate of Ptolema´is; and there were slain of the heathen about three thousand men, whose spoils he took. [23]And those that were in Galilee, and in Arbat´tis, with their wives and their children, and all that they had, took he away with him, and brought them into Judea with great joy.

[24]Judas Maccabe´us also and his brother Jonathan went over Jordan, and traveled three days' journey in the wilderness, [25]where they met with the Nabate´ans, who came unto them in a peaceable manner, and told them every thing that had happened to their

brethren in the land of Gil´e-ad: [26]and
how that many of them were shut up in
Bozrah, and Bezer, and Alema,
Casphor, Maked, and Carnaim; all
these cities are strong and great: [27]and
that they were shut up in the rest of
the cities of the country of Gil´e-ad, and
that against tomorrow they had
appointed to bring their host against the
forts, and to take them, and to destroy
them all in one day.
[28]Hereupon Judas and his host turned
suddenly by the way of the wilderness
unto Bozrah; and when he had won the
city, he slew all the males with the edge
of the sword, and took all their spoils,
and burned the city with fire. [29]From
whence he removed by night, and went
till he came to the fortress. [30]And
betimes in the morning they looked up,
and, behold, there was an innumerable
people bearing ladders and other
engines of war, to take the fortress: for
they assaulted them. [31]When Judas
therefore saw that the battle was begun,
and that the cry of the city went up to
heaven, with trumpets, and a great
sound, [32]he said unto his host, Fight
this day for your brethren. [33]So he went
forth behind them in three companies,
who sounded their trumpets, and cried
with prayer. [34]Then the host of
Timo´theus, knowing that it was
Maccabe´us, fled from him: wherefore
he smote them with a great slaughter; so
that there were killed of them that day
about eight thousand men.
[35]This done, Judas turned aside to
Mizpah; and after he had assaulted it,
he took it, and slew all the males therein,
and received the spoils thereof, and
burnt it with fire. [36]From thence went
he, and took Casphon, Ma´ged, Bezer,
and the other cities of the country of
Gil´e-ad. [37]After these things gathered
Timo´theus another host, and encamped
against Raphon beyond the brook. [38]So
Judas sent men to espy the host, who
brought him word, saying, All the
heathen that be round about us are
assembled unto them, even a very great
host. [39]He hath also hired the Arabians
to help them, and they have pitched
their tents beyond the brook, ready
to come and fight against thee. Upon
this Judas went to meet them. [40]Then
Timo´theus said unto the captains of
his host, When Judas and his host
come near the brook, if he pass over
first unto us, we shall not be able to
withstand him; for he will mightily
prevail against us: [41]but if he be afraid,
and camp beyond the river, we shall go
over unto him, and prevail against him.
[42]Now when Judas came near the brook,
he caused the scribes of the people to
remain by the brook: unto whom he
gave commandment, saying, Suffer no
man to remain in the camp, but let all
come to the battle. [43]So he went first
over unto them, and all the people after
him: then all the heathen, being
discomfited before him, cast away their
weapons, and fled unto the temple that
was at Carnaim. [44]But they took the
city, and burned the temple with all that
were therein. Thus was Carnaim
subdued, neither could they stand any
longer before Judas.
[45]Then Judas gathered together all the
Israelites that were in the country of
Gil´e- ad, from the least unto the
greatest, even their wives, and their
children, and their stuff, a very great
host, to the end they might come into
the land of Judea. [46]Now when they
came unto Ephron, (this was a great
city in the way as they should go, very
well fortified) they could not turn from
it, either on the right hand or the left,

but must needs pass through the midst
of it. 47 Then they of the city shut them
out, and stopped up the gates with
stones. 48 Whereupon Judas sent unto
them in peaceable manner, saying, Let
us pass through your land to go into our
own country, and none shall do you any
hurt; we will only pass through on foot:
howbeit they would not open unto him.
49 Wherefore Judas commanded a
proclamation to be made throughout
the host, that every man should pitch his
tent in the place where he was. 50 So the
soldiers pitched, and assaulted the city
all that day and all that night, till at the
length the city was delivered into his
hands: 51 who then slew all the males
with the edge of the sword, and rased
the city, and took the spoils thereof, and
passed through the city over them that
were slain. 52 After this went they over
Jordan into the great plain before Beth–
shan. 53 And Judas gathered together
those that came behind, and exhorted
the people all the way through, till they
came into the land of Judea. 54 So they
went up to Mount Zion with joy and
gladness, where they offered burnt
offerings, because not one of them
were slain until they had returned in
peace.

55 Now what time as Judas and Jonathan
were in the land of Gil′e-ad, and
Simon his brother in Galilee before
Ptolema′is, 56 Joseph the son of
Zachari′as, and Azari′as, captains of
the garrisons, heard of the valiant acts
and warlike deeds which they had
done. 57 Wherefore they said, Let us
also get us a name, and go fight against
the heathen that are round about us. 58 So
when they had given charge unto the
garrison that was with them, they went
toward Jabneh. 59 Then came Gorgias
and his men out of the city to fight
against them. 60 And so it was, that
Joseph and Azari′as were put to flight,
and pursued unto the borders of Judea:
and there were slain that day of the
people of Israel about two thousand
men. 61 Thus was there a great
overthrow among the children of Israel,
because they were not obedient unto
Judas and his brethren, but thought to
do some valiant act. 62 Moreover these
men came not of the seed of those, by
whose hand deliverance was given unto
Israel.

63 Howbeit the man Judas and his
brethren were greatly renowned in the
sight of all Israel, and of all the heathen,
wheresoever their name was heard
of; 64 insomuch as the people
assembled unto them with joyful
acclamations. 65 Afterward went Judas
forth with his brethren, and fought
against the children of Esau in the land
toward the south, where he smote
Hebron, and the towns thereof, and
pulled down the fortress of it, and
burned the towers thereof round about.
66 From thence he removed to go into
the land of the Philistines, and passed
through Samaria. 67 At that time certain
priests, desirous to show their valor,
were slain in battle, for that they went
out to fight unadvisedly. 68 So Judas
turned to Ashdod in the land of the
Philistines, and when he had pulled
down their altars, and burned their
carved images with fire, and spoiled
their cities, he returned into the land of
Judea.

CHAPTER 6

1 About that time king An-ti′ochus
traveling through the high countries
heard say, that Elyma′is in the country
of Persia was a city greatly renowned
for riches, silver, and gold; 2 and that

there was in it a very rich temple,
wherein were coverings of gold, and
breastplates, and shields, which
Alexander, son of Philip, the
Macedo´nian king, who reigned first
among the Greeks, had left there.
3 Wherefore he came and sought to take
the city, and to spoil it; but he was not
able, because they of the city, having
had warning thereof, 4 rose up against
him in battle: so he fled, and departed
thence with great heaviness, and
returned to Babylon.
5 Moreover there came one who brought
him tidings into Persia, that the armies,
which went against the land of Judea,
were put to flight: 6 and that Lys´i-as,
who went forth first with a great power,
was driven away of the Jews; and that
they were made strong by the armor,
and power, and store of spoils, which
they had gotten of the armies, whom
they had destroyed: 7 also that they had
pulled down the abomination, which he
had set up upon the altar in Jerusalem,
and that they had compassed about the
sanctuary with high walls, as before,
and his city Beth–zur.
8 Now when the king heard these words,
he was astonished and sore moved:
whereupon he laid him down upon his
bed, and fell sick for grief, because it
had not befallen him as he looked for.
9 And there he continued many days: for
his grief was ever more and more, and
he made account that he should die.
10 Wherefore he called for all his friends,
and said unto them, The sleep is gone
from mine eyes, and my heart faileth for
very care. 11 And I thought with myself,
Into what tribulation am I come, and
how great a flood of misery is it,
wherein now I am! for I was bountiful
and beloved in my power. 12 But now I
remember the evils that I did at
Jerusalem, and that I took all the
vessels of gold and silver that were
therein, and sent to destroy the
inhabitants of Judea without a cause. 13 I
perceive therefore that for this cause
these troubles are come upon me, and,
behold, I perish through great grief in a
strange land.
14 Then called he for Philip, one of his
friends, who he made ruler over all his
realm, 15 and gave him the crown, and
his robe, and his signet, to the end he
should bring up his son An-ti´ochus,
and nourish him up for the kingdom.
16 So king An- ti´ochus died there in the
hundred forty and ninth year. 17 Now
when Lys´i-as knew that the king was
dead, he set up An- ti´ochus his son,
whom he had brought up being young,
to reign in his stead, and his name he
called Eu´pator.
18 About this time they that were in
the tower shut up the Israelites round
about the sanctuary, and sought always
their hurt, and the strengthening of the
heathen. 19 Wherefore Judas, purposing
to destroy them, called all the people
together to besiege them. 20 So they
came together, and besieged them in
the hundred and fiftieth year, and he
made mounts for shot against them,
and other engines. 21 Howbeit certain of
them that were besieged got forth, unto
whom some ungodly men of Israel
joined themselves: 22 and they went
unto the king, and said, How long will
it be ere thou execute judgment, and
avenge our brethren? 23 We have been
willing to serve thy father, and to do as
he would have us, and to obey his
commandments; 24 for which cause they
of our nation besiege the tower, and are
alienated from us: moreover as many of
us as they could light on they slew, and
spoiled our inheritance. 25 Neither have

they stretched out their hand against us
only, but also against their borders.
26 And, behold, this day are they
besieging the tower at Jerusalem, to take
it: the sanctuary also and Beth–zur have
they fortified. 27 Wherefore if thou dost
not prevent them quickly, they will do
greater things than these, neither shalt
thou be able to rule them.

28 Now when the king heard this, he was
angry, and gathered together all his
friends, and the captains of his army,
and those that had charge of the horse.
29 There came also unto him from other
kingdoms, and from isles of the sea,
bands of hired soldiers. 30 So that the
number of his army was an hundred
thousand footmen, and twenty
thousand horsemen, and two and thirty
elephants exercised in battle. 31 These
went through Idume′a, and pitched
against Beth–zur, which they assaulted
many days, making engines of war; but
they of Beth–zur came out, and burned
them with fire, and fought valiantly.

32 Upon this Judas removed from the
tower, and pitched in Bath–zach-ari′as,
over against the king's camp. 33 Then
the king rising very early marched
fiercely with his host toward Bath–
zach-ari′as, where his armies made
them ready to battle, and sounded the
trumpets. 34 And to the end they might
provoke the elephants to fight, they
showed them the blood of grapes and
mulberries. 35 Moreover they divided
the beasts among the armies, and for
every elephant they appointed a
thousand men, armed with coats of
mail, and with helmets of brass on their
heads; and beside this, for every
beast were ordained five hundred
horsemen of the best. 36 These were
ready at every occasion: wheresoever
the beast was, and whithersoever the
beast went, they went also, neither
departed they from him. 37 And upon
the beasts were there strong towers of
wood, which covered every one of
them, and were girt fast unto them with
devices: there were also upon every
one two and thirty strong men, that
fought upon them, beside the Indian
that ruled him. 38 As for the remnant
of the horsemen, they set them on this
side and that side at the two parts of the
host giving them signs what to do, and
being harnessed all over amidst the
ranks. 39 Now when the sun shone upon
the shields of gold and brass, the
mountains glistened therewith, and
shined like lamps of fire. 40 So part of
the king's army being spread upon the
high mountains, and part on the valleys
below, they marched on safely and in
order. 41 Wherefore all that heard the
noise of their multitude, and the
marching of the company, and the
rattling of the harness, were moved: for
the army was very great and mighty.
42 Then Judas and his host drew near,
and entered into battle, and there were
slain of the king's army six hundred
men.

43 Ele-a′zar also, surnamed Sav′aran,
perceiving that one of the beasts, armed
with royal harness, was higher than all
the rest, and supposing that the king
was upon him, 44 put himself in
jeopardy, to the end he might deliver his
people, and get him a perpetual name:
45 wherefore he ran upon him
courageously through the midst of the
battle, slaying on the right hand and on
the left, so that they were divided from
him on both sides. 46 Which done, he
crept under the elephant, and thrust him
under, and slew him: whereupon the
elephant fell down upon him, and there
he died. 47 Howbeit the rest of the Jews

seeing the strength of the king, and the
violence of his forces, turned away
from them.
48 Then the king's army went up to
Jerusalem to meet them, and the king
pitched his tents against Judea, and
against Mount Zion. 49 But with them
that were in Beth–zur he made peace:
for they came out of the city, because
they had no victuals there to endure the
siege, it being a year of rest to the land.
50 So the king took Beth–zur, and set a
garrison there to keep it. 51 As for the
sanctuary, he besieged it many days:
and set there artillery with engines and
instruments to cast fire and stones, and
pieces to cast darts and slings.
52 Whereupon they also made engines
against their engines, and held them
battle a long season. 53 Yet at the last,
their vessels being without victuals,
(for that it was the seventh year, and
they in Judea, that were delivered from
the Gentiles, had eaten up the residue
of the store;) 54 there were but a few left
in the sanctuary, because the famine
did so prevail against them, that they
were fain to disperse themselves, every
man to his own place.
55 At that time Lys´i-as heard say, that
Philip, whom An-ti´ochus the king,
while he lived, had appointed to bring up
his son An-ti´ochus, that he might be
king, 56 was returned out of Persia and
Me´di-a, and the king's host also that
went with him, and that he sought to
take unto him the ruling of the affairs.
57 Wherefore he went in all haste, and
said to the king and the captains of the
host and the company, We decay daily,
and our victuals are but small, and the
place we lay siege unto is strong, and
the affairs of the kingdom lie upon us:
58 now therefore let us be friends with
these men, and make peace with them,
and with all their nation; 59 and
covenant with them, that they shall live
after their laws, as they did before: for
they are therefore displeased, and have
done all these things, because we
abolished their laws.
60 So the king and the princes were
content: wherefore he sent unto them to
make peace; and they accepted thereof.
61 Also the king and the princes made an
oath unto them: whereupon they went
out of the stronghold. 62 Then the king
entered into Mount Zion; but when he
saw the strength of the place, he brake
his oath that he had made, and gave
commandment to pull down the wall
round about. 63 Afterward departed he in
all haste, and returned unto An´ti-och,
where he found Philip to be master of
the city: so he fought against him, and
took the city by force.

CHAPTER 7

1 In the hundred and one and fiftieth year
Deme´tri-us the son of Seleu´cus
departed from Rome, and came up with
a few men unto a city of the sea coast,
and reigned there. 2 And as he entered
into the palace of his ancestors, so it
was, that his forces had taken An-
ti´ochus and Lys´i-as, to bring them
unto him. 3 Wherefore, when he knew
it, he said, Let me not see their faces.
4 So his host slew them.
Now when Deme´tri-us was set upon
the throne of his kingdom, 5 there came
unto him all the wicked and ungodly
men of Israel, having Al´cimus, who
was desirous to be high priest, for their
captain: 6 and they accused the people to
the king, saying, Judas and his brethren
have slain all thy friends, and driven us
out of our own land. 7 Now therefore
send some man whom thou trustest,

and let him go and see what havoc he
hath made among us, and in the king's
land, and let him punish them with all
them that aid them.
8 Then the king chose Bac´chi-des, a
friend of the king, who ruled beyond
the flood, and was a great man in the
kingdom, and faithful to the king. 9 And
him he sent with that wicked Al´cimus,
whom he made high priest, and
commanded that he should take
vengeance of the children of Israel.
10 So they departed, and came with a
great power into the land of Judea,
where they sent messengers to Judas
and his brethren with peaceable words
deceitfully. 11 But they gave no heed to
their words; for they saw that they were
come with a great power.
12 Then did there assemble unto
Al´cimus and Bac´chi-des a company
of scribes, to require justice. 13 Now the
Hasideans were the first among the
children of Israel that sought peace of
them: 14 for said they, One that is a priest
of the seed of Aaron is come with this
army, and he will do us no wrong. 15 So
he spake unto them peaceably, and
sware unto them, saying, We will
procure the harm neither of you nor
your friends. 16 Whereupon they
believed him: howbeit he took of them
threescore men, and slew them in one
day, according to the words which he
wrote, 17 The flesh of thy saints have
they cast out, and their blood have they
shed round about Jerusalem, and there
was none to bury them. 18 Wherefore
the fear and dread of them fell upon all
the people, who said, There is neither
truth nor righteousness in them; for they
have broken the covenant and oath that
they made.
19 After this, removed Bac´chi-des from
Jerusalem, and pitched his tents in
Bezeth, where he sent and took many
of the men that had forsaken him, and
certain of the people also, and when he
had slain them, he cast them into the
great pit. 20 Then committed he the
country to Al´cimus, and left with him
a power to aid him: so Bac´chi-des went
to the king. 21 But Al´cimus contended
for the high priesthood. 22 And unto him
resorted all such as troubled the people,
who, after they had gotten the land of
Judah into their power, did much hurt in
Israel. 23 Now when Judas saw all the
mischief that Al´cimus and his company
had done among the Israelites, even
above the heathen, 24 he went out into all
the coasts of Judea round about, and
took vengeance of them that had
revolted from him, so that they durst no
more go forth into the country. 25 On the
other side, when Al´cimus saw that
Judas and his company had gotten the
upper hand, and knew that he was not
able to abide their force, he went again
to the king, and said all the worst of
them that he could.
26 Then the king sent Nica´nor, one of
his honorable princes, a man that bare
deadly hate unto Israel, with
commandment to destroy the people.
27 So Nica´nor came to Jerusalem with
a great force; and sent unto Judas and
his brethren deceitfully with friendly
words, saying, 28 Let there be no battle
between me and you; I will come with
a few men, that I may see you in peace.
29 He came therefore to Judas, and they
saluted one another peaceably.
Howbeit the enemies were prepared to
take away Judas by violence. 30 Which
thing after it was known to Judas, to
wit, that he came unto him with deceit,
he was sore afraid of him, and would
see his face no more. 31 Nica´nor also,
when he saw that his counsel was

discovered, went out to fight against
Judas beside Caphar-sal′ama: [32]where
there were slain of Nica′nor's side
about five thousand men, and the rest
fled into the city of David.
[33]After this went Nica′nor up to Mount
Zion, and there came out of the
sanctuary certain of the priests and
certain of the elders of the people,
to salute him peaceably, and to show
him the burnt sacrifice that was offered
for the king. [34]But he mocked them,
and laughed at them, and abused them
shamefully, and spake proudly, [35]and
sware in his wrath, saying, Unless
Judas and his host be now delivered
into my hands, if ever I come again in
safety, I will burn up this house: and
with that he went out in a great rage.
[36]Then the priests entered in, and stood
before the altar and the temple,
weeping, and saying, [37]Thou, O Lord,
didst choose this house to be called by
thy name, and to be a house of prayer
and petition for thy people: [38]be avenged
of this man and his host, and let them
fall by the sword: remember their
blasphemies, and suffer them not to
continue any longer.
[39]So Nica′nor went out of Jerusalem,
and pitched his tents in Beth–ho′ron,
where an host out of Syria met him.
[40]But Judas pitched in Adasa with three
thousand men, and there he prayed,
saying, [41]O Lord, when they that were
sent from the king of the Assyrians
blasphemed, thine angel went out, and
smote an hundred fourscore and five
thousand of them. [42]Even so destroy
thou this host before us this day, that
the rest may know that he hath spoken
blasphemously against thy sanctuary,
and judge thou him according to his
wickedness.
[43]So the thirteenth day of the month
Adar the hosts joined battle: but
Nica′nor's host was discomfited, and
he himself was first slain in the battle.
[44]Now when Nica′nor's host saw that
he was slain, they cast away their
weapons, and fled. [45]Then they
pursued after them a day's journey,
from Adasa unto Gezer, sounding an
alarm after them with their trumpets.
[46]Whereupon they came forth out of all
the towns of Judea round about, and
closed them in; so that they, turning
back upon them that pursued them,
were all slain with the sword, and not
one of them was left. [47]Afterwards they
took the spoils, and the prey, and
smote off Nica′nor's head, and his right
hand, which he stretched out so proudly,
and brought them away, and hanged
them up toward Jerusalem. [48]For this
cause the people rejoiced greatly, and
they kept that day a day of great
gladness. [49]Moreover they ordained to
keep yearly this day, being the
thirteenth of Adar. [50]Thus the land of
Judah was in rest a little while.

CHAPTER 8

[1]Now Judas had heard of the fame of
the Romans, that they were mighty and
valiant men, and such as would
lovingly accept all that joined
themselves unto them, and make a
league of amity with all that came unto
them; [2]and that they were men of great
valor. It was told him also of their wars
and noble acts which they had done
among the Galatians, and how they had
conquered them, and brought them
under tribute; [3]and what they had done
in the country of Spain, for the winning
of the mines of the silver and gold
which is there; [4]and that by their policy
and patience they had conquered all the

place, though it were very far from them;
and the kings also that came against
them from the uttermost part of the
earth, till they had discomfited them,
and given them a great overthrow, so
that the rest did give them tribute every
year: 5beside this, how they had
discomfited in battle Philip, and
Perseus, king of the Kittim, with others
that lifted up themselves against them,
and had overcome them: 6how also
An-ti´ochus the great king of Asia, that
came against them in battle, having an
hundred and twenty elephants, with
horsemen, and chariots, and a very
great army, was discomfited by them;
7and how they took him alive, and
covenanted that he and such as reigned
after him should pay a great tribute, and
give hostages, and that which was
agreed upon, 8and the country of India,
and Me´di-a, and Lydia, and of the
goodliest countries, which they took of
him, and gave to king Eu´menes:
9moreover how the Greeks had
determined to come and destroy them;
10and that they, having knowledge
thereof, sent against them a certain
captain, and fighting with them slew
many of them, and carried away
captives their wives and their children,
and spoiled them, and took possession
of their lands, and pulled down their
strongholds, and brought them to be
their servants unto this day: 11it was
told him besides, how they destroyed
and brought under their dominion all
other kingdoms and isles that at any
time resisted them;
12but with their friends and such as
relied upon them they kept amity: and
that they had conquered kingdoms both
far and nigh, insomuch as all that heard
of their name were afraid of them:
13also that, whom they would help to a
kingdom, those reign; and whom again
they would, they displace: finally, that
they were greatly exalted: 14yet for all
this none of them wore a crown, or was
clothed in purple, to be magnified
thereby: 15moreover how they had
made for themselves a senate house,
wherein three hundred and twenty men
sat in council daily, consulting alway
for the people, to the end they might be
well ordered: 16and that they committed
their government to one man every
year, who ruled over all their country,
and that all were obedient to that one,
and that there was neither envy nor
emulation among them.
17In consideration of these things, Judas
chose Eupol´emus the son of John,
the son of Hakkoz, and Jason the son of
Ele- a´zar, and sent them to Rome, to
make a league of amity and
confederacy with them, 18and to intreat
them that they would take the yoke from
them; for they saw that the kingdom of
the Greeks did oppress Israel with
servitude. 19They went therefore to
Rome, which was a very great journey,
and came into the senate, where they
spake and said, 20Judas Maccabe´us
with his brethren, and the people of the
Jews, have sent us unto you, to make a
confederacy and peace with you, and
that we might be registered your
confederates and friends. 21So that
matter pleased the Romans well. 22And
this is the copy of the epistle which the
senate wrote back again in tables of
brass, and sent to Jerusalem, that there
they might have by them a memorial
of peace and confederacy: 23Good
success be to the Romans, and to the
people of the Jews, by sea and by
land for ever: the sword also and
enemy be far from them. 24If there
come first any war upon the Romans or

any of their confederates throughout
all their dominion, 25 the people of the
Jews shall help them, as the time shall
be appointed, with all their heart:
26 neither shall they give any thing unto
them that make war upon them, or aid
them with victuals, weapons, money, or
ships, as it hath seemed good unto the
Romans; but they shall keep their
covenants without taking any thing
therefore. 27 In the same manner also, if
war come first upon the nation of the
Jews, the Romans shall help them with
all their heart, according as the time
shall be appointed them: 28 neither shall
victuals be given to them that take part
against them, or weapons, or money, or
ships, as it hath seemed good to the
Romans; but they shall keep their
covenants, and that without deceit.
29 According to these articles did the
Romans make a covenant with the
people of the Jews. 30 Howbeit if
hereafter the one party or the other shall
think meet to add or diminish any thing,
they may do it at their pleasures, and
whatsoever they shall add or take away
shall be ratified.

31 And as touching the evils that
Deme´tri- us doeth to the Jews, we have
written unto him, saying, Wherefore
hast thou made thy yoke heavy upon
our friends and confederates the Jews?
32 If therefore they complain any more
against thee, we will do them justice,
and fight with thee by sea and by land.

CHAPTER 9

1 Furthermore when Deme´tri-us heard
that Nica´nor and his host were slain in
battle, he sent Bac´chi-des and
Al´cimus into the land of Judea the
second time, and with them the chief
strength of his host: 2 who went forth
by the way that leadeth to Gilgal, and
pitched their tents before Mas´aloth,
which is in Arbela, and after they had
won it, they slew much people. 3 Also
the first month of the hundred fifty and
second year they encamped before
Jerusalem: 4 from whence they removed,
and went to Berea, with twenty
thousand footmen and two thousand
horsemen.

5 Now Judas had pitched his tents at
Ele- a´sa, and three thousand chosen
men with him: 6 who seeing the
multitude of the other army to be so
great were sore afraid; whereupon
many conveyed themselves out of the
host, insomuch as there abode of them
no more but eight hundred men. 7 When
Judas therefore saw that his host slipt
away, and that the battle pressed upon
him, he was sore troubled in mind, and
much distressed, for that he had no time
to gather them together. 8 Nevertheless
unto them that remained he said, Let us
arise and go up against our enemies, if
peradventure we may be able to fight
with them. 9 But they exhorted him
against it, saying, We shall never be
able: let us now rather save our lives,
and hereafter we will return with our
brethren, and fight against them: for we
are but few. 10 Then Judas said, God
forbid that I should do this thing, and
flee away from them: if our time be
come, let us die manfully for our
brethren, and let us not stain our honor.
11 With that the host of Bac´chi-des
removed out of their tents, and stood
over against them, their horsemen
being divided into two troops, and their
slingers and archers going before the
host, and they that marched in the
foreward were all mighty men. 12 As for
Bac´chi-des, he was in the right wing:
so the host drew near on the two parts,

and sounded their trumpets. 13 They also
of Judas' side, even they sounded their
trumpets also, so that the earth shook at
the noise of the armies, and the battle
continued from morning till night.
14 Now when Judas perceived that
Bac´chi-des and the strength of his
army were on the right side, he took
with him all the hardy men, 15 who
discomfited the right wing, and pursued
them unto the Mount Azo´tus. 16 But
when they of the left wing saw that they
of the right wing were discomfited,
they followed upon Judas and those
that were with him hard at the heels
from behind: 17 whereupon there was a
sore battle, insomuch as many were slain
on both parts. 18 Judas also was killed,
and the remnant fled.

19 Then Jonathan and Simon took Judas
their brother, and buried him in the
sepulchre of his fathers in Modin.
20 Moreover they bewailed him, and all
Israel made great lamentation for him,
and mourned many days, saying,
21 How is the valiant man fallen, that
delivered Israel! 22 As for the other
things concerning Judas and his wars,
and the noble acts which he did, and his
greatness, they are not written: for they
were very many.

23 Now after the death of Judas the
wicked began to put forth their heads in
all the coasts of Israel, and there arose
up all such as wrought iniquity. 24 In
those days also was there a very great
famine, by reason whereof the country
revolted, and went with them. 25 Then
Bac´chi-des chose the wicked men, and
made them lords of the country. 26 And
they made inquiry and search for Judas'
friends, and brought them unto
Bac´chi-des, who took vengeance of
them, and used them despitefully. 27 So
was there a great affliction in Israel, the
like whereof was not since the time that
a prophet was not seen among them.

28 For this cause all Judas' friends came
together, and said unto Jonathan,
29 Since thy brother Judas died, we have
no man like him to go forth against our
enemies, and Bac´chi-des, and against
them of our nation that are adversaries
to us. 30 Now therefore we have chosen
thee this day to be our prince and
captain in his stead, that thou mayest
fight our battles. 31 Upon this Jonathan
took the governing upon him at that
time, and rose up instead of his brother
Judas.

32 But when Bac´chi-des got knowledge
thereof, he sought for to slay him.
33 Then Jonathan, and Simon his
brother, and all that were with him,
perceiving that, fled into the wilderness
of Teko´a, and pitched their tents by the
water of the pool Asphar. 34 Which
when Bac´chi-des understood, he came
near to Jordan with all his host upon the
sabbath day.

35 Now Jonathan had sent his brother
John, a captain of the people, to pray his
friends the Nabate´ans, that they might
leave with them their carriage, which
was much. 36 But the children of Jambri
came out of Me´deba, and took John, and
all that he had, and went their way with
it. 37 After this came word to Jonathan
and Simon his brother, that the children
of Jambri made a great marriage, and
were bringing the bride from
Nadab´atha with a great train, as being
the daughter of one of the great princes
of Canaan. 38 Therefore they
remembered John their brother, and
went up, and hid themselves under the
covert of the mountain: 39 where they
lifted up their eyes, and looked, and,
behold, there was much ado and great
carriage: and the bridegroom came

forth, and his friends and brethren, to
meet them with drums, and instruments
of music, and many weapons. 40 Then
Jonathan and they that were with him
rose up against them from the place
where they lay in ambush, and made a
slaughter of them in such sort, as many
fell down dead, and the remnant fled
into the mountain, and they took all
their spoils. 41 Thus was the marriage
turned into mourning, and the noise of
their melody into lamentation. 42 So
when they had avenged fully the blood
of their brother, they turned again to the
marsh of Jordan.
43 Now when Bac´chi-des heard hereof,
he came on the sabbath day unto the
banks of Jordan with a great power.
44 Then Jonathan said to his company,
Let us go up now and fight for our
lives, for it standeth not with us today,
as in time past: 45 for, behold, the battle
is before us and behind us, and the water
of Jordan on this side and that side, the
marsh likewise and wood, neither is
there place for us to turn aside.
46 Wherefore cry ye now unto heaven,
that ye may be delivered from the hand
of your enemies. 47 With that they
joined battle, and Jonathan stretched
forth his hand to smite Bac´chi-des, but
he turned back from him. 48 Then
Jonathan and they that were with him
leapt into Jordan, and swam over unto
the farther bank: howbeit the other
passed not over Jordan unto them. 49 So
there were slain of Bac´chi-des' side
that day about a thousand men.
50 Afterward returned Bac´chi-des to
Jerusalem and, repaired the strong cites
in Judea; the fort in Jericho, and
Emma´us, and Beth–ho´ron, and Beth–
el, and Timnah, Pira´thon, and Taphon,
these did he strengthen with high walls,
with gates, and with bars. 51 And in
them he set a garrison, that they might
work malice upon Israel. 52 He fortified
also the city Beth–zur, and Gezer, and
the tower, and put forces in them, and
provision of victuals. 53 Besides, he
took the chief men's sons in the country
for hostages, and put them into the
tower at Jerusalem to be kept.
54 Moreover in the hundred fifty and
third year, in the second month,
Al´cimus commanded that the wall of
the inner court of the sanctuary should
be pulled down; he pulled down also
the works of the prophets. 55 And as he
began to pull down, even at that time
was Al´cimus plagued, and his
enterprises hindered: for his mouth was
stopped, and he was taken with a palsy,
so that he could no more speak any
thing, nor give order concerning his
house. 56 So Al´cimus died at that time
with great torment. 57 Now when
Bac´chi-des saw that Al´cimus was
dead, he returned to the king:
whereupon the land of Judea was in rest
two years.
58 Then all the ungodly men held a
council, saying, Behold, Jonathan and
his company are at ease, and dwell
without care: now therefore we will
bring Bac´chi-des hither, who shall
take them all in one night. 59 So they
went and consulted with him. 60 Then
removed he, and came with a great
host, and sent letters privily to his
adherents in Judea, that they should
take Jonathan and those that were with
him: howbeit they could not, because
their counsel was known unto them.
61 Wherefore they took of the men of the
country, that were authors of that
mischief, about fifty persons, and slew
them. 62 Afterward Jonathan, and
Simon, and they that were with him,
got them away to Beth-ba´si, which is

in the wilderness, and they repaired the
decays thereof, and made it strong.
63 Which thing when Bac´chi-des knew,
he gathered together all his host, and
sent word to them that were of Judea.
64 Then went he and laid siege against
Beth-ba´si; and they fought against it a
long season and made engines of war.
65 But Jonathan left his brother Simon in
the city, and went forth himself into the
country, and with a certain number
went he forth. 66 And he smote
Odonar´kes and his brethren, and the
children of Phas´iron in their tent.
67 And when he began to smite them,
and came up with his forces,
Simon and his company went out of the
city, and burned up the engines of war,
68 and fought against Bac´chi-des, who
was discomfited by them, and they
afflicted him sore: for his counsel and
travail was in vain. 69 Wherefore he was
very wroth at the wicked men that gave
him counsel to come into the country,
insomuch as he slew many of them,
and purposed to return into his own
country.
70 Whereof when Jonathan had
knowledge, he sent ambassadors unto
him, to the end he should make peace
with him, and deliver them the
prisoners. 71 Which thing he accepted,
and did according to his demands, and
sware unto him that he would never do
him harm all the days of his life.
72 When therefore he had restored unto
him the prisoners that he had taken
aforetime out of the land of Judea, he
returned and went his way into his own
land, neither came he any more into
their borders. 73 Thus the sword ceased
from Israel: but Jonathan dwelt at
Michmash, and began to govern the
people; and he destroyed the ungodly
men out of Israel.

CHAPTER 10

1 In the hundred and sixtieth year
Alexander, the son of An- ti´ochus
surnamed E-piph´anes, went up and
took Ptolema´is: for the people had
received him, by means whereof he
reigned there. 2 Now when king
Deme´tri- us heard thereof, he gathered
together an exceeding great host, and
went forth against him to fight.
3 Moreover Deme´tri- us sent letters
unto Jonathan with loving words, so as
he magnified him. 4 For said he, Let us
first make peace with him, before he
join with Alexander against us: 5 else he
will remember all the evils that we have
done against him, and against his
brethren and his people. 6 Wherefore he
gave him authority to gather together
an host, and to provide weapons, that
he might aid him in battle: he
commanded also that the hostages that
were in the tower should be delivered
him.
7 Then came Jonathan to Jerusalem, and
read the letters in the audience of all
the people, and of them that were in the
tower: 8 who were sore afraid, when
they heard that the king had given him
authority to gather together an host.
9 Whereupon they of the tower delivered
their hostages unto Jonathan, and he
delivered them unto their parents.
10 This done, Jonathan settled himself in
Jerusalem, and began to build and
repair the city. 11 And he commanded
the workmen to build the walls and the
Mount Zion round about with square
stones for fortification; and they did so.
12 Then the strangers, that were in the
fortresses which Bac´chi-des had built,
fled away; 13 insomuch as every man
left his place, and went into his own
country. 14 Only at Beth–zur certain of

those that had forsaken the law and the
commandments remained still: for it
was their place of refuge.
[15]Now when king Alexander had heard
what promises Deme´tri-us had sent
unto Jonathan: when also it was told
him of the battles and noble acts which
he and his brethren had done, and of the
pains that they had endured, [16]he said,
Shall we find such another man? now
therefore we will make him our friend
and confederate. [17]Upon this he wrote a
letter, and sent it unto him, according to
these words, saying, [18]King Alexander
to his brother Jonathan sendeth
greeting: [19]We have heard of thee, that
thou art a man of great power, and meet
to be our friend. [20]Wherefore now this
day we ordain thee to be the high priest
of thy nation, and to be called the king's
friend; (and therewithal he sent him a
purple robe and a crown of gold:) and
require thee to take our part, and keep
friendship with us. [21]So in the seventh
month of the hundred and sixtieth year,
at the feast of the tabernacles, Jonathan
put on the holy robe, and gathered
together forces, and provided much
armor.
[22]Whereof when Deme´tri-us heard, he
was very sorry, and said, [23]What have
we done, that Alexander hath prevented
us in making amity with the Jews to
strengthen himself? [24]I also will write
unto them words of encouragement,
and promise them dignities and gifts,
that I may have their aid. [25]He sent unto
them therefore to this effect: King
Deme´tri- us unto the people of the
Jews sendeth greeting: [26]Whereas ye
have kept covenants with us, and
continued in our friendship, not joining
yourselves with our enemies, we have
heard hereof, and are glad. [27]Wherefore
now continue ye still to be faithful unto
us, and we will well recompense you
for the things ye do in our behalf, [28]and
will grant you many immunities, and
give you rewards. [29]And now do I free
you, and for your sake I release all the
Jews, from tributes, and from the
customs of salt, and from crown taxes,
[30]and from that which appertaineth unto
me to receive for the third part of the
seed, and the half of the fruit of the trees,
I release it from this day forth, so that
they shall not be taken of the land of
Judea, nor of the three governments
which are added thereunto out of the
country of Samaria and Galilee, from
this day forth for evermore. [31]Let
Jerusalem also be holy and free, with
the borders thereof, both from tenths
and tributes. [32]And as for the tower
which is at Jerusalem, I yield up
authority over it, and give it to the high
priest, that he may set in it such men as
he shall choose to keep it. [33]Moreover I
freely set at liberty every one of the
Jews, that were carried captives out of
the land of Judea into any part of my
kingdom, and I will that all my officers
remit the tributes even of their cattle.
[34]Furthermore I will that all the feasts,
and sabbaths, and new moons, and
solemn days, and the three days before
the feast, and the three days after the
feast, shall be all days of immunity and
freedom for all the Jews in my realm.
[35]Also no man shall have authority to
meddle with them, or to molest any of
them in any matter.
[36]I will further, that there be enrolled
among the king's forces about thirty
thousand men of the Jews, unto whom
pay shall be given, as belongeth to all
the king's forces. [37]And of them some
shall be placed in the king's strongholds,
of whom also some shall be set over
the affairs of the kingdom, which are of

trust: and I will that their overseers and
governors be of themselves, and that
they live after their own laws, even as
the king hath commanded in the land of
Judea.
38 And concerning the three
governments that are added to Judea
from the country of Samaria, let them be
joined with Judea, that they may be
reckoned to be under one, nor bound to
obey other authority than the high
priest's. 39 As for Ptolema´is, and the
land pertaining thereto, I give it as a
free gift to the sanctuary at Jerusalem
for the necessary expenses of the
sanctuary. 40 Moreover I give every year
fifteen thousand shekels of silver out of
the king's accounts from the places
appertaining. 41 And all the overplus,
which the officers paid not in as in
former time, from henceforth shall be
given toward the works of the temple.
42 And beside this, the five thousand
shekels of silver, which they took from
the uses of the temple out of the
accounts year by year, even those
things shall be released, because they
appertain to the priests that minister.
43 And whosoever they be that flee unto
the temple at Jerusalem, or be within
the liberties thereof, being indebted
unto the king, or for any other matter,
let them be at liberty, and all that they
have in my realm.
44 For the building also and repairing of
the works of the sanctuary expenses
shall be given of the king's accounts.
45 Yea, and for the building of the walls
of Jerusalem, and the fortifying thereof
round about, expenses shall be given
out of the king's accounts, as also for
the building of the walls in Judea.
46 Now when Jonathan and the
people heard these words, they gave
no credit unto them, nor received
them, because they remembered the
great evil that he had done in Israel; for
he had afflicted them very sore. 47 But
with Alexander they were well pleased,
because he was the first that entreated
of true peace with them, and they
were confederate with him always.
48 Then gathered king Alexander great
forces, and camped over against
Deme´tri-us. 49 And after the two
kings had joined battle, Deme´tri-us'
host fled: but Alexander followed after
him, and prevailed against them. 50 And
he continued the battle very sore until the
sun went down: and that day was
Deme´tri-us slain.
51 Afterward Alexander sent
ambassadors to Ptol´emy king of Egypt
with a message to this effect:
52 forasmuch as I am come again to my
realm, and am set in the throne of my
progenitors, and have gotten the
dominion, and overthrown Deme´tri-
us, and recovered our country; 53 for
after I had joined battle with him, both
he and his host was discomfited by us,
so that we sit in the throne of his
kingdom: 54 now therefore let us make a
league of amity together, and give me
now thy daughter to wife: and I will be
thy son-in-law, and will give both thee
and her gifts according to thy dignity.
55 Then Ptol´emy the king gave answer,
saying, Happy be the day wherein thou
didst return into the land of thy
fathers, and satest in the throne of their
kingdom. 56 And now will I do to thee,
as thou hast written: meet me therefore
at Ptolema´is, that we may see one
another; for I will marry my daughter to
thee according to thy desire.
57 So Ptol´emy went out of Egypt with
his daughter Cleopatra, and they came
unto Ptolema´is in the hundred
threescore and second year: 58 where

king Alexander meeting him, he gave
unto him his daughter Cleopatra, and
celebrated her marriage at Ptolema´is
with great glory, as the manner of kings
is.
59Now king Alexander had written unto
Jonathan, that he should come and meet
him. 60Who thereupon went
honorably to Ptolema´is, where he met
the two kings, and gave them and their
friends silver and gold, and many
presents, and found favor in their sight.
61At that time certain pestilent fellows
of Israel, men of a wicked life,
assembled themselves against him, to
accuse him: but the king would not hear
them. 62Yea more than that, the king
commanded to take off his garments,
and clothe him in purple: and they did
so. 63Also he made him sit by himself,
and said into his princes, Go with him
into the midst of the city, and make
proclamation, that no man complain
against him of any matter, and that no
man trouble him for any manner of
cause. 64Now when his accusers saw
that he was honored according to the
proclamation, and clothed in purple,
they fled all away. 65So the king
honored him, and wrote him among his
chief friends, and made him a duke, and
partaker of his dominion. 66Afterward
Jonathan returned to Jerusalem with
peace and gladness.
67Furthermore in the hundred
threescore and fifth year came
Deme´tri-us son of Demetrius out of
Crete into the land of his fathers:
68whereof when king Alexander heard
tell, he was right sorry, and returned into
An´ti-och. 69Then Deme´tri-us made
Apol-lo´nius the governor of
Coelesyr´ia his general, who gathered
together a great host, and camped in
Jabneh, and sent unto Jonathan the high
priest, saying,
70Thou alone liftest up thyself against
us, and I am laughed to scorn for thy
sake, and reproached: and why dost
thou vaunt thy power against us in the
mountains? 71Now therefore, if thou
trustest in thine own strength, come
down to us into the plain field, and
there let us try the matter together: for
with me is the power of the cities. 72Ask
and learn who I am, and the rest that
take our part, and they shall tell thee that
thy foot is not able to stand before our
face; for thy fathers have been twice put
to flight in their own land. 73Wherefore
now thou shalt not be able to abide the
horsemen and so great a power in the
plain, where is neither stone nor flint,
nor place to flee unto.
74So when Jonathan heard these
words of Apol-lo´nius, he was moved
in his mind, and choosing ten thousand
men he went out of Jerusalem, where
Simon his brother met him for to help
him. 75And he pitched his tents against
Joppa: but they of Joppa shut him out of
the city, because Apol-lo´nius had a
garrison there. 76Then Jonathan laid
siege unto it: whereupon they of the
city let him in for fear: and so Jonathan
won Joppa.
77Whereof when Apol-lo´nius heard, he
took three thousand horsemen, with a
great host of footmen, and went to
Ashdod as one that journeyed, and
therewithal drew him forth into the
plain, because he had a great number of
horsemen, in whom he put his trust.
78Then Jonathan followed after him to
Ashdod, where the armies joined battle.
79Now Apol-lo´nius had left a thousand
horsemen in ambush. 80And Jonathan
knew that there was an ambushment
behind him; for they had compassed in
his host, and cast darts at the people, from

morning till evening. 81 But the people
stood still, as Jonathan had commanded
them: and so the enemies' horses were
tired. 82 Then brought Simon forth his
host, and set them against the
footmen, (for the horsemen were
spent,) who were discomfited by him,
and fled. 83 The horsemen also, being
scattered in the field, fled to Ashdod,
and went into Beth–da′gon, their idol's
temple, for safety. 84 But Jonathan set
fire on Ashdod, and the cities round
about it, and took their spoils; and the
temple of Dagon, with them that were
fled into it, he burned with fire. 85 Thus
there were burned and slain with the
sword well nigh eight thousand men.
86 And from thence Jonathan removed
his host, and camped against
Ash′kelon, where the men of the city
came forth, and met him with great
pomp. 87 After this returned Jonathan
and his host unto Jerusalem, having
many spoils. 88 Now when king
Alexander heard these things, he
honored Jonathan yet more, 89 and sent
him a buckle of gold, as the use is to be
given to such as are of the king's blood:
he gave him also Ekron with the
borders thereof in possession.

CHAPTER 11

1 And the king of Egypt gathered
together a great host, like the sand
that lieth upon the sea shore, and
many ships, and went about through
deceit to get Alexander's kingdom, and
join it to his own. 2 Whereupon he took
his journey into Syria in peaceable
manner, so as they of the cities opened
unto him, and met him: for king
Alexander had commanded them so to
do, because he was his father-in-law.
3 Now as Ptol′emy entered into the
cities, he set in every one of them a
garrison of soldiers to keep it. 4 And
when he came near to Ashdod, they
showed him the temple of Dagon that
was burned, and Ashdod and the
suburbs thereof that were destroyed,
and the bodies that were cast abroad,
and them that he had burned in the
battle; for they had made heaps of
them by the way where he should pass.
5 Also they told the king whatsoever
Jonathan had done, to the intent he
might blame him: but the king held his
peace. 6 Then Jonathan met the king
with great pomp at Joppa, where they
saluted one another, and lodged.
7 Afterward Jonathan, when he had gone
with the king to the river called
Eleu′therus, returned again to
Jerusalem. 8 King Ptol′emy therefore,
having gotten the dominion of the
cities by the sea unto Seleu′cia upon
the sea coast, imagined wicked
counsels against Alexander.
9 Whereupon he sent ambassadors unto
king Deme′tri- us, saying, Come, let us
make a league betwixt us, and I will
give thee my daughter whom Alexander
hath, and thou shalt reign in thy father's
kingdom: 10 for I repent that I gave my
daughter unto him, for he sought to slay
me. 11 Thus did he slander him, because
he was desirous of his kingdom.
12 Wherefore he took his daughter from
him, and gave her to Deme′tri-us, and
forsook Alexander, so that their hatred
was openly known. 13 Then Ptol′emy
entered into An′ti-och, where he set
two crowns upon his head, the crown of
Asia, and of Egypt. 14 In the mean season
was king Alexander in Cili′cia, because
those that dwelt in those parts had
revolted from him. 15 But when
Alexander heard of this, he came to war
against him: whereupon king Ptol′emy

brought forth his host, and met him with
a mighty power, and put him to flight.
16 SoAlexander fled into Arabia, there to
be defended; but king Ptol′emy was
exalted: 17 for Zab′di- el the Arabian
took off Alexander's head, and sent it
unto Ptol′emy. 18 King Ptol′emy also
died the third day after, and they that
were in the strongholds were slain one
of another. 19 By this means Deme′tri-
us reigned in the hundred threescore
and seventh year.
20 At the same time Jonathan gathered
together them that were in Judea, to
take the tower that was in Jerusalem:
and he made many engines of war
against it. 21 Then certain ungodly
persons, who hated their own people,
went unto the king, and told him that
Jonathan besieged the tower.
22 Whereof when he heard, he was
angry, and immediately removing, he
came to Ptolema′is, and wrote unto
Jonathan, that he should not lay siege to
the tower, but come and speak with him
at Ptolema′is in great haste.
23 Nevertheless Jonathan, when he heard
this, commanded to besiege it still: and
he chose certain of the elders of Israel
and the priests, and put himself in peril;
24 and took silver and gold, and raiment,
and divers presents besides, and went to
Ptolema′is unto the king, where he
found favor in his sight. 25 And though
certain ungodly men of the people had
made complaints against him, 26 yet the
king treated him as his predecessors
had done before, and promoted him in the
sight of all his friends, 27 and confirmed
him in the high priesthood, and in all
the honors that he had before, and gave
him pre-eminence among his chief
friends. 28 Then Jonathan desired the
king, that he would make Judea free
from tribute, as also the three
governments, with the country of
Samaria; and he promised him three
hundred talents. 29 So the king
consented, and wrote letters unto
Jonathan of all these things after this
manner:
30 King Deme′tri-us unto his brother
Jonathan, and unto the nation of the
Jews, sendeth greeting: 31 We send you
here a copy of the letter which we did
write unto our cousin Las′thenes
concerning you, that ye might see it.
32 King Deme′tri-us unto his father
Las′thenes sendeth greeting: 33 We are
determined to do good to the people
of the Jews, who are our friends, and
keep covenants with us, because of
their good will toward us. 34 Wherefore
we have ratified unto them the borders
of Judea, with the three governments of
E′phra-im and Lud and Ramatha′im,
that are added unto Judea from the
country of Samaria, and all things
appertaining unto them, for all such as
do sacrifice in Jerusalem, instead of the
payments which the king received of
them yearly aforetime out of the fruits
of the earth and of trees. 35 And as for
other things that belong unto us, of the
tithes and customs pertaining unto us, as
also the saltpits, and the crown taxes,
which are due unto us, we discharge
them of them all for their relief. 36 And
nothing hereof shall be revoked from
this time forth for ever. 37 Now
therefore see that thou make a copy of
these things, and let it be delivered unto
Jonathan, and set upon the holy mount
in a conspicuous place. 38 After this,
when king Deme′tri-us saw that the
land was quiet before him, and that no
resistance was made against him, he
sent away all his forces, every one to his
own place, except certain bands of
strangers, whom he had gathered from

the isles of the heathen: wherefore all
the forces of his fathers hated him.
39 Moreover there was one Tryphon,
that had been of Alexander's part afore,
who, seeing that all the host murmured
against Deme´tri-us, went to Simal´cu-
e the Arabian, that brought up An-
ti´ochus the young son of Alexander,
40 and lay sore upon him to deliver him
this young An-ti´ochus, that he might
reign in his father's stead: he told him
therefore all that Deme´tri-us had done,
and how his men of war were at enmity
with him, and there he remained a long
season. 41 In the mean time Jonathan
sent unto king Deme´tri-us, that he
would cast those of the tower out of
Jerusalem, and those also in the
fortresses: for they fought against
Israel. 42 So Deme´tri-us sent unto
Jonathan, saying, I will not only do this
for thee and thy people, but I will
greatly honor thee and thy nation, if
opportunity serve. 43 Now therefore
thou shalt do well, if thou send me men
to help me; for all my forces are gone
from me. 44 Upon this Jonathan sent him
three thousand strong men unto An´ti-
och: and when they came to the king,
the king was very glad of their coming.
45 Howbeit they that were of the city
gathered themselves together into the
midst of the city, to the number of an
hundred and twenty thousand men, and
would have slain the king. 46 Wherefore
the king fled into the court, but they of the
city kept the passages of the city, and
began to fight. 47 Then the king called to
the Jews for help, who came unto him
all at once, and dispersing themselves
through the city slew that day in the city
to the number of an hundred thousand.
48 Also they set fire on the city, and got
many spoils that day, and delivered the
king. 49 So when they of the city saw that
the Jews had got the city as they would,
their courage was abated: wherefore
they made supplication to the king, and
cried, saying, 50 Grant us peace, and let
the Jews cease from assaulting us and
the city. 51 With that they cast away
their weapons, and made peace; and the
Jews were honored in the sight of the
king, and in the sight of all that were in
his realm; and they returned to
Jerusalem, having great spoils. 52 So
king Deme´tri-us sat on the throne of
his kingdom, and the land was quiet
before him. 53 Nevertheless he
dissembled in all that ever he spake,
and estranged himself from Jonathan,
neither rewarded he him according to
the benefits which he had received of
him, but troubled him very sore. 54 After
this returned Tryphon, and with him the
young child An-ti´ochus, who reigned,
and was crowned. 55 Then there
gathered unto him all the men of war,
whom Deme´tri-us had put away, and
they fought against Deme´tri-us, who
turned his back and fled. 56 Moreover
Tryphon took the elephants, and won
An´ti- och. 57 At that time young An-
ti´ochus wrote unto Jonathan, saying, I
confirm thee in the high priesthood,
and appoint thee ruler over the four
governments, and to be one of the king's
friends. 58 Upon this he sent him golden
vessels to be served in, and gave him
leave to drink in gold, and to be clothed
in purple, and to wear a golden buckle.
59 His brother Simon also he made
captain from the place called The
ladder of Tyrus unto the borders of
Egypt. 60 Then Jonathan went forth, and
passed through the cities beyond the
water, and all the forces of Syria
gathered themselves unto him for to
help him: and when he came to
Ash´kelon, they of the city met him

honorably. 61 From whence he went to
Gaza, but they of Gaza shut him out;
wherefore he laid siege unto it, and
burned the suburbs thereof with fire,
and spoiled them. 62 Afterward, when
they of Gaza made supplication unto
Jonathan, he made peace with them, and
took the sons of their chief men for
hostages, and sent them to Jerusalem,
and passed through the country unto
Damascus. 63 Now when Jonathan
heard that Deme′tri-us' princes were
come to Kedesh, which is in Galilee,
with a great power, purposing to
remove him out of the country, 64 he
went to meet them, and left Simon his
brother in the country. 65 Then Simon
encamped against Beth–zur, and fought
against it a long season, and shut it up:
66 but they desired to have peace with
him, which he granted them, and then
put them out from thence, and took the
city, and set a garrison in it. 67 As for
Jonathan and his host, they pitched at
the water of Chin′nereth, from whence
betimes in the morning they got them to
the plain of Hazor. 68 And, behold, the
host of strangers met them in the plain,
who, having laid men in ambush for him
in the mountains, came themselves
over against him. 69 So when they that
lay in ambush rose out of their places,
and joined battle, all that were of
Jonathan's side fled; 70 insomuch as
there was not one of them left, except
Mattathi′as the son of Ab′salom, and
Judas the son of Calphi, the captains of
the host. 71 Then Jonathan rent his
clothes, and cast earth upon his head,
and prayed. 72 Afterwards turning again
to battle, he put them to flight, and so
they ran away. 73 Now when his own men
that were fled saw this, they turned
again unto him, and with him pursued
them to Kedesh, even unto their own
tents, and there they camped. 74 So there
were slain of the heathen that day about
three thousand men: but Jonathan
returned to Jerusalem.

CHAPTER 12

1 Now when Jonathan saw that time
served him, he chose certain men, and
sent them to Rome, for to confirm and
renew the friendship that they had with
them. 2 He sent letters also to the
Lacede- mon′ians, and to other places,
for the same purpose. 3 So they went
unto Rome, and entered into the senate,
and said, Jonathan the high priest, and
the people of the Jews, sent us unto
you, to the end ye should renew the
friendship, which ye had with them,
and league, as in former time. 4 Upon
this the Romans gave them letters unto
the governors of every place, that they
should bring them into the land of
Judea peaceably.
5 And this is the copy of the letters
which Jonathan wrote to the Lacede-
mon′ians: 6 Jonathan the high priest,
and the elders of the nation, and the
priests, and the other people of the
Jews, unto the Lacede-mon′ians their
brethren send greeting: 7 There were
letters sent in times past unto Oni′as the
high priest from Dari′us, who reigned
then among you, to signify that ye are
our brethren, as the copy here
underwritten doth specify. 8 At which
time Oni′as treated the ambassador that
was sent honorably, and received the
letters, wherein declaration was made
of the league and friendship. 9 Therefore
we also, albeit we need none of
these things, for that we have the holy
books of scripture in our hands to
comfort us, 10 have nevertheless
attempted to send unto you for the

renewing of brotherhood and
friendship, lest we should become
strangers unto you altogether: for there
is a long time passed since ye sent unto
us. 11We therefore at all times without
ceasing, both in our feasts, and other
convenient days, do remember you in
the sacrifices which we offer, and in
our prayers, as reason is, and as it
becometh us to think upon our
brethren: 12and we are right glad of
your honor. 13As for ourselves, we have
had great troubles and wars on every
side, forsomuch as the kings that are
round about us have fought against us.
14Howbeit we would not be
troublesome unto you, nor to others of
our confederates and friends, in these
wars: 15for we have help from heaven
that succoreth us, so as we are delivered
from our enemies, and our enemies are
brought under foot. 16For this cause we
chose Nume′nius the son of An-
ti′ochus, and An-tip′ater the son of
Jason, and sent them unto the Romans,
to renew the amity that we had with
them, and the former league. 17We
commanded them also to go unto you,
and to salute you, and to deliver you our
letters concerning the renewing of our
brotherhood. 18Wherefore now ye shall
do well to give us an answer thereto.
19And this is the copy of the letters
which Oni′as sent. 20Ar′eus king of the
Lacede-mon′ians to Oni′as the high
priest, greeting: 21It is found in writing,
that the Lacede-mo′nians and Jews
are brethren, and that they are of the
stock of Abraham: 22now therefore,
since this is come to our knowledge, ye
shall do well to write unto us of your
prosperity. 23We do write back again to
you, that your cattle and goods are ours,
and ours are yours. We do command
therefore our ambassadors to make
report unto you on this wise.
24Now when Jonathan heard that
Deme′tri- us' princes were come to
fight against him with a greater host
than afore, 25he removed from
Jerusalem, and met them in the land of
Hamath: for he gave them no respite to
enter his country. 26He sent spies also
unto their tents, who came again, and
told him that they were appointed to
come upon them in the night season.
27Wherefore so soon as the sun was
down, Jonathan commanded his men to
watch, and to be in arms, that all the
night long they might be ready to fight:
also he sent forth sentinels round about
the host. 28But when the adversaries
heard that Jonathan and his men were
ready for battle, they feared, and
trembled in their hearts, and they
kindled fires in their camp. 29Howbeit
Jonathan and his company knew it not
till the morning: for they saw the lights
burning. 30Then Jonathan pursued after
them, but overtook them not: for they
were gone over the river Eleu′therus.
31Wherefore Jonathan turned to the
Arabians, who were called Zabade′ans,
and smote them, and took their spoils.
32And removing thence, he came to
Damascus, and so passed through all the
country. 33Simon also went forth, and
passed through the country unto
Ash′kelon, and the holds there
adjoining, from whence he turned aside
to Joppa, and won it. 34For he had heard
that they would deliver the hold unto
them that took Deme′tri-us' part;
wherefore he set a garrison there to
keep it.
35After this came Jonathan home again,
and calling the elders of the people
together, he consulted with them about
building strongholds in Judea, 36and
making the walls of Jerusalem higher,

and raising a great mount between the
tower and the city, for to separate it
from the city, that so it might be alone,
that men might neither sell nor buy in
it. 37 Upon this they came together to
build up the city, forasmuch as part of
the wall toward the brook on the east
side was fallen down, and they repaired
that which was called Caphen´atha.
38 Simon also set up Hadid in
Shephe´lah, and made it strong with
gates and bars.

39 Now Tryphon went about to get the
kingdom of Asia, and to kill An-
ti´ochus the king, that he might set the
crown upon his own head. 40 Howbeit he
was afraid that Jonathan would not
suffer him, and that he would fight
against him; wherefore he sought a way
how to take Jonathan, that he might kill
him. So he removed, and came to Beth–
shan. 41 Then Jonathan went out to meet
him with forty thousand men chosen
for the battle, and came to Beth–shan.
42 Now when Tryphon saw Jonathan
came with so great a force, he durst not
stretch his hand against him; 43 but
received him honorably, and
commended him unto all his friends,
and gave him gifts, and commanded his
men of war to be as obedient unto him,
as to himself. 44 Unto Jonathan also he
said, Why hast thou put all this people
to so great trouble, seeing there is no
war betwixt us? 45 Therefore send them
now home again, and choose a few men
to wait on thee, and come thou with me
to Ptolema´is, for I will give it thee, and
the rest of the strongholds and forces,
and all that have any charge: as for me,
I will return and depart: for this is the
cause of my coming. 46 So Jonathan
believing him did as he bade him, and
sent away his host, who went into the
land of Judea. 47 And with himself he
retained but three thousand men, of
whom he sent two thousand into
Galilee, and one thousand went with
him. 48 Now as soon as Jonathan entered
into Ptolema´is, they of Ptolema´is
shut the gates, and took him, and all
them that came with him they slew with
the sword. 49 Then sent Tryphon an host
of footmen and horsemen into Galilee,
and into the great plain, to destroy all
Jonathan's company. 50 But when they
knew that Jonathan and they that were
with him were taken and slain, they
encouraged one another; and went
close together, prepared to fight.
51 They therefore that followed upon
them, perceiving that they were ready
to fight for their lives, turned back
again. 52 Whereupon they all came into
the land of Judea peaceably, and there
they bewailed Jonathan, and them that
were with him, and they were sore
afraid; wherefore all Israel made great
lamentation. 53 Then all the heathen that
were round about them sought to
destroy them: for said they, They have
no captain, nor any to help them: now
therefore let us make war upon them,
and take away their memorial from
among men.

CHAPTER 13

1 Now when Simon heard that Tryphon
had gathered together a great host to
invade the land of Judea, and destroy it,
2 and saw that the people was in great
trembling and fear, he went up to
Jerusalem, and gathered the people
together. 3 And gave them exhortation,
saying, Ye yourselves know what great
things I, and my brethren, and my
father's house, have done for the laws
and the sanctuary, the battles also and
troubles which we have seen, 4 by

reason whereof all my brethren are
slain for Israel's sake, and I am left
alone. 5 Now therefore be it far from me,
that I should spare mine own life in any
time of trouble: for I am no better than
my brethren. 6 Doubtless I will avenge
my nation, and the sanctuary, and our
wives, and our children: for all the
heathen are gathered to destroy us of
very malice. 7 Now as soon as the people
heard these words, their spirit revived.
8 And they answered with a loud voice,
saying, Thou shalt be our leader instead
of Judas and Jonathan thy brother.
9 Fight thou our battles, and whatsoever
thou commandest us, that will we do.
10 So then he gathered together all the
men of war, and made haste to finish the
walls of Jerusalem, and he fortified it
round about. 11 Also he sent Jonathan
the son of Ab′salom, and with him a
great power, to Joppa: who casting out
them that were therein remained there in
it.

12 So Tryphon removed from Ptolema′is
with a great power to invade the land
of Judea, and Jonathan was with him
in ward. 13 But Simon pitched his tents
at Hadid, over against the plain. 14 Now
when Tryphon knew that Simon was
risen up instead of his brother Jonathan,
and meant to join battle with him, he
sent messengers unto him, saying,
15 Whereas we have Jonathan thy brother
in hold, it is for money that he is owing
unto the king's treasure, concerning the
business that was committed unto him.
16 Wherefore now send an hundred
talents of silver, and two of his sons for
hostages, that when he is at liberty he
may not revolt from us, and we will let
him go. 17 Hereupon Simon, albeit he
perceived that they spake deceitfully
unto him, yet sent he the money and the
children, lest peradventure he should
procure to himself great hatred of the
people: 18 who might have said,
Because I sent him not the money and
the children, therefore is Jonathan
dead. 19 So he sent them the children and
the hundred talents: howbeit Tryphon
dissembled, neither would he let
Jonathan go.

20 And after this came Tryphon to
invade the land, and destroy it, going
round about by the way that leadeth
unto Adora′im: but Simon and his host
marched against him in every place,
wheresoever he went. 21 Now they that
were in the tower sent messengers
unto Tryphon, to the end that he should
hasten his coming unto them by the
wilderness, and send them victuals.
22 Wherefore Tryphon made ready all
his horsemen to come that night: but
there fell a very great snow, by reason
whereof he came not. So he departed,
and came into the country of Gil′e-ad.
23 And when he came near to Bascama,
he slew Jonathan, who was buried
there. 24 Afterward Tryphon returned
and went into his own land.

25 Then sent Simon, and took the bones
of Jonathan his brother, and buried
them in Modin, the city of his fathers.
26 And all Israel made great lamentation
for him, and bewailed him many days.
27 Simon also built a monument upon the
sepulchre of his father and his brethren,
and raised it aloft to the sight, with
hewn stone behind and before.
28 Moreover he set up seven pyramids,
one against another, for his father, and
his mother, and his four brethren. 29 And
in these he made cunning devices,
about the which he set great pillars, and
upon the pillars he made all their armor
for a perpetual memory, and by the
armor ships carved, that they might be
seen of all that sail on the sea. 30 This is

the sepulchre which he made at Modin,
and it standeth yet unto this day.
[31]Now Tryphon dealt deceitfully with
the young king An-ti´ochus, and slew
him. [32]And he reigned in his stead, and
crowned himself king of Asia, and
brought a great calamity upon the land.
[33]Then Simon built up the strongholds
in Judea, and fenced them about with
high towers, and great walls, and gates,
and bars, and laid up victuals therein.
[34]Moreover Simon chose men, and sent
to king Deme´tri-us, to the end he
should give the land an immunity,
because all that Tryphon did was to
spoil. [35]Unto whom king Deme´tri-us
answered and wrote after this manner:
[36]King Deme´tri-us unto Simon the
high priest, and friend of kings, as also
unto the elders and nation of the Jews,
sendeth greeting: [37]The golden crown,
and the scarlet robe, which ye sent unto
us, we have received: and we are ready
to make a steadfast peace with you,
yea, and to write unto our officers, to
confirm the immunities which we have
granted. [38]And whatsoever covenants
we have made with you shall stand; and
the strongholds, which ye have builded,
shall be your own. [39]As for any
oversight or fault committed unto this
day, we forgive it, and the crown tax
also, which ye owe us: and if there were
any other tribute paid in Jerusalem, it
shall no more be paid. [40]And look who
are meet among you to be in our court,
let then be enrolled, and let there be
peace betwixt us. [41]Thus the yoke of the
heathen was taken away from Israel in
the hundred and seventieth year. [42]Then
the people of Israel began to write in
their instruments and contracts, In the
first year of Simon the high priest, the
governor and leader of the Jews.
[43]In those days Simon camped against
Gaza, and besieged it round about; he
made also an engine of war, and set it
by the city, and battered a certain tower,
and took it. [44]And they that were in the
engine leaped into the city; whereupon
there was a great uproar in the city:
[45]insomuch as the people of the city
rent their clothes, and climbed upon the
walls with their wives and children, and
cried with a loud voice, beseeching
Simon to grant them peace. [46]And they
said, Deal not with us according to our
wickedness, but according to thy
mercy. [47]So Simon was appeased
toward them, and fought no more
against them, but put them out of the
city, and cleansed the houses wherein
the idols were, and so entered into it
with songs and thanksgiving. [48]Yea, he
put all uncleanness out of it, and placed
such men there as would keep the law,
and made it stronger than it was before,
and built therein a dwelling place for
himself.
[49]They also of the tower in Jerusalem
were kept so strait, that they could
neither come forth, nor go into the
country, nor buy, nor sell: wherefore
they were in great distress for want of
victuals, and a great number of them
perished through famine. [50]Then cried
they to Simon, beseeching him to be at
one with them: which thing he granted
them; and when he had put them out
from thence, he cleansed the tower
from pollutions: [51]and entered into it
the three and twentieth day of the
second month, in the hundred seventy
and first year, with thanksgiving, and
branches of palm trees, and with harps,
and cymbals, and with viols, and
hymns, and songs: because there was
destroyed a great enemy out of Israel.
[52]He ordained also that that day should
be kept every year with gladness.

Moreover the hill of the temple that was
by the tower he made stronger than
it was, and there he dwelt himself with
his company. 53 And when Simon saw
that John his son was a valiant man, he
made him captain of all the hosts: and
he dwelt in Gezer.

CHAPTER 14

1 Now in the hundred threescore and
twelfth year king Deme´tri-us gathered
his forces together, and went into
Me´di-a to get him help to fight against
Tryphon. 2 But when Ar´sa-ces, the
king of Persia and Me´di-a, heard that
Deme´tri-us was entered within his
borders, he sent one of his princes to
take him alive: 3 who went and smote
the host of Deme´tri-us, and took him,
and brought him to Ar´sa-ces, by whom
he was put in ward.
4 As for the land of Judea, that was quiet
all the days of Simon; for he sought the
good of his nation in such wise, as that
evermore his authority and honor
pleased them well. 5 And as he was
honorable in all his acts, so in this, that he
took Joppa for an haven, and made an
entrance to the isles of the sea, 6 and
enlarged the bounds of his nation, and
recovered the country, 7 and gathered
together a great number of captives,
and had the dominion of Gezer, and
Beth–zur, and the tower, out of the
which he took all uncleanness, neither
was there any that resisted him. 8 Then
did they till their ground in peace, and
the earth gave her increase, and the
trees of the field their fruit. 9 The
ancient men sat all in the streets,
communing together of good things,
and the young men put on glorious and
warlike apparel. 10 He provided victuals
for the cities, and set in them all
manner of munition, so that his
honorable name was renowned unto the
end of the world. 11 He made peace in
the land, and Israel rejoiced with great
joy: 12 for every man sat under his vine
and his fig tree, and there was none to
fray them: 13 neither was there any left
in the land to fight against them: yea,
the kings themselves were overthrown
in those days. 14 Moreover he
strengthened all those of his people that
were brought low: the law he searched
out; and every contemner of the law and
wicked person he took away. 15 He
beautified the sanctuary, and multiplied
the vessels of the temple.
16 Now when it was heard at Rome, and
as far as Sparta, that Jonathan was dead,
they were very sorry. 17 But as soon as
they heard that his brother Simon was
made high priest in his stead, and ruled
the country, and the cities therein:
18 they wrote unto him in tables of brass,
to renew the friendship and league
which they had made with Judas and
Jonathan his brethren: 19 which writings
were read before the congregation at
Jerusalem.
20 And this is the copy of the letters that
the Lacede-mon´ians sent; The rulers
of the Lacede-mon´ians, with the city,
unto Simon the high priest, and the
elders, and priests, and residue of the
people of the Jews, our brethren, send
greeting: 21 The ambassadors that were
sent unto our people certified us of your
glory and honor: wherefore we were
glad of their coming, 22 and did register
the things that they spake in the council
of the people in this manner;
Nume´nius son of An-ti´ochus, and
An-tip´ater son of Jason, the
Jews'ambassadors, came unto us to
renew the friendship they had with us.
23 And it pleased the people to entertain

the men honorably, and to put the copy
of their ambassage in public records, to
the end the people of the Lacede-
mon´ians might have a memorial
thereof: furthermore we have written a
copy thereof unto Simon the high
priest.
24 After this Simon sent Nume´nius to
Rome with a great shield of gold of a
thousand pound weight, to confirm the
league with them.
25 Whereof when the people heard, they
said, What thanks shall we give to
Simon and his sons? 26 For he and his
brethren and the house of his father
have established Israel, and chased
away in fight their enemies from them,
and confirmed their liberty. 27 So then
they wrote it in tables of brass, which
they set upon pillars in Mount Zion:
and this is the copy of the writing; The
eighteenth day of the month Elul, in the
hundred threescore and twelfth year,
being the third year of Simon the high
priest, 28 at Sar´amel in the great
congregation of the priests, and people,
and rulers of the nation, and elders of
the country, were these things notified
unto us. 29 Forasmuch as oftentimes
there have been wars in the country,
wherein for the maintenance of their
sanctuary, and the law, Simon the son
of Mattathi´as, of the posterity of
Joi´arib, together with his brethren, put
themselves in jeopardy, and resisting
the enemies of their nation did their
nation great honor: 30 (for after that
Jonathan, having gathered his nation
together, and been their high priest,
was added to his people, 31 their
enemies purposed to invade their
country, that they might destroy it, and
lay hands on the sanctuary: 32 at which
time Simon rose up, and fought for his
nation, and spent much of his own
substance, and armed the valiant men of
his nation, and gave them wages, 33 and
fortified the cities of Judea, together
with Beth–zur, that lieth upon the
borders of Judea, where the armor of
the enemies had been before; but he set
a garrison of Jews there: 34 moreover he
fortified Joppa, which lieth upon the
sea, and Gezer, that bordereth upon
Ashdod, where the enemies had dwelt
before: but he placed Jews there, and
furnished them with all things
convenient for the reparation thereof.)
35 The people therefore, seeing the acts
of Simon, and unto what glory he
thought to bring his nation, made him
their governor and chief priest, because
he had done all these things, and for the
justice and faith which he kept to his
nation, and for that he sought by all
means to exalt his people. 36 For in his
time things prospered in his hands, so
that the heathen were taken out of their
country, and they also that were in the
city of David in Jerusalem, who had
made themselves a tower, out of which
they issued, and polluted all about the
sanctuary, and did much hurt in the
holy place: 37 but he placed Jews
therein, and fortified it for the safety of
the country and the city, and raised up
the walls of Jerusalem. 38 King
Deme´tri-us also confirmed him in the
high priesthood according to those
things, 39 and made him one of his
friends, and honored him with great
honor. 40 For he had heard say, that the
Romans had called the Jews their
friends and confederates and brethren;
and that they had entertained the
ambassadors of Simon honorably;
41 also that the Jews and priests were
well pleased that Simon should be their
governor and high priest for ever, until
there should arise a faithful prophet;

42moreover that he should be their
captain, and should take charge of the
sanctuary, to set them over their works,
and over the country, and over the
armor, and over the fortresses, that, I
say, he should take charge of the
sanctuary; 43beside this, that he should
be obeyed of every man, and that all the
writings in the country should be made
in his name, and that he should be
clothed in purple, and wear gold: 44also
that it should be lawful for none of the
people or priests to break any of these
things, or to gainsay his words, or to
gather an assembly in the country
without him, or to be clothed in purple,
or wear a buckle of gold: 45and
whosoever should do otherwise, or
break any of these things, he should be
punished. 46Thus it liked all the people
to deal with Simon, and to do as hath
been said.
47Then Simon accepted hereof, and was
well pleased to be high priest, and
captain and governor of the Jews and
priests, and to defend them all. 48So
they commanded that this writing
should be put in tables of brass, and
that they should be set up within the
compass of the sanctuary in a
conspicuous place; 49also that the
copies thereof should be laid up in the
treasury, to the end that Simon and his
sons might have them.

CHAPTER 15

1Moreover An-ti´ochus son of
Deme´tri- us the king sent letters from
the isles of the sea unto Simon the
priest and prince of the Jews, and to all
the people; 2the contents whereof were
these: King An-ti´ochus to Simon the
high priest and prince of his nation,
and to the people of the Jews, greeting:
3Forasmuch as certain pestilent men
have usurped the kingdom of our
fathers, and my purpose is to challenge
it again, that I may restore it to the old
estate, and to that end have gathered a
multitude of foreign soldiers together,
and prepared ships of war; 4my
meaning also being to go through the
country, that I may be avenged of them that
have destroyed it, and made many
cities in the kingdom desolate: 5now
therefore I confirm unto thee all the
oblations which the kings before me
granted thee, and whatsoever gifts
besides they granted. 6I give thee leave
also to coin money for thy country with
thine own stamp. 7And as concerning
Jerusalem and the sanctuary, let them
be free; and all the armor that thou hast
made, and fortresses that thou hast
built, and keepest in thine hands, let
them remain unto thee. 8And if any
thing be, or shall be, owing to the king,
let it be forgiven thee from this time
forth for evermore. 9Furthermore,
when we have obtained our kingdom,
we will honor thee, and thy nation, and
thy temple, with great honor, so that
your honor shall be known throughout
the world.
10In the hundred threescore and
fourteenth year went An-ti´ochus into
the land of his fathers: at which time all
the forces came together unto him, so
that few were left with Tryphon.
11Wherefore being pursued by king An-
ti´ochus, he fled unto Dor, which lieth
by the sea side: 12for he saw that
troubles came upon him all at once, and
that his forces had forsaken him.
13Then camped An-ti´ochus against
Dor, having with him an hundred and
twenty thousand men of war, and eight
thousand horsemen. 14And when he had
compassed the city round about, and

joined ships close to the town on the sea
side, he vexed the city by land and by
sea, neither suffered he any to go out or
in.
15In the mean season came Nume´nius
and his company from Rome, having
letters to the kings and countries;
wherein were written these things:
16Lucius, consul of the Romans unto
king Ptol´emy, greeting: 17The Jews'
ambassadors, our friends and
confederates, came unto us to renew
the old friendship and league, being
sent from Simon the high priest, and
from the people of the Jews: 18and they
brought a shield of gold of a thousand
pound. 19We thought it good therefore
to write unto the kings and countries,
that they should do them no harm, nor
fight against them, their cities, or
countries, nor yet aid their enemies
against them. 20It seemed also good to
us to receive the shield of them. 21If
therefore there be any pestilent fellows,
that have fled from their country unto
you, deliver them unto Simon the high
priest, that he may punish them
according to their own law. 22The same
things wrote he likewise unto
Deme´tri-us the king, and At´talus, to
Ariara´thes, and Ar´sa-ces, 23and to all
the countries and to Samp´sames, and
the Lacede-mon´ians, and to Delos, and
Myndos, and Sic´yon, and Caria, and
Samos, and Pamphyl´i-a, and Ly´ci-a,
and Halicarnas´sus, and Rhodes, and
Phaselis, and Cos, and Side, and
Aradus, and Gorty´na, and Cnidus, and
Cyprus, and Cyre´ne. 24And the copy
hereof they wrote to Simon the high
priest.
25So An-ti´ochus the king camped
against Dor the second day,
assaulting it continually, and making
engines, by which means he shut up
Tryphon, that he could neither go out
nor in. 26At that time Simon sent him
two thousand chosen men to aid him;
silver also, and gold, and much armor.
27Nevertheless he would not receive
them, but brake all the covenants which
he had made with him afore, and
became strange unto him.
28Furthermore he sent unto him
Atheno´bius, one of his friends, to
commune with him, and say, Ye
withhold Joppa and Gezer, with the
tower that is in Jerusalem, which are
cities of my realm. 29The borders
thereof ye have wasted, and done great
hurt in the land, and got the dominion
of many places within my kingdom.
30Now therefore deliver the cities
which ye have taken, and the tributes
of the places, whereof ye have gotten
dominion without the borders of Judea:
31or else give me for them five
hundred talents of silver; and for the
harm that ye have done, and the tributes
of the cities, other five hundred talents:
if not, we will come and fight against
you. 32So Atheno´bius the king's friend
came to Jerusalem: and when he saw
the glory of Simon, and the cupboard of
gold and silver plate, and his great
attendance, he was astonished, and told
him the king's message. 33Then
answered Simon, and said unto him,
We have neither taken other men's
land, nor holden that which
appertaineth to others, but the
inheritance of our fathers, which our
enemies had wrongfully in possession a
certain time. 34Wherefore we, having
opportunity, hold the inheritance of our
fathers. 35And whereas thou demandest
Joppa and Gezer, albeit they did great
harm unto the people in our country,
yet will we give an hundred talents for
them. Hereunto Atheno´bius answered

him not a word; 36but returned in a rage
to the king, and made report unto him
of these speeches, and of the glory of
Simon, and of all that he had seen:
whereupon the king was exceeding
wroth.
37In the mean time fled Tryphon by
ship unto Ortho´sias. 38Then the king
made Cendebe´us captain of the sea
coast, and gave him an host of footmen
and horsemen, 39and commanded him
to remove his host toward Judea; also
he commanded him to build up
Gede´rah, and to fortify the gates, and to
war against the people; but as for the
king himself, he pursued Tryphon. 40So
Cendebe´us came to Jabneh, and began
to provoke the people, and to invade
Judea, and to take the people prisoners,
and slay them. 41And when he had built
up Gede´rah, he set horsemen there,
and an host of footmen, to the end that
issuing out they might make outroads
upon the ways of Judea, as the king had
commanded him.

CHAPTER 16

1Then came up John from Gezer, and
told Simon his father what Cendebe´us
had done. 2Wherefore Simon called his
two eldest sons, Judas and John, and
said unto them, I, and my brethren, and
my father's house, have ever from my
youth unto this day fought against the
enemies of Israel; and things have
prospered so well in our hands, that we
have delivered Israel oftentimes. 3But
now I am old, and ye, by God's mercy,
are of a sufficient age: be ye instead of
me and my brother, and go and fight for
our nation, and the help from heaven be
with you. 4So he chose out of the
country twenty thousand men of war
with horsemen, who went out against
Cendebe´us, and rested that night at
Modin. 5And when as they rose in the
morning, and went into the plain,
behold, a mighty great host both of
footmen and horsemen came against
them: howbeit there was a water brook
betwixt them. 6So he and his people
pitched over against them: and when he
saw that the people were afraid to go
over the water brook, he went first over
himself, and then the men seeing him
passed through after him. 7That done,
he divided his men, and set the
horsemen in the midst of the footmen:
for the enemy's horsemen were very
many. 8Then sounded they with the
holy trumpets: whereupon Cendebe´us
and his host were put to flight, so that
many of them were slain, and the
remnant got them to the stronghold. 9At
that time was Judas John's brother
wounded; but John still followed after
them, until he came to Gede´rah, which
Cendebe´us had built. 10So they fled
even unto the towers in the fields of
Ashdod; wherefore he burned it with
fire: so that there were slain of them
about two thousand men. Afterward he
returned into the land of Judea in peace.
11Moreover in the plain of Jericho was
Ptol´emy the son of Abu´bus made
captain, and he had abundance of silver
and gold: 12for he was the high priest's
son-in-law. 13Wherefore his heart being
lifted up, he thought to get the country
to himself, and thereupon consulted
deceitfully against Simon and his sons
to destroy them. 14Now Simon was
visiting the cities that were in the
country, and taking care for the good
ordering of them; at which time he
came down himself to Jericho with his
sons, Mattathi´as and Judas, in the
hundred threescore and seventeenth
year, in the eleventh month, called

Sebat: 15where the son of Abu´bus
receiving them deceitfully into a little
hold, called Dok, which he had built,
made them a great banquet: howbeit he
had hid men there. 16So when Simon
and his sons had drunk largely,
Ptol´emy and his men rose up, and took
their weapons, and came upon Simon
into the banqueting place, and slew him,
and his two sons, and certain of his
servants. 17In which doing he
committed a great treachery, and
recompensed evil for good.
18Then Ptol´emy wrote these things,
and sent to the king, that he should send
him an host to aid him, and he would
deliver him the country and cities. 19He
sent others also to Gezer to kill John:
and unto the tribunes he sent letters to
come unto him, that he might give them
silver, and gold, and rewards. 20And
others he sent to take Jerusalem, and the
mountain of the temple. 21Now one had
run afore to Gezer, and told John that his
father and brethren were slain, and,
quoth he, Ptol´emy hath sent to slay
thee also. 22Hereof when he heard, he
was sore astonished: so he laid hands
on them that were come to destroy him,
and slew them; for he knew that they
sought to make him away. 23As
concerning the rest of the acts of John,
and his wars, and worthy deeds which
he did, and the building of the walls
which he made, and his doings,
24behold, these are written in the
chronicles of his priesthood, from the
time he was made high priest after his
father.

II MACCABEES

CHAPTER 1

[1]The brethren, the Jews that be at Jerusalem and in the land of Judea, wish unto the brethren, the Jews that are throughout Egypt, health and peace: [2]God be gracious unto you, and remember his covenant that he made with Abraham, Isaac, and Jacob, his faithful servants; [3]and give you all an heart to serve him, and to do his will, with a good courage and a willing mind; [4]and open your hearts in his law and commandments, and send you peace, [5]and hear your prayers, and be at one with you, and never forsake you in time of trouble. [6]And now we be here praying for you. [7]What time as Deme´tri- us reigned, in the hundred threescore and ninth year, we the Jews wrote unto you in the extremity of trouble that came upon us in those years, from the time that Jason and his company revolted from the holy land and kingdom, [8]and burned the porch, and shed innocent blood: then we prayed unto the Lord, and were heard; we offered also sacrifices and fine flour, and lighted the lamps, and set forth the loaves. [9]And now see that ye keep the feast of tabernacles in the month Chislev. [10]In the hundred fourscore and eighth year, the people that were at Jerusalem and in Judea, and the council, and Judas, sent greeting and health unto Aristob´ulus, king Ptolemy's master, who was of the stock of the anointed priests, and to the Jews that were in Egypt: [11]insomuch as God hath delivered us from great perils, we thank him highly, as having been in battle against a king. [12]For he cast them out that fought within the holy city. [13]For when the leader was come into Persia, and the army with him that seemed invincible, they were slain in the temple of Nane´a by the deceit of Nane´a's priests. [14]For An- ti´ochus, as though he would marry her, came into the place, and his friends that were with him, to receive money in name of a dowry. [15]Which when the priests of Nane´a had set forth, and he was entered with a small company into the compass of the temple, they shut the temple as soon as An-ti´ochus was come in: [16]and opening a privy door of the roof, they threw stones like thunderbolts, and struck down the captain, hewed them in pieces, smote off their heads, and cast them to those that were without. [17]Blessed be our God in all things, who hath delivered up the ungodly. [18]Therefore whereas we are now purposed to keep the purification of the temple upon the five and twentieth day of the month Chislev, we thought it necessary to certify you thereof, that ye also might keep it, as the feast of the tabernacles, and of the fire, which was given us when Nehemi´ah offered sacrifice, after that he had builded the temple and the altar.

[19]For when our fathers were led into Persia, the priests that were then devout took the fire of the altar privily, and hid it in an hollow place of a pit without water, where they kept it sure, so that the place was unknown to all men. [20]Now after many years, when it pleased God, Nehemi´ah, being sent from the king of Persia, did send of the posterity of those priests that had hid it to the fire: but when they told us they found no fire, but thick water; [21]then

commanded he them to draw it up, and
to bring it; and when the sacrifices were
laid on, Nehemi'ah commanded the
priests to sprinkle the wood and the
things laid thereupon with the water.
22 When this was done, and the time
came that the sun shone, which afore
was hid in the cloud, there was a great
fire kindled, so that every man
marveled. 23 And the priests made a
prayer whilst the sacrifice was
consuming, I say, both the priests, and
all the rest, Jonathan beginning, and the
rest answering thereunto, as Nehemi'ah
did.
24 And the prayer was after this manner;
O Lord, Lord God, Creator of all
things, who art fearful and strong, and
righteous, and merciful, and the only
and gracious King, 25 the only giver of
all things, the only just, almighty, and
everlasting, thou that deliverest Israel
from all trouble, and didst choose the
fathers, and sanctify them: 26 receive the
sacrifice for thy whole people Israel,
and preserve thine own portion, and
sanctify it. 27 Gather those together that
are scattered from us, deliver them that
serve among the heathen, look upon
them that are despised and abhorred, and
let the heathen know that thou art our
God. 28 Punish them that oppress us, and
with pride do us wrong. 29 Plant thy
people again in thy holy place, as
Moses hath spoken. 30 And the priests
sung psalms of thanksgiving. 31 Now
when the sacrifice was consumed,
Nehemi'ah commanded the water that
was left to be poured on the great stones.
32 When this was done, there was
kindled a flame: but it was consumed by
the light that shone from the altar. 33 So
when this matter was known, it was
told the king of Persia, that in the place,
where the priests that were led away
had hid the fire, there appeared water,
and that Nehemi'ah had purified the
sacrifices therewith. 34 Then the king,
inclosing the place, made it holy, after
he had tried the matter. 35 And the king
took many gifts, and bestowed thereof
on those whom he would gratify. 36 And
Nehemi'ah called this thing Naphthar,
which is as much as to say, a cleansing:
but many men call it naphtha.

CHAPTER 2

1 It is also found in the records, that Jeremiah
the prophet commanded them that were
carried away to take of the fire, as it
hath been signified: 2 and how that the
prophet, having given them the law,
charged them not to forget the
commandments of the Lord, and that
they should not err in their minds, when
they see images of silver and gold, with
their ornaments. 3 And with other such
speeches exhorted he them, that the law
should not depart from their hearts. 4 It
was also contained in the same writing,
that the prophet, being warned of God,
commanded the tabernacle and the ark
to go with him, as he went forth into the
mountain, where Moses climbed up,
and saw the heritage of God. 5 And
when Jeremiah came thither, he found an
hollow cave, wherein he laid the
tabernacle, and the ark, and the altar of
incense, and so stopped the door. 6 And
some of those that followed him came
to mark the way, but they could not find
it. 7 Which when Jeremiah perceived, he
blamed them, saying, As for that place,
it shall be unknown until the time that
God gather his people again together,
and receive them unto mercy. 8 Then
shall the Lord show them these things,
and the glory of the Lord shall appear,
and the cloud also, as it was showed

under Moses, and as when Solomon
desired that the place might be
honorably sanctified.
9 It was also declared, that he being wise
offered the sacrifice of dedication, and
of the finishing of the temple. 10 And as
when Moses prayed unto the Lord, the
fire came down from heaven, and
consumed the sacrifices: even so
prayed Solomon also, and the fire came
down from heaven, and consumed the
burnt offerings. 11 And Moses said,
Because the sin offering was not to be
eaten, it was consumed. 12 So Solomon
kept those eight days.
13 The same things also were reported
in the writings and commentaries of
Nehemi´ah; and how he founding a
library gathered together the acts of the
kings, and the prophets, and of David,
and the epistles of the kings concerning
the holy gifts. 14 In like manner also
Judas gathered together all those things
that were lost by reason of the war we
had, and they remain with us.
15 Wherefore if ye have need thereof,
send some to fetch them unto you.
16 Whereas we then are about to
celebrate the purification, we have
written unto you, and ye shall do well,
if ye keep the same days. 17 We hope
also, that the God, that delivered all his
people, and gave them all an heritage,
and the kingdom, and the priesthood,
and the sanctuary, 18 as he promised in
the law, will shortly have mercy upon
us, and gather us together out of every
land under heaven into the holy place:
for he hath delivered us out of great
troubles, and hath purified the place.
19 Now as concerning Judas
Maccabe´us, and his brethren, and the
purification of the great temple, and the
dedication of the altar, 20 and the wars
against An-ti´ochus E-piph´anes, and
Eu´pator his son, 21 and the manifest
signs that came from heaven unto those
that behaved themselves manfully to
their honor for Judaism: so that, being
but a few, they overcame the whole
country, and chased barbarous
multitudes, 22 and recovered again the
temple renowned all the world over,
and freed the city, and upheld the laws
which were going down, the Lord being
gracious unto them with all favor: 23 all
these things, I say, being declared by
Jason of Cyre´ne in five books, we will
assay to abridge in one volume. 24 For
considering the infinite number, and the
difficulty which they find that desire to
look into the narrations of the story, for
the variety of the matter, 25 we have been
careful, that they that will read may
have delight, and that they that are
desirous to commit to memory might
have ease, and that all into whose hands
it comes might have profit. 26 Therefore
to us, that have taken upon us this
painful labor of abridging, it was not
easy, but a matter of sweat and
watching; 27 even as it is no ease unto
him that prepareth a banquet, and
seeketh the benefit of others: yet for the
pleasure of many we will undertake
gladly this great pains; 28 leaving to the
author the exact handling of every
particular, and laboring to follow the
rules of an abridgement. 29 For as the
master builder of a new house must
care for the whole building; but he that
undertaketh to set it out, and paint it,
must seek out fit things for the adorning
thereof: even so I think it is with us.
30 To stand upon every point, and go
over things at large, and to be curious
in particulars, belongeth to the first
author of the story: 31 but to use brevity,
and avoid much laboring of the work,
is to be granted to him that will make

an abridgment. [32]Here then will we begin the story: only adding thus much to that which hath been said, that it is a foolish thing to make a long prologue, and to be short in the story itself.

CHAPTER 3

[1]Now when the holy city was inhabited with all peace, and the laws were kept very well, because of the godliness of Oni´as the high priest, and his hatred of wickedness, [2]it came to pass that even the kings themselves did honor the place, and magnify the temple with their best gifts; [3]insomuch that Seleu´cus king of Asia of his own revenues bare all the costs belonging to the service of the sacrifices. [4]But one Simon of the tribe of Benjamin, who was made governor of the temple, fell out with the high priest about disorder in the city. [5]And when he could not overcome Oni´as, he got him to Apol-lo´nius the son of Thra-se´as, who then was governor of Coelesyr´ia and Phoeni´cia, [6]and told him that the treasury in Jerusalem was full of infinite sums of money, so that the multitude of their riches, which did not pertain to the account of the sacrifices, was innumerable, and that it was possible to bring all into the king's hand. [7]Now when Apol-lo´nius came to the king, and had showed him of the money whereof he was told, the king chose out Heliodor´us his treasurer, and sent him with a commandment to bring him the foresaid money. [8]So forthwith Heliodor´us took his journey, under a color of visiting the cities of Coelesyr´ia and Phoeni´cia, but indeed to fulfil the king's purpose.

[9]And when he was come to Jerusalem, and had been courteously received of the high priest of the city, he told him what intelligence was given of the money, and declared wherefore he came, and asked if these things were so indeed. [10]Then the high priest told him that there was such money laid up for the relief of widows and fatherless children: [11]and that some of it belonged to Hyrca´nus son of Tobias, a man of great dignity, and not as that wicked Simon had misinformed: the sum whereof in all was four hundred talents of silver, and two hundred of gold: [12]and that it was altogether impossible that such wrongs should be done unto them, that had committed it to the holiness of the place, and to the majesty and inviolable sanctity of the temple, honored over all the world. [13]But Heliodor´us, because of the king's commandment given him, said, That in any wise it must be brought into the king's treasury. [14]So at the day which he appointed he entered in to order this matter.

Wherefore there was no small agony throughout the whole city. [15]But the priests, prostrating themselves before the altar in their priests' vestments, called unto heaven upon him that made a law concerning things given to he kept, that they should safely be preserved for such as had committed them to be kept. [16]Then whoso had looked the high priest in the face, it would have wounded his heart: for his countenance and the changing of his color declared the inward agony of his mind. [17]For the man was so compassed with fear and horror of the body, that it was manifest to them that looked upon him, what sorrow he had now in his heart. [18]Others ran flocking out of their houses to the general supplication, because the place was like to come into

contempt. 19 And the women, girt with
sackcloth under their breasts, abounded
in the streets, and the virgins that were
kept in ran, some to the gates, and some
to the walls, and others looked out of
the windows. 20 And all, holding their
hands toward heaven, made
supplication. 21 Then it would have
pitied a man to see the falling down of
the multitude of all sorts, and the fear of
the high priest, being in such an agony.
22 They then called upon the Almighty
Lord to keep the things committed of
trust safe and sure for those that had
committed them.
23 Nevertheless Heliodor´us executed
that which was decreed. 24 Now as he
was there present himself with his
guard about the treasury, the Lord of
spirits, and the Prince of all power,
caused a great apparition, so that all
that presumed to come in with him were
astonished at the power of God, and
fainted, and were sore afraid. 25 For
there appeared unto them an horse with
a terrible rider upon him, and adorned
with a very fair covering, and he ran
fiercely, and smote at Heliodor´us with
his forefeet, and it seemed that he that
sat upon the horse had complete
harness of gold. 26 Moreover two other
young men appeared before him,
notable in strength, excellent in beauty,
and comely in apparel, who stood by
him on either side; and scourged him
continually, and gave him many sore
stripes. 27 And Heliodor´us fell
suddenly unto the ground, and was
compassed with great darkness: but
they that were with him took him up,
and put him into a litter. 28 Thus him,
that lately came with a great train and
with all his guard into the said treasury,
they carried out, being unable to help
himself with his weapons: and
manifestly they acknowledged the
power of God: 29 for he by the hand of
God was cast down, and lay speechless
without all hope of life. 30 But they
praised the Lord, that had miraculously
honored his own place: for the temple,
which a little afore was full of fear and
trouble, when the Almighty Lord
appeared, was filled with joy and
gladness.
31 Then straightway certain of
Heliodor´us' friends prayed Oni´as,
that he would call upon the most High
to grant him his life, who lay ready to
give up the ghost. 32 So the high priest,
suspecting lest the king should
misconceive that some treachery had
been done to Heliodor´us by the Jews,
offered a sacrifice for the health of the
man. 33 Now as the high priest was
making an atonement, the same young
men in the same clothing appeared and
stood beside Heliodor´us, saying, Give
Oni´as the high priest great thanks,
insomuch as for his sake the Lord hath
granted thee life: 34 and seeing that thou
hast been scourged from heaven,
declare unto all men the mighty power
of God. And when they had spoken these
words, they appeared no more.
35 So Heliodor´us, after he had offered
sacrifice unto the Lord, and made great
vows unto him that had saved his life,
and saluted Oni´as, returned with his
host to the king. 36 Then testified he to
all men the works of the great God,
which he had seen with his eyes. 37 And
when the king asked Heliodor´us, who
might be a fit man to be sent yet once
again to Jerusalem, he said, 38 If thou
hast any enemy or traitor, send him
thither, and thou shalt receive him well
scourged, if he escape with his life: for
in that place, no doubt, there is an
especial power of God. 39 For he that

dwelleth in heaven hath his eye on that
place, and defendeth it; and he beateth
and destroyeth them that come to hurt
it. [40]And the things concerning
Heliodor´us, and the keeping of the
treasury, fell out on this sort.

CHAPTER 4

[1]This Simon now, of whom we spake
afore, having been a betrayer of the
money, and of his country, slandered
Oni´as, as if he had terrified
Heliodor´us, and been the worker of
these evils. [2]Thus was he bold to call
him a traitor, that had deserved well of
the city, and tendered his own nation,
and was so zealous of the laws. [3]But
when their hatred went so far, that by
one of Simon's faction murders were
committed, [4]Oni´as seeing the danger of
this contention, and that Apol-lo´nius,
as being the governor of Coelesyr´ia
and Phoeni´cia, did rage, and increase
Simon's malice, [5]he went to the king,
not to be an accuser of his countrymen,
but seeking the good of all, both public
and private: [6]for he saw that it was
impossible that the state should
continue quiet, and Simon leave his
folly, unless the king did look
thereunto.
[7]But after the death of Seleu´cus, when
An-ti´ochus, called E-piph´anes, took
the kingdom, Jason the brother of
Oni´as labored underhand to be high
priest, [8]promising unto the king by
intercession three hundred and
threescore talents of silver, and of
another revenue eighty talents: [9]beside
this, he promised to assign an hundred
and fifty more, if he might have license
to set him up a place for exercise, and
for the training up of youth in the
fashions of the heathen, and to write
them of Jerusalem by the name of Anti-
o´chians. [10]Which when the king had
granted, and he had gotten into his hand
the rule, he forthwith brought his own
nation to the Greek fashion. [11]And the
royal privileges granted of special favor
to the Jews by the means of John the
father of Eupol´emus, who went
ambassador to Rome for amity and aid,
he took away; and putting down the
governments which were according to
the law, he brought up new customs
against the law: [12]for he built gladly
a place of exercise under the tower
itself, and brought the chief young men
under his subjection, and made them
wear a hat. [13]Now such was the height
of Greek fashions, and increase of
heathenish manners, through the
exceeding profaneness of Jason, that
ungodly wretch, and no high priest;
[14]that the priests had no courage to
serve any more at the altar, but despising
the temple, and neglecting the
sacrifices, hastened to be partakers of
the unlawful allowance in the place of
exercise, after the game of discus called
them forth; [15]not setting by the honors
of their fathers, but liking the glory of
the Greeks best of all. [16]By reason
whereof sore calamity came upon
them: for they had them to be their
enemies and avengers, whose custom
they followed so earnestly, and unto
whom they desired to be like in all
things. [17]For it is not a light thing to do
wickedly against the laws of God: but
the time following shall declare these
things.
[18]Now when the game that was used
every fifth year was kept at Tyre, the
king being present, [19]this ungracious
Jason sent special messengers from
Jerusalem, who were Anti-o´chians, to
carry three hundred drachms of silver to

the sacrifice of Hercules, which even
the bearers thereof thought fit not to
bestow upon the sacrifice, because it
was not convenient, but to be reserved
for other charges. [20]This money then, in
regard of the sender, was appointed to
Hercules' sacrifice; but because of the
bearers thereof, it was employed to
the making of galleys. [21]Now when
Apol-lo´nius the son of Menestheus was
sent into Egypt for the coronation of king
Ptoleme´us Philome´tor, An-ti´ochus,
understanding him not to be well
affected to his affairs, provided for his
own safety: whereupon he came to
Joppa, and from thence to Jerusalem:
[22]where he was honorably received of
Jason, and of the city, and was brought
in with torch light, and with great
shoutings: and so afterward went with
his host unto Phoeni´cia.
[23]Three years afterward Jason sent
Menela´us, the aforesaid Simon's
brother, to bear the money unto the
king, and to put him in mind of certain
necessary matters. [24]But he being
brought to the presence of the king,
when he had magnified him for the
glorious appearance of his power, got the
priesthood to himself, offering more than
Jason by three hundred talents of silver.
[25]So he came with the king's mandate,
bringing nothing worthy the high
priesthood, but having the fury of a
cruel tyrant, and the rage of a savage
beast. [26]Then Jason, who had
undermined his own brother, being
undermined by another, was compelled
to flee into the country of the
Ammonites. [27]So Menela´us got the
principality: but as for the money that
he had promised unto the king, he took
no good order for it, albeit Sos´tratus the
ruler of the castle required it: [28]for unto
him appertained the gathering of the
customs. Wherefore they were both
called before the king. [29]Now
Menela´us left his brother
Lysim´achus in his stead in the
priesthood; and Sos´tratus left Crates,
who was governor of the Cyprians.
[30]While those things were in doing,
they of Tarsus and Mallos made
insurrection, because they were given
to the king's concubine, called An´ti-
ochis. [31]Then came the king in all haste
to appease matters, leaving
Andron´icus, a man in authority, for
his deputy. [32]Now Menela´us,
supposing that he had gotten a
convenient time, stole certain vessels of
gold out of the temple, and gave some
of them to Andron´icus, and some he
sold into Tyre and the cities round
about. [33]Which when Oni´as knew of a
surety, he reproved him, and withdrew
himself into a sanctuary at Daphne,
that lieth by An´ti-och. [34]Wherefore
Menela´us, taking Andron´icus apart,
prayed him to get Oni´as into his hands;
who being persuaded thereunto, and
coming to Oni´as in deceit, gave him
his right hand with oaths; and though he
were suspected by him, yet persuaded
he him to come forth of the sanctuary:
whom forthwith he shut up without
regard of justice. [35]For the which cause
not only the Jews, but many also of
other nations, took great indignation,
and were much grieved for the unjust
murder of the man. [36]And when the
king was come again from the places
about Cili´cia, the Jews that were in
the city, and certain of the Greeks
that abhorred the fact also, complained
because Oni´as was slain without
cause. [37]Therefore An-ti´ochus was
heartily sorry, and moved to pity, and
wept, because of the sober and
modest behavior of him that was dead.

38 And being kindled with anger,
forthwith he took away Andron´icus his
purple, and rent off his clothes, and
leading him through the whole city unto
that very place, where he had
committed impiety against Oni´as,
there slew he the cursed murderer.
Thus the Lord rewarded him his
punishment, as he had deserved.
39 Now when many sacrileges had been
committed in the city by Lysim´achus
with the consent of Menela´us, and the
bruit thereof was spread abroad, the
multitude gathered themselves together
against Lysim´achus, many vessels of
gold being already carried away.
40 Whereupon the common people
rising, and being filled with rage,
Lysim´achus armed about three
thousand men, and began first to offer
violence; one Aura´nus being the
leader, a man far gone in years, and no
less in folly. 41 They then seeing the
attempt of Lysim´achus, some of them
caught stones, some clubs, others taking
handfuls of dust, that was next at hand,
cast them all together upon
Lysim´achus, and those that set upon
them. 42 Thus many of them were
wounded, and some they struck to the
ground, and all of them they forced to
flee: but as for the churchrobber
himself, him they killed beside the
treasury.
43 Of these matters therefore there was
an accusation laid against Menela´us.
44 Now when the king came to Tyre,
three men that were sent from the
senate pleaded the cause before him:
45 but Menela´us, being now convicted,
promised Ptol´emy the son of
Dorym´enes to give him much money,
if he would pacify the king toward him.
46 Whereupon Ptol´emy taking the king
aside into a certain gallery, as it were to
take the air, brought him to be of
another mind: 47 insomuch that he
discharged Menela´us from the
accusations, who notwithstanding was
cause of all the mischief: and those
poor men, who, if they had told their
cause, yea, before the Scyth´i-ans,
should have been judged innocent,
them he condemned to death. 48 Thus
they that followed the matter for the city,
and for the people, and for the holy
vessels, did soon suffer unjust
punishment. 49 Wherefore even they of
Tyre, moved with hatred of that wicked
deed, caused them to be honorably
buried. 50 And so through the
covetousness of them that were of
power Menela´us remained still in
authority, increasing in malice, and
being a great traitor to the citizens.

CHAPTER 5

1 About the same time An-ti´ochus
prepared his second voyage into Egypt:
2 and then it happened, that through all
the city, for the space almost of forty
days, there were seen horsemen running
in the air, in cloth of gold, and armed
with lances, like a band of soldiers, 3 and
troops of horsemen in array,
encountering and running one against
another, with shaking of shields, and
multitude of pikes, and drawing of
swords, and casting of darts, and
glittering of golden ornaments, and
harness of all sorts. 4 Wherefore every
man prayed that that apparition might
turn to good.
5 Now when there was gone forth a
false rumor, as though An-ti´ochus had
been dead, Jason took at the least a
thousand men, and suddenly made an
assault upon the city; and they that were
upon the walls being put back, and the city

at length taken, Menela´us fled into the
castle: 6 but Jason slew his own citizens
without mercy, not considering that to
get the day of them of his own nation
would be a most unhappy day for him;
but thinking they had been his
enemies, and not his countrymen, whom
he conquered. 7 Howbeit for all this he
obtained not the principality, but at the
last received shame for the reward of
his treason, and fled again into the
country of the Ammonites. 8 In the end
therefore he had an unhappy return,
being accused before Ar´etas the king
of the Arabians, fleeing from city to
city, pursued of all men, hated as a
forsaker of the laws, and being had in
abomination as an open enemy of his
country and countrymen, he was cast
out into Egypt. 9 Thus he that had driven
many out of their country perished in a
strange land, retiring to the Lacede-
mon´ians, and thinking there to find
succor by reason of his kindred: 10 and
he that had cast out many unburied had
none to mourn for him, nor any solemn
funerals at all, nor sepulchre with his
fathers.
11 Now when this that was done came to
the king's ear, he thought that Judea
had revolted: whereupon removing out
of Egypt in a furious mind, he took the
city by force of arms, 12 and
commanded his men of war not to spare
such as they met, and to slay such as
went up upon the houses. 13 Thus there
was killing of young and old, making
away of men, women, and children,
slaying of virgins and infants. 14 And
there were destroyed within the space of
three whole days fourscore thousand,
whereof forty thousand were slain in
the conflict; and no fewer sold than
slain. 15 Yet was he not content with
this, but presumed to go into the most
holy temple of all the world;
Menela´us, that traitor to the laws, and
to his own country, being his guide:
16 and taking the holy vessels with
polluted hands, and with profane hands
pulling down the things that were
dedicated by other kings to the
augmentation and glory and honor of
the place, he gave them away. 17 And so
haughty was An-ti´ochus in mind, that
he considered not that the Lord was
angry for a while for the sins of them
that dwelt in the city, and therefore his
eye was not upon the place. 18 For had
they not been formerly wrapped in
many sins, this man, as soon as he had
come, had forthwith been scourged,
and put back from his presumption, as
Heliodor´us was, whom Seleu´cus the
king sent to view the treasury.
19 Nevertheless God did not choose the
people for the place's sake, but the
place for the people's sake. 20 And
therefore the place itself, that was
partaker with them of the adversity that
happened to the nation, did afterward
communicate in the benefits sent from
the Lord: and as it was forsaken in the
wrath of the Almighty, so again, the
great Lord being reconciled, it was set
up with all glory.
21 So when An-ti´ochus had carried out
of the temple a thousand and eight
hundred talents, he departed in all haste
unto An´ti-och, weening in his pride to
make the land navigable, and the sea
passable by foot: such was the
haughtiness of his mind. 22 And he left
governors to vex the nation: at
Jerusalem, Philip, for his country a
Phryg´i-an, and for manners more
barbarous than he that set him there;
23 and at Ger´izim, Andron´icus; and
besides, Menela´us, who worse than all
the rest bare an heavy hand over the
citizens, having a malicious mind

against his countrymen the Jews. [24]He
sent also that detestable ringleader
Apol-lo′nius with an army of two and
twenty thousand, commanding him to
slay all those that were in their best age,
and to sell the women and the younger
sort: [25]who coming to Jerusalem, and
pretending peace, did forbear till the
holy day of the sabbath, when taking
the Jews keeping holy day, he
commanded his men to arm themselves.
[26]And so he slew all them that were
gone to the celebrating of the sabbath,
and running through the city with
weapons slew great multitudes.
[27]But Judas Maccabe′us with nine
others, or thereabout, withdrew himself
into the wilderness, and lived in the
mountains after the manner of beasts,
with his company, who fed on herbs
continually, lest they should be
partakers of the pollution.

CHAPTER 6

[1]Not long after this the king sent an old
man of Athens to compel the Jews to
depart from the laws of their fathers,
and not to live after the laws of God:
[2]and to pollute also the temple in
Jerusalem, and to call it the temple of
Jupiter Olympius; and that in Ger′izim,
of Jupiter the Defender of Strangers, as
they did desire that dwelt in the place.
[3]The coming in of this mischief was
sore and grievous to the people: [4]for
the temple was filled with riot and
reveling by the Gentiles, who dallied
with harlots, and had to do with women
within the circuit of the holy places, and
besides that brought in things that were
not lawful. [5]The altar also was filled
with profane things, which the law
forbiddeth. [6]Neither was it lawful
for a man to keep sabbath days or
ancient feasts, or to profess himself at
all to be a Jew. [7]And in the day of the
king's birth every month they were
brought by bitter constraint to eat of the
sacrifices; and when the feast of
Bacchus was kept, the Jews were
compelled to go in procession to
Bacchus, carrying ivy. [8]Moreover there
went out a decree to the neighbor cities
of the heathen, by the suggestion of
Ptol′emy, against the Jews, that they
should observe the same fashions, and
be partakers of their sacrifices: [9]and
whoso would not conform themselves
to the manners of the Gentiles should
be put to death. Then might a man have
seen the present misery.
[10]For there were two women brought,
who had circumcised their children;
whom when they had openly led round
about the city, the babes handing at
their breasts, they cast them down
headlong from the wall. [11]And others,
that had run together into caves near
by, to keep the Sabbath day secretly,
being discovered to Philip, were all
burned together, because they made a
conscience to help themselves for the
honor of the most sacred day.
[12]Now I beseech those that read this
book, that they be not discouraged for
these calamities, but that they judge
those punishments not to be for
destruction, but for a chastening of our
nation. [13]For it is a token of his great
goodness, when wicked doers are not
suffered any long time, but forthwith
punished. [14]For not as with other
nations, whom the Lord patiently
forbeareth to punish, till they be come
to the fulness of their sins, so dealeth he
with us, [15]lest that, being come to the
height of sin, afterwards he should take
vengeance of us. [16]And therefore he
never withdraweth his mercy from us:
and though he punish with adversity,

yet doth he never forsake his people.
17 But let this that we have spoken be for
a warning unto us. And now will we
come to the declaring of the matter in a
few words.
18 Ele-a´zar, one of the principal scribes,
an aged man, and of a well-favored
countenance, was constrained to open
his mouth, and to eat swine's flesh.
19 But he, choosing rather to die
gloriously, than to live stained with
such an abomination, spit it forth, and
came of his own accord to the torment,
20 as it behoved them to come, that are
resolute to stand out against such
things, as are not lawful for love of life
to be tasted. 21 But they that had the
charge of that wicked feast, for the old
acquaintance they had with the man,
taking him aside, besought him to
bring flesh of his own provision, such
as was lawful for him to use, and make
as if he did eat of the flesh taken from
the sacrifice commanded by the king;
22 that in so doing he might be delivered
from death, and for the old friendship
with them find favor. 23 But he began
to consider discreetly, and as became
his age, and the excellency of his
ancient years, and the honor of his gray
head, whereunto he was come, and his
most honest education from a child, or
rather the holy law made and given by
God: therefore he answered
accordingly, and willed them
straightway to send him to the grave.
24 For it becometh not our age, said he,
in any wise to dissemble, whereby
many young persons might think that
Ele-a´zar, being fourscore years old and
ten, were now gone to a strange
religion; 25 and so they through mine
hypocrisy, and desire to live a little
time and a moment longer, should be
deceived by me, and I get a stain to
mine old age, and make it abominable.
26 For though for the present time I
should be delivered from the
punishment of men: yet should I not
escape the hand of the Almighty,
neither alive, nor dead. 27 Wherefore
now, manfully changing this life, I will
show myself such an one as mine age
requireth, 28 and leave a notable
example to such as be young to die
willingly and courageously for the
honorable and holy laws. And when he
had said these words, immediately he
went to the torment: 29 they that led him
changing the good will they bare him a
little before into hatred, because the
foresaid speeches proceeded, as they
thought, from a desperate mind. 30 But
when he was ready to die with stripes,
he groaned, and said, It is manifest unto
the Lord, that hath the holy knowledge,
that whereas I might have been delivered
from death, I now endure sore pains in
body by being beaten: but in soul am
well content to suffer these things,
because I fear him. 31 And thus this man
died, leaving his death for an example
of a noble courage, and a memorial of
virtue, not only unto young men, but
unto all his nation.

CHAPTER 7

1 It came to pass also, that seven
brethren with their mother were taken,
and compelled by the king against the
law to taste swine's flesh, and were
tormented with scourges and whips.
2 But one of them that spake first said
thus, What wouldest thou ask or learn
of us? we are ready to die, rather than
to transgress the laws of our fathers.
3 Then the king, being in a rage,
commanded pans and caldrons to be
made hot: 4 which forthwith being

heated, he commanded to cut out the
tongue of him that spake first, and to
cut off the utmost parts of his body, the
rest of his brethren and his mother
looking on. 5 Now when he was thus
maimed in all his members, he
commanded him being yet alive to be
brought to the fire, and to be fried in the
pan: and as the vapor of the pan was for
a good space dispersed, they exhorted
one another with the mother to die
manfully, saying thus, 6 The Lord God
looketh upon us, and in truth hath
comfort in us, as Moses in his song,
which witnessed to their faces,
declared, saying, And he shall be
comforted in his servants.
7 So when the first was dead after this
manner, they brought the second to
make him a mocking stock: and when
they had pulled off the skin of his head
with the hair, they asked him, Wilt thou
eat, before thou be punished throughout
every member of thy body? 8 But he
answered in his own language, and
said, No. Wherefore he also received
the next torment in order, as the former
did. 9 And when he was at the last gasp,
he said, Thou like a fury takest us out of
this present life, but the King of the
world shall raise us up, who have died
for his laws, unto everlasting life.
10 After him was the third made a
mocking stock: and when he was
required, he put out his tongue, and that
right soon, holding forth his hands
manfully, 11 and said courageously,
These I had from heaven; and for his
laws I despise them; and from him I
hope to receive them again.
12 Insomuch that the king, and they
that were with him, marveled at the
young man's courage, for that he
nothing regarded the pains.
13 Now when this man was dead also,
they tormented and mangled the fourth
in like manner. 14 So when he was ready
to die he said thus, It is good, being put
to death by men, to look for hope from
God to be raised up again by him: as for
thee, thou shalt have no resurrection to
life.
15 Afterward they brought the fifth also,
and mangled him. 16 Then looked he
unto the king, and said, Thou hast
power over men, thou art corruptible,
thou doest what thou wilt; yet think not
that our nation is forsaken of God;
17 but abide a while, and behold his
great power, how he will torment thee
and thy seed.
18 After him also they brought the sixth,
who being ready to die said, Be
not deceived without cause: for we
suffer these things for ourselves,
having sinned against our God:
therefore marvelous things are done
unto us. 19 But think not thou, that
takest in hand to strive against God,
that thou shalt escape unpunished.
20 But the mother was marvelous
above all, and worthy of honorable
memory: for when she saw her seven
sons slain within the space of one day,
she bare it with a good courage,
because of the hope that she had in the
Lord. 21 Yea, she exhorted every one of
them in her own language, filled with
courageous spirits; and stirring up her
womanish thoughts with a manly
stomach, she said unto them, 22 I cannot
tell how ye came into my womb; for
I neither gave you breath nor life,
neither was it I that formed the members
of every one of you; 23 but doubtless
the Creator of the world, who formed
the generation of man, and found out
the beginning of all things, will also
of his own mercy give you breath and
life again, as ye now regard not your

own selves for his laws' sake.
24 Now An-ti´ochus, thinking himself
despised, and suspecting it to be a
reproachful speech, whilst the youngest
was yet alive, did not only exhort him
by words, but also assured him with
oaths, that he would make him both a
rich and a happy man, if he would turn
from the laws of his fathers; and that
also he would take him for his friend,
and trust him with affairs. 25 But when
the young man would in no case
hearken unto him, the king called his
mother, and exhorted her that she
would counsel the young man to save
his life. 26 And when he had exhorted
her with many words, she promised
him that she would counsel her son.
27 But she bowing herself toward him,
laughing the cruel tyrant to scorn, spake
in her country language on this manner;
O my son, have pity upon me that bare
thee nine months in my womb, and
gave thee suck three years, and
nourished thee, and brought thee up
unto this age, and endured the troubles
of education. 28 I beseech thee, my son,
look upon the heaven and the earth, and
all that is therein, and consider that God
made them of things that were not; and
so was mankind made likewise. 29 Fear
not this tormentor, but, being worthy of
thy brethren, take thy death, that I may
receive thee again in mercy with thy
brethren.
30 While she was yet speaking these
words, the young man said, Whom wait
ye for? I will not obey the king's
commandment: but I will obey the
commandment of the law that was
given unto our fathers by Moses. 31 And
thou, that hast been the author of all
mischief against the Hebrews, shalt not
escape the hands of God. 32 For we suffer
because of our sins. 33 And though the
living Lord be angry with us a little
while for our chastening and
correction, yet shall he be at one
again with his servants. 34 But thou, O
godless man, and of all other most
wicked, be not lifted up without a
cause, nor puffed up with uncertain
hopes, lifting up thy hand against the
servants of God: 35 for thou hast not yet
escaped the judgment of Almighty
God, who seeth all things. 36 For our
brethren, who now have suffered a
short pain, are dead under God's
covenant of everlasting life: but thou,
through the judgment of God, shalt
receive just punishment for thy pride.
37 But I, as my brethren, offer up my
body and life for the laws of our fathers,
beseeching God that he would speedily
be merciful unto our nation; and that
thou by torments and plagues mayest
confess, that he alone is God; 38 and that
in me and my brethren the wrath of the
Almighty, which is justly brought upon
all our nation, may cease. 39 Then the
king, being in a rage, handled him
worse than all the rest, and took it
grievously that he was mocked. 40 So
this man died undefiled, and put his
whole trust in the Lord.
41 Last of all after the sons the mother
died. 42 Let this be enough now to have
spoken concerning the idolatrous
feasts, and the extreme tortures.

CHAPTER 8

1 Then Judas Maccabe´us, and they that
were with him, went privily into the
towns, and called their kinsfolk
together, and took unto them all such as
continued in the Jews' religion, and
assembled about six thousand men.
2 And they called upon the Lord, that he
would look upon the people that was

trodden down of all; and also pity the
temple profaned of ungodly men; 3 and
that he would have compassion upon the
city, sore defaced, and ready to be made
even with the ground; and hear the
blood that cried unto him, 4 and
remember the wicked slaughter of
harmless infants, and the blasphemies
committed against his name; and that
he would show his hatred against the
wicked. 5 Now when Maccabe′us had
his company about him, he could not be
withstood by the heathen: for the wrath
of the Lord was turned into mercy.
6 Therefore he came at unawares, and
burnt up towns and cities, and got into his
hands the most commodious places,
and overcame and put to flight no small
number of his enemies. 7 But specially
took he advantage of the night for such
privy attempts, insomuch that the bruit
of his manliness was spread every
where.

8 So when Philip saw that this man
increased little by little, and that things
prospered with him still more and
more, he wrote unto Ptolemy, the
governor of Coelesyr′ia and
Phoeni′cia, to yield more aid to the
king's affairs. 9 Then forthwith
choosing Nica′nor the son of
Patro′clus, one of his special friends, he
sent him with no fewer than twenty
thousand of all nations under him, to
root out the whole generation of the
Jews; and with him he joined also
Gorgias a captain, who in matters of
war had great experience. 10 So
Nica′nor undertook to make so much
money of the captive Jews, as should
defray the tribute of two thousand
talents, which the king was to pay to
the Romans. 11 Wherefore immediately
he sent to the cities upon the sea
coast, proclaiming a sale of the captive
Jews, and promising that they should
have fourscore and ten bodies for one
talent, not expecting the vengeance that
was to follow upon him from the
Almighty God. 12 Now when word was
brought unto Judas of Nica′nor's
coming, and he had imparted unto
those that were with him that the army
was at hand, 13 they that were fearful,
and distrusted the justice of God, fled,
and conveyed themselves away.
14 Others sold all that they had left, and
withal besought the Lord to deliver
them, being sold by the wicked
Nica′nor before they met together:
15 and if not for their own sakes, yet for
the covenants he had made with their
fathers, and for his holy and glorious
name's sake, by which they were
called.

16 So Maccabe′us called his men
together unto the number of six
thousand, and exhorted them not to be
stricken with terror of the enemy, nor
to fear the great multitude of the
heathen, who came wrongly against
them; but to fight manfully, 17 and to set
before their eyes the injury that they had
unjustly done to the holy place, and the
cruel handling of the city, whereof they
made a mockery, and also the taking
away of the government of their
forefathers: 18 for they, said he, trust in
their weapons and boldness; but our
confidence is in the Almighty God,
who at a beck can cast down both them
that come against us, and also all the
world. 19 Moreover, he recounted unto
them what helps their forefathers had
found, and how they were delivered,
when under Sennach′erib an hundred
fourscore and five thousand perished.
20 And he told them of the battle that they
had in Babylon with the Galatians, how
they came but eight thousand in all to

the business, with four thousand
Macedo´nians, and that the
Macedo´nians being perplexed, the
eight thousand destroyed an hundred
and twenty thousand because of the
help that they had from heaven, and so
received a great booty.
21 Thus when he had made them bold
with these words, and ready to die for
the laws and the country, he divided his
army into four parts; 22 and joined with
himself his own brethren, leaders of each
band, to wit, Simon, and Joseph, and
Jonathan, giving each one fifteen
hundred men. 23 Also he appointed Ele-
a´zar to read the holy book: and when
he had given them this watchword, The
help of God; himself leading the first
band, he joined battle with Nica´nor.
24 And by the help of the Almighty they
slew above nine thousand of their
enemies, and wounded and maimed the
most part of Nica´nor's host, and so put
all to flight; 25 and took their money that
came to buy them, and pursued them
far: but lacking time they returned: 26 for
it was the day before the sabbath, and
therefore they would no longer pursue
them. 27 So when they had gathered
their armor together, and spoiled their
enemies, they occupied themselves
about the sabbath, yielding exceeding
praise and thanks to the Lord, who had
preserved them unto that day, which
was the beginning of mercy distilling
upon them. 28 And after the sabbath,
when they had given part of the spoils
to the maimed, and the widows, and
orphans, the residue they divided
among themselves and their servants.
29 When this was done, and they had
made a common supplication, they
besought the merciful Lord to be
reconciled with his servants for ever.
30 Moreover of those that were with
Timo´theus and Bac´chi-des, who
fought against them, they slew above
twenty thousand, and very easily got
high and strongholds, and divided
among themselves many spoils more,
and made the maimed, orphans,
widows, yea, and the aged also, equal
in spoils with themselves. 31 And when
they had gathered their armor together,
they laid them up all carefully in
convenient places, and the remnant of
the spoils they brought to Jerusalem.
32 They slew also Philar´ches, that
wicked person, who was with
Timo´theus, and had annoyed the Jews
many ways. 33 Furthermore at such time
as they kept the feast for the victory in
their country they burnt Callis´the-nes,
that had set fire upon the holy gates,
who had fled into a little house; and so
he received a reward meet for his
wickedness.
34 As for that most ungracious Nica´nor,
who had brought a thousand merchants
to buy the Jews, 35 he was through the
help of the Lord brought down by them,
of whom he made least account; and
putting off his glorious apparel, and
discharging his company, he came like
a fugitive servant through the
midland unto An´ti-och, having very
great dishonor, for that his host was
destroyed. 36 Thus he, that took upon
him to make good to the Romans their
tribute by means of the captives in
Jerusalem, told abroad, that the Jews
had God to fight for them, and therefore
they could not be hurt, because they
followed the laws that he gave them.

CHAPTER 9

1 About that time came An-ti´ochus
with dishonor out of the country of
Persia. 2 For he had entered the city

called Persep´olis, and went about to
rob the temple, and to hold the city;
whereupon the multitude running to
defend themselves with their weapons
put them to flight; and so it happened,
that An-ti´ochus being put to flight of
the inhabitants returned with shame.
3 Now when he came to Ecbatana, news
was brought him what had happened unto
Nica´nor and Timo´theus. 4 Then
swelling with anger, he thought to
avenge upon the Jews the disgrace done
unto him by those that made him flee.
Therefore commanded he his
chariotman to drive without ceasing,
and to dispatch the journey, the
judgment of God now following him.
For he had spoken proudly in this sort,
That he would come to Jerusalem, and
make it a common burying place of the
Jews.
5 But the Lord Almighty, the God of
Israel, smote him with an incurable and
invisible plague: for as soon as he had
spoken these words, a pain of the
bowels that was remediless came upon
him, and sore torments of the inner
parts; 6 and that most justly: for he had
tormented other men's bowels with
many and strange torments. 7 Howbeit
he nothing at all ceased from his
bragging, but still was filled with pride,
breathing out fire in his rage against the
Jews, and commanding to haste the
journey: but it came to pass that he fell
down from his chariot, carried
violently; so that having a sore fall, all
the members of his body were much
pained. 8 And thus he that a little afore
thought he might command the waves
of the sea, (so proud was he beyond the
condition of man) and weigh the high
mountains in a balance, was now cast
on the ground, and carried in an horse-
litter, showing forth unto all the
manifest power of God. 9 So that the
worms rose up out of the body of this
wicked man, and while he lived in
sorrow and pain, his flesh fell away,
and the filthiness of his smell was
noisome to all his army. 10 And the man,
that thought a little afore he could reach
to the stars of heaven, no man could
endure to carry for his intolerable stink.
11 Here therefore, being plagued, he
began to leave off his great pride, and
to come to the knowledge of himself by
the scourge of God, his pain increasing
every moment. 12 And when he himself
could not abide his own smell, he said
these words, It is meet to be subject unto
God, and that a man that is mortal
should not proudly think of himself, as
if he were God. 13 This wicked person
vowed also unto the Lord, who now no
more would have mercy upon him,
saying thus, 14 that the holy city (to the
which he was going in haste, to lay it
even with the ground, and to make it a
common burying place,) he would set
at liberty: 15 and as touching the Jews,
whom he had judged not worthy so
much as to be buried, but to be cast out
with their children to be devoured of the
fowls and wild beasts, he would make
them all equals to the citizens of
Athens: 16 And the holy temple, which
before he had spoiled, he would garnish
with goodly gifts, and restore all the
holy vessels with many more, and out
of his own revenue defray the charges
belonging to the sacrifices: 17 yea, and
that also he would become a Jew
himself, and go through all the world
that was inhabited, and declare the
power of God.
18 But for all this his pains would not
cease: for the just judgment of God was
come upon him: therefore despairing of
his health, he wrote unto the Jews the

letter underwritten, containing the form
of a supplication, after this manner:
19 An- ti´ochus, king and governor, to
the good Jews his citizens wisheth
much joy, health, and prosperity: 20 If ye
and your children fare well, and your
affairs be to your contentment, I give
very great thanks to God, having my
hope in heaven. 21 As for me, I was
weak, or else I would have
remembered kindly your honor and
good will. Returning out of Persia, and
being taken with a grievous disease, I
thought it necessary to care for the
common safety of all: 22 not distrusting
mine health, but having great hope to
escape this sickness. 23 But considering
that even my father, at what time he
led an army into the high
countries, appointed a successor, 24 to
the end that, if any thing fell out
contrary to expectation, or if any tidings
were brought that were grievous, they
of the land, knowing to whom the state
was left, might not be troubled: 25 again,
considering how that the princes that
are borderers and neighbors unto my
kingdom wait for opportunities, and
expect what shall be the event, I have
appointed my son An-ti´ochus king,
whom I often committed and
commended unto many of you, when I
went up into the high provinces; to
whom I have written as followeth:
26 therefore I pray and request you to
remember the benefits that I have done
unto you generally, and in special, and
that every man will be still faithful to me
and my son. 27 For I am persuaded that
he understanding my mind will
favorably and graciously yield to your
desires.
28 Thus the murderer and blasphemer
having suffered most grievously, as he
treated other men, so died he a
miserable death in a strange country in
the mountains. 29 And Philip, that was
brought up with him, carried away his
body, who also fearing the son of An-
ti´ochus went into Egypt to Ptoleme´us
Philome´tor.

CHAPTER 10

1 Now Maccabe´us and his company,
the Lord guiding them, recovered the
temple and the city: 2 but the altars
which the heathen had built in the open
street, and also the chapels, they pulled
down. 3 And having cleansed the temple
they made another altar, and striking
stones they took fire out of them, and
offered a sacrifice after two years, and
set forth incense, and lights, and
showbread. 4 When that was done, they
fell flat down, and besought the Lord that
they might come no more into such
troubles; but if they sinned any more
against him, that he himself would
chasten them with mercy, and that they
might not be delivered unto the
blasphemous and barbarous nations.
5 Now upon the same day that the
strangers profaned the temple, on the
very same day it was cleansed again,
even the five and twentieth day of the
same month, which is Chislev. 6 And
they kept eight days with gladness, as
in the feast of the tabernacles,
remembering that not long before they
had held the feast of the tabernacles,
when as they wandered in the
mountains and dens like beasts.
7 Therefore they bare branches, and
fair boughs, and palms also, and sang
psalms unto him that had given them
good success in cleansing his place.
8 They ordained also by a common
statute and decree, That every year
those days should be kept of the whole

nation of the Jews. 9 And this was the
end of An-ti´ochus, called E-
piph´anes. 10 Now will we declare the
acts of An-ti´ochus Eu´pator, who was
the son of this wicked man, gathering
briefly the calamities of the wars.
11 So when he was come to the crown,
he set one Lys´i-as over the affairs of his
realm, and appointed him his chief
governor of Coelesyr´ia and Phoeni´cia.
12 For Ptolemy, that was called Macron,
choosing rather to do justice unto the
Jews for the wrong that had been
done unto them, endeavored to
continue peace with them.
13 Whereupon being accused of the
king's friends before Eu´pator, and
called traitor at every word, because he
had left Cyprus, that Philome´tor had
committed unto him, and departed to
An-ti´ochus E-piph´anes, and seeing
that he was in no honorable place, he
was so discouraged, that he poisoned
himself and died.

14 But when Gorgias was governor of
the holds, he hired soldiers, and
nourished war continually with the
Jews: 15 and therewithal the Idume´ans,
having gotten into their hands the most
commodious holds, kept the Jews
occupied, and receiving those that were
banished from Jerusalem, they went
about to nourish war. 16 Then they that
were with Maccabe´us made
supplication, and besought God that he
would be their helper; and so they ran
with violence upon the strongholds of
the Idume´ans, 17 and assaulting them
strongly, they won the holds, and kept
off all that fought upon the wall, and
slew all that fell into their hands, and
killed no fewer than twenty thousand.
18 And because certain, who were no less
than nine thousand, were fled together
into two very strong castles, having all
manner of things convenient to sustain
the siege, 19 Maccabe´us left Simon and
Joseph, and Zacche´us also, and them
that were with him, who were enough
to besiege them, and departed himself
unto those places which more needed
his help. 20 Now they that were with
Simon, being led with covetousness,
were persuaded for money through
certain of those that were in the castle,
and took seventy thousand drachms,
and let some of them escape. 21 But
when it was told Maccabe´us what
was done, he called the governors of the
people together, and accused those
men, that they had sold their brethren
for money, and set their enemies free to
fight against them. 22 So he slew those
that were found traitors, and
immediately took the two castles.
23 And having good success with his
weapons in all things he took in hand,
he slew in the two holds more than
twenty thousand.

24 Now Timo´theus, whom the Jews had
overcome before, when he had
gathered a great multitude of foreign
forces, and horses out of Asia not a few,
came as though he would take Judea by
force of arms. 25 But when he drew near,
they that were with Maccabe´us turned
themselves to pray unto God, and
sprinkled earth upon their heads, and
girded their loins with sackcloth, 26 And
fell down at the foot of the altar, and
besought him to be merciful to them,
and to be an enemy to their enemies,
and an adversary to their adversaries, as
the law declareth.

27 So after the prayer they took their
weapons, and went on further from the
city: and when they drew near to their
enemies, they kept by themselves.
28 Now the sun being newly risen, they
joined both together; the one part having

together with their virtue their refuge
also unto the Lord for a pledge of their
success and victory: the other side
making their rage leader of their battle.
29But when the battle waxed strong,
there appeared unto the enemies from
heaven five comely men upon horses,
with bridles of gold, and two of them
led the Jews, 30and took Maccabe´us
betwixt them, and covered him on
every side with their weapons, and kept
him safe, but shot arrows and
lightnings against the enemies: so that
being confounded with blindness, and
full of trouble, they were killed. 31And
there were slain of footmen twenty
thousand and five hundred, and six
hundred horsemen.
32As for Timo´theus himself, he fled
into a very stronghold, called Gezer,
where Cher´eas was governor. 33But they
that were with Maccabe´us laid siege
against the fortress courageously four
days. 34And they that were within,
trusting to the strength of the place,
blasphemed exceedingly, and uttered
wicked words. 35Nevertheless upon the
fifth day early twenty young men of
Maccabe´us' company, inflamed with
anger because of the blasphemies,
assaulted the wall manly, and with a
fierce courage killed all that they met
withal. 36Others likewise ascending
after them, while they were busied with
them that were within, burned the
towers, and kindling fires burned the
blasphemers alive; and others broke open
the gates, and, having received in the
rest of the army, took the city, 37and
killed Timo´theus, that was hid in a
certain pit, and Cher´eas his brother,
with Apol-lo´phan-es. 38When this was
done, they praised the Lord with psalms
and thanksgiving, who had done so
great things for Israel, and given them
the victory.

CHAPTER 11

1Not long after this, Lys´i-as the king's
protector and cousin, who also
managed the affairs, took sore
displeasure for the things that were
done. 2And when he had gathered
about fourscore thousand with all the
horsemen, he came against the Jews,
thinking to make the city an habitation
of the Gentiles, 3and to make a gain of
the temple, as of the other chapels of the
heathen, and to set the high priesthood
to sale every year: 4not at all
considering the power of God, but
puffed up with his ten thousands of
footmen, and his thousands of
horsemen, and his fourscore elephants.
5So he came to Judea, and drew near to
Beth–zur, which was a strong town, but
distant from Jerusalem about five
furlongs, and he laid sore siege unto it.
6Now when they that were with
Maccabe´us heard that he besieged
the holds, they and all the people with
lamentation and tears besought the
Lord that he would send a good angel to
deliver Israel. 7Then Maccabe´us
himself first of all took weapons,
exhorting the other that they would
jeopardize themselves together with
him to help their brethren: so they went
forth together with a willing mind. 8And
as they were at Jerusalem, there
appeared before them on horseback one
in white clothing, shaking his armor of
gold. 9Then they praised the merciful
God all together, and took heart,
insomuch that they were ready not only
to fight with men, but with most cruel
beasts, and to pierce through walls of
iron. 10Thus they marched forward in
their armor, having an helper from

heaven: for the Lord was merciful unto
them. 11And giving a charge upon their
enemies like lions, they slew eleven
thousand footmen, and sixteen hundred
horsemen, and put all the other to flight.
12Many of them also being wounded
escaped naked; and Lys′i-as himself
fled away shamefully, and so escaped.
13Who, as he was a man of
understanding, casting with himself
what loss he had had, and considering
that the Hebrews could not be
overcome, because the Almighty God
helped them, he sent unto them, 14and
persuaded them to agree to all
reasonable conditions, and promised
that he would persuade the king that he
must needs be a friend unto them.
15Then Maccabe′us consented to all
that Lys′i- as desired, being careful of
the common good; and whatsoever
Maccabe′us wrote unto Lys′i-as
concerning the Jews, the king granted
it.
16For there were letters written unto
the Jews from Lys′i-as to this effect:
Lys′i-as unto the people of the
Jews sendeth greeting: 17John and
Ab′salom, who were sent from you,
delivered me the petition subscribed,
and made request for the performance
of the contents thereof. 18Therefore
what things soever were meet to be
reported to the king, I have declared them,
and he hath granted as much as might
be. 19If then ye will keep yourselves
loyal to the state, hereafter also will I
endeavor to be a means of your good.
20But of the particulars I have given
order both to these, and the other that came
from me, to commune with you. 21Fare
ye well. The hundred and eight and
fortieth year, the four and twentieth
day of the month Di′os-corin′thius.
22Now the king's letter contained these
words: King An-ti′ochus unto his
brother Lys′i-as sendeth greeting:
23Since our father is translated unto the
gods, our will is, that they that are in our
realm live quietly, that every one may
attend upon his own affairs. 24We
understand also that the Jews would not
consent to our father, for to be brought
unto the custom of the Gentiles, but had
rather keep their own manner of living:
for the which cause they require of us,
that we should suffer them to live after
their own laws. 25Wherefore our mind
is, that this nation shall be in rest, and we
have determined to restore them their
temple, that they may live according to
the customs of their forefathers. 26Thou
shalt do well therefore to send unto
them, and grant them peace, that when
they are certified of our mind, they
may be of good comfort, and ever go
cheerfully about their own affairs.
27And the letter of the king unto the
nation of the Jews was after this
manner: King An-ti′ochus sendeth
greeting unto the council, and the rest
of the Jews: 28If ye fare well, we
have our desire; we are also in good
health. 29Menela′us declared unto us,
that your desire was to return home,
and to follow your own business:
30wherefore they that will depart shall
have safe conduct till the thirtieth day
of Xan′thicus with security. 31And the
Jews shall use their own kind of meats
and laws, as before; and none of them
any manner of ways shall be molested
for things ignorantly done. 32I have
sent also Menela′us, that he may
comfort you. 33Fare ye well. In the
hundred forty and eighth year, and the
fifteenth day of the month Xan′thicus.
34The Romans also sent unto them a
letter containing these words: Quintus
Memm′ius and Titus Man′lius,

ambassadors of the Romans, send
greeting unto the people of the Jews.
35 Whatsoever Lys´i-as the king's
cousin hath granted, therewith we also
are well pleased. 36 But touching such
things as he judge to be referred to the
king, after ye have advised thereof, send
one forthwith, that we may declare as it
is convenient for you: for we are now
going to An´ti-och. 37 Therefore send
some with speed, that we may know
what is your mind. 38 Farewell. This
hundred and eight and fortieth year, the
fifteenth day of the month Xan´thicus.

CHAPTER 12

1 When these covenants were made,
Lys´i-as went unto the king, and the
Jews were about their husbandry. 2 But
of the governors of several places,
Timo´theus, and Apol-lo´nius the son
of Gen-ne´us, also Hieron´ymus, and
Dem´ophon, and beside them Nica´nor
the governor of Cyprus, would not
suffer them to be quiet, and live in peace.
3 The men of Joppa also did such an
ungodly deed: they prayed the Jews that
dwelt among them to go with their
wives and children into the boats which
they had prepared, as though they had
meant them no hurt. 4 Who accepted of it
according to the common decree of the
city, as being desirous to live in peace,
and suspecting nothing: but when they
were gone forth into the deep, they
drowned no less than two hundred of
them. 5 When Judas heard of this cruelty
done unto his countrymen, he
commanded those that were with him to
make them ready. 6 And calling upon
God the righteous Judge, he came
against those murderers of his brethren,
and burned the haven by night, and set
the boats on fire, and those that fled
thither he slew. 7 And when the town
was shut up, he went backward, as if he
would return to root out all them of the
city of Joppa. 8 But when he heard that
the people of Jabneh were minded to do
in like manner unto the Jews that dwelt
among them, 9 he came upon the people
of Jabneh also by night, and set fire on
the haven and the navy, so that the light
of the fire was seen at Jerusalem two
hundred and forty furlongs off.
10 Now when they were gone from
thence nine furlongs in their journey
toward Timo´theus, no fewer than five
thousand men on foot and five hundred
horsemen of the Arabians set upon
him. 11 Whereupon there was a very
sore battle; but Judas' side by the help
of God got the victory; so that the
nomads of Arabia, being overcome,
besought Judas for peace, promising
both to give him cattle, and to pleasure
him otherwise. 12 Then Judas, thinking
indeed that they would be profitable in
many things, granted them peace:
whereupon they shook hands, and so
they departed to their tents.
13 He went also about to make a bridge
to a certain strong city, which was
fenced about with walls, and inhabited
by people of divers countries; and the
name of it was Caspis. 14 But they that
were within it put such trust in the
strength of the walls and provision of
victuals, that they behaved themselves
rudely toward them that were with
Judas, railing and blaspheming, and
uttering such words as were not to be
spoken. 15 Wherefore Judas with his
company, calling upon the great Lord
of the world, who without rams or
engines of war did cast down Jericho in
the time of Joshua, gave a fierce assault
against the walls, 16 and took the city by
the will of God, and made unspeakable

slaughters, insomuch that a lake two
furlongs broad near adjoining thereunto,
being filled full, was seen running with
blood.
17Then departed they from thence
seven hundred and fifty furlongs, and
came to Char´aca unto the Jews that are
called Tubi-e´ni. 18But as for
Timo´theus, they found him not in the
places: for before he had dispatched
any thing, he departed from thence,
having left a very strong garrison in a
certain hold. 19Howbeit Dosith´eus and
Sosip´ater, who were of Maccabe´us'
captains, went forth, and slew those that
Timo´theus had left in the fortress,
above ten thousand men. 20And
Maccabe´us ranged his army by bands,
and set them over the bands, and went
against Timo´theus, who had about him
an hundred and twenty thousand men
of foot, and two thousand and five
hundred horsemen. 21Now when
Timo´theus had knowledge of Judas'
coming, he sent the women and children
and the other baggage unto a fortress
called Carnaim: for the town was hard
to besiege, and uneasy to come unto, by
reason of the straitness of all the places.
22But when Judas his first band came in
sight, the enemies, being smitten with
fear and terror through the appearance
of him that seeth all things, fled amain,
one running this way, another that way,
so as that they were often hurt of their
own men, and wounded with the points
of their own swords. 23Judas also was
very earnest in pursuing them, killing
those wicked wretches, of whom he
slew about thirty thousand men.
24Moreover Timo´theus himself fell
into the hands of Dosith´eus and
Sosip´ater, whom he besought with
much craft to let him go with his life,
because he had many of the Jews'
parents, and the brethren of some of
them, who, if they put him to death,
should not be regarded. 25So when he
had assured them with many words that
he would restore them without hurt,
according to the agreement, they let
him go for the saving of their brethren.
26Then Maccabe´us marched forth to
Carnaim, and to the temple of
Atar´gatis, and there he slew five and
twenty thousand persons. 27And after he
had put to flight and destroyed them,
Judas removed the host toward Ephron,
a strong city, wherein Lys´i-as abode,
and a great multitude of divers nations,
and the strong young men kept the
walls, and defended them mightily:
wherein also was great provision of
engines and darts. 28But when Judas
and his company had called upon
Almighty God, who with his power
breaketh the strength of his enemies,
they won the city, and slew twenty and
five thousand of them that were within.
29From thence they departed to
Scythop´olis, which lieth six hundred
furlongs from Jerusalem. 30But when
the Jews that dwelt there had testified
that the Scythopol´itans dealt lovingly
with them, and treated them kindly in
the time of their adversity; 31they gave
them thanks, desiring them to be
friendly still unto them: and so they
came to Jerusalem, the feast of the
weeks approaching.
32And after the feast, called Pentecost,
they went forth against Gorgias the
governor of Idume´a, 33who came out
with three thousand men of foot and
four hundred horsemen. 34And it
happened that in their fighting together
a few of the Jews were slain. 35At
which time Dosith´eus, one of Ba-
ce´nor's company, who was on
horseback, and a strong man, was still

upon Gorgias, and taking hold of his
coat drew him by force; and when he
would have taken that cursed man
alive, a horseman of Thracia coming
upon him smote off his shoulder, so
that Gorgias fled unto Mare´shah.
36 Now when they that were with
Gorgias had fought long, and were
weary, Judas called upon the Lord, that
he would show himself to be their
helper and leader of the battle. 37 And
with that he began in his own language,
and sung psalms with a loud voice, and
rushing unawares upon Gorgias' men,
he put them to flight.
38 So Judas gathered his host, and came
into the city of Adul´lam. And
when the seventh day came, they
purified themselves, as the custom was,
and kept the sabbath in the same place.
39 And upon the day following, as the
use had been, Judas and his company
came to take up the bodies of them that
were slain, and to bury them with their
kinsmen in their fathers' graves. 40 Now
under the coats of every one that was
slain they found things consecrated to
the idols of the people of Jabneh, which
is forbidden the Jews by the law. Then
every man saw that this was the cause
wherefore they were slain. 41 All men
therefore praising the Lord, the
righteous Judge, who had opened the
things that were hid, 42 betook
themselves unto prayer, and besought
him that the sin committed might
wholly be put out of remembrance.
Besides, that noble Judas exhorted the
people to keep themselves from sin,
forsomuch as they saw before their
eyes the things that came to pass for the
sins of those that were slain. 43 And
when he had made a gathering
throughout the company to the sum
of two thousand drachms of silver, he
sent it to Jerusalem to offer a sin
offering, doing therein very well and
honestly, in that he was mindful of the
resurrection: 44 for if he had not hoped
that they that were slain should have
risen again, it had been superfluous and
vain to pray for the dead. 45 And also in
that he perceived that there was great
favor laid up for those that died godly,
it was an holy and good thought.
Whereupon he made a reconciliation
for the dead, that they might be
delivered from sin.

CHAPTER 13

1 In the hundred forty and ninth year it
was told Judas, that An-ti´ochus
Eu´pator was coming with a great power
into Judea, 2 and with him Lys´i-as his
protector, and ruler of his affairs,
having either of them a Greek force of
footmen, an hundred and ten thousand,
and horsemen five thousand and three
hundred, and elephants two and twenty,
and three hundred chariots armed with
hooks.
3 Menela´us also joined himself with
them, and with great dissimulation
encouraged An-ti´ochus, not for the
safeguard of the country, but because
he thought to have been made
governor. 4 But the King of kings
moved An-ti´ochus' mind against this
wicked wretch, and Lys´i-as informed
the king that this man was the cause of
all mischief, so that the king
commanded to bring him unto Berea,
and to put him to death, as the manner
is in that place. 5 Now there was in that
place a tower of fifty cubits high, full
of ashes, and it had a round
instrument, which on every side
hanged down into the ashes. 6 And
whosoever was condemned of

sacrilege, or had committed any other
grievous crime, there did all men thrust
him unto death. [7]Such a death it
happened that wicked man to die, not
having so much as burial in the earth;
and that most justly: [8]for inasmuch as he
had committed many sins about the
altar, whose fire and ashes were holy,
he received his death in ashes.
[9]Now the king came with a barbarous
and haughty mind to do far worse
to the Jews, than had been done in his
father's time. [10]Which things when
Judas perceived, he commanded the
multitude to call upon the Lord night
and day, that if ever at any other time,
he would now also help them, being at
the point to be put from their law, from
their country, and from the holy
temple: [11]and that he would not suffer
the people, that had even now been but
a little refreshed, to be in subjection
to the blasphemous nations. [12]So when
they had all done this together, and
besought the merciful Lord with
weeping and fasting, and lying flat
upon the ground three days long, Judas,
having exhorted them, commanded
they should be in a readiness. [13]And
Judas, being apart with the elders,
determined, before the king's host
should enter into Judea, and get the
city, to go forth and try the matter in
fight by the help of the Lord. [14]So when
he had committed all to the Creator of
the world, and exhorted his soldiers to
fight manfully, even unto death, for the
laws, the temple, the city, the country,
and the commonwealth, he camped by
Modin: [15]and having given the
watchword to them that were about
him, Victory is of God; with the most
valiant and choice young men he went
in into the king's tent by night, and slew
in the camp about four thousand men,
and the chiefest of the elephants, with
all that were upon him. [16]And at last they
filled the camp with fear and tumult,
and departed with good success. [17]This
was done in the break of the day,
because the protection of the Lord did
help him. [18]Now when the king had
taken a taste of the manliness of the
Jews, he went about to take the holds by
policy, [19]and marched toward Beth–zur,
which was a stronghold of the Jews: but
he was put to flight, failed, and lost of
his men: [20]for Judas had conveyed unto
them that were in it such things as were
necessary. [21]But Rhod′ocus, who was in
the Jews' host, disclosed the secrets to
the enemies; therefore he was sought
out, and when they had gotten him,
they put him in prison.
[22]The king treated with them in Beth–
zur the second time, gave his hand, took
theirs, departed, fought with Judas, was
overcome; [23]heard that Philip, who was
left over the affairs in An′ti-och, was
desperately bent, confounded, intreated
the Jews, submitted himself, and sware
to all equal conditions, agreed with
them, and offered sacrifice, honored the
temple, and dealt kindly with the place,
[24]and accepted well of Maccabe′us,
made him principal governor from
Ptolema′is unto the Gerar; [25]came to
Ptolema′is: the people there were
grieved for the covenants; for they
stormed, because they would make their
covenants void: [26]Lys′i-as went up to
the judgment seat, said as much as
could be in defense of the cause,
persuaded, pacified, made them well
affected, returned to An′ti-och. Thus it
went touching the king's coming and
departing.

CHAPTER 14

1After three years was Judas informed,
that Deme´tri-us the son of Seleu´cus,
having entered by the haven of
Trip´olis with a great power and navy,
2had taken the country, and killed An-
ti´ochus, and Lys´i-as his protector.
3Now one Al´cimus, who had been
high priest, and had defiled himself
wilfully in the times of their mingling
with the Gentiles, seeing that by no
means he could save himself, nor have
any more access to the holy altar, 4came
to king Deme´tri-us in the hundred and
one and fiftieth year, presenting unto
him a crown of gold, and a palm, and
also of the boughs which were used
solemnly in the temple: and so that day
he held his peace. 5Howbeit, having
gotten opportunity to further his foolish
enterprise, and being called into
counsel by Deme´tri-us, and asked how
the Jews stood affected, and what they
intended, he answered thereunto:
6Those of the Jews that be called
Hasideans, whose captain is Judas
Maccabe´us, nourish war, and are
seditious, and will not let the realm be
in peace. 7Therefore I, being deprived
of mine ancestors' honor, I mean the
high priesthood, am now come hither:
8first, verily for the unfeigned care I
have of things pertaining to the king; and
secondly, even for that I intend the good
of mine own countrymen: for all our
nation is in no small misery through the
unadvised dealing of them aforesaid.
9Wherefore, O king, seeing thou
knowest all these things, be careful for
the country, and our nation, which is
pressed on every side, according to the
clemency that thou readily showest unto
all. 10For as long as Judas liveth, it is
not possible that the state should be
quiet. 11This was no sooner spoken
of him, but others of the king's friends,
being maliciously set against Judas, did
more incense Deme´tri-us.
12And forthwith calling Nica´nor, who
had been master of the elephants, and
making him governor over Judea, he
sent him forth, 13commanding him to
slay Judas, and to scatter them that
were with him, and to make Al´cimus
high priest of the great temple. 14Then
the heathen, that had fled out of Judea
from Judas, came to Nica´nor by flocks,
thinking the harm and calamities of the
Jews to be their welfare.
15Now when the Jews heard of
Nica´nor's coming, and that the
heathen were up against them, they
cast earth upon their heads, and made
supplication to him that had
established his people for ever, and
who always helpeth his portion with
manifestation of his presence. 16So at
the commandment of the captain they
removed straightway from thence,
and came near unto them at the
town of Dessau. 17Now Simon, Judas'
brother, had joined battle with Nica´nor,
but was somewhat discomfited
through the sudden silence of his
enemies. 18Nevertheless Nica´nor,
hearing of the manliness of them that
were with Judas, and the
courageousness that they had to fight
for their country, durst not try the
matter by the sword. 19Wherefore he
sent Posido´nius, and The-od´otus,
and Mattathi´as, to make peace. 20So
when they had taken long advisement
thereupon, and the captain had made
the multitude acquainted therewith, and
it appeared that they were all of one
mind, they consented to the covenants,
21and appointed a day to meet in
together by themselves: and when the

day came, and stools were set for
either of them, 22Judas placed armed
men ready in convenient places, lest
some treachery should be suddenly
practiced by the enemies: so they made
a peaceable conference. 23Now
Nica´nor abode in Jerusalem, and did
no hurt, but sent away the people that
came flocking unto him. 24And he
would not willingly have Judas out of
his sight: for he loved the man from his
heart. 25He prayed him also to take a
wife, and to beget children: so he
married, was quiet, and took part of this
life.

26But Al´cimus, perceiving the love
that was betwixt them, and considering
the covenants that were made, came to
Deme´tri-us, and told him that Nica´nor
was not well affected toward the state;
for that he had ordained Judas, a traitor
to his realm, to be the king's successor.
27Then the king being in a rage, and
provoked with the accusations of the
most wicked man, wrote to Nica´nor,
signifying that he was much displeased
with the covenants, and commanding
him that he should send Maccabe´us
prisoner in all haste unto An´ti-och.
28When this came to Nica´nor's
hearing, he was much confounded in
himself, and took it grievously that he
should make void the articles which
were agreed upon, the man being in no
fault. 29But because there was no
dealing against the king, he watched
his time to accomplish this thing by
policy. 30Notwithstanding, when
Maccabe´us saw that Nica´nor began to
be churlish unto him, and that he
treated him more roughly than he was
wont, perceiving that such sour
behavior came not of good, he gathered
together not a few of his men, and
withdrew himself from Nica´nor.

31But the other, knowing that he was
notably prevented by Judas' policy,
came into the great and holy temple,
and commanded the priests, that were
offering their usual sacrifices, to deliver
him the man. 32And when they sware
that they could not tell where the man
was whom he sought, 33he stretched out
his right hand toward the temple, and
made an oath in this manner: If ye will
not deliver me Judas as a prisoner, I
will lay this temple of God even with
the ground, and I will break down the
altar, and erect a notable temple unto
Bacchus. 34After these words he
departed. Then the priests lifted up their
hands toward heaven, and besought
him that was ever a defender of their
nation, saying in this manner; 35Thou,
O Lord of all things, who hast need of
nothing, wast pleased that the temple of
thine habitation should be among us:
36therefore now, O holy Lord of all
holiness, keep this house ever undefiled,
which lately was cleansed, and stop
every unrighteous mouth.

37Now was there accused unto Nica´nor
one Razis, one of the elders of
Jerusalem, a lover of his countrymen,
and a man of very good report, who for
his kindness was called a father of the
Jews. 38For in the former times, when
they mingled not themselves with the
Gentiles, he had been accused of
Judaism, and did boldly jeopardize his
body and life with all vehemency for
the religion of the Jews. 39So Nica´nor,
willing to declare the hate that he bare
unto the Jews, sent above five hundred
men of war to take him: 40for he
thought by taking him to do the Jews
much hurt. 41Now when the multitude
would have taken the tower, and
violently broken into the outer door,
and bade that fire should be brought to

burn it, he being ready to be taken on
every side fell upon his sword;
42choosing rather to die manfully, than
to come into the hands of the wicked,
to be abused otherwise than beseemed
his noble birth: 43but missing his stroke
through haste, the multitude also
rushing within the doors, he ran boldly
up to the wall, and cast himself down
manfully among the thickest of them.
44But they quickly giving back, and a
space being made, he fell down into
the midst of the void place.
45Nevertheless, while there was yet
breath within him, being inflamed with
anger, he rose up; and though his blood
gushed out like spouts of water, and his
wounds were grievous, yet he ran
through the midst of the throng; and
standing upon a steep rock, 46when as his
blood was now quite gone, he plucked
out his bowels, and taking them in both
his hands, he cast them upon the throng,
and calling upon the Lord of life and
spirit to restore him those again, he thus
died.

CHAPTER 15

1But Nica´nor, hearing that Judas and
his company were in the strong
places about Samaria, resolved without
any danger to set upon them on the
sabbath day. 2Nevertheless the Jews
that were compelled to go with him
said, O destroy not so cruelly and
barbarously, but give honor to that day,
which he, that seeth all things, hath
honored with holiness above all other
days. 3Then the most ungracious wretch
demanded, if there were a Mighty one
in heaven, that had commanded the
sabbath day to be kept. 4And when they
said, There is in heaven a living Lord,
and mighty, who commanded the
seventh day to be kept; 5then said the
other, And I also am mighty upon earth,
and I command to take arms, and to do
the king's business. Yet he obtained not
to have his wicked will done. 6So
Nica´nor in exceeding pride and
haughtiness determined to set up a
public monument of his victory over
Judas and them that were with him.

7But Maccabe´us had ever sure
confidence that the Lord would help
him: 8wherefore he exhorted his people
not to fear the coming of the heathen
against them, but to remember the help
which in former times they had
received from heaven, and now to
expect the victory and aid, which should
come unto them from the Almighty.
9And so comforting them out of the law
and the prophets, and withal putting
them in mind of the battles that they won
afore, he made them more cheerful.
10And when he had stirred up their
minds, he gave them their charge,
showing them therewithal the
falsehood of the heathen, and the
breach of oaths. 11Thus he armed every
one of them, not so much with defense
of shields and spears, as with
comfortable and good words: and
beside that, he told them a dream
worthy to be believed, as if it had been
so indeed, which did not a little rejoice
them.

12And this was his vision: That Oni´as,
who had been high priest, a virtuous
and a good man, revered in
conversation, gentle in condition,
well spoken also, and exercised from
a child in all points of virtue, holding
up his hands prayed for the whole body
of the Jews. 13This done, in like
manner there appeared a man with
gray hairs, and exceeding glorious,
who was of a wonderful and excellent

majesty. 14Then Oni´as answered,
saying, This is a lover of the
brethren, who prayeth much for the
people, and for the holy city, to wit,
Jeremiah the prophet of God.
15Whereupon Jeremiah holding forth
his right hand gave to Judas a sword of
gold, and in giving it spake thus, 16Take
this holy sword, a gift from God, with
the which thou shalt wound the
adversaries. 17Thus being well
comforted by the words of Judas, which
were very good, and able to stir them
up to valor, and to encourage the hearts
of the young men, they determined not
to pitch camp, but courageously to set
upon them, and manfully to try the
matter by conflict, because the city
and the sanctuary and the temple were
in danger. 18For the care that they took
for their wives, and their children, their
brethren, and kinsfolk, was in least
account with them: but the greatest and
principal fear was for the holy temple.
19Also they that were in the city took
not the least care, being troubled for the
conflict abroad.

20And now, when as all looked what
should be the trial, and the enemies were
already come near, and the army was set
in array, and the beasts conveniently
placed, and the horsemen set in wings,
21Maccabe´us seeing the coming of the
multitude, and the divers preparations
of armor, and the fierceness of the
beasts, stretched out his hands toward
heaven, and called upon the Lord that
worketh wonders, knowing that victory
cometh not by arms, but even as it
seemeth good to him, he giveth it to
such as are worthy: 22therefore in his
prayer he said after this manner; O
Lord, thou didst send thine angel in the
time of Hezeki´ah king of Judah, and
didst slay in the host of Sennach´erib an
hundred fourscore and five thousand:
23wherefore now also, O Lord of
heaven, send a good angel before us for
a fear and dread unto them; 24and
through the might of thine arm let those
be stricken with terror, that come
against thy holy people to blaspheme.
And he ended thus.

25Then Nica´nor and they that were
with him came forward with trumpets
and songs. 26But Judas and his
company encountered the enemies with
invocation and prayer. 27So that
fighting with their hands, and praying
unto God with their hearts, they slew
no less than thirty and five thousand
men: for through the appearance of
God they were greatly cheered. 28Now
when the battle was done, returning
again with joy, they knew that Nica´nor
lay dead in his harness. 29Then they
made a great shout and a noise, praising
the Almighty in their own language.
30And Judas, who was ever the chief
defender of the citizens both in body
and mind, and who continued his love
toward his countrymen all his life,
commanded to strike off Nica´nor's
head, and his hand with his shoulder,
and bring them to Jerusalem. 31So when
he was there, and called them of his
nation together, and set the priests before
the altar, he sent for them that were of
the tower, 32and showed them vile
Nica´nor's head, and the hand of that
blasphemer, which with proud brags he
had stretched out against the holy
temple of the Almighty. 33And when he
had cut out the tongue of that ungodly
Nica´nor, he commanded that they
should give it by pieces unto the fowls,
and hang up the reward of his madness
before the temple. 34So every man
praised toward the heaven the glorious
Lord, saying, Blessed be he that hath

kept his own place undefiled. 35He
hanged also Nica´nor's head upon the
tower, an evident and manifest sign
unto all of the help of the Lord. 36And
they ordained all with a common
decree in no case to let that day pass
without solemnity, but to celebrate the
thirteenth day of the twelfth month,
which in the Syrian tongue is called
Adar, the day before Mor´decai's day.
37Thus went it with Nica´nor: and from
that time forth the Hebrews had the city
in their power. And here will I make an
end. 38And if I have done well, and as
is fitting the story, it is that which I
desired: but if slenderly and meanly,
it is that which I could attain unto.
39For as it is hurtful to drink wine or
water alone; and as wine mingled with
water is pleasant, and delighteth the
taste: even so speech finely framed
delighteth the ears of them that read the
story. And here shall be an end.

Printed in Great Britain
by Amazon

59108925R00150